Engendering the
Chinese Revolution

Engendering the Chinese Revolution

Radical Women, Communist
Politics, and Mass Movements
in the 1920s

Christina Kelley Gilmartin

UNIVERSITY OF CALIFORNIA PRESS

Berkeley / Los Angeles / London

Chapters 1 and 4 are reprinted in significantly expanded form from "Gender in the Formation of a Communist Body Politic," *Modern China* 19, no. 3 (July 1993): 299–329 (© 1993 Sage Publications, Inc.), by permission of Sage Publications, Inc.

Chapter 6 is reprinted with changes from "Gender, Political Culture, and Women's Mobilization in the Chinese Nationalist Revolution, 1924–1927," in *Engendering China: Women, Culture, and the State* (Cambridge: Harvard University Press, 1994), 195–225, by permission of Harvard University Press.

University of California Press
Berkeley and Los Angeles, California

University of California Press, Ltd.
London, England

Library of Congress Cataloging-in-Publication Data

Gilmartin, Christina K.
    Engendering the Chinese revolution : radical women, communist politics, and mass movements in the 1920s / Christina Kelley Gilmartin.
        p.   cm.
    Includes bibliographical references and index.
    ISBN 0-520-08981-2 (alk. paper); ISBN 0520-20346-1 (pbk: alk. paper)
    1. Women and socialism—China.   2. Communism—China—History.   3. China—History—1912–1928.   I. Title.
    HX546.G54   1995
    335.43'082—dc20   94-24723

Printed in the United States of America
9 8 7 6 5 4 3 2 1

The paper used in this publication meets the minimum requirements of American National Standard for Information Sciences— Permanence of Paper for Printed Library Materials, ANSI Z39.48–1984.

*In memory of Arthur T. Bisson and
Adele Austin Rickett, for their intellectual
inspiration, devotion to teaching, and
moral courage.*

Contents

Maps

Acknowledgments

This work would not have reached the printed page without the help of many friends and colleagues who encouraged me, provided me with invaluable advice and moral support, and commented on my numerous drafts. Special thanks go to Gail Hershatter, Carma Hinton, Emily Honig, and Marilyn Young, who patiently waded through various renditions of this manuscript as it evolved from a doctoral dissertation into a book. This work was also immeasurably improved by the criticisms and suggestions made by Kathryn Bernhardt, Laura Frader, Kandice Hauf, Tony Saich, Konstantin V. Schevelyoff, Vera Schwarcz, Mark Selden, Lynda Shaffer, Rubie Watson, and Weili Ye.

My work has benefited from the assistance of many institutions. I am very grateful for the generous financial support I have received over the years. The Committee for Scholarly Communication with the People's Republic of China funded the initial dissertation research, the American Council of Learned Societies provided me with a postdoctoral fellowship to expand and rewrite the dissertation, and the University of Houston awarded me a summer research grant that allowed me to use the Nationalist Party Archives at Yangmingshan in Taiwan. The University of Houston and Northeastern University also provided funding for assistance from several graduate students: He Zhigong, who conscientiously read through some Hunan and Guangdong newspapers, He Hongfei, who helped me locate some important sources in the Yenching Library at Harvard University, Michael O'Connor, who assisted me in the final preparation of the bibliography and checking citations in the notes, Barbara Clough, who sat in front of a computer for a good number of hours typing in revisions of an earlier draft, and Cheng Yinghong, who checked the information in the directory.

Over the years I enjoyed the hospitality of many libraries and archives. I wish to thank the staffs at the Beijing National Library, the Beijing Normal University Library, the Guangzhou Municipal Library, the Guangdong Revolutionary History Museum, the Hunan Revolutionary History Museum, the Modern History Institute Library at the Chinese Academy of Social Sciences, and the Shanghai Municipal Library, all in the People's Republic of China; Harvard University's Fairbank Center for East Asian Research Library, Yenching Library, and Widner Library; the Modern History Institute Library at the Academia Sinica and the Nationalist Party Archives at Yangmingshan in Taiwan; and the Russian Centre for the Preservation and Study of Records of Modern History in Moscow.

I would also like to express my gratitude to those who helped me with the writing of my doctoral dissertation, on which this present work is partially based. Professors Allyn Rickett and Susan Naquin unstintingly gave me their time, attention, and valuable advice. To Ding Shou of the Chinese Academy of Social Sciences in Beijing, I owe a special debt for his generous sharing of ideas, insights, and advice on sources.

The most enjoyable part of researching and writing this book was the time I spent talking with elderly Chinese women and their families about their political experiences in the 1920s. I am very grateful for their valuable input and support. As most of the interviews occurred in the early 1980s, when little regard was paid to women's role in the revolution, we were drawn together by the common goal of drawing attention to a historical moment that had largely been forgotten.

A number of people contributed in significant ways to this text during its final stages of preparation. Sheila Levine, Laura Driussi, and Scott Norton of the University of California Press made the entire process of publishing this work a humane experience. Freelance editors Carlotta Shearson and Anne Canright offered fine suggestions to improve the readability of this work. Many thanks go as well to He Xiuwen, who labored tirelessly to produce three fine maps, Zhang Shaoqing, who churned out a computerized rendition of my glossary in record time, and Zhang Jiaxuan, whose elegant calligraphy adorns the cover of this book.

Finally I owe the greatest personal debt to my inner circle of friends and to my family—Peter, Benjamin, and Beth—who provided tremendous encouragement and support from beginning to end of this project.

Note on Romanization

The system of romanization employed in this book is pinyin, which has gradually gained international acceptance since the Chinese government's decision in 1979 to adopt it in its foreign publications and thereby encourage its use as the standard romanization system. In most Western works on modern Chinese history, it has replaced the more cumbersome Wade-Giles system.

The Wade-Giles spelling of Mao Tse-tung is rendered as Mao Zedong in pinyin, and Peking, Canton, and the Yangtze River become Beijing, Guangzhou, and Yangzi. In this book, however, in the case of the very well accepted names of Sun Yatsen, Chiang Kaishek, and Soong Qingling, exceptions to the pinyin system have been allowed in recognition of their general familiarity in the West. (Most Western works that put Sun Yatsen's name into standard Mandarin pinyin use his revolutionary nom de guerre, Sun Zhongshan, rather than the proper pinyin for Sun Yatsen, which is Sun Yixian.)

The other notable exception in this book to the employment of pinyin is in the notes and bibliography, where the authors' names are presented as cited. Thus, Xie Bingying is rendered as Hsieh Ping-ying, and Chen Hansheng as Chen Han-seng.

Introduction

This book began in Beijing in the autumn of 1979 with a set of lengthy discussions with Wang Yizhi, a retired principal of No. 101 Middle School and a veteran woman Communist. It was my good fortune to have been recommended to her by Carma Hinton, one of her former students, and before long I found myself interviewing her about the story of her life. Many times over the next two years I rode my bike up that long dusty road past Zhongguancun and Beida (Beijing University) to Wang Yizhi's modest home at the edge of a small pond on the rambling campus of No. 101 Middle School and listened to her reminiscing about her experiences of growing up female in China and becoming a revolutionary.

Wang Yizhi ultimately entrusted me with much more than her autobiography; she opened up a whole new chapter in Chinese women's history. Most intriguing were her reflections on the first phase of the Chinese Communist movement (1920–1927), which took me far from the beaten track of Chinese Communist party history I had traveled in graduate school. I found myself in a maze of uncharted avenues and alleyways peopled with a host of unfamiliar women and lined with a multitude of vital revolutionary organizations for politicizing women, such as the Shanghai Pingmin Girls' School, the Women's Rights League, Shanghai University, the Women's Movement Training Institute, and the women's class of the Wuhan Central Military and Political Institute.

The world of women Communists seemed intrinsically appealing as a research project, but at first I doubted that sufficient written documentation existed to warrant such an undertaking. Fortuitously, the dramatic change in research conditions for Westerners in the early 1980s included the opening of Chinese libraries and archives. At the same time, Chinese researchers produced a massive outpouring of scholarly and documentary publications about the Chinese Communist party, including an impressive collection of works on Communist women put out by a special research team of the All-China Women's Federation. From these materials I was able to draw a road map to the untapped resources scattered through China on women and the Communist party in the 1920s. Convinced that the project was viable, I began full-scale research in the autumn of 1981.[1] Focusing my attention exclusively on women revolutionaries seemed eminently fitting at first. Making women visible and restoring them to history was a major endeavor of women's studies when I initiated this project. Once I became fully immersed in the relevant periodical and documentary literature, however, the limitations of this approach for this study became evident. In order to comprehend fully women's roles in the formation of the Chinese Communist party and in the mass mobilization campaigns of the National Revolution, I needed to understand the ways in which the world of Communist women of the 1920s intersected with—and in crucial ways was created by—the world of Communist men. Thus, the use of the word "gender" in the title of this book is not meant as a synonym for "women." Rather "gender" is invoked as an essential analytical conceptual framework for the exploration of relations between men and women in the Chinese Communist party and in other revolutionary mass mobilization organizations of the 1920s. It is used to map the hierarchy of the newly created Communist polity, the dimensions of power, the boundaries in revolutionary organizations, competing notions of the proper place of women in public and private life, and the multiple meanings associated with masculinity and femininity.[2]

Examining the experiences of women in the early Chinese Communist revolutionary movement through the lens of gender does not merely augment our understanding of party activities, as a study of the peasant mobilization campaigns might do, but rather, it forces a shift in perspective. In this book, in contrast to other studies of the Chinese Communist party, the deliberations, decisions, and directives of the Central Committee[3] and party congresses often appear less significant than the ideological, cultural, and social facets of party life and programs. To the first generation of Communists, changing what they understood as "traditional" or "feudal" culture and society was inextricably connected with the task of political transformation.[4] Thus, many Communists of the 1920s were just as concerned with reconstituting their social relationships in accordance with egalitarian principles as they were with constructing a political organization. Dedicated to the proposition that "modern" marriages had to be based on love and free choice, they created a party that functioned at once as a radical subculture for social experimentation and as a revolutionary political organization.

This new perspective on the early Chinese Communist party and the cultural preoccupations of its members broadens our understanding of the extent to which cultural contention was at the core of the revolutionary process in twentieth-century China. It makes visible the enormous attention devoted to gender issues in the revolutionary discourse and practice of the 1920s, issues such as male-female relations, marriage, women's political, social, and legal status, the nature of the family, and women's roles in the public domain. In so doing, it shows that these issues often proved much more contentious at a grassroots level than matters related to political rule and the nature of the state.[5]

Examining the party-building and revolutionary actions of the Chinese Communist party in the 1920s through the lens of gender also suggests new ways to think about important historical events and their meanings in China during the course of this century. Through its examination of the Chinese Communist party's gender relations, women's program, and role in the large-scale mobilization of women in the National Revolution, this book makes visible one aspect of the dramatic transformation of the political order that occurred in China during the 1920s. It argues that the 1920s in China was not just "a decade of challenge," to borrow the scholar Teng Ssu-yü's phrase, but a period of peak influence of feminism on Communist and Nationalist revolutionaries, and a seminal period in setting critical features of the relationship of women to the Chinese Communist party.[6]

This study seeks to integrate what have up to now remained more or less disparate scholarly endeavors—Chinese modern political history and gender studies. Despite the pioneering work of women scholars,[7] Western specialists writing on the Chinese Communist revolution (1920–1949) have thus far given little consideration to gender issues. Many pioneering and innovative works on the Chinese Communist movement published in the last decade have overlooked the ways in which gender figures into revolutionary discourse and practice. This book does not purport to present a comprehensive history of the Chinese Communist party in the 1920s, but it does at least begin to place the challenge of engendering the Chinese Communist revolution on the scholarly agenda.

When I began my work, the dominant conceptual framework employed by historians for examining women's roles and the articulation of women's issues in Communist revolutionary movements was the incompatibility of Marxism and feminism.[8] This theoretical approach exerted a discernible influence on the pioneering scholarly articles and books published in the China field in the 1970s concerning the Communist treatment of gender issues in the 1920s.[9] Given the well-documented Western research on the experiences of women in other Communist parties and Chinese Communist ideological treatments of the "woman question" since 1949, it seemed eminently reasonable to assume that the Chinese case represented yet one more example of proletarian ideology meeting and overcoming bourgeois feminism.

After many months in the libraries of China during the early 1980s sorting through materials that had previously been unavailable to Western scholars, it became clear that we had been looking at the early years of the Chinese Communist party through the prism of late-twentieth-century feminist concerns. We had failed to recognize the vast differences between the party policies on women's issues in the 1920s and those that came later. Ultimately, the tensions between gender and class in classical Marxist theory proved much less influential on early Communist policies and practices than the feminist ideals that had been nurtured in Chinese political culture since the turn of the century. The founders of the Chinese Communist party were strongly influenced by the blossoming of feminist thought during the May Fourth era (1915–1921) and by the countless instances of female activism that ripped through the political and social fabric of China in the 1920s. Under their auspices women's emancipatory issues were integrated into the political action program of the new party, and women were given command of this area of work.

The Chinese women Communists of the 1920s were less troubled by Marxist theoretical tensions between gender and class than were either of their closest contemporary counterparts in the socialist world—the "reluctant feminists" of the German Social Democratic party, such as Clara Zetkin, and the "Bolshevik feminists" represented by Alexandra Kollontai.[10] Moreover, women's presence in the Chinese Communist party, in contrast to the major European socialist parties in the first decades of the twentieth century, had a distinct impact on setting the party's revolutionary agenda for women's issues, particularly after the formation of an alliance between the Communist and Nationalist parties in 1923. In fact, Communist women played a critical role in weaving together thousands of discrete incidents of women's independent struggles into a massive social mobilization of women. Ultimately, hundreds of thousands, if not millions, of women were drawn into political action through their efforts. The tremendous popular response to this campaign attested to the drawing power, especially among younger women, of May Fourth feminist issues and the way in which these issues were fused with socialist ideals to formulate a fundamental assault on certain aspects of the kinship system and gender hierarchy.

Indeed, even Xiang Jingyu, the most prominent Communist woman leader of the era, ultimately decided to embrace the feminist orientation of the Communist women's program. In contrast to other Western studies, which generally portray Xiang Jingyu as disdainful of feminist issues, this study demonstrates that her main contribution as director of the Chinese Communist Women's Bureau was the formulation of a strong program for promoting a radical alteration of gender relations in the revolutionary movement as well as for combating gender oppression within the party.[11] Despite occasional twinges of reluctance, she persevered in building a feminist-oriented Communist women's program. Understanding the feminist leanings of Xiang Jingyu and her fellow male and female associates requires attention to the remarkable power of Chinese nationalism. Indeed, it had become an overarching political imperative in China by the last years of the Qing dynasty and facilitated the grounding of feminism in the first decades of the twentieth century. The influence of this historical connection between nationalism and feminism was far-reaching in Chinese political culture of the 1920s and proved to be a compelling factor in shaping the feminist ideological formulations and program of the Chinese Communist party in its first years of operation.

The connection between gender issues and nationalism in the revolutionary movement of the 1920s was strengthened by the introduction of Lenin's thesis on the colonial question. As E. J. Hobsbawm has noted, in the post–World War I era, when nationalist movements were proliferating and "the radicalism of the Russian Revolution took

over from that of the French Revolution as the main ideology of glo-
bal emancipation," Lenin discovered that the anti-imperialist nationalist struggles of colonial and semicolonial peoples in the third world
were a tremendous potential asset to the cause of world revolution
because they could seriously weaken Western imperialist power and
influence.[12] Communist revolutionaries in many parts of the world
embraced nationalist struggles on the grounds that they would ultimately prove beneficial to the industrial proletariat. In China, Lenin's
thesis had a strong impact on the policies of the Communist party,
particularly its decision to form an alliance with the Nationalist party
in 1923. His thesis also provided further justification for the Communists' continuing support for feminist positions and programs, including a wide variety of women's groups that espoused anti-imperialist
views, regardless of the groups' class composition.

My use of the word "feminism" in this study is not meant to imply
that feminism in a Chinese context is synonymous with Western feminism. Disparate historical experiences and profound cultural differences between China and the West have given rise to substantially
different variants of feminism. Understanding early-twentieth-century
Chinese feminism on its own terms requires a break with a universal-
ist outlook that presumes that only one type of female emancipatory
experience, that based on Western criteria, can be deemed truly feminist. Recently, some scholars have raised strong objections to the use
of the Western definition of feminism as the sole yardstick to determine whether social-change movements in the third world have a
feminist character. In contesting the very meaning of the term
"feminism," these scholars draw attention to the fact that feminist
movements in the non-Western world have been compelled by their
localities to address the intersection of gender oppression with imperialist, racial, and class oppression.[13] Perhaps the most articulate
spokesperson for this approach to third-world feminism has been
Chandra Talpade Mohanty, who has noted:

Unlike the history of Western (white, middle-class) feminisms, which has
been explored in great detail over the last few decades, histories of third
world women's engagement with feminism are in short supply.... Constructing such histories often requires reading against the grain of a number of intersecting progressive discourses (e.g., white feminist, third-world
nationalist and socialist).... In fact, the challenge of third world feminisms to white, Western feminisms has been precisely this inescapable link
between feminist and political liberation movements. In fact, black, white,

and other third world women have very different histories with respect to the particular inheritance of post-fifteenth-century Euro-American hegemony: the inheritance of slavery, enforced migration, plantation, and indentured labor, colonialism, imperial conquest, and genocide.[14]

In other words, modern feminist movements in the third world have been compelled by the realities of western hegemony to broaden their agendas by connecting their effort to end gender oppression with struggles for national liberation.

From the vantage point of the late twentieth century, it seems curious to use the word "feminism" in conjunction with the Chinese Communist experience. Indeed, Chinese Communists have generally avoided contact with feminist groups and expressed great scorn at being identified in any form or fashion with feminism, which they commonly render into Chinese as *nüquan zhuyi*. However, this strong disdain was not in evidence during the formative phase of the Chinese Communist party, in large part because of the historical development of the term in China and its political connotations in the late nineteenth and early twentieth centuries. *Nüquan yundong* was a term that was first coined around the turn of the century as a translation for the Western phrase "women's rights movement." However, the ideograph *quan* connoted both "rights" and "power." This nuance allowed Chinese of later generations to use the term to refer at once to women's rights and to the feminist movement. Thus, although it is possible for Nancy Cott to talk about the specific historical moment in American history when the term "feminism" entered the political vocabulary as a break with the ideology of the suffrage movement, in China no such clear-cut moment can be identified.[15] Instead, the movement for women's rights, including the right to vote, merged with the feminist movement.

Chinese Communists of the 1920s did not reject the *nüquan yundong*; in fact, they participated in the establishment of a nationwide organization in 1922 that bore the name *Nüquan yundong tongmenghui* (variably translated as either the Feminist League or Women's Rights League). To Communists of that era, one appealing feature of the *nüquan yundong* groups was that they saw women's issues from a nationalist perspective. An improvement in women's conditions was always viewed as an integral component of strengthening the state.[16] However, to most cultural revolutionaries of the late 1910s and early 1920s, the *nüquan yundong* was not as in step with the times as the *funü jiefang yundong* (women's emancipation movement). This women's movement was seen as broader than *nüquan yundong* because it drew adherents from all social classes. Perhaps because this term was preferred by Communists, *funü jiefang yundong* continued in popular usage throughout most of the twentieth century, although its English rendition changed from the "women's emancipation movement"— a phrase that to our ears sounds somewhat archaic—to "women's liberation movement." In order to remain faithful to the historical tenor of the 1920s, however, this study will use the term "women's emancipation."

Format

This study weaves portraits of early Communist revolutionaries into a chronological treatment of the gendered dimension of the making of a Communist polity, the social mobilization of women in the revolutionary upsurge of the mid-1920s, and the immediate aftermath of this social ferment. Part 1 contains four chapters that focus primarily on gender issues in the making of the Shanghai Communist organization between 1920 and 1925. It deals with the tensions between the feminist aspects of the ideology and program of the party on the one hand and patriarchal attitudes and behaviors on the other hand. The founders of the Chinese Communist party were committed to challenging many aspects of their own culture, including male-female relations, the patriarchal family structure, and the social and legal status of women.[17] At the same time that they formulated a radical program on gender transformation that challenged the dominant culture, however, they reproduced and reinscribed central aspects of the gender system from the larger society within their own party organizations. This contradiction was mirrored in the personal lives of these revolutionaries: they conducted themselves in a radical egalitarian fashion but at the same time replicated certain traditional aspects of gender hierarchy. As a result, a patriarchal gender system that proved to be enduring grew within the body politic of the Chinese Communist party.

Part 2 consists of three chapters that probe the gender dynamics of the revolutionary upsurge of 1925–1927 under the rubric of the First United Front, the term for the alliance between the Nationalist and Communist parties. These chapters demonstrate the decisive impact of politics on the emergence of a massive social mobilization of women for the National Revolution in certain parts of China. Beginning in Shanghai with the May Thirtieth Incident (1925), Part 2 traces the unfolding of mass women's movements in Shanghai, Beijing, and the southern provinces of Guangdong, Jiangxi, Hunan, and Hubei. The mass mobilization of women was pursued through a strikingly innovative use of cultural symbols, propaganda, and organization, tools that were derived from the Soviet revolutionary model. The explicit aim of this intense effort of mass mobilization was to bring women into the political process, usually for the first time, and make them feel like they were an integral part of the making of the new state. We can discern in this process the gendered contours of the state that was created through this revolutionary process and established as the legitimate political authority twenty-some years later.

Part 2 also pinpoints the difficulties encountered by these mass women's movements from within the political parties that spawned them. From the removal of Xiang Jingyu to the problems in funding that He Xiangning faced to the unwillingness of labor and peasant organizers to focus on gender issues, both the Chinese Communist and Nationalist parties exhibited the strength of traditional attitudes and behaviors that pervaded their political organizations. To be sure, the mass women's movement also experienced public opposition to its programs. But the defeat of the women's movement was due less to public opposition or internal weaknesses than to the collapse—in blood—of the first United Front.

The concluding chapter summarizes the main issues presented in this book and then examines the impact of the acrimonious and bloody breakdown of the Nationalist-Communist collaboration on the fate of feminism in Chinese politics. The tragic struggle that ensued between the two parties included a propaganda war over the politicization of gender issues. The Nationalists, discovering that the issue of alleged Communist sexual immorality was an extremely effective weapon, accused the Communists of promoting sexual chaos. One of the many issues under attack was the conduct of women political organizers, who were portrayed as sexually promiscuous and dangerous to the moral order. The identification of morality as an issue of contention had far-reaching consequences for both parties. The Nationalist party embraced traditional values once again, and promoted domesticity, as was most clearly revealed in the New Life Movement of 1934.[18] The Communist party itself became puritanical in the 1930s, modifying or

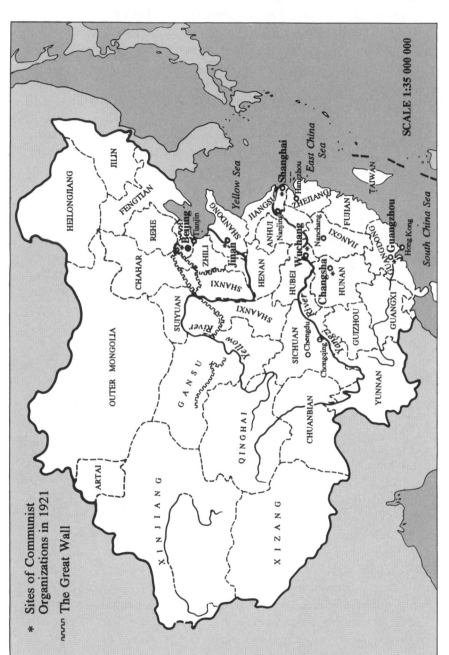

* Sites of Communist
   Organizations in 1921

⌒⌒⌒ The Great Wall

SCALE 1:35 000 000

1. China

abandoning much of its original women's program. Thenceforth, both parties set definite limits on women's political roles and the use of gender issues in political and social campaigns. Not only were female political identities restricted but patriarchal conceptions of political power became unassailable.

Yet neither party entirely abandoned the cause of women's emancipation. As the Nationalists became the rulers of the country in 1928, they enacted a civil code that granted women full citizenship rights in the new state, and Chinese women achieved suffrage and extensive legal rights—on paper at least—years before their counterparts in the Catholic countries of Western Europe. Meanwhile, the outlawed Chinese Communist party, in its continued efforts at revolution, kept alive much of the language and rituals of women's emancipation, a fact that was to have an enduring impact on the political and social order of post-1949 China, as well as on revolutionary movements in other third-world countries.

women granted political rights.

PART I

Gender in the Formation of a Communist Body Politic, 1920–1925

Introduction to Part One

Marxist to feminism apathy to feminism

Why do Communist revolutionary movements exhibit such a glaring discrepancy between their theoretical positions on gender equality and their political practice? This question has absorbed the attention of a considerable number of scholars, many of whom focus on the tensions between Marxism and feminism.[1] These theorists contend that Marxism and feminism are basically incompatible, that their union, to paraphrase Heidi Hartmann, has been problematic from the start and like all unhappy marriages should be dissolved.[2] Other scholars attribute the incongruity between word and deed to the subordination of gender issues to "larger" political goals on socialist revolutionary agendas.[3]

Both these interpretations, despite their differences, proceed from the premise that Communists have generally lacked sufficient commitment to the cause of gender equality to permit its realization in the postrevolutionary state. These interpretations reflect a profound skepticism of the capacity of socialist revolutions to establish gender equality. Both analyses also pay little attention to political culture as such, or to the ways in which gender issues are interpolated into a revolutionary movement.

Out of a desire to probe more deeply into the gender interactions of the Chinese Communist revolutionary movement in the 1920s, I have found the work of several scholars of the French Revolution to be useful. In particular, Lynn Hunt's treatment of political culture, which she defines as "the values, expectations, and implications that expressed and shaped collective action," allows for a much more dynamic approach to revolutionary occasions and their possibilities, even when the outcome is already well established.[4] Perhaps most important for my study, Hunt's methodology draws attention to the ways in which revolutionaries make meaning out of their own experience, and in so doing it provides insights into their fashioning of a compelling logic for their revolutionary actions.

Part I of this study examines the making of the Chinese Communist party from its inception in 1920 until the upsurge of the revolutionary mass mobilizations in 1925. It grapples with two simultaneous processes that shaped the formation of the Communist body politic. It examines the ways in which the explicit, radical break Communists made with tradition, including a rejection of paternalist and patriarchal models of society, created a fertile environment for the entry of feminist women into the party and for the construction of a women's program informed by feminism. At the same time, the study finds evidence of the persistence of traditional gender patterns of political attitudes and behavior in the party, which were not merely archaic remnants but became central organizing principles of the Chinese Communist polity. The new political culture of twentieth-century China incorporated this contradiction, and in time the gap between Communist rhetoric and practice on gender issues became starkly evident.

The geographical focus of the first part of this book is Shanghai. Although data exist for other localities that hosted a Communist organization by the convening of the first congress of the Chinese Communist party in 1921 (Beijing, Changsha, Guangzhou, Jinan, Shanghai, Tokyo, and Wuhan), it was Communist experiences in Shanghai that produced the richest historical material for this study.[5] The industrial capital of China and a haven for Chinese radicals since the turn of the century, Shanghai quickly became the political, cultural, and social center of the Chinese Communist world. It was also in Shanghai that the greatest number of Communist feminists, both male and female, congregated. Moreover, Shanghai served as the home of the Chinese feminist press, a sizable assembly of women's groups, an active student movement, and the largest concentration of women workers in China.

To understand the interactions between feminist politics and traditional attitudes and behaviors, we must first probe into the origins and attributes of the feminist ideals that permeated the party at its inception. Chapter 1 examines how gender issues were constructed in the political and revolutionary Communist male discourse during the first years of the Communist movement, drawing attention to the ways in which May Fourth feminist categories shaped this discussion. This chapter explores some of the personal reasons motivating these male Communists to embrace feminist issues, as well as the political reasons compelling them to draw women into their organization.

Chapter 2 examines the tentative and paradoxical beginnings of the Chinese Communist women's action program. It focuses on the way Wang Huiwu and Gao Junman, the first women activists in the Shanghai Communist organization, worked to create a women's voice in the copious Communist literature on women's emancipation, establish a presence in the Shanghai women's circles, and develop a rudimentary infrastructure for involving women in Communist programs. Despite their accomplishments, these activists faced strong impediments to developing egalitarian political roles within the Communist polity and gaining the full support of male Communists for their undertakings. Only outside intervention by the Comintern effected a significant breakthrough, compelling the Chinese Communist party to grant legitimate status to this area of work by establishing a formal bureau with officially appointed leaders to oversee the party's women's program.

Chapter 3 explores Xiang Jingyu's search for a meaningful role in the Chinese Communist party. Her struggle to come to terms with the potentially painful contradictions between gender and class in theory and practice had a pronounced impact on the Communist women's program and on other Communist women leaders.

Chapter 4 looks at the experiences of women Communists in the creation of a gender hierarchy within the Communist body politic. It discusses their political background, their motivations for joining the Communist party, and their experiences in the political organization and the party's subculture. The chapter also addresses the question of why male and female Communists tolerated the development of a discrepancy between their ideological stance on women's emancipation and the unequal power hierarchy in the Shanghai Communist organization.

CHAPTER I

In a Different Voice

*Male Communist Rhetoric
on Women's Emancipation*

As the Chinese Communist party emerged from scattered study societies to become a rudimentary political organization during 1920 and 1921, the ideal of women's emancipation was closely intertwined with the party's overall goal of societal transformation. This ideal was invoked to attest to the compelling power of socialism to obliterate both the traditional modes of female oppression in the family and capitalist exploitation of women in the industrial workplace. Moreover, women's emancipation came to symbolize a critical distinction between "feudal" China and China as a "modern" nation-state. As such, it was closely tied to the groundswell of nationalism that rippled through China in the first decades of the twentieth century and pervaded the Communist movement.[1]

This chapter explores the impact of Chinese feminism on the first generation of Communists. It argues that the temporal juxtaposition of the blossoming of feminism in China during the mid-1910s—a time of great political, cultural, and social ferment that came to be termed the May Fourth era—and the founding of the Chinese Communist party in the early 1920s forged a greater compatibility between Marxism and feminism during the formative period of the Chinese Communist party than has generally been the case in other communist and socialist movements. Thus, leading Chinese intellectuals did not abandon their strong commitment to transforming the gender order once they became Communists. Rather, they produced a voluminous literature on the topic of women's emancipation, which integrated many of the May Fourth feminist issues with Marxist formulations on the "woman question."

The torrent of words that poured from their pens not only set the terms of the radical discussion on women's emancipation within the nascent Communist polity but also was ultimately instrumental in shaping the party's political culture. The great passion the first generation of Communist intellectuals displayed in their essays revealed the extent to which the issue of women's emancipation possessed great personal meaning, as well as political significance, for them. Their writings guided them through a problematic reality in gender relations as well as allowed them to create a stronger sense of ideological connection between their May Fourth radicalism and their newfound Marxist convictions.

A distinct characteristic of this Communist discourse to begin with was that its participants were overwhelmingly male.[2] Admittedly, the male domination of the discourse on women's issues was not unusual for the times; in fact most writers for the Chinese feminist press in those years were male. Nonetheless, that these Communist writings invariably reflected male concerns about and perspectives on gender issues raises questions about the probable readership of this male Communist rhetoric and its function in the nascent party.

The Historical Connection between Nationalism and Feminism

The male Communists' propensity to reflect seriously on women's issues did not emerge suddenly out of a vacuum but can be traced back to the late nineteenth century, when notions of state making, nationalism, and feminism became thoroughly intertwined in the quest for modernity. During the tumultuous 1890s, when Western and Japanese imperialists were scrambling for concessions in China, male would-be modernizers subjected the traditional political and social order to harsh scrutiny as they searched for a way to transform their politically weak civilization into an independent "modern" nation-state. To this end, they focused on the overarching need for China to separate itself from its traditional past by reconstituting both its society and its individuals.[3]

It was in the context of their discussions on China's confrontation

women's equality

with the modern world that Chinese intellectuals began to rephrase certain women's social issues discussed during previous centuries into a new discourse that was markedly modern in its premises.[4] Constitutional reformers and political revolutionaries alike began to advocate women's equality as a means to increase the strength of the nation. Liang Qichao was perhaps the most prominent of the political theorists of that era to articulate the connections between nationalism and feminism. Equating the lives of Chinese women with the miserable lot of slaves or domesticated animals, he argued that China could not survive the Western challenge and become a powerful state in the world community until its female "parasites"—symbolized by their bound feet—were transformed into independent and productive citizens.[5] This nationalist rationale for unfettering Chinese women may well have proved effective in reaching normally unsympathetic male ears.[6] In any event, it created fertile ground for the sowing of feminist seeds. But, from its inception, modern feminism in China was a hand-maiden of nationalism.[7]

During the first two decades of the twentieth century, feminism became more firmly planted in Chinese soil. It was nourished both by male proponents and by female nationalist and anarchist radicals such as Qiu Jin and He Zhen.[8] As Peter Zarrow has convincingly demonstrated, anarchists contributed much to the redefining of feminism during those years. They not only offered a piercing critique of traditional morality and the Chinese family but also challenged the essentialist nature of the bond between nationalism and feminism. In so doing, they played a role in the rendering of the "woman question" into one of the major issues of the late 1910s and foreshadowed the unequivocal iconoclastic indictment of tradition during the May Fourth era. They did not, however, succeed in their aim of irrevocably breaking the tight connection between nationalism and feminism.[9]

The May Fourth era encompassed both a complex cultural and social ferment and a renewed sense of national urgency that swept through the country in the wake of Japan's ultimatum of 1915 (commonly referred to as the Twenty-One Demands), which compelled China to surrender certain sovereign rights, and the decision of the victors of World War I to hand over German interests in the Chinese province of Shandong to the Japanese. When student demonstrations broke out in Beijing on May 4, 1919, to protest the terms of the postwar treaty drawn up in Versailles, they set off a large-scale campaign that came to be known as the May Fourth Movement. The seemingly disparate cultural, intellectual, political, and social dimensions of the May Fourth Movement became closely linked together in the minds of many intellectuals and students who believed that the only way China could become an independent modern state was if they declared full-scale war on the entire Chinese cultural heritage.

For May Fourth cultural revolutionaries, the identification of the family as the fundamental social institution perpetuating traditional values and customs quickly led to a consideration of women's oppression, which was commonly discussed under the rubric of the "woman question" (*funü wenti*). Indeed, an entire chorus of voices turned the *funü wenti* into a cause célèbre during the May Fourth era, and in so doing, helped to stimulate the proliferation of journals that made women's issues their major or sole focus.[10] The deluge of words let loose in print at this time was filled with certain specific terms that signified the intention of these cultural revolutionaries to make a radical break with the past. Hallmarks of this revolutionary language used in reference to women were words like progress (*jinbu*), emancipation (*jiefang*), new (*xin*), feudal (*fengjian*), tradition (*chuantong*), enlightenment (*qimeng*), national salvation (*jiuguo*), science (*kexue*), democracy (*minzu*), awakening (*juewu*), woman's personhood (*nüzi ren'ge*), and social contact between men and women (*nannü shejiao*). These key words reflected reconstructed images of society, which were useful to revolutionaries in their efforts to gain public acceptance of the urgent need to transform the Chinese polity, economy, and society.[11]

Another significant language invention of the period was the appearance of new words associated with female identity. Amidst the effort to establish a vernacular Chinese to replace the antiquated classical written form, Liu Bannong, a leading iconoclastic intellectual of the May Fourth period, is credited with creating a gendered pronoun in the vernacular by adapting an ancient ideogram to denote "she" (*ta*).[12] The pronoun eventually came into common usage. However, in May Fourth radical discourse less concern was exhibited for utilizing the female *ta* than for expounding on the "woman question." As the "woman question" was elevated into one of the most important issues of the period, the word *funü* (woman) became inextricably linked with the nationalist agenda.

Probing beneath the iconoclastic veneer of the writings of the cultural revolutionaries reveals the strong connection created between nationalism and feminism. For instance, Francesca Cini's study of *New*

Youth (Xin qingnian), one of the most influential journals of the day and a powerful vehicle for popularizing the "woman question," showed that most of *New Youth*'s articles approached the issue of women's emancipation from the utilitarian perspective that it was a general benefit to the nation. Even the call for women to become more "conscious" of their oppression and work for emancipation was justified on the basis of promoting China's salvation.[13]

The strong connection between nationalist and feminist issues in this period facilitated the expansion of the exploration of women's exploitation. Within a short time, the May Fourth critique of the oppressive nature of the Chinese family system became quite extensive and included such gender issues as the common practices of parental arrangement of marriages, polygamy, and "one-sided chastity"—a common code word of the times for the double standard in the sexual mores of men and women. It was socially acceptable for men to frequent brothels, have concubines, and remarry, but women were expected to be impeccable exemplars of virtue by remaining faithful to their husbands, even to the point of adhering to strict chastity codes in widowhood and committing suicide in the event of rape. Other traditional standards of virtuous conduct that these radical iconoclasts singled out for criticism were the notions that the ideal woman should strive to be an excellent wife and virtuous mother (*xianqi liangmu*) and that a daughter should exhibit flawless filial piety towards her parents (*xiaonü*).

A distinguishing characteristic of this cultural critique of women's oppression is that it was largely a male discourse. It was very difficult, for instance, to discern a female voice in the pages of *New Youth*. Indeed, according to Francesca Cini, no serious attempt was made by its editors to develop a women's perspective on gender oppression during the May Fourth era. Personalized accounts of growing up female in early-twentieth-century China were not included in this journal, for instance. Rather, the oppression of women was portrayed as yet one more example of the inhumanity of Confucian culture and society. Thus, the solution to women's problems was exactly the same as the solution to the general national crisis.[14]

This problem of male voice was not totally ignored by the writers of the times. Zhang Shenfu was one of a number of men who questioned the purpose of all these writings. An admirer of Bertrand Russell and later one of the founding members of the Communist organization in Beijing, Zhang Shenfu asked in his essay of 1919 entitled "The Great

Inappropriateness of Women's Emancipation" whether it was possible for men to emancipate women.[15] Moreover, he questioned the extent to which self-proclaimed male emancipators recognized that they were actually just as much a part of the problem as the solution for women. From Zhang Shenfu's perspective, most women were not ready for or interested in emancipation.

For at least some of these May Fourth male feminists, it seems that writing about women's oppression was a means to express their own fears and desires about the plight of their country. Vera Schwarcz has suggested some of these men often identified with the social predicament of women because it symbolized their own feelings of powerlessness in the face of the all-embracing family system that entrapped them in social roles of submission to authority.[16] Indeed, as it did for their Ming and Qing dynasty predecessors, bemoaning the plight of women served as a metaphor for expressing concerns about other dilemmas.[17]

The Emergence of a Male-Feminist Core within the Party

It was in the context of the May Fourth Movement that the founders of the Chinese Communist party originally developed an appreciation for the importance of women's emancipation. Indeed, some of them played a leading role in elevating it to a pivotal issue in the radical discourse. This section examines the views of Chen Duxiu, Yun Daiying, and Mao Zedong, three May Fourth male feminists, on the eve of their embracing Marxism. It then traces the emergence of Shanghai as the center for the discussion of women's issues in the Chinese Communist world.

Chen Duxiu, who would become the first secretary-general of the Chinese Communist party in 1921, was one of the foremost May Fourth cultural revolutionaries. He exerted enormous influence over Chinese students through his iconoclastic writings in the widely read *New Youth* magazine and his position as dean of Beijing University. In his articles, Chen lambasted the Confucian familial norms for regulating women to an inferior social position, restricting them to physically and spiritually abnormal lives through cloistering, barring them from participating in public discussions, and inculcating in them the value of total submission to patriarchal authority. In his view, these traditional principles of proper social conduct for women were incompatible with a modern way of life, which must be based on the concepts of equality and independence.[18]

A distinguishing characteristic of Chen's consideration of women's exploitation was that it was placed firmly in the context of his attack on Chinese tradition. He discussed women's plight only as an example of the debauched nature of Confucian cultural norms and practices. His "totalistic anti-Confucianism," to borrow a phrase of Lin Yü-sheng, was premised on the interplay between his commitment to nationalism and his commitment to individualism.[19] Although he was disgusted by displays of mindless patriotism, his iconoclasm was shaped by a profound concern for the welfare of the Chinese nation. His commitment to individualism was based on a belief that personhood could only be achieved by emancipation from traditional shackles. In that he saw women's emancipation as beneficial for the survival of the nation, his views about women bore some resemblance to those of Liang Qichao.

In central China, Yun Daiying quickly emerged as one of the most influential May Fourth radicals to take up the cause of women's emancipation. He rose to prominence in leftist circles as a student leader of the 1915 mass protest in Hankou against the Twenty-One Demands and as a founding member of the Benefit the Masses Society (Liqun she), a coalition of progressive study societies. His translations, particularly his selections from Friedrich Engels's *The Origin of the Family, Private Property, and the State*, and his essays on women's affairs were influential in enlarging the scope of the May Fourth feminist discourse in central China. A self-professed anarchist until he joined the Chinese Communist party in 1922, Yun was particularly vocal in his condemnation of the family and of marriage. One of his searing indictments was published in an essay entitled "Research on the Marriage Issue," which appeared in 1917. To Yun Daiying, a marriage without love was meaningless and should be dissolved. He believed that families constructed around forced marriages had an evil impact on children. In later articles, he expounded at great length about the need to have public child care in order to protect children from the pernicious effects of the family.[20]

In Hunan, Mao Zedong also became well known as a May Fourth proponent of women's emancipation, but he supported women's emancipation in a somewhat different manner than Chen Duxiu or

Yun Daiying. Rather than engage in theoretical expositions, Mao seized upon a sensational event in the small provincial capital of Changsha— the suicide of Zhao Wuzhen in November 1919—to heighten public opposition to the traditional marriage practices. In a series of ten essays he published on this event, he portrayed the suicide of Zhao Wuzhen, whom he chose to call Miss Zhao (*Zhao nüshi*), as an act of despair against an evil system. In so doing, he transformed her into a revolutionary martyr who struck a blow for the cause of women's emancipation.[21]

Of the several female suicides that occurred that autumn, Mao selected Miss Zhao's because of its spectacular and very public nature. She slit her throat with a razor, which had been concealed in her foot bindings, while she was being carried in the bridal sedan to her husband's house. Mao's interpretation of this suicide touched off a major discussion on the significance of the event in the pages of a local newspaper, *Dagongbao* (Public interest), where nine of his articles on this topic appeared, with the result that Miss Zhao's case gained national exposure.

It is instructive that other commentators who contributed some fifteen articles on this event to *Dagongbao* did not necessarily agree with Mao Zedong's interpretation.[22] They revealed that the Miss Zhao whom Mao portrayed as a despairing victim of the hegemonic Confucian system apparently looked upon suicide as a weapon of female empowerment.[23] A strong believer in the eight immortals and a vegetarian on religious grounds, Miss Zhao believed that her ghost would have greater power to seek revenge both upon her parents and upon the Wu family if she ended her life while en route to her future in-laws' house rather than while still residing in her parents' home.

Indeed, Miss Zhao succeeded in her purpose: her suicide brought about the ruin of both families. The prosperous Wu family was so concerned about her ghost haunting their house that they immediately sold it at a great loss. Moreover, they were ordered by local authorities to adorn her corpse for the funeral with expensive gold jewelry as would normally be fitting for a wealthy bride. These financial expenditures in combination with the wedding costs already incurred impoverished the family and caused them great difficulty in arranging another marriage for their son. Similarly, Miss Zhao's family suffered a major financial catastrophe. In addition to covering the expensive funeral costs, they lost the bride price that they had planned to use for arranging their son's wedding. Initially they were unwilling to let their fear of their daughter's ghost force them to abandon their home, but eventually the ostracism of the neighbors forced them to sell their house at a substantial loss.[24]

Ironically, the Zhaos might have been able to avoid this catastrophe if they had been willing to break with traditional conventions dictating social propriety between the sexes. Because the first hospital they brought her to did not have a female doctor on duty, the Zhaos decided to take her to another medical facility rather than suffer the embarrassment of having a male doctor examine and care for their daughter. But by the time they arrived at the Yale Medical Hospital in Changsha, she had expired.[25]

Mao Zedong's portrayal of Miss Zhao's suicide as an act of despair was closely connected to a perspective on women generally held by May Fourth men. Indeed, it was often difficult for May Fourth feminists to see any signs of female empowerment. Rather, women were viewed as the prey of a cruel system that had robbed them of their personhood and their independence. Mao and others of his persuasion, however, believed that it was possible for women to become conscious of their oppression and take steps to alter their condition. Thus, Mao sought to use Miss Zhao's case, regardless of the specifics, to rally other men and women to the cause of women's emancipation. To this end, he made her a May Fourth revolutionary martyr.

These three May Fourth male feminists were representative of the first generation of male Communists before their conversion to Marxism. Others were just as vocal and instrumental in attributing such importance to the cause of women's emancipation in this radical discourse. To elaborate, one of the most influential proponents of women's emancipation in Shanghai at this time was Shao Lizi, a professor at Fudan University and a founder of the *Republican Daily* (Minguo ribao), the Nationalist party organ, in 1915. In June 1919 he began publishing *Awakening* (Juewu) as a supplement to the newspaper and filled it with articles on women's issues. Shao Lizi himself wrote approximately fifty such pieces. Other soon-to-be-Communist intellectuals who contributed to the deliberations on women's issues and the development of a feminist press in China during the May Fourth era were Li Dazhao, Mao Dun, Li Da, Shen Cuntong, Xuan Shenlu, Zhang Shenfu, Chen Wangdao, and Tian Han.[26]

Most of the seven localities that spawned Communist organizations between the late summer of 1920 and the convening of the first congress in July 1921 had a few ardent proponents of the cause of women's emancipation. Indeed, even the fledgling Communist grouping in Jinan had at least one supporter of women's rights who published a piece concerned with women's education.[27] However, the most vocal male feminists in this new political organization were clustered in Beijing and Shanghai. Beijing had functioned as an important center of intellectual ferment in China during the late 1910s, in large part because of the presence of leading iconoclastic scholars at Beijing University and writers for some influential May Fourth periodicals. Important forums for discussing women's issues in Beijing during the May Fourth era were *New Tide* (Xin chao), *Young China* (Shaonian Zhongguo), and the supplement of *Morning Post* (Chen bao), which carried articles on women's human worth (*ren'ge*) and the oppressive nature of the family, chastity, and marriage.[28] In such an atmosphere, many budding Communists, including Chen Duxiu, Li Dazhao, Zhang Shenfu, and Deng Zhongxia, took up the cause of women's rights.

By the fall of 1920, however, when Li Dazhao, inspired by the building of the Communist party in Shanghai, decided to establish a Communist organization in Beijing, warlord political repression hampered much of its public activities. The frustration of Communist organizers was reflected in their propaganda materials, with one leaflet complaining that "Beijing is a prison."[29] This repression soon stifled written expression as well. Beijing police monitored publishing activities quite closely, keeping a vigilant watch on all printing establishments, with the result that Beijing Communists were completely frustrated in their efforts to engage in the main endeavor of the early party, the creation of propaganda. Communist reports from this city complained about the failure to publish even translations of important Communist texts, such as *The Communist Party Program*, that members of the Beijing organization had completed.[30] Had it not been for tight political controls, the Beijing Communist organization might well have put out its own women's publication. Certainly the interest of Li Dazhao and some of the other members was sufficient to warrant such an undertaking. However, Beijing Communists were forced to publish their writings on women in the established newspapers of the city, such as *Social Welfare* (Yishibao) and *Morning Post*, and its supplement, or they sent their pieces to Shanghai publications.[31]

The harsh political climate in Beijing compelled Communists in the early 1920s to make Shanghai the political center of their party. For this reason, Shanghai also eclipsed Beijing as the main center of intellectual discourse in the party. Much larger than Beijing, Shanghai was

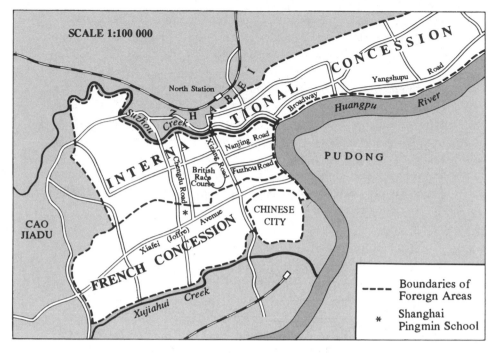

SCALE 1:100 000

North Station

ZHABEI CONCESSION

Suzhou Creek

INTERNATIONAL CONCESSION

Broadway

Yangshupu Road

Huangpu River

PUDONG

Nanjing Road

Xizang Road

Chengdu Road

British Race Course

Fuzhou Road

CHINESE CITY

CAO JIADU

* Avenue

Xiafei (Joffre)

FRENCH CONCESSION

Xujiahui Creek

- - - - Boundaries of Foreign Areas

* Shanghai Pingmin School

2. Shanghai

a bustling, cosmopolitan semicolonial city with a complex blending of Western and non-Western culture, society, and polity. To be more exact, Shanghai was not one city but at least three. The International Settlement was an amalgamation of the British and American enclaves that had been established in the mid–nineteenth century after China's defeat in the first Opium War. By the 1920s it had expanded to 8.3 square miles and hosted Western commercial houses, banks, and corporate headquarters along the Bund, the Huangpu River waterfront promenade commonly referred to as China's Wall Street. The separate and politically independent French Concession was well known for its elegant residences and bohemian, Montmartre-style café life and pleasure palaces. The Chinese municipality consisted of the outlying factory districts of Zhabei and Pudong plus the more centrally located Chinese walled city of approximately three and a half miles in circumference, with densely packed housing, narrow streets, and crowded teahouses and shops.

Even though Shanghai in those days was often characterized as a "Sin City" because of rampant crime, including kidnapping, murder, and smuggling, and its powerful underworld gangs, its foreign settlements had served as a political haven for radical intellectuals for several decades.[32] The International Settlement in Shanghai would not allow taxpaying Chinese to vote, but it was much more tolerant of free speech and the expression of public dissent than was any other city in China. Publications flourished here, the most notable for the airing of Communist views on women's issues being *New Youth*, *Awakening*, *Women's Critic* (Funü pinglun), and *Women's Magazine* (Funü zazhi).[33] Thus, the largest cluster of prominent Communist male feminists in the early days of the party congregated in Shanghai, because it provided the most conducive environment for the production of their theoretical writings.

The Making of a Communist Ideology on Women's Emancipation

The gender ideology of the early Chinese Communist party was not adopted ready-made from European socialist and communist parties, nor was it created ex nihilo. Rather, it was synthesized from a number of sources, the most important of which were May Fourth feminism and the Marxist critique of the family that was based primarily on the writings of Friedrich Engels. These two currents mingled in the Chinese Communist movement as part of a single historical trend and served to enshrine the ideal of women's emancipation within the movement itself.

Although a complete Chinese translation of Friedrich Engels's *Origin of the Family, Private Property, and the State* did not appear until 1929, the gist of his argument was conveyed in partial translations and summaries and was echoed in the translations of August Bebel's writings.[34] Chinese Communist writers placed much emphasis on Engels's materialist theory, which attributed the historic defeat of women's independence and autonomy to the emergence of significant holdings of private property and the advent of class society.[35] Chinese Communists were enchanted with this Engelsian analysis in part because it served to denaturalize Chinese patriarchal power and open up the possibility of its demise at some time in the foreseeable future.

Engels's materialist analysis of the family as the prime locus of female oppression resonated well with the antifamily orientation of many Chinese Communists. They found in this materialist interpretation a theoretical framework for their May Fourth critique of the patriarchal family as a despotic institution that perpetuated the odious practices of foot binding, concubinage, arranged marriages, and the enforcement of women's illiteracy, seclusion, and submission to male authority. Thus, Engels's theory not only justified the continuing condemnation of the family in Chinese Communist writings but also facilitated the retention of other May Fourth feminist issues in the Communist gender discourse, at least until 1927. A brief perusal of a few representative titles by Communists exemplifies this phenomenon: "The Deplorable Evils of the Marriage System," "The Event of Ms. Xi Shangzhen's Suicide in the Office of the Commercial Press," "Women's Consciousness," "The Relationship between Love and Virginity," "An Admonition to Modern Style Men Who Denigrate Social Contact between the Sexes," "Social Contact between Men and Women and Old Ethics," "The Tragedy of the Old Style of Marriage," "The Issue of a Love Triangle," "A Discussion of the Co-Educational School Issue," "The Problem of Preventing Women Students from Getting a Divorce," and "How to Solve the Dilemma of Social Contact Between Men and Women."[36]

The apparent compatibility of May Fourth and Marxist ideas about women's emancipation in certain respects facilitated the acceptance of some Engelsian theories among influential non-Communist intellectuals. An instructive illustration of this phenomenon is the pervasiveness of the contention that women's economic independence was the decisive determinant of genuine gender equality. At roughly the same time that Communists like Li Hanjun, Mao Dun, Chen Wangdao, and Shen Zemin were writing about the importance of women's acquiring the education and job skills to become self-supporting, published non-Communist writers such as Lu Xun, Hu Shi, Chen Youqin, Gao Xian, Li Xiaofeng, and Wu Yu were making the same point. Lu Xun's memorable speech "What Happens after Nora Leaves Home" to the students at Beijing Normal Women's College and his poignant story "Regret for the Past" contained graphic accounts of the sorry fate that awaited those Chinese women who tried to escape the control of their families without having acquired the capacity or means to support themselves. For Lu Xun, the outcome was patently clear: such women would either become irreparably debased or have to resubmit to their families' controls.[37]

Another Engelsian idea that received great attention in the early

Chinese Communist movement was the comparison of the institution of marriage with prostitution. The notion that the difference between a wife and a streetwalker was only in the length of time that her sexual services were secured seemed to capture the inhumanity of the arranged-marriage system and strip it of any lingering legitimacy it might hold for radical intellectuals. Shen Zemin, the younger brother of the well-known writer Mao Dun, published one of the most impassioned indictments of the marriage system that adhered to this interpretation. He charged:

The present system turns women into prostitutes. This is because the system is alive and expanding, purposely and incessantly swallowing innocent people into its bloody mouth. The present number of people who have fallen victim will increase. In such a social reality, this system noiselessly forces upper-class women to unconsciously sell their most precious "sex." It forces working-class women who can barely subsist to turn directly into prostitutes.... Money, of course, is not the only reason why women degenerate into this deplorable status, as women do not necessarily always demand money. Women have their own reasons for exchanging their only possession—their sexual services. In order to avoid the isolation of remaining single, or to fulfill a desire to become a mother, or to have their vanity indulged, women often marry men they do not love. Emotionally their predicament is similar to the experiences of prostitutes, for they have to painfully submit to their husbands and put up with fondling caresses in the absence of love.[38]

The natural progression of this argument led Mao Dun and other Communists of his era to call for the abolition of marriage. They believed that family-controlled marriages only served family interests and often resulted in unhappy unions for the individuals involved. In this respect, they were revealing certain anarchist inclinations, which Arif Dirlik has conclusively shown to have been quite strong in the early Communist movement.[39] Such traits, for example, can be identified in the writings of Shi Cuntong, who was more candid than most budding Communists in acknowledging his anarchist inclinations. In several articles on marriage that he published in May of 1920, also the time he joined the Shanghai Marxist Research Society, he argued that marriage was the main instrument shackling individuals to the family system. Moreover, in Shi's view, marriage essentially required the subordination of one individual's emotions and sexuality to another person—a situation that nobody should be forced to tolerate.[40]

As Arif Dirlik has noted, Chen Duxiu was one of the few early members of the party who was not influenced by anarchist ideas.[41] But even though he did not call for the dissolution of the family, Chen Duxiu was well known for his critique of the family's virtual enslavement of women.[42] After his conversion to Communism in early 1920, Chen Duxiu no longer expounded at length on May Fourth feminist ideas in his writings the way he had when he was the editor of *New Youth* a year or two before. Rather, beginning in May 1920, he focused his attention on the exploitation of women workers, publishing an article on the procurement of Hunanese women workers by the Shanghai cotton mills in a special edition of *New Youth* devoted to factory conditions. Nine months later, he founded the Communist periodical *Labor and Women* (Laodong yu funü) in Guangzhou and contributed several articles that explored the connections between gender exploitation and class. Even after this journal folded a few months later, Chen continued to publish on this topic.[43]

It might well be surmised from this progression in Chen's thinking on women's issues that he was representative of, even that he fostered, a trend in the Chinese Communist party to subsume gender issues totally into an all-encompassing class analysis. Indeed, many Chinese male Communists during the early 1920s published articles on the harsh exploitation of women in the industrial workplace in order to heighten public awareness about the dangers of capitalism. However, what is distinctive about the Chinese Communist experience is that May Fourth feminist categories of analysis remained relevant throughout most of the 1920s. Chen Duxiu did not completely abandon his May Fourth feminist perspective when he became a Communist. A close reading of his works reveals indications of a continuing commitment to certain May Fourth issues, such as the importance of women's attaining a sense of personhood and dignity (*ren'ge*), the need for women's education, and the value of developing coeducational schools.[44]

Perhaps the strongest legacy of his May Fourth feminist orientation was Chen's lack of hostility to women's rights groups and suffrage groups, an attitude that sharply contrasted with that of European male communists and socialists at that time.[45] Rather he looked upon these groups as natural allies of the party and encouraged Communists to work with them.[46] In this endeavor, Chen was encouraged and supported by Li Dazhao, who published some very influential positive assessments of women's suffrage groups and women's rights groups in Western countries.[47] As a result, a greater compatibility between

Marxism and feminism was created in the early Chinese Communist party than in communist and socialist parties in other countries of that era.

Romantic Revolutionaries and the Emergence of a Communist Subculture

These writings on women's issues played a significant role in guiding male Communists through a very problematic new social reality in gender relations.[48] During the late 1910s and 1920s, the erosion of social barriers to heterosocial interaction, the establishment of coeducational schools, the appearance of free-choice marriages and consensual unions, the growing public knowledge of birth control (especially after the speaking tour of Margaret Sanger in 1922), the expansion of prostitution, and the expression of public concern about venereal disease reflected an increasing public awareness of sexual matters in urban society, which was especially pronounced in the Western enclaves of Shanghai.

The male Communist rhetoric on women's emancipation served in part as a coping strategy. Their discussion of women was a way to talk about conflicts in their personal lives. Male-female relations was a topic of urgency to these young men, many in their early twenties, who sought to reconcile their lives with their notions of modernity. These writings were an expression of heartfelt anxiety about being trapped between two eras and were also a set of guidelines about how to deal with this dilemma. The sexual revolution in urban China had an impact not just on the ideological views of Chinese Communist males but also on their lives, particularly in the areas of heterosocial interaction, free-choice marriages, and consensual unions.

Many Communists had a personal stake in the issue of family reform and found the issue of marriage particularly agonizing. Chen Duxiu, for instance, was very unhappy with his arranged marriage to Gao Dazhong, an illiterate rural woman three years his elder.[49] Their constant bickering left deep grudges. At first he sought relief in writing, and he published an essay denouncing the Chinese marriage system in 1904. Finally in 1910 he decided to leave her, at which point he took the highly unconventional step of entering into a consensual union with his wife's younger sister, Gao Junman, a graduate of

Beijing Women's Normal Institute. Described by Lee Feigon in his biography of Chen Duxiu as one of the few women of her era who was willing to partake "in a revolutionary life style," Gao Junman had to endure public censure and even the rebuke of her family because of her strong commitment to becoming a "new woman" who defied social conventions and lived her own life.[50] She became absorbed in the bohemian culture of the 1910s and was an enthusiastic adherent of the New Culture Movement.

The scandal of their relationship continued to haunt the couple long after they began to live together. By the early 1920s, Chen Duxiu was portrayed in conservative circles as a flagrant transgressor of morality. Chen Gongbo, a founding member of the Chinese Communist party, remembered that Chen Duxiu was hounded by conservative critics in Guangzhou where he served as education minister in the progressive warlord government of Chen Jiongming in 1920 and 1921. Rumors of his "immoral" conduct with women abounded and fueled calls in the newspapers for his resignation.[51] Also at issue here was Chen's advocacy of gender change in the school system. Chen's appointment of Yuan Zhenying, a well-known radical, as the principal of the First Middle School provoked much opposition, especially when Yuan integrated May Fourth ideas into the curriculum and made the school coeducational. Particularly objectionable to the established elite of the city was the practice of having boys and girls sit at the same desks.[52]

Chen was not the only Communist who left an arranged marriage. But some, like Gao Junyu and Chen Wangdao, chose to go one step further and do it in a more "modern" way by seeking to divorce their illiterate rural wives. Gao Junyu, for instance, a member of the Beijing Communist organization, fell in love with Shi Pingmei, a graduate of Beijing Higher Normal Institute, and promptly decided to divorce his wife of ten years through a letter to his father-in-law.[53] His letter demonstrated the typical outlook of early male Communists on this issue.

I have already explained to your daughter that I have decided to seek a divorce.... I have never felt that your daughter and I had a compatible marriage. Besides, I travel extensively and am seldom home. As a result, your daughter has a miserable life. I like to travel and can easily find a new woman. The only person who is suffering from loneliness is your daughter! Of course, she could live her entire life as a servant to my family. But your daughter is a human being. How could I allow this to happen to her?

In consideration of her future and on humanitarian grounds, I am determined to obtain a divorce.

From Gao's perspective, it was preferable to dissolve a relationship than to maintain a fictitious marriage. He may well have sincerely
believed his wife's prospects in the future were better as a divorcée
than as a de facto widow. In this respect, he was representative of this
first generation of Communists, who believed that challenging the
existing marriage system in one way or another was a fundamental
component of their overall rebellion against Chinese traditional norms.

No evidence remains on the effect of the divorce on the life of Gao
Junyu's illiterate wife. Perhaps Gao's humanitarian hopes for her to
find a more suitable mate were realized. In Chen Wangdao's case,
however, the decision to seek a divorce proved tragic. His wife found
the prospect of being a divorcée in a rural community so humiliating
that she committed suicide. Understandably, a number of Communist
males reacted to such tragedies by refusing to formalize their separa-
tion from their first wives, particularly when children were involved.
Zhang Tailei, for instance, allowed his wife the dignity of remaining in
his home community with the status of his wife and the mother of
his three children when he terminated his relationship with her and
married Wang Yizhi.

Most Communists wrestled in private with the various ways to
handle their arranged marriages, but on occasion scandals resulting
from their unconventional practices did reach the newspapers. One of
the most infamous cases in Shanghai involved Zhou Fuhai, a delegate
to the first party congress. News of his love affair with the daughter
of the chief secretary of the Shanghai Chamber of Commerce was
printed in the *Shanghai Eastern Times* (Shishi xinbao). According to
Zhang Guotao, the newspaper reported that a young Hunanese man
"who claimed to be the most progressive disciple of socialism in China
. . . already had a wife in his home village and was said to be a father."
When the chief secretary of the Shanghai Chamber of Commerce
threatened to sue Zhou for seducing his daughter, Zhang Guotao
hastened to explain the new morality that was common in the party at
that time:

I could see how furious Yang (the young women's father) was, and I tried
to calm him. If Chou Fo-hai [Zhou Fuhai] was really married, I said, and
had hidden the fact while carrying on a love affair with another girl, then
that, of course, was not right. But, I added, there were many young

men these days with old-fashioned wives at home, whose marriages were arranged by their parents. Even though they loathed their wives, the old moral code enslaved them and they could not get a divorce. So, many of them sought love away from home and perhaps even married again.[54]

To be sure, not every male Communist flouted traditional marriage practices. Mao Dun and Li Dazhao continued in their arranged marriages, for instance. Mao Dun chose to respect the wishes of his mother, who not only picked out an illiterate wife, Kong Dezhi, for him but also decided to move her to Shanghai rather than allow Mao Dun to continue with his bachelorlike existence. Although on the instructions of her husband Kong Dezhi attended a school in order to become literate and subsequently participated in certain party activities, Mao Dun always felt that a large cultural divide separated them and inhibited the development of a close marriage.

These radical Communist males who reconciled their marriages with traditional practices may well have represented a large number of the early membership. Nonetheless, they did not prove instrumental in shaping the interior social life of the new political organization. Rather, the fledgling Chinese Communist party quickly gained a reputation as a haven for those wishing to lead unconventional lives. As a result, the party emerged as a subculture in Shanghai and other large Chinese cities at the same time that it developed as a revolutionary political institution.

Production of Propaganda as a Means of Reaching Women

Although it was indeed true that these May Fourth male Communists were sometimes speaking metaphorically when they discussed women's problems, others clearly had more concrete intentions. In this respect, they were influenced by a distinct recognition in the political culture of twentieth-century China that the press, if used effectively as a propaganda instrument, could have a profound impact on the public.[55] Thus, they were acting in accordance with the contention of the well-known reformer Liang Qichao on the role of publications when he said: "One must intend to use one's words to change the world. Otherwise, why utter them?"[56]

Communists placed their writings on women's issues as widely as possible, with the great bulk appearing in party-sponsored journals, feminist periodicals, and political newspapers. Because of the political repression of most Communist journals, their circulation and influence were far more limited than those of women's publications and newspapers that focused on political issues. Indeed feminist and nationalist presses had grown hand in hand since the late 1890s, when for the first time in Chinese history newspapers were established with the specific purpose of promoting reform. The event that triggered this new development in journalism was the historic crisis caused by China's humiliating defeat by Japan in 1895. The ensuing scramble for concessions by imperialist powers during the last few years of the nineteenth century strengthened the resolve of Chinese reformers and revolutionaries for publications that were not commercially driven, such as *Shanghai News* (Shen bao), but would serve as forums for discussing solutions to the national dilemma. To this end, both political newspapers (such as *Journal of National Strengthening* [Qiangxue bao], which commenced under Kang Youwei's auspices in 1895) and women's periodicals (such as *Women's Studies News* [Nüxue bao], which Kang Tongwei, Kang Youwei's daughter, helped to establish in 1898) began to appear in Shanghai.[57] During the next two decades, political and feminist periodicals continued to flourish, particularly in Shanghai, providing an important vehicle for the dissemination of Communist writings on women's issues.

Articles on women's issues in Communist-sponsored publications in the early 1920s for the most part linked them with working-class concerns. One of the first acts of the Communist organizations in Beijing and Shanghai was to establish labor journals as a means to reach the industrial work force, which had grown rapidly in size during the 1910s and displayed increasing militancy beginning in 1919 with the holding of strikes in support of the May Fourth student protests. The large number of women workers—in Shanghai alone more than one-half of the three hundred thousand workers were women—made them an obvious target of any party that professed to represent the interests of the working class.

Ultimately, however, it was in Guangzhou that the first Communist journal specifically dedicated to exploring the interconnections between class and gender exploitation was established. When Chen Duxiu went to Guangzhou in 1920 to serve as education minister in Chen Jiongming's government, he and Shen Xuanlu founded the journal *Labor and Women*, the first of its kind in the Chinese Communist movement. Both Chen and Shen had written extensively on women's issues and had served as editors of influential May Fourth journals: Chen on *New Youth*, and Shen on the Nationalist party journal *Weekly Review* (Xingqi pinglun). A progressive Zhejiang landowner, Shen was the chief financial supporter of the *Weekly Review* and through his influence made it a center for radical discourse in Shanghai in late 1919 and 1920.

The effectiveness of both *New Youth* and *Weekly Review* in Shanghai may well have prompted Chen Duxiu and Shen Xuanlu to found this journal in Guangzhou as a tool of party building. The journal offered the possibility of extending the influence of the all-male Guangzhou Communist organization, which Chen Duxiu established soon after he arrived there in November 1920, to women workers and women intellectuals. Guangzhou had a strong reputation for women's activism, dating back to the 1911 Revolution, and at this time contained the largest and most influential independent women's group in China, the Guangdong Federation of Women's Circles.[58]

Although Chen Gongbo and Tan Pingshan, two other members of the Guangdong Communist organization, were invited to serve on the editorial board of *Labor and Women*, the actual work of writing and editing this journal fell on Chen Duxiu's and particularly Shen Xuanlu's shoulders. Shen wrote the bulk of the articles for the twelve issues, and the general position he took on women's issues was remarkably similar to that he had expounded in the pages of *Weekly Review* several months earlier. His message was simple: women suffered from both class and gender oppression. He equated the struggle of women against patriarchy with the struggle of workers against the capitalist class. Thus the situations of women and workers were not mutually exclusive but rather interconnected. He held that most women were by virtue of their gender for all intents and purposes part of the propertyless class (*wuchan jieji*), and both gender and class oppression would ultimately be eradicated by the advent of socialism.

After twelve issues, this pioneering Communist journal folded. Although Chen Duxiu and Shen Xuanlu had created an interesting and vibrant publication, it had failed to develop a strong institutional basis of support within the Guangzhou Communist organization or the women's movement. Normally this lack of support would not have been a fatal flaw; in fact it was quite common in those years for journals to be the product of a few strong editors. However, in this case, neither Shen Xuanlu nor Chen Duxiu was willing to make a long-term commitment to political involvement in this southern city. For both, this stay in Guangzhou was merely a brief respite from their party-building activities in Shanghai. Their tenuous relationship with Guangzhou coupled with the lack of sufficient local interest in this project caused the journal's speedy demise.

In contrast to the ephemeral character of most Communist labor publications, the well-established *Women's Magazine* (Funü zazhi) provided a much more visible and legitimate forum for Communist writers on women's issues. Founded in January 1915 under the auspices of Shanghai's Commercial Press, by 1920 it had gradually shifted its focus from fiction to the examination of women's lives.[59] As a result, Communist male feminists such as Mao Dun, Li Da, and Shen Zemin published a number of pieces in this reputable journal.[60] In addition, they were also inclined to contribute to the less established, but often more radical, women's journals that had sprung up after the May Fourth demonstrations, including *New Woman* (Xin funü), Suzhou's *Women's Critic*, and *Contemporary Woman* (Xiandai funü).[61] However appealing Communists found the women's press as a vehicle for disseminating their writings on women's issues, they preferred the political newspapers of the day, particularly the Nationalist-run *Republican Daily*, which had been established in Shanghai by Ye Chucang and Shao Lizi in 1915. At first, the newspaper's new culture movement supplement, *Awakening*, was popular among Shanghai Communist members for voicing their positions on women's emancipation. However, in August of 1921, the *Republican Daily* established yet another supplement, which was devoted specifically to women's issues. Entitled *Women's Critic*, it consisted of a special four-page insert edited by Chen Wangdao that was folded into the newspaper once a week. Chen Wangdao had come to Shanghai from Zhejiang, where he had become radicalized in the May Fourth revolutionary tempest at First Normal School in Hangzhou. Joining the Shanghai Communist organization soon after its founding, he quickly distinguished himself as the translator of the first complete Chinese edition of *The Communist Manifesto*.[62] A few weeks after the convening of the first congress of the Chinese Communist party, Chen Wangdao drew further attention to himself by launching *Women's Critic*. For the next few years, it served as the primary forum for Communist writings on women's issues. It covered a wide range of issues, focusing considerable attention on the evolution of the family as an oppressive institution, the practices of the patriarchal family that were so damaging to its female members, the importance of female education and employment, the social and legal status of women, the onerous exploitation of women factory workers, and the activities of women's organizations.

The articles in *Women's Critic* represented for the most part a male perspective on women's issues. To be sure, this pattern of male domination of the intellectual prose on women's issues was not out of keeping with the times. Most of the feminist press of the May Fourth era, in fact, was dominated by men. Even the *Women's Magazine*, which claimed to be the major mouthpiece for women, did not conceal the fact that most of its articles were written and edited by men. Although a few independent women's groups established magazines that primarily carried articles by women members, such ventures were short-lived and attained only minuscule circulations. In contrast, the women's periodicals that were run by men and featured male writers were much more influential, both in terms of distribution and intellectual clout. *Women's Magazine*, for instance, enjoyed a circulation of one thousand in 1922, and the circulation had risen to ten thousand by 1925; the circulations of *Women's Critic* and *Awakening*, which were inserted in the newspaper *Republican Daily* on a weekly basis, shot up from three thousand in 1920 to almost twenty thousand a few years later.[63]

Men not only shaped feminist writings in the early 1920s but also, from the little evidence available, appear to have constituted the bulk of the readership. Bao Tianxiao, the editor of *Women's Times* (Funü shibao), for instance, estimated that only 10 percent of the readership for his magazine was female. While no such estimate exists for *Women's Magazine*, one of its surveys on the social background of its readership in 1923 elicited only 26 responses from women in comparison to 155 from men.[64] No doubt the high female-illiteracy rate of the era was a major factor for the preponderance of male readers of this literature.

Nevertheless, a strong challenge to male perspectives on women's issues in Communist writings was delivered by several female readers of *Women's Critic*. They objected to an essay by Shen Zemin in early 1922 ostensibly supporting the recently announced YWCA campaign to eradicate prostitution.[65] The main argument of the article, as discussed earlier in this chapter, was that in the present deteriorating economic situation, all women, with the sole exception of those who had achieved a high level of consciousness, were in essence being turned into prostitutes. Shen Zemin's articles provoked a furious response from one woman reader and more measured criticisms from several others. Han Ying, who identified herself as a believer in the Communist party and socialism, an advocate of class struggle, and a woman who had spent time in Japan, immediately voiced her immense displeasure with Shen Zemin's assertion that "all women are in essence prostitutes," which she labeled as a gross insult to all woman.[66] She further accused him of confusing oppression with prostitution, for in her opinion oppressed women performing unpaid housework in the family and educating their children were distinctly different from prostitutes. Moreover, she argued that most women did not choose to sell their sexual services but were forced into it by "unscrupulous men." Though careful to clarify that she was a proponent of proletarian revolution and was not advocating all-out war between the sexes, Han Ying nevertheless felt it was important to recognize the male role in female prostitution as well as in the general economic and social subordination of women in the family.

Her letter and those of other readers prompted Shen to rephrase his argument slightly. In a subsequent clarification of his views, Shen explained: "In my [original] statement on the status of women under the present system, what I really meant to say is: 'The present system has a *tendency* [my emphasis] of turning women into prostitutes.'"[67] However, he brushed off Han Ying's objection to the use of the word "prostitute" as an indication that she was still too heavily influenced by old-fashioned notions of chastity. Equating her views to those held by old village women who would not flinch at being called a slave but would regard it as a supreme insult to be labeled a prostitute, Shen charged that Han Ying's sensitivity revealed her thinking was still poisoned by the belief that women should be sexually pure and virtuous.

Most readers who responded to this debate were women and they did not agree with Shen. Clearly, this Engelsian formulation was offensive to many educated women, even those who had little difficulty accepting other Marxist propositions. More importantly, Shen Zemin unwittingly revealed the dilemma of male writers on women's issues, as numerous as they were in China at that time; as much as these men empathized with the plight of women, they lacked a sensitivity to the actual realities that women faced on a day-to-day basis. The last thing that women who were stepping into any area of public life wanted to contend with was the insinuation that women outside the brothels might also be labeled as a type of prostitute.

The pervasiveness of the male perspective on women's issues was a general problem in the pages of *Women's Critic*. Only the male voice was articulated in its special issue on the problem of divorce, for instance, and *Women's Magazine* included only one essay, by a woman, that contained a clear female perspective on the problem.[68] After the flare-up over Shen Zemin's insensitive portrayal of married women as prostitutes, however, the editors strove to give the image that *Women's Critic* was truly a women's journal. First of all, they published more articles under female pseudonyms.[69] At the same time, Chen Wangdao also began soliciting contributions from female writers. Before long, he actually did manage to publish some essays by women, most notably Cheng Wanzhen, an activist for the YWCA, and Yang Zhihua, the daughter-in-law of Shen Xuanlu. In so doing, he manifested an awareness that the party needed to incorporate female voices and perspectives into its political discourse if it was going to reach women, and certainly if it ever expected to exert a strong influence over the ideas and actions of large numbers of women. It was no longer possible for Communist male feminists to imagine that their attempt to speak in a different voice could succeed.

CHAPTER 2

Tentative Programmatic Beginnings

Wang Huiwu's Leadership

In March of 1921, forty-two-year-old Chen Duxiu addressed a dynamic women's group in the southern city of Guangzhou. His message to the membership of the Guangdong Federation of Women's Circles (Guangdong nüjie lianhehui) was simple and straightforward. Chinese daughters, he told the gathering, were like decorative objects on their father's tables: they had no clear purpose to their lives and were bartered or given away as wives or concubines without any consideration of their own aspirations. Young women, Chen argued, could only develop independent personalities (*ren'ge*) if they could escape the domination of male oppressors and the old morality, which inculcated female compliance. Because present-day Chinese society would not permit women's pursuit of independence, their only hope, he maintained, lay with socialism, which would sweep away all social inequalities, including authoritarian patriarchal power. For this reason he urged the women sitting before him and those who would eventually read the published text of his remarks to involve themselves in the struggle for the realization of socialism.[1]

At the time of this speech, Chen Duxiu was in Guangzhou to serve as the minister of education in the provincial government of Chen Jiongming, a progressive Guangdong warlord. At the same time, he also sought to use his presence in the city to strengthen the local Communist organization, which had been corrupted by anarchists. As the most prestigious of the May Fourth intellectuals to become involved with the fledgling Communist movement, his presence at this gathering of the Guangdong Federation of Women's Circles signified his interest in attracting Chinese feminists to participate in a Communist-inspired revolutionary movement.[2] It also suggested that Chen Duxiu was contemplating the prospect of establishing an informal affiliation between his party and the Guangdong Federation of Women's Circles.

Five months later Chen Duxiu took steps to concretize these aspirations. Upon his return to Shanghai, where he assumed his new role as secretary-general of the Chinese Communist party, a position which had been conferred upon him in absentia at the party's first congress in July 1921, he encouraged several women to take charge of the newly conceived Communist women's action program by forming a connection with the Shanghai Federation of Women's Circles. In so doing, Chen Duxiu revealed an appreciation for the need for women to assume leadership positions in any outreach activities to female constituencies, even before the Han Ying controversy alerted Communist leaders to the problems connected with the male domination of the party's ideological formulations of women's issues. No doubt Chen Duxiu was guided in part by the realization that the strict gender segregation in Chinese society prevented the possibility of men's serving as prime organizers for women workers, a major target group of any Communist women's program.

The woman who emerged as the first leader in the Communist polity was Wang Huiwu.[3] Twenty-three years old at that time, she had already evinced through her May Fourth radical activism some of the salient characteristics that would be manifested in her leadership of the Communist women's program: deep political commitment, journalistic abilities, feminism, and seemingly boundless energy. Moreover, she possessed the determination and skills necessary to accomplish the feat of establishing a program of this nature. Her efforts to breathe life into this Communist endeavor during its first year of operation reveal much about the process of developing a program informed by feminist ideals and about the impediments to female power in the new polity.

The Political Context for the Rise of a Woman Leader

Just as May Fourth feminist discourse left a distinct imprint on the new party's ideological formulations, female activism in this period impressed Chen Duxiu and other Communist leaders with the potential for women's involvement in political actions. In the wake of the May Fourth mass protests, independent women's organizations bearing the name Federation of Women's Circles (*nüjie lianhehui*) sprang up in Shanghai, Guangdong, Zhejiang, and Hunan.[4] Invigorated by nationalist, anti-imperialist politics, they quickly widened their scope of operation to include issues of women's civil rights. Both their achievements and their internal difficulties were widely reported in the press. Much national attention, for instance, was focused on the conflict that erupted in the Guangdong Federation of Women's Circles over the issue of admitting concubines, with one-third of the membership, including the chairperson, voting against their inclusion.[5] Equally newsworthy was the tremendous coup of the Hunan Federation of Women's Circles, which stunned the nation by actually engineering the election of several women to the provincial assembly. But from a Communist perspective the most significant aspect of these organizations was their capacity to bring out hundreds and occasionally even thousands of women to demonstrate for a variety of women's causes.[6]

Chen Duxiu's speech to the membership of the Guangdong Federation of Women's Circles in the spring of 1921 indicated that Communists were heedful of this upsurge in women's political activism and also possibly interested in cultivating some sort of ties with these women's organizations. In Changsha, Mao Zedong responded positively to the efforts of the Hunanese women's organization to agitate for constitutional measures guaranteeing women's rights.[7] However, the Communist reaction to this new development was not uniformly affirmative. In Shanghai, Mao Dun was quite critical of the efforts of the All-Zhejiang Federation of Women's Circles (Quan Zhe nüjie lianhehui) to pressure its provincial assembly into extending certain civil rights to women. In his view, the three proposals developed by Wang Bihua, the chairperson of the organization, represented the interests of a small aristocratic elite and constituted a type of "ideological poison." Thus, Mao Dun put himself on record as being against the group's aim to extend suffrage to women, end prostitution, and establish coeducational schools. The only aspect of Wang Bihua's effort that Mao Dun found praiseworthy was her threat to call on women (especially the wives of the legislators) to resort to divorce if these three proposals were not included in the provincial constitution.[8]

Mao Dun was representative of those in the Chinese Communist party who saw certain aspects of Chinese feminist thought as antagonistic to Marxism. Because of his knowledge of foreign languages and the history of the women's movement in Europe, he, more than any other Chinese Communist, was aware of the hostility that had developed in the European context between socialist and feminist groups.[9] Yet his views seemed to have had little practical effect in the Chinese Communist movement at this time, perhaps because they were grounded in a European context that had little bearing on the Chinese radical political environment, which was greatly influenced by Chinese feminist thought.

While Communist males were voicing different assessments of the character and worth of the Federations of Women's Circles, they spoke in unison about the revolutionary potential of women workers. It was in Shanghai, with the largest concentration of women workers in China, that Communists publications focused increasing attention on the exploitative work conditions that women faced on a daily basis in Chinese factories. Chen Duxiu commenced this examination by publishing an article in 1920 in *New Youth* (Xin qingnian) on the exploitative practices involved in the hiring of fifty Hunanese women for a Shanghai cotton mill. He also drew attention to their onerous work load after arriving in Shanghai, where they were contractually obligated to work twelve hours a day for a minimum of three years at a mere pittance of eight *yuan* a week.[10] After the convening of the first congress of the Chinese Communist party in July 1921, similarly detailed explorations of various work hazards women had to endure in Shanghai industries began to be published in *Labor Weekly* (Laodong zhoukan), the organ of the party's Shanghai Labor Secretariat. The journal voiced indignation, for instance, when a checker at the gate of a cotton mill in west Shanghai forced a pregnant woman to take off her clothes because he suspected she was smuggling goods out of the factory.[11] It also reported the deaths of a ten-year-old girl whose braids became entangled in a machine at another Shanghai cotton mill and a woman named Yang who was crushed in an accident directly related to a foreman's negligence in a Japanese-owned cotton mill on West Suzhou Road.[12]

From Chen Duxiu's purview, the potential for organizing women workers that existed in the early 1920s stood in stark contrast to the capacity of the Shanghai Communist organization to do so because it had a dearth of women members. Indeed, at the time of the first congress, of the fifty-seven reported members only two were female: Miao Boying, a Hunanese who was drawn into radical politics while studying at the Beijing Normal Women's College and joined the Chinese Communist party in November of 1920, and Liu Qingyang, a prominent activist of the May Fourth era who had been a member of at least two study societies (the Awakening Society and the New Citizen's Study Society) and was recruited in Paris in January of 1921.[13]

Ironically, the percentage of women members in the party at its inception was lower than that of some of the study societies from which it was spawned. The New Citizen's Study Society (Xinmin xuehui), which was established in April 1918 by twelve men, began to admit women soon after the demonstrations on May 4, 1919, and by the early 1920s at least fourteen out of its sixty or seventy members were women.[14] Similarly, five of the eight Tianjin students who founded the Awakening Society (Juewu she) in September of 1919 were women, and thereafter women constituted about 50 percent of the membership.[15] Although, some of these women in the study societies were slowly recruited into Communist organizations over the next few years, at the time of the party's inception it was clearly a male-centered enterprise.

It was this total absence of women members in the Shanghai organization in 1920 and 1921 that allowed Wang Huiwu and Gao Junman to emerge as leaders of a Communist women's program soon after the first congress, largely in response to the beckoning of their spouses. Although these two women did not hold formal Communist membership, they were involved in companionate marital relationships with the two highest-ranking male leaders in the party, Chen Duxiu and Li Da. These two women developed a warm friendship after the two couples took up residence together in 1920 in a house at No. 6 Yuyang Lane in the French Concession and turned it into a headquarters for the Shanghai Communist organization.[16]

Wang Huiwu and Gao Junman were years apart in age, but because they shared a strong iconoclastic and feminist outlook and spent many hours together preparing meals for their husbands, a strong supportive relationship developed between the two. However, in many ways, these two women were very different. Gao graduated from a women's normal school before the 1911 Revolution, wrote poetry, was a staunch advocate of the adoption of the vernacular in literature, and enjoyed playing majong. In contrast, Wang Huiwu—who had spent time in missionary schools, where she converted to Christianity, developed a strong command of English, was a political activist, and held several positions as an English teacher—boldly championed the cause of women's rights and social change, and penned social commentaries.[17] Although Gao Junman was "married" to the highest-ranking Communist leader in the party and was older than Wang Huiwu, the political interests and leadership skills that Wang Huiwu developed during the May Fourth Movement made her more suitable for heading up the women's program.[18]

Like many of her generation, Wang Huiwu was radicalized through her involvement in the student protests against the post–World War I Paris peace conference at her school—the Hujun Academy for Girls (Hujun nüshi) in Huzhou, Zhejiang—but what distinguished her from many other female student activists of her era was not her participation in student politics but her decision to begin writing about the social injustices imposed upon Chinese women. Her most prominent essay, a critique of the arranged-marriage system entitled "The Chinese Woman Question: Liberation from a Trap," was published in the autumn of 1919 in *Young China* (Shaonian Zhongguo), a new journal put out by the Young China Study Society, whose membership included a number of future Communists, such as Li Dazhao, Mao Zedong, Deng Zhongxia, Liu Renjing, and Yun Daiying.[19] In this essay she bitterly assailed the arranged-marriage system as a form of lifelong imprisonment for women. In her view, women were blinded to the real nature of their subjugation and easily fell into the trap of arranged marriages because of their acceptance of certain traditional norms about womanhood, such as the Confucian ideal of female obedience to male authority figures in the family, the notion that wives should obey their husbands at all times, and the belief that women should aspire only to become virtuous wives and excellent mothers and should disdain the acquisition of knowledge (*nüzi wucai bian shi de*).[20]

This essay not only contained Wang Huiwu's condemnation of Chinese customs for women's enfetterment but also focused on the oppressive role that men played in using marriage to ensnare women. In so doing, she bluntly assailed traditional morality's contribution to this process of confining women within the household, as the following passage shows:

Some people say: "Women are devoid of a philosophy of life and do not deserve to have their own personality [*ren'ge*]." This is absurd. Who has concealed women's philosophy of life—the selfish, deceptive hearts of men created this trap and put us in it. . . . Men feared that women would work hard and be successful, acquire savings and break down the economic restrictions, whereupon the trap would be jeopardized. So household jobs like "sewing" and "cooking" were entrusted to women with the result that women no longer had the opportunity of achieving victory. . . . Men's selfishness was far-reaching. They feared that women would get involved in political power and frustrate their operations. Luckily, they had "morality," "sages," "books and records" as charms so they could fabricate omens that would restrict women's entry into politics. Because of their jealous natures, men built "interior and exterior defenses" to sever women's social relations that have continued up to the present. Women were inextricably caught in this trap and never have been able to extract themselves.[21]

Wang Huiwu's sentiments about the institution of marriage and the passion with which they were expressed reflected those of her generation of educated women in the post–World War I period, but her own personal experience did not conform to this common practice. Unlike the families of many of her classmates, her family had not forced her into an arranged marriage but rather had fostered her independence. No doubt, the death of her father, an impoverished local school teacher, during her childhood facilitated her avoidance of an arranged marriage because her family relied on the income she was able to bring in as a teacher. Nevertheless, she shared the hatred of her generation of May Fourth students for this parentally controlled system of marriage.

Wang Huiwu met Li Da in Shanghai in 1920. This young Communist from Hubei impressed her with his erudition and his political commitment, particularly to the cause of women's emancipation in China. He had become well known in scholarly circles for his deep interest in this topic with the publication in 1919 of "On Women's Emancipation" (Lun funü jiefang), which put forth an Engelsian interpretation of the historical connections between women's oppression and the emergence of the private-property system. Much of Li's own writing over the next two years, as well as his translations of articles by the Japanese socialist Yamakawa Kikuei, emphasized Engels's approach to the "woman question." One concept he found particularly appealing was that in the early period of human history, the social order had been matriarchal.[22]

Wang Huiwu was quite taken by this Communist male feminist, and in the fall of 1920 she agreed to marry him. Theirs was a free-choice marriage that was totally devoid of family controls—his family did not even attend the small party they held in Shanghai to mark the occasion.[23] They shared a conviction that their relationship should be egalitarian and that their political lives should be closely intertwined. Li Da introduced her to party life by including her in all his political meetings during the early days of the Communist movement, even though his doing so was considered highly irregular. Because Chen Duxiu's home served as the main meeting place for the Shanghai Communist organization, she quickly became knowledgeable about the inner workings of the party and the members of the Shanghai cell.

However, Wang Huiwu's views on women's issues did not meet with complete acceptance within the Shanghai Communist organization. A year earlier she had received a strong rebuke from Mao Dun in the form of an article that he had placed in the most well-established women's publication in Shanghai, *Women's Magazine* (Funü zazhi).[24] He argued that her conceptualization of human history as presented in her article "The Chinese Woman Question: Liberation from a Trap" was flawed. He particularly objected to her assertion that men were afraid that women would be successful and had therefore intentionally entrapped them in household tasks, arguing that this process had been dictated not by male intentions but by the need for someone to carry out domestic tasks to improve the well-being of humanity. Men might use women as playtoys, he argued, but they had not subordinated women as a result of their pernicious male natures. In this essay Mao Dun was careful to show that although he was a defender of the cause of women's emancipation, he was deeply concerned that Wang's article would encourage women to see men as inherently evil enemies. His objections were not limited to Wang Huiwu's beliefs, and in essays he published in *Women's Critic* (Funü pinglun), he argued at much greater length that blaming men for women's oppression could prompt women to refuse to join the revolutionary movement and to focus instead exclusively on gender issues.[25]

However, despite his aversion to her anti-male orientation, Mao Dun may well have been unwilling to voice strong disapproval of Wang Huiwu's assumption of a leadership position in the Chinese Communist party because she was his cousin. If other male members of the Shanghai Communist organization had any hesitations about Wang Huiwu's political credibility, her efforts at the party's first congress earned their respect. She secured two sites for the meetings. First she used her connections in Shanghai women's circles to arrange for space in the Bowen Girls' School in the French Concession; and when police officers raided the meeting, she organized the reconvening of the congress on a houseboat on West Lake in Zhejiang, where the delegates could pass as tourists and avoid police surveillance. Zhang Guotao, a delegate from Beijing, was clearly impressed by her cool-headedness and her strong problem solving during the most difficult moments.[26] Thus, her role at the congress paved the way for her acceptance as the leader of the women's program.

Origins of the Communist Women's Program

The Shanghai Communist group organized several activities that concerned women's issues before the first congress, but it was in August of 1921 that the party's women's action program commenced in earnest under the direction of Wang Huiwu and Gao Junman. In January 1921 a commemoration of the death of the Communist woman martyr Rosa Luxemburg was held; and in March an International Women's Day meeting featuring Gao Junman as the main speaker was convened at Chen Duxiu's home at No. 6 Yuyang Lane.[27] The party's first congress opted to leave the issue of "women's movement work" to the newly appointed Central Committee, which was composed of Chen Duxiu, Li Da, and Zhang Guotao.[28] This body's first decision was to empower Wang Huiwu and Gao Junman to revitalize the Shanghai Federation of Women's Circles. In so doing, the committee set a policy of commencing a Communist women's program under the rubric of an existing independent women's organization.

In the late summer of 1921 Wang Huiwu and Gao Junman initiated the Communist women's program by directing in an unobtrusive fashion the reorganization meetings of the Federation of Women's Circles in Shanghai.[29] Although this women's organization had fallen into a period of inertia after its initial flurry of activity during the May Fourth protests, Shanghai Communist leaders were optimistic about reviving it in large part because its chairperson, Huang Zonghan, was amenable to the idea of Communist participation.[30] Huang's willingness to allow Communists to develop their women's program in an almost parasitic fashion by using the resources and reputation of the Shanghai Federation of Women's Circles may well have been prompted by her earlier revolutionary experiences.

The daughter of a wealthy tea merchant in Zhongshan, Guang-dong, Huang Zonghan did not become involved in public affairs until after the early death of her husband, who had come from a Qing official family. She converted to Christianity while working with a famous Chinese woman doctor, Zhang Zhujun, to advance women's rights and to establish several hospitals and a girls' school in Guang-zhou. In 1907 she joined Sun Yatsen's Revolutionary Alliance and earned a reputation as one of the party's prominent anti-Manchu female revolutionaries. During an armed uprising against the imperial government in early 1911, she met and fell in love with Huang Xing, an influential leader of the Revolutionary Alliance. As he already had a family in Hunan, she became his second wife and worked closely with him until his death in 1916.[31]

After the May Fourth nationalist protests, Huang Zonghan par-ticipated in the founding of the Shanghai Federation of Women's Circles and was chosen as its chairperson. However, in a little over a year the group was racked by dissension, and much of its vitality was sapped by the sudden death of its vice-chairperson in 1920. After a year of inaction, Huang Zonghan willingly gave her approval to Wang Huiwu's proposal to revive the Shanghai Federation of Women's Circles by involving it in Communist-sponsored activities.[32]

The first public indication of any link between the Chinese Com-munist party and this independent women's group came with the publication of an announcement about the reorganization meeting in a leading Communist organ, New Youth.[33] The Communist imprint could be discerned in the new declaration and constitution that were drafted at that gathering. The declaration, for instance, emphasized the need to combat the inhuman conditions of women and child workers in the factories, to organize women workers and peasants, and to oppose warlord governments and foreign domination. But this reconstituted women's group not only pledged to focus on working-class issues but also called for equal educational opportunities for women, self-determination in marriage, the right of women to in-herit property and be employed, and women's suffrage. Its principles reflected the belief of Wang Huiwu and Gao Junman that it was the duty of conscious women to embrace the issues of working-class women while continuing to agitate for those causes that would im-prove the political, economic, and social status of women from other class backgrounds as well.

The declaration and constitution of the Shanghai Federation of

Women's Circles were circulated by Chen Duxiu, along with a short directive, to other Communist organizations to be used as a basis to develop their work on women's issues.[34] The inference in Chen's directive in November 1921 was that Communist organizations in other cities should either form such a woman's organization or influence an existing group to expand its mandate in accordance with the guidelines established by the Shanghai Federation of Women's Circles. Only the Wuhan Communist organization seems to have given any heed to Chen Duxiu's circular. Chen Tanqiu, one of its founding members, issued a public call for establishing a Wuhan Federation of Women's Circles in an article entitled "The Women's Movement" published in *Wuhan Weekly Critic* (Wuhan xingqi pinglun).[35] This particular Communist organization had already evidenced some interest in developing a women's program through its establishment of a Women's Study Society and its cultivation of a group of female students at the Hubei Provincial Girls' Normal School.[36] However, nothing concrete materialized in Wuhan, or in those cities, like Guangzhou and Hunan, where Federations of Women's Circles already existed. Thus, it was only in Shanghai that Communists were able to tap the resources of this women's organization for building their own program.

Wang Huiwu and Gao Junman gained the approval of the twenty-three members of the Shanghai Federation of Women's Circles who participated in the reorganization to sponsor two projects: a women's journal entitled *Women's Voice* (Funü sheng) and a school for girls, which was named Shanghai Pingmin Girls' School (Shanghai pingmin nüxuexiao). They also succeeded in attracting Wang Jianhong, one of the members of the federation, to play a leading role in these two endeavors. Having recently come to Shanghai after graduating from the No. 2 Hunan Provincial Girls' Normal School in Taoyuan, she was a strong-minded young Sichuanese woman whose father had encouraged her to seek her own way in the world and had provided the financial support to underwrite her living costs in Shanghai.[37] For Wang Jianhong, the journal presented an opportunity for her to facilitate women's speaking out on issues of importance to women. Moreover, she had strong opinions on women's issues that she wanted to express and a flair for writing. The girls' school had a powerful personal appeal as well, for like many women normal-school graduates in the early 1920s, Wang Jianhong had not been able to gain entrance into one of the few women's colleges that existed at that time.

Because this new school provided her with a rare chance to continue her education, she was highly motivated to make it succeed.

During the autumn of 1921, as the advertisements for these two undertakings were placed in various publications in Shanghai, especially the *Republican Daily* (Minguo ribao) and its supplements, no critical opinions were expressed in print by male Communists. However, *Women's Critic*, which was under the editorial control of Communists, did carry one article that echoed previous concerns articulated by Mao Dun about the dangers of this type of women's organization's becoming an instrument of a small aristocratic elite. It urged the federation:

Try to do something different. Don't just hold meetings.... There are issues women ought to take up right now. For instance, in education, there are many schools for girls—both public and private—that are not suited to the demands of new women and ought to be run by women themselves.... Yours should not be an organization of aristocratic women. The most able and conscious women in China now come from the third class [middle class]. Women workers in silk and cotton factories do not know what consciousness is. They feel nothing but their fetters, making it difficult to rely on them as pioneers. The pioneers definitely are among the conscious people of the third class.... The past Federation of Women's Circles had a very strong aristocratic tendency. We hope that from now on it will be an organization of the fourth class [working class].[38]

A Journal with a Distinctly Female Perspective

In December of 1921 the clandestine institutional affiliation between the Chinese Federation of Women's Circles of Shanghai and the Chinese Communist party produced its first concrete project with the publication of the first issue of *Women's Voice*, edited by Wang Huiwu and Wang Jianhong. This affiliation had distinct advantages for Communists in Shanghai, as it provided them with a propaganda organ that was officially identified with a legitimate women's group and could be legally disseminated. Significantly this was the first party-sponsored journal that really presented female voices. Not only were its editors female but its authors were also primarily women. The journal provided a forum for women in and around the Communist movement to express their ideas and develop their abilities to craft essays

and formulate arguments on important women's issues. It offered a
strong contrast with *Women's Critic*, the Nationalist publication that
was under the control of Chen Wangdao and other Communists.

In the beginning, however, the bulk of the essays were written by
Wang Huiwu and Wang Jianhong. They clearly faced the same problem that Chen Wangdao and Mao Dun had with *Women's Critic* and
Shen Xuanlu had with *Labor and Women* (Laodong yu funü): pro-
spective writers needed to be cultivated. However, once the Shanghai
Pingmin Girls' School opened its doors in early 1922, Wang Huiwu
and Wang Jianhong were able to create a talented writing staff from
the students, who were all encouraged to submit articles. They also
succeeded in soliciting articles from some women social activists and
students in Shanghai.[39]

Women's Voice was aimed at women educated in the May Fourth
period who viewed themselves as having attained "consciousness."
Wang Huiwu and her core of writers were quick to disassociate
themselves from "aristocratic" women and their causes, which they
argued had been left behind in the dustbin of history. The main message conveyed in the journal was that conscious women needed to
broaden their political orientation and become leaders for the causes
of working-class women, who were depicted as belonging to the
fourth estate, in the terminology of the French Revolution. Although
these women workers were portrayed in the journal as unknowledge-
able, lacking consciousness, and illiterate to the extent that they
"don't even recognize their own names," in the view of the authors
these women workers were nevertheless beginning to show signs of
consciousness, particularly in their willingness to engage in economic
struggles.[40] Wang Huiwu asserted, for instance, that in China, just as
in Europe after World War I, the rise of political women's movements
with strong working-class participation was now the order of the day,
and working-class women's movements were quickly overtaking those
of the third estate (that is, the bourgeoisie). Wang Huiwu pinpointed
the event marking the change from bourgeois to proletarian women's
movements as having recently occurred in China with the outbreak
of the strike at the British-American Tobacco Company (B.A.T.) in
Hankou, which involved more than three thousand women.[41]

The editorials and articles of *Women's Voice* elucidated Engels's and
Bebel's general historical schematic approaches to women's oppression that were presented in other Communist publications in the early
1920s. Much stress was placed on the existence of matriarchal societies

early in human history as proof that women had not always been the weaker sex. The writers strove to convince their readership that women's oppression was the result of a protracted historical process that began with the emergence of class divisions and private property rather than a natural expression of women's biological inferiority. They portrayed women as "the first workers" in human history, who had served as family slaves up until the present. Because most women were without property, they could in many ways be considered members of the "propertyless class" (*wuchan jieji*), a term that served for the word "proletariat" in Chinese. The interests and the influence of the journal were primarily limited to Shanghai, although it did carry a few articles on women's activities in Hankou, Guangzhou, and Hunan. It also strove to convey an international perspective by reporting on women's organizations in the Soviet Union and extolling the virtues of the female revolutionary martyr Rosa Luxemburg on the anniversary of her death in January 1919. However, its readership as reflected in the letters to the editor was mainly limited to Shanghai residents.

During the first half of 1922, Wang Huiwu and Wang Jianhong fashioned *Women's Voice* into a useful forum within Shanghai for women to express their ideas in writing. In comparison to the leading Shanghai women's publications of the early 1920s, such as *Women's Magazine* and *Women's Critic*, it really lived up to its name. The clearest manifestation of a difference between male and female perspectives on a woman's issue occurred when Margaret Sanger came to China in 1922 to advocate birth control. Both Wang Huiwu and Wang Jianhong published essays in *Women's Voice* expressing strong support for this cause. Wang Jianhong's piece, which she entitled "Birth Control and the Preservation of Love," stressed that the adoption of birth-control measures would enable women to reclaim their humanity. In a moving analogy, she likened Chinese women to sows that always had a sizable number of small ones hanging from their teats.

Wedged tightly under the control of men's heels, women are tools that satisfy male carnal desires.... Women constantly raise small children for men and aside from this role are nothing but ignorant animals. Chinese society is built upon this kind of slave system that lacks any compassion and human character.[42]

In Wang Jianhong's view, Chinese women would not be able to

achieve equality in marriage unless they limited the number of their children. Numerous offspring not only had a detrimental impact on women's ability to develop their own distinct personalities and capabilities but also removed all possibilities for women to become economically independent. Without economic independence, there was no possibility for "pure love" in marriage to be maintained because it would quickly be undermined by the unequal economic nature of the relationship.[43]

In her essay, Wang Huiwu echoed the theme of economic independence and stressed that birth control would improve the quality of life for the entire human race as well as give much greater freedom to women. Moreover, Wang Huiwu believed that the practice of birth control actually served to enhance rather than detract from women's maternal instincts (*muxing*) by reducing the physiological and psychological pain associated with numerous births and thereby allowing the mother to enjoy nurturing one or two children with the love and devotion similar to what one might lavish on a work of art. She also combated the view put forth by Margaret Sanger in her lectures that Marxists and socialists opposed the practice of birth control.[44] In so doing, Wang Huiwu was clearly saying that at least some women in the Chinese Communist movement supported this issue.

This female perspective on birth control presented in *Women's Voice* stood in stark contrast to the viewpoint of Mao Dun, who presented in *Women's Critic* what was becoming the standard Communist critique of birth control, a position that had been formulated in European socialist parties before World War I.[45] He argued that it was not excessive population but rather the unequal distribution of wealth and services that was the reason for poverty. The issue of birth control, in Mao Dun's view, diverted women from engaging in the struggle to bring about fundamental social and economic change. Once socialism was instituted, he maintained, there would be enough for everyone, and the large size of the Chinese population would no longer be considered a problem.[46]

These differences of opinion on birth control within the early Communist movement have a familiar ring. Similar arguments were voiced in China in the first several decades after the establishment of the People's Republic of China in 1949. Although Mao Zedong and other male Communists did not express their opinion on this issue in the 1920s, they were influenced by these early debates and accepted a utopian solution to the problem of birth control, with the result that the Chinese population is much larger today than it would have been if the female perspective in the Communist movement on the question in 1922 had prevailed.

Mixing Revolutionary Politics and Education

The Shanghai Pingmin Girls' School opened its doors to students immediately following the Chinese New Year holiday in early 1922. The main objective of the school was to develop a core of women cadres for the party, yet its curriculum and general orientation hardly resembled a cadre training institute. Rather than instilling specific mass-mobilization skills and revolutionary doctrine in students, the Shanghai Pingmin Girls' School strove to enrich its women students with a broad spectrum of knowledge that would not only encourage consciousness of class and gender oppression but also impart a sound general education.

Li Da was chosen as principal of the school by the Communist leadership, who clearly felt it was appropriate to appoint a man to such a leadership position, but Wang Huiwu did all the legwork and provided much of the day-to-day intellectual direction. For all intents and purposes, Li Da was a figurehead, and Wang Huiwu actually ran the school. While Li Da concerned himself with overseeing the operations of the Shanghai Communist organization, she rented a two-story building at 32 Fude Lane in the French Concession, designed the curriculum, found a core of qualified teachers, oversaw the recruitment of students, and set up a work-study program that provided the necessary funds for financially needy students.

Wang Huiwu was highly committed to making the school a success because of her own personal educational experiences in exclusive women's schools and her belief that all women should have an opportunity to be educated.[47] In contrast to elitist schools, which Wang criticized for training a small group of upper-class women to become good wives and mothers and for perpetuating traditional rules of propriety, the Shanghai Pingmin Girls' School would offer young women a "modern," scientifically oriented education, which would feature courses in sociology, English, mathematics, economics, Chinese, physics, and chemistry. In addition, the work program was designed to supply instruction, equipment, and materials for three kinds of jobs: sock knitting, tailoring, and weaving. Ideologically, the work program stood as a concrete embodiment of Engels's principle that women ultimately would be liberated by achieving economic independence. Wang's women would have the opportunity to learn a skill that would help remove them from patriarchal control. For Wang Huiwu, these reasons served as a justification for the tremendous outlay of her time and energy that was required to set up and run the program.

Realizing that the school could not survive without the active support and participation of the male membership of the Shanghai Communist organization, many of whom she hoped to recruit as teachers, Wang Huiwu strove to fend off two major concerns that existed within the party at that time: its impracticality and its excessive emphasis on education. She published one article to combat the skepticism about the school's feasibility in which she attributed the origin of these nagging doubts among Communists to the collapse of a similar work-study program in Beijing in 1920. Indeed, the failure of the Work-Study Mutual-Aid Corps, which had been supported by prominent intellectuals such as Cai Yuanpei, Hu Shi, and Li Dazhao, had stunned radical communities in China and set off a wide-ranging discussion about the reasons for the catastrophe.

In her article, Wang Huiwu argued that the Beijing experiment had been plagued by what she termed "pure anarchist" tendencies. She cited the example of members having been paid according to their needs rather than according to how much or how long they had worked. Such practices, she argued, were idealistic and totally impractical. Therefore, the work program of the Shanghai Pingmin Girls' School, she maintained, would be well supervised, and good records would be kept on what the participants produced and what they earned. As proof that she would keep to her word, Wang Huiwu published elaborate rules and procedures for the work program in subsequent issues of *Women's Voice*.[48]

A second step Wang Huiwu took to shore up support for her school was to invite leading Communists in the Shanghai organization to contribute articles to a special issue of *Women's Voice* hailing the opening of the school and underscoring the importance of its mission. They responded enthusiastically, allowing her to dedicate the sixth issue of the journal to this topic. Many pieces emphasized the widespread belief among male Communists that knowledge was critical to the development of consciousness (*juewu*), which was the first step to becoming a social revolutionary. At least some party members were willing to assert that education was valuable for its own sake. Li Da expressed his support for any effort that would universalize women's education, as the existing school system for women still was aimed primarily at a small elite.[49] Chen Duxiu evinced an even more liberal approach to the issue of women's education in his essay acclaiming the founding of the school:

Education has to be recognized as an important tool for social change, the ultimate tool for changing society. I am a person who is superstitious about education so I don't even oppose aristocratic education, especially in China where education is undeveloped. Having said this, we, however, hope that the educational world will move from aristocratic to universal.[50]

Li Da's and Chen Duxiu's championing of universal education (*pingmin jiaoyu*) was persuasive to many Communists in the early 1920s because they saw it as addressing the needs of the common people (*pingmin*), who were seen as possessing interests similar to those of the proletariat. Thus, this endeavor represented the mingling of May Fourth ideals with the Marxist preoccupation with the proletariat. The concept of universal education had gained great popularity in China after John Dewey promoted his philosophy of education in lectures at Beijing University in 1919. In the next year associations dedicated to the popularization of education proliferated. Some of the most well-known organizations were the Popular Education Association, the Cooperative Study Society, the Mass Education Speech Corps at Beijing University, the Society for Popular Education at Beijing Higher Normal College, the Common People's Night School at Beijing University, and the Common People's School run by the Chinese Association for the Promotion of Plain Education.[51]

However, one male Communist used the special edition of *Women's Voice* to voice his concerns about the tendency of the school to overemphasize its goal of educating women over its political mandate. Writing under a pen name, Shi Cuntong asserted: "I hope that we can train some female pioneers for the women's movement, the more the better. If they can only recognize a few characters or read a few books, in my opinion there is nothing of great significance in the school."[52] He was challenging Wang Huiwu's basic contention that educating women was in essence a worthwhile and revolutionary undertaking in itself.

Wang Huiwu's efforts to assuage the doubts of male Communists initially proved quite successful. In all she was able to sign up ten members of the Shanghai party as teachers, with others agreeing to occasionally give lectures (see table 1 for a list of teachers). Some, such as Chen Duxiu, Chen Wangdao, Li Da, Mao Dun, and Shao Lizi, were well known for their writings in the Shanghai feminist press. Their names were used in the extensive publicity effort that was undertaken at the time of the school's opening. Younger and less established party members like Gao Yuhan and Shen Zemin became mainstays of the teaching staff. In order to fill in gaps in the curriculum and strengthen the caliber of the staff, Wang Huiwu also invited three Chinese graduates of the Japanese Imperial University to teach at the school as well.[53]

Wang Huiwu devoted as much effort to finding students as she had to signing up teachers. As we reconstruct it, students were attracted to the school through three channels: the party network that was slowly being constructed in Jiangsu, Zhejiang, and Anhui; the efforts of Wang Jianhong, who made a special trip to Hunan to encourage former classmates and relatives to enroll; and a substantial publicity effort in progressive journals of Shanghai, including an advertisement in the *Republican Daily*, which ran for nineteen days. Through these efforts, approximately thirty women attended the school in the spring of 1922.

Wang Huiwu strove to create an environment in the school that encouraged students to become independent of traditional roles and family constraints. In this way, she was clearly emulating the Beijing work-study project, which had aimed to create a new life style.[54] Some students opted to shed their surnames as soon as they arrived at the school in order to signal their complete rejection of the patriarchal kinship system. Later, discovering that the lack of surnames proved too inconvenient in a culture where it was conventional to greet a stranger with the question "What is your surname" (*Nin guixing*), they decided to adopt very common, simple ones instead, like Ding (Ding Ling) and Wang (Wang Yizhi).

At least six students saw the Shanghai Pingmin Girls' School as a refuge from the system of arranged marriages. Ding Ling, Fu Yixing, Gao Yuhan, Huang Yuheng, Pan Yun, and Wang Yizhi had cut off relations with their families over this issue and desperately wanted an education in order to secure a means to earn their livelihoods. The poignancy with which the dilemma of arranged marriages was felt by these students was aptly revealed in a letter that one of them wrote to her parents and then published in the *Women's Critic*:

Table 1. *Teachers at Shanghai Pingmin Girls' School*

Teachers	Subject	Party or Other Affiliation
Agatha Harrison	English conversation (2nd term)	YWCA
Chen Duxiu	Sociology	Communist party
Chen Wangdao	Chinese language	Communist party
Cheng Wanzhen	English (2nd term)	YWCA
Fan Shoukang	Education	Graduate of Japan Imperial University
Gao Junman	Elementary Chinese	Shanghai Federation of Women's Circles, wife of Communist party member
Ke Qingshi	Elementary arithmetic	Communist party
Li Da	Mathematics and sociology	Communist party
Li Xixian	Economics	Graduate of Japan Imperial University
Mao Dun	English	Chinese Communist party
Shao Lizi	Chinese	Communist party and Nationalist party
Shen Zemin	English	Communist party and Nationalist party
Wang Huiwu	Elementary English and Chinese	Shanghai Federation of Women's Circles, wife of Communist party member
Zhang Qiuren	Elementary English	Communist party and Nationalist party
Zhang Shoubai	Chinese grammar	Communist party and Nationalist party
Zhou Changshou	Physics and chemistry	Graduate of Japan Imperial University, physics editor of Commercial Press

The reason I have left home is because of my arranged marriage with Mr. Wang. This matter ought to be based on love.... Although our country is corrupt, our civil law stipulates that marriage is to be decided by the people involved and only then is the permission of the parents gained. In April of 1916 the Supreme Court decided in favor of a daughter who objected to an arranged marriage. Although Mr. Wang and I are relatives, we have no feelings toward one another. Our relationship is like ice. Such a marriage could not produce love. Mr. Wang is the same generation as my grandfather. According to old conventions, this is not a good marriage. I argued against this marriage agreement both before and after the engagement, but my pleas fell on deaf ears. As parents, you were concerned about my honor, but not my feelings. I am a person and have my rights. For my future happiness, I have no choice but to leave home.... My suffering is unbearable. I hope you won't do this to my sister.[55]

The school attracted both women with relatively strong educational backgrounds and illiterate women of lower social status. Although the students were drawn from different class backgrounds, it was assumed that gender issues would serve as a common uniting bond. In practice, this proved to be only partially true. Qian Xijun perhaps more than any other lower-class student was able to identify with the May Fourth family rebellion issues because, by happenstance, she had been betrothed as a child to Zhang Qiuren, who was radicalized in the May Fourth protests and joined the Communist party. He opposed the entire system of minor marriages and arranged for Qian to attend the Shanghai Pingmin Girls' School specifically because he wanted her to acquire an education.

However, a number of poor women did not feel entirely comfortable in this school environment. Zhang Huaide, an older woman with two children who was also married to a Communist, lived in the kitchen of the school like a maidservant and claimed the dubious distinction of being the only student who was willing to clean the toilets. Lu Liang, who was attracted to the school by the advertisements placed in the newspaper, was quite evasive about her background and always seemed ill at ease. Later Wang Huiwu discovered that she was a concubine. Another woman was enrolled in the school by her husband, who wanted her to become educated. However, he was afraid that she might be contaminated by the emancipated behavior and views of the other students, so he demanded that she live in Wang Huiwu's home rather than in the dorm rooms.[56] As the only educated woman from an elite background who was in the work program, Wang Yizhi found that a strong cultural division existed in the student body. Of the students who had to earn their keep, she was the only one who was accepted socially by the more affluent girls, in large part because she was from a similar class background and a product of the provincial school system that had evolved in the early years of the twentieth century. Also, like them, she strove to be a liberated women in the May Fourth fashion.[57] Thus, a serious cultural clash developed along class lines in the school, and this clash revealed deep differences of opinions on gender issues.

Wang Huiwu tried to overcome some of these class antagonisms by creating a common concern among the students of all class backgrounds for the conditions of working-class women in Shanghai. When three thousand women workers struck at the Pudong Sino-Japanese Cotton Mill in May of 1922, she urged her students to form a strike-support team. They responded enthusiastically at first by writing up a leaflet that they circulated at one of the large rallies. But strike-support work proved more difficult than expected. Because most of the students came from distant provinces, they could not communicate with women workers in the Shanghai mills. Ding Ling recalled:

[We] went out to do propaganda for the strike, to encourage the workers and explain the reasons for their action. We went from one group of the girl-workers to another, but it was hard to talk with them because of different dialects [Ding Ling spoke with a Hunanese accent], and some of us had to have an interpreter.[58]

Students were also demoralized by organizational problems. Their goal of raising eight thousand *yuan*, which would have permitted the dispensing of two *yuan* to each striker, proved unrealistic; they collected one-eighth that amount. Further problems occurred when students failed to devise a system for distributing those funds that they had managed to raise.[59] This demoralization was a harbinger of much more deep-seated problems that would surface in *Women's Voice* and the Shanghai Pingmin Girls' School during the summer of 1922.

The school experienced serious problems when Wang Huiwu was unable to maintain an unwavering commitment among the voluntary teaching staff of male Communists. The upper-class students were quite vocal in their criticism about the irregularity and low standards of the classes. Ding Ling was particularly harsh in her indictment of Mao Dun, who she claimed rarely met with his English class and frequently came late at night, making the students get out of bed.

Moreover, he could not actually speak any English, he could only read it. Nor was he particularly loquacious in Chinese, she complained, since he frequently had difficulty with stuttering.[60] Thus, within a short time of the school's starting up, at least some male Communists began to question whether devoting such a large expenditure of time to a small girls' school was warranted.

Things Fall Apart

Signs that Wang Huiwu and Gao Junman's women's program had run into serious difficulty became apparent in late June when *Women's Voice* suddenly ceased publication after only ten issues. Soon thereafter most students in the upper class left the Shanghai Pingmin Girls' School in disgust. Although its academic and work programs continued to operate during the fall term, the school was permanently closed down at the end of 1922. Clearly, organizational weaknesses were an important factor contributing to the unraveling of this first women's program. The deathblow was struck at the second congress of the Chinese Communist party in July of 1922, when a major shift in leadership had a devastating impact on Wang Huiwu's power and status in the party. Ding Ling believed that the Communist male leadership was unhappy with the content of some of the articles in *Women's Voice*, which the leaders perceived as manifesting certain anarchist tendencies.[61] Ding Ling and Wang Jianhong were indeed gravitating towards the Anarchist party and were quite sensitive to the severe critique of anarchism that party leaders were engaging in at that time. Ding and Wang prudently kept their anarchist leanings hidden from their friends because of the efforts of Chinese Communist leaders in 1921, and even continuing into early 1922, to root out anarchist points of view in the party. Numerous essays were published attacking anarchism in party journals, and the Socialist Youth League was disbanded because of its strong anarchist leanings. Indeed, it was in the Shanghai Communist organization that the polemics against the anarchists were the most strongly argued.[62]

However, it seems unlikely that suspicions about anarchist tendencies in the women's program were strong enough by themselves to bring about the termination of the program's two major projects. Significantly, Communists' critiques of anarchism did not touch on women's issues, and no clear distinction was drawn in their writings between Marxist and anarchist feminism. Nor was there much recognition of the role that anarchists had played in defining feminism as a distinct political creed in China in the era of the 1911 Revolution.[63] The issues seized upon by the party leaders to distinguish Communists from anarchists were the endorsement of the Bolshevik Revolution, the belief in the short-term necessity of state power, the necessity for a dictatorship of the proletariat, and the use of the state apparatus as a vehicle for social change.[64]

The most crucial reason for the collapse of these two projects was the serious erosion of Wang Huiwu's power in the party that occurred when her husband was not reelected to the Central Committee at the party's second congress. The deterioration of Li Da's relationship with Chen Duxiu over the previous year finally resulted in the decision to replace Li with Cai Hesen, a Hunanese who had played a leading role in the New Citizen's Study Society and the work-study movement in France. A close friend of Mao Zedong and an ardent Marxist, he had joined the Shanghai Communist organization shortly after returning from France in late 1921.

This congress also decided to legitimate the women's program by establishing a Women's Bureau, which later came to be called the Central Women's Bureau (Zhongyang funübu).[65] This decision might well be interpreted as a vindication of Wang Huiwu and Gao Junman's work during the previous year. However, the text of the "Resolution on the Women's Movement" that was passed at the congress clearly stated that the main impetus for the creation of this women's office came from the Comintern.[66] If we are to believe the opinion of Chen Gongbo, one of the delegates to the party's second congress, there was little, if any, support among male Communists for establishing this organization.[67] This opinion seems curious in light of the initial achievements of Wang Huiwu and Gao Junman and in light of the fact that so many members of the party had expressed their concern in writing for improving women's status and transforming traditional norms. If true, this lack of support suggests that certain unarticulated traditional assumptions about women's political roles were militating against formalizing a women's program and legitimizing women's status in the Shanghai Communist organization.

Indeed, the entry of Chinese women into politics since the turn of the century had challenged a deeply embedded gender code of political behavior in Chinese culture—that the realm of politics was strictly a male domain. In the male-oriented, traditional world view, the mixing of woman and power—either political or domestic—actually violated the natural order of the world. For centuries, women had been barred from holding formal power in the imperial government. The wielding of power, which is rendered into Chinese as *quan*, was defined as a male prerogative and was central to the Chinese social construction of male political identity.

To be sure, much of the Communist ideology on women's emancipation consisted of a radical critique of this patriarchal tradition. However, the party's treatment of Wang Huiwu, particularly its failure to accord her full membership status and its termination of her projects once it was clear that Li Da would be stepping down from the inner sanctum of Communist decision makers, suggests that lingering traditional assumptions about women and power still influenced the attitudes and behavior of many party members. Indeed, Wang Huiwu proved much more adept at overcoming resistance to her leadership that stemmed from classical Marxist concerns about feminism than at combating traditional attitudes about women and power. A further indication of invisible patriarchal impediments to women was revealed in the party's decision to pass over Wang Huiwu for the position of director of the Communist Women's Bureau and appoint Xiang Jing-yu in her stead. In terms of experience, Wang Huiwu was the most qualified, but it seemed inconceivable for male leaders to allow her to hold a more important position than her husband did. As the spouse of Cai Hesen, Xiang Jingyu seemed much more appropriate. Thus, in one stroke, one couple replaced another at the top echelon of the party.

However, it is clear from the "Resolution on the Women's Movement" that the congress did affirm the continuation of much of the basic approach to women's organizing that Wang Huiwu had formulated over the previous year. In the congress's resolution, for instance, Communists pledged to help women achieve the right to vote and other political rights and freedoms, to protect the interests of women and child workers, and to destroy the bonds of all feudal customs of the old society.

The women of the entire nation are still imprisoned in the yoke of the feudal ethical code and lead lives similar to prostitutes. Women of every class in China are unable to obtain political, economic, and educational rights. Therefore the Chinese Communist party in addition to ardently protecting and struggling for the interests of women workers—like striving for equal wages and drafting laws for women and children, also should struggle for the interests of all oppressed women.[68]

After the congress, Wang Huiwu did not immediately withdraw from the party's women's work. In fact, she was more visible in this domain than Xiang Jingyu for the next few months. Most notably, she played a prominent role in founding the Women's Rights League in Shanghai (discussed in chapter 3) and tried to salvage the Shanghai Pingmin Girls' School. When the school reopened after summer recess, its programs were significantly curtailed. Although the literacy classes were continued, no upper-class curriculum was offered, nor were new students admitted into the work program, an indication of the heavy administrative burden entailed in running such an operation. Throughout the fall, Wang Huiwu and Li Da made efforts to shore up the school, particularly by trying to set up a new foreign languages program that was to feature courses in German, French, Japanese, English, and Esperanto.[69] Wang Huiwu used her connections in the Christian community to invite two members of the YWCA to teach English at the school: Agatha Harrison and Cheng Wanzhen.

Cheng Wanzhen was a potentially very significant contact for the Shanghai Communist organization because she was one of the most knowledgeable female social activists in the city on the subject of the conditions of women factory workers. Following her attendance at an international conference on female labor issues in October 1921 as a delegate of the Chinese YWCA, Cheng Wanzhen began to write extensive reports on some of the most horrendous conditions in Shanghai factories that women workers had to endure. The male feminists of the party eagerly published some of her studies in *Women's Critic*, but no effort was made to involve her in the Communist women's action program.

Nor was Wang Huiwu able to convince party members, including the new director of the Women's Bureau, that this school was worth the effort and expense of maintaining. At the end of the fall term, the Shanghai Pingmin Girls' School closed its doors permanently. Its most tangible benefit to the party was the politicalization of some of the students, including Wang Yizhi, who became the first women to be accepted formally into the Shanghai organization in August 1922.[70] Qian Xijun joined in 1925, and Ding Ling, in 1931. But for Wang Huiwu and Gao Junman, this collapse of their projects marked the end of their organizational relationships with the Chinese Communist party. Wang Huiwu moved to Changsha with Li Da at the end of 1921 and did not become involved politically with women organizers in the city. Gao Junman ended her relationship with Chen Duxiu and moved to Nanjing. While it is unclear whether the party's decision to terminate the projects she was involved with contributed to her decision to leave Chen Duxiu, she was unequivocal in her refusal to have any future dealings with the Chinese Communist party. A decade later she died in poverty, scorned by her family, who in conventional patriarchal fashion still respected Chen Duxiu.[71]

CHAPTER 3

Xiang Jingyu's Dilemma

I have real doubts about the demands of the Guangdong Federation of Women's Circles that women should acquire political rights and be able to establish their own separate households. These advocates believe that the emancipation and remaking of women must start with educational equality and economic independence. But ultimately such prerequisites will be difficult to achieve without women holding power in the legislatures, which will necessitate their engaging in a suffrage campaign. This agenda cannot be labeled as thoughtless or ill-conceived. However, in my estimation, the representative system of government, which originally was a revolutionary product of the middle class, has now become an impediment of the proletariat.

Xiang Jingyu, "Nüzi jiefang yu
gaizao de shangque," 1920

When Xiang Jingyu crafted this rather classical Communist stance on an influential Chinese women's rights group, she was still in France, where the animosity between feminists and socialists was intense and long-standing. Moreover, Xiang's stance was certainly in accord with the general sentiments of Alexandra Kollontai, appointed in 1920 as head of the Zhenotdel (women's section of the Soviet Communist party), who was much more vituperative in her indictment of bourgeois feminists than this newly appointed director of the Chinese Communist Women's Bureau. Indeed, one of the most difficult issues for Xiang Jingyu when she was appointed to this post in the summer of 1922 was to define the direction of this program, particularly its relationship to the diffuse and disconnected independent women's organizations that had mushroomed throughout Chinese urban centers in the wake of the May Fourth protests. Now that she was back in China, the orthodox Communist stance that she had found so compelling in 1920 no longer seemed so absolute, particularly because it was being called into question by some members of her own party.

The naming of Xiang Jingyu as the director of the newly established Women's Bureau seemed eminently reasonable from the standpoint of her May Fourth political and personal experiences but posed a serious dilemma for this recent convert to communism who was attentive to the incompatibility of Marxism and feminism. The daughter of a prosperous businessman in western Hunan, she had been deeply influenced by the nationalist-feminist atmosphere in Zhounan Girls' School in Changsha. Upon graduation, she demonstrated her commitment to women's education by taking the unusual step of starting a girls' primary school in her hometown of Xupu in 1916.[1] Her commitment to eliminating women's oppression was also manifested in her impassioned speech at the Zhounan memorial service for the tragic Miss Zhao, who had committed suicide to avoid an arranged marriage (discussed in chapter 1). Xiang herself refused to allow her father to arrange her marriage, delaying this step until the late age, by contemporary Chinese standards, of twenty-five. When she did decide to marry in May of 1920, she chose Cai Hesen, a man of similar political interests whom she had originally met several years earlier during her radical student days in Changsha.[2]

During her tenure as director of the Women's Bureau of the Chinese Communist party from 1922 until 1925, Xiang Jingyu struggled to come to terms with the theoretical and practical incompatibilities between gender and class. In so doing, she had to take into consideration the mixed views of her comrades, the impact of the formation of an alliance between the Nationalist and Communist parties (the United Front), the practical realities of women's organizing at that time, and the sentiments of her husband and close comrade, Cai Hesen. This chapter examines Xiang Jingyu's quandary and the resolution she reached in defining a women's program.

Growing Up in Hunan

Born in 1895, the year of the disastrous Sino-Japanese War, Xiang Jingyu began her life during a period when the imperial order was deteriorating, Western pressure was acute, and nationalism emerged as a vigorous force in China. She grew up in a province that was well known for its particularly intense nationalist political culture. Indeed, this culture helped to shape a unique political part for Hunan—one that has been likened to the role played by the daimyo of Satsuma in the Japanese Meiji Restoration (1868)—in the unfolding drama of twentieth-century Chinese history.[3] The fear of imminent colonization that swept through China in the wake of the humiliating defeat by Japan in 1895 and the intensification of Western efforts to carve out spheres of influence was particularly strong in Hunan because it could no longer prevent foreign penetration into its territory.

These nationalist sentiments were strongly articulated in the home of Xiang Jingyu. Her father, who may have been Tujia, had risen from humble origins to become one of Xupu's most successful businessmen and head of its chamber of commerce.[4] As a prominent member of the community, he maintained a keen interest in national affairs and encouraged his children to do likewise. As the ninth child (and first daughter) in the family, Xiang Jingyu grew up listening to her father's and brothers' ongoing discussions at the dinner table about foreigners' pursuit of privilege and Chinese responses.

In 1900, when Xiang Jingyu was five years old, foreign missionaries finally gained entry to Hunan, and although the total number of missionaries grew relatively slowly, reaching 123 in 1907, the dominant public impression was that a massive intrusion was underway.[5] This climate set the stage for a number of clashes between the local populace and Western missionaries, one of the nastiest of which occurred in 1902 at Chenzhou, a town in western Hunan not far from Xupu. Two British missionaries settled in Chenzhou and attempted to attract converts by establishing both a church and a hospital. It was generally believed that these two missionaries had gained entry to the town through connections with an ill-reputed landlord in the area, and Chenzhou residents were reluctant to become involved with either the church or the hospital. In the late summer of 1902, when a cholera epidemic spread through Chenzhou, some people became suspicious of the missionaries' housekeeper, widow Xiao, whom they had noticed putting a white powdery substance in the town well. A crowd of more than two thousand people gathered to accuse her and the missionaries of poisoning the well. Before long, the horde descended on the two missionaries and clubbed them to death.

According to other historical accounts, this event had a significant impact on western Hunan,[6] especially because of the reaction of the British consulate in Hankou, which decided to use the case as an example for all antiforeign elements in Hunan. The consulate's protests compelled the Qing imperial authorities to dismiss many officials and arrest three hundred people, including the widow Xiao. She perished in prison; ten others were executed. The British officials, in their effort to strike fear in the Hunanese inhabitants, even demanded that the court execute a fourteen-year-old waiter solely for kicking one of the corpses. Because the Qing officials appeared so acquiescent, if not downright obsequious, to the British, local indignation was quite impassioned. The incident even was reportedly discussed in Xiang Jingyu's home. However, it is questionable how much effect this event had on shaping the political consciousness of the seven-year-old Xiang Jingyu, although one of her brothers recalled it had inspired her to emulate the feats of Hua Mulan, a legendary female warrior who disguised herself as a man in order to join the battle against foreign invaders.[7]

Although it is difficult to judge the extent of this incident's impact on Xiang Jingyu, it certainly served to intensify the nationalist sentiments in Hunan. The person in the Xiang family who was the most galvanized by this heightened political environment and also the most influential in shaping Xiang Jingyu's ideas was her oldest brother, Xiang Xianyue. A follower of Liang Qichao, he went abroad to study at Waseda University in Tokyo, where he joined the Revolutionary Alliance and become a strong supporter of Sun Yatsen. Upon his return to China, he became one of the leading representatives of the Revolutionary Alliance in western Hunan.[8] Soon afterwards, Xiang Xianyue accepted a teaching post at the newly established Changde Girls' Normal School and facilitated his younger sister's admittance in 1907. It was during her school years that he exerted the most pronounced influence on Xiang Jingyu's political ideas. He furnished her with an abundance of nationalist newspapers, particularly *People's Journal* (Minbao) and *Renovation of the People* (Xinmin congbao), which emphasized the danger of national ruin by foreigners. During this time, he reportedly also had long talks with her about the French Revolution, entertaining her with stories of valiant French women revolutionaries.[9]

Thus, certain critical features of Xiang Jingyu's political makeup took shape while she was a student in Changde. For one thing, her identity as a woman revolutionary, which began to emerge in these years, was strengthened by the death of her mother. This very sad event in Xiang Jingyu's early life inadvertently facilitated her development as a strong independent personality who paid little heed to conventional women's roles. Secondly, the environment at the Chang-de Girls' Normal School proved particularly powerful in encouraging Xiang Jingyu and some of her classmates, including Ding Ling's mother, to link their quest for an education with patriotic goals. Xiang Jingyu felt compelled to make a solemn pledge with six other students at the school to devote herself to intensive study in order to achieve equality between the sexes and save the country through education.[10]

In 1912 Xiang Jingyu transferred to the First Provincial Girls' Normal School in the Hunanese capital of Changsha. Here she came under the tutelage of Zhu Jianfan, a progressive educator who had studied in Japan and was strongly influenced by Liang Qichao's nationalist approach to women's emancipation. He reportedly used to tell his students: "Half of China's four hundred million are women. If China is to become strong, it must educate and employ its two hundred million women. Women will then leave their homes and go out to run schools. They will wholeheartedly walk down the path of saving the nation through education."[11] Xiang was so enamored of Zhu Jianfan that when he was dismissed by the Hunan Ministry of Education for his novel ideas and went back to his previous post as principal of Zhounan Girls' School, she followed him.

At Zhounan, Xiang Jingyu was inspired to discard the traditional name that she had been given at birth, Junxian, which extolled the values of beauty and virtue, and assume the more modern sounding name of Jingyu, which connoted a state of alertness. Her new name revealed her strong concern with women's consciousness at this early stage in her life by expressing her belief that women needed to wake themselves up and end their somnambulance.[12] Her heightened political awareness was also reflected in the diary Xiang Jingyu kept while at Zhounan. Several entries testify to her strong identification with Sun Yatsen's Nationalist party and her belief that women had to assume responsibility for the sad state of national affairs:

Four years ago today our Republic of China was proclaimed.... Teacher Li told us about the problems and all the work that have gone into the Republic in these four years. In his view the reason that the country has steadily been sinking is because of us; we are unable to help the country because we cannot support ourselves. The country is a congregation of individuals. How can we let the country collapse? Hearing Teacher Li tell us that we should strive for independence, I suddenly felt a great hope that I could help create a new China.[13]

Xiang Jingyu's nationalist aspiration to participate in the creation of a new China manifested itself regularly during the next five years as she laid the foundation for her later political career. In the spring of 1915, she became a leading student activist at Zhounan in the effort to organize popular opposition to what became known as Japan's Twenty-One Demands. Japanese demands for all German rights in Shandong province, control of mineral exploration in southern Manchuria, the construction of railroads in central China, and part ownership of the Han Yeping Iron Company in Hubei, among others, galvanized Xiang Jingyu to address student assemblies, write leaflets, and organize a boycott of Japanese goods in Changsha.

After her graduation from Zhounan in 1916, Xiang Jingyu took the unusual action of founding an upper-primary girls' school in her hometown of Xupu. Here she combined her nationalist and feminist objectives. At the opening ceremony, Xiang Jingyu frankly stated that the girls at her school "were not studying for the sake of education or to get a husband, but rather to become part of a new citizenry."[14] This message was further developed during the daily morning assembly, where she reportedly focused on national affairs and urged the student body to devote itself to China's salvation.[15] At the same time, Xiang Jingyu promoted ideas about women's emancipation by demanding that all students unbind their feet and by arguing they should strive to be equal with men. The school anthem, which she helped to compose, captured this sentiment when it proclaimed, "Prepare for the advent of a glorious new world for women."[16]

Similarly, Xiang Jingyu's involvement in the New Citizen's Study Society manifested strong nationalist inclinations. The members of this Hunanese association, which was established in April of 1918, were interested in acquiring knowledge in order to help strengthen the nation. The group's name reflected the influence of Liang Qichao's work "The Way of the New Citizen."[17] Although she was not officially admitted as a member into the society until the autumn of 1919, when it decided to allow women to join, she came under its influence in the fall of 1918, when she participated in preliminary efforts to establish a work-study group.[18] When the May Fourth protests broke out in Changsha, Xiang Jingyu played a leading role, largely under the guidance of the New Citizen's Study Society. She often took to the podium to denounce the Duan Qirui warlord government in Beijing and to call for greater student supervision of the boycott of Japanese goods. Her feminist leanings were also revealed through her keynote address at the Zhounan memorial service for Miss Zhao in 1919. Through these activities, Xiang Jingyu earned such a reputation as a rabble-rouser that her father decided the time had come to marry her off to a local army commander. Her refusal to comply with this patriarchal mandate caused a grave rupture with her family and marked her first steps towards becoming a radical.

Becoming a Communist

Xiang Jingyu's decision to become a Communist was largely due to the influence of Cai Hesen. Although he was known to be aloof and stern, what she found most attractive in him was his political sophistication.[19] He was well known for his voracious consumption of Marxist literature and as the most theoretical of the Communists in the New Citizen's Study Society in France. More than any other single individual, he was responsible for creating the theoretical basis among these Chinese students in France for founding the European Chinese-Communist organizations in 1922. Moreover, he was reputed to be the first of his generation of radicals to speak specifically of founding "the Chinese Communist party."[20] During the time he spent in France, he developed a reputation as a zealous propagator of his newfound beliefs. His frequent letters to friends in China, which were filled with his thoughts on Marxism-Leninism and the Bolshevik Revolution, had a profound impact on Mao Zedong.[21] Cai also dedicated much effort to converting his compatriots in France. A few months after his conversion to Marxism in 1920, he called a five-day study session of the Chinese work-study students in Montargis, during which he distributed more than one hundred pieces of Western Marxist theoretical literature in order to convince the students to found a Communist party.[22]

Similarly, Cai Hesen's influence on the shaping of Xiang Jingyu's political views was enormous. Even before they traveled to France together, she had been drawn into the network of New Citizen's Study Society friends who met regularly at his home in Changsha. In

1918 she followed Cai Hesen to Beijing to participate in the training classes set up by the Franco-Chinese Society for Hunanese students interested in going to France as part of the work-study program. After returning to Changsha in the spring of 1919, Xiang Jingyu reportedly spent many hours at Cai Hesen's home and often studied with both Cai Hesen and Mao Zedong.[23]

According to Dai Xugong, Xiang Jingyu moved into Cai Hesen's home in August of 1919, when she refused the marriage arranged by her father.[24] Conceivably Xiang and Cai's romance could have started at this time, but the pristine and platonic cultural environment of the New Citizen's Study Society militated against such love matches. It was at this time, for instance, that Cai Chang, the younger sister of Cai Hesen who also joined the New Citizen's Study Society, renounced marriage and pledged to remain celibate for her whole life.[25] But even if Xiang Jingyu was not romantically attached to Cai Hesen in the late 1910s, she did develop a very close relationship with his mother and sister, which no doubt paved the way for her being brought into the family as Cai Hesen's wife in France. Indeed, they all set sail for France from Shanghai together in December of 1919. The political basis of her free-choice, "revolutionary" marriage to Cai Hesen was indicated in their wedding picture, which was sent to their family and friends back in Hunan—a photograph of the couple reading Marx's *Das Kapital*. Their declaration of their right to decide their marriage was widely hailed by their friends as thoroughly "modern" and a strike against patriarchal control of this family institution.[26]

When Xiang Jingyu left China, she was a strong advocate of the importance of education as a vehicle of social change. Her decision to participate in the work-study program was firmly based on this belief. However, once she married Cai Hesen, she became an almost instant convert to Marxism. Through his influence, she became an avid reader of publications like *L'Humanité*, *The Communist Manifesto*, and Engels's *The Origin of the Family, Private Property, and the State*.[27] By August of 1920, Xiang Jingyu believed that fundamental social change in China could best be brought about by emulating the Bolshevik Revolution.

Xiang Jingyu expressed this idea in "A Discussion of Women's Emancipation and Transformation," which represented the first piece of her writing that reflected her new political orientation. Published in 1920 in the journal *Young China* (Shaonian Zhongguo), this essay condemned the system of representative government as "an impediment of the proletariat" and denounced the private property system as "the source of countless evils." Her views on "bourgeois" women's groups seemed similarly characteristic of those of European communists. She declared that the cause of women's suffrage "was a dead end road" that should be avoided at all costs. Moreover, her May Fourth antifamily views were now infused with an Engelsian theoretical analysis of the family. She argued in this essay, for instance, that women could not be genuinely emancipated until collective institutions, such as public nurseries, replaced the family. Despite the strong influence of her newfound Communist orientation on women's issues, this article reflected some indication of the continuation of her May Fourth feminist ideals, particularly her proposal that women establish associations to promote free-choice marriage and thereby facilitate the termination of the arranged-marriage system.[28]

Xiang Jingyu returned to China in late 1921 after almost two years in France and settled in Shanghai, just as Wang Huiwu was publishing the first issue of *Women's Voice* (Funü sheng) and preparing to open the Shanghai Pingmin Girls' School. Despite her previous interest in women's issues, Xiang Jingyu chose to distance herself from Wang Huiwu's projects. Indeed, she did not create any sort of presence for herself at the school, although two Hunanese students, Wang Yizhi and Ding Ling, did pay her a visit in the early spring of 1922. Both Hunanese women were interested in meeting Xiang Jingyu because of knowledge they had of her through personal connections: Wang had first heard about Xiang Jingyu when she accepted a teaching position at Xiang's school in Xupu after she had departed for France; Ding Ling's mother had been a close friend and classmate of Xiang Jingyu ten years earlier.[29]

After her selection as director of the Women's Bureau in the summer of 1922, Xiang Jingyu remained deeply ambivalent about involving herself in women's work.[30] To be sure, it was a chaotic time in her life. The birth of her daughter in April of 1922 had placed a severe strain on her political activities, particularly because she and Cai Hesen were quite strapped financially and frequently had to move.[31] She soon decided to turn her child over to her mother-in-law in order to devote herself full time to her political career. However, taking her baby back to Hunan in August proved more complicated than Xiang had envisioned. She immediately found herself besieged by family requests, for her eighty-year-old father and sickly stepmother urged her to extend her visit and care for them and her ailing brother. Thus, no sooner had she resolved her unsettled feelings over her role as a mother when she was torn by internal conflict over fulfilling her obligations as a daughter. For two months she bowed to their behests, but then she could no longer suppress her desire to resume her political life in Shanghai. Extricating herself from her family proved emotionally difficult, however, and her sense of guilt was compounded when she learned that her brother had died soon after her departure.[32]

These personal problems, however difficult, do not sufficiently explain Xiang Jingyu's failure to involve herself with women's work in the party during the first year of her tenure as director of the Communist Women's Bureau. Most notably, she was able to find time to launch the new Communist theoretical journal *The Weekly Guide* (Xiangdao zhoubao), which was started soon after the second congress under the editorship of Cai Hesen.[33] Writing under the pen name of Zhenyu, Xiang contributed twenty-three articles to *The Weekly Guide* in the fall of 1922 and the spring of 1923 on topics related to the domineering role of the foreign powers in China.[34] In her essays for *The Weekly Guide*, Xiang presented herself as a virulent enemy of Western expansionism, which she argued had intensified in China since the Washington Conference. Through her writings, she sought to arouse the discontent of her country's populace against British and American policies to exploit the Chinese market under the pretext of pursuing cooperative interests. In her view, the Chinese people had been lured into a state of numbness by unsubstantiated stories in the foreign-controlled press. As a result, they were unable to perceive the extent to which China had been sold out by the various warlord governments, whom she mocked for the servile way in which they carried out the bidding of the imperialist powers with the ultimate result of ruining the country.[35]

While Xiang Jingyu was busy helping to establish *The Weekly Guide*, she ignored all women's work, even when it was occurring right in front of her. Most notably, she refused to become involved with the upsurge of a new wave of women's groups in the second half of 1922 and the beginning of 1923. The initial stimulus for this movement was the announcement by Wu Peifu's warlord regime in Beijing to reinstate the old parliament of 1913 and the former president of the republic, Li Yuanhong. It also announced it would reconvene the Constitutional Conference. Women from Beijing University, the Beijing Law Institute, and the Beijing Normal Women's College decided this was the opportune moment to press for women's legal rights. As they tried to hammer out a statement of principles at a meeting on July 15, 1922, serious disagreements, which proved unresolvable, caused them to split into two different groups, which were named the Women's Suffrage Association (Nüzi canzheng xiejinhui) and the Women's Rights League (Nüquan yundong tongmenghui). The Women's Suffrage Association promoted three goals: suffrage, women's inheritance rights, and the elimination of the traditional curriculum from girls' schools. Zhou Min, Zhang Renrui, and Miao Boying, who headed the Women's Rights League, developed a broader program. The main goals of their organization were the suspension of all laws that subjugated women to men; legal equality in marriage; prohibition of prostitution, concubinage, girl slavery, and foot binding; and the enactment of legislation protecting female laborers from wage discrimination, granting paid maternity leave for female factory workers, and providing legal guarantees for women's access to all educational institutions.[36]

From the inception of this political agitation, Communists showed a preference for the Women's Rights League over the Women's Suffrage Association, ostensibly because instead of focusing just on suffrage issues, the former advocated sweeping legislative changes for women in the areas of politics, family, education, and labor reform. However, according to the recollections of Zhou Min, a founding member of the Women's Rights League, the actual—though unstated—reason for the split into two groups was more personal than political: it ultimately boiled down to who was friends with whom.[37] From the inception of this upsurge of activity in Beijing, Miao Boying, a student at Beijing Normal Women's College and the first woman to have joined the Chinese Communist party (1920), worked closely with Zhou Min, her classmate, to found the Beijing Women's Rights League. When they succeeded in increasing the Beijing membership to more than three hundred, Miao Boying then traveled to Shanghai and Nanjing in the fall of 1922, where she helped to establish new chapters.

In Shanghai, Xiang Jingyu distanced herself from this endeavor of founding a Women's Rights League even though Zhang Renrui, one of her former classmates who had provided Xiang with housing during her stay in Beijing in 1918–1919, was among the Beijing league's founders. Rather, it was Wang Huiwu and Wang Yizhi who responded to Miao Boying's stimulus and took up the cause on behalf of the Shanghai Communist organization and became founding members of the Shanghai Women's Rights League when the organization was officially established on October 22, 1922.[38] In this endeavor, they cooperated with other prominent women activists in Shanghai with whom Wang Huiwu had cultivated political ties, such as Shen Yibin, the wife of a Nationalist party leader; Cheng Wanzhen, the YWCA activist who specialized in labor conditions and taught at the Shanghai Pingmin Girls' School in the fall of 1922; and Huang Shaolan, principal of the Bowen Girls' School, where the party's first congress had convened. In early November 1922, these Shanghai women took their first action by issuing a petition on behalf of the league that in essence called on members of the constitution committee in Beijing to include provisions in their draft constitution that extended civil rights to women and upheld the principle of gender equality.[39]

Wang Yizhi, who had recently decided to seek membership in the Shanghai Communist organization, expounded her reasons for participating in the league in her essay for *Women's Critic* (Funü pinglun) in late September 1922. She wrote:

We Shanghai sisters ought to take advantage of this opportunity to strive together with our sisters from Beijing for the rights we ought to have.... All rights in the constitution should be held equally by men and women. ... When we obtain the right to participate in government, we can elect representatives to all levels of the legislative assemblies who will formulate laws beneficial to us and advocate rights that will benefit us. Thus, now in particular, we should struggle for our suffrage rights.[40]

Moreover, Wang Yizhi also used this opportunity to express her opinion that men were the principal oppressors of women, thereby echoing the message that Wang Huiwu had expounded in "The Chinese Woman Question: Liberation from a Trap." "In this male-oriented society, the laws guarantee the interests of men," Wang charged. "Many men consider us ignoramuses and despicable."[41]

Although Xiang Jingyu did not share Wang Yizhi's clear bond with the women of the league, she could not criticize Wang's position, as it was in full accord with the women's resolution passed at the second party congress (July 1922). For this reason, Xiang Jingyu may have decided not to air her opinions on the Women's Rights League for the time being. However, some male members of the Shanghai Communist organization felt compelled to raise their concerns and objections. Chen Wangdao, for instance, in his role as editor of *Women's Critic*, stated that this "unrevolutionary political movement" did nothing to advance the cause of "the disinherited," even though it did have the redeeming value of advocating the rights of women.[42] Gao Junyu, a member of the party's Central Committee, published a more critical assessment in the Communist organ *The Weekly Guide*. He assailed the leaders of the Women's Rights League for their lack of socialist and class consciousness. He was particularly critical of the group's first aim: to achieve equality between men and women. It showed, he argued, that the members of the group aspired for equality with capitalists, not coolies.[43]

As the Women's Rights League continued to expand during the autumn of 1922 and the spring of 1923, establishing branches in Tianjin, Nanjing, Shandong, Hubei, and Sichuan, one of the most influential Communist male leaders decided to enter the public debate. Li Dazhao, the head of the Beijing Communist organization, accepted an invitation from the Hubei Women's Rights League to address its membership in February 1923 and used this occasion to counter the notion that the aims of these Chinese women's rights organizations were at odds with the interests of proletarian women. In his view, as long as China was under warlord control, all civil rights groups of this type essentially promoted the interests of the public and should be supported. He therefore advocated that women's rights organizations, whether under the rubric of the Women's Rights League or the Women's Suffrage Association, be established in every province in China.[44] The definitive pronouncement of this eminent Communist leader on the political merits of these women's rights organizations quelled the discussion by the few critical male Communists on this subject in the public media.

Although these two women's organizations were not able to fulfill Li Dazhao's invocation to spread throughout China, collectively they constituted the largest organized women's movement to develop since the toppling of the empire a decade earlier. When no concrete gains were exacted from the warlord regime in Beijing, which simply ignored their demands, many of these groups lapsed into inertia and allowed their publications to perish. Nonetheless, their upsurge succeeded in drawing many women intellectuals, professionals, students, and social activists into the effort, thereby significantly expanding these women's networks, which had slowly been constructed in China after the 1911 Revolution. Illustrative of the women leaders who emerged in this upsurge in women's rights activity was Deng Yingchao. A member of the Awakening Society in Tianjin during the May

Fourth period, she surfaced as a prominent leader of the Tianjin chapter of the Women's Rights League when it commenced operations on October 28, 1922. Partially as a result of her efforts, this chapter became one of the most active in the country through such undertakings as running a vocational school for women and publishing a journal. At the same time, Deng Yingchao gained some national prestige as a leader in the women's rights movement through her writings for the league's journal, which carried a number of her essays on the evils of the traditional marriage system.[45]

Capitulation or Change of Heart?

After watching these developments from the sidelines for many months, Xiang Jingyu, on the occasion of the party's third congress in June of 1923, suddenly signaled her willingness to relate to women's rights activists as well as to assume her position as director of the Communist women's program. She drafted a resolution on women's work for this congress, in which she specified that an important function of the party's work among women would be to gain influence over the "general women's movement" (*yiban funü yundong*), which she defined as comprising women's rights, suffrage, and social reform groups. Moreover, her resolution presented a wide array of slogans for this general women's movement to adopt, including the May Fourth appeals for freedom for men and women to have social contact with one another, the eradication of the traditional ethical code (*lijiao*), and equality of education for men and women.[46]

What motivated Xiang Jingyu to make such a dramatic shift? Did it reflect a genuine change in her political stance? Or did she finally bow to party pressures and grudgingly accept the leadership position that she had avoided since the summer of 1922? Her husband's comments on her sentiments suggest that Xiang Jingyu was quite averse to assuming the directorship of the Communist women's program. Shortly after her death in 1928, Cai Hesen wrote: "She was responsible for the women's work of the party, yet she herself was never happy to do 'women's work.' "[47] However, Cai Hesen's statement may have been motivated by certain political considerations, as this piece was written in Moscow in 1928 around the time of the party's sixth congress, which issued a strong condemnation of the Communist women's program during the previous five years. In order to assure that Xiang Jingyu would be enshrined in the annals of the party as the most revered Communist woman martyr of her era, Cai may have felt it necessary to dissociate her to some extent from the tarnished women's program, which stood accused of succumbing to bourgeois influences. Moreover, Cai Hesen was not a strong supporter of this women's program,[48] or of the alliance with the Nationalist party, which provided the main political context for Xiang Jingyu's women's work. In contrast to Cai, Xiang Jingyu's two biographers have marshaled a significant body of evidence, independently of each other, about her stance on the alliance with the Nationalist party and her formative political experiences in Hunan to support the contention that her decision to assume leadership of the women's program in June 1923 was sincere.

First and foremost, Xiang Jingyu was very much affected by the circumstances of the third congress, which came at an important juncture in the party's history. The year 1922 had witnessed a spate of labor strikes, prompting the Central Committee and some other leading Communists from the Shanghai organization, including Xiang Jingyu, to move to Beijing in late 1922 to take advantage of the opportune political moment provided by warlord Wu Peifu, who indicated he was amenable to Communist labor organizers. However, when the Beijing-Hankou Railway workers went on strike in February 1923, Wu Peifu decided the radicals had gone too far. He had his soldiers brutally suppress the strike on February 7, 1923, causing almost two hundred injuries and fifty deaths. The collapse of Communist labor organizing in the winter of 1923 had damped prospects for the party's ambition to lead a working-class revolution. Thus, the third congress was convened at a time when a distinct demoralization pervaded the party.[49]

This defeat helped to consolidate support for the Comintern proposal that the Chinese Communist party enter into an alliance with Sun Yatsen's Nationalist party. The issue of cooperation with Sun Yatsen's party had set off a major controversy in the party when first raised by the Comintern representative Maring at a special plenary session in Hangzhou in August 1922. The issue was placed on the agenda once again for the third congress, which was convened in June of 1923 in Guangzhou, the political center of the Nationalist party. After another heated discussion, the congress decided to pursue the collaboration. It also ratified the policy of having individual

Communists join the Nationalist party. Xiang gave her wholehearted endorsement to the United Front despite the strong objections of her husband, Cai Hesen, to this policy.[50] Thus, it was in the context of the formation of the United Front that Xiang Jingyu decided to assume the leadership of the women's program of the Chinese Communist party and begin working with "the general women's movement." Clearly now that the Chinese Communist party had committed itself to promoting a national revolution, it seemed quite feasible and appropriate to begin women's work and especially to strengthen ties with independent women's groups. Xiang's willingness to differ with her husband on this matter of utmost importance to the party has been explained by her biographers, Dai Xugong and Gu Ci, primarily in terms of the strong nationalist sentiments that she acquired while growing up in Hunan. The nationalist influences that shaped Xiang Jingyu's early political views provide much insight into her reasons for supporting the proposal before the third congress that the Chinese Communist party collaborate with the Nationalist party for the purposes of launching a nationalist revolution, even when it meant opposing her husband's stance. Moreover, now that the Communist party was resolved to bring about a national, rather than proletarian, revolution, Xiang saw a political purpose for working with women's organizations. However persuasive these renditions of her pre-Communist years, an even stronger indicator of her attitude about leading the women's program can be gained by examining the actual role that she carved out for herself.

The Politics of Collaboration

The formation of the Communist alliance with the Nationalist party galvanized Xiang Jingyu into women's work. She seems to have been guided not by a sense of defeat or compliance as much as by a dedication to a new mission. From the third party congress until mid-1925, she poured an extraordinary amount of energy into creating a voice for herself in the world of independent women's groups in Shanghai, establishing a foundation for a broad-based women's movement, and utilizing the resources of the Nationalist party to consolidate her program. What is most striking about her actions is that they were more strongly focused on developing the institutional infrastructure of the Nationalist rather than the Communist women's program. Indeed, one of Xiang Jingyu's most significant achievements during her tenure as director of the Communist Women's Bureau was to construct the first viable women's program in the Nationalist party.

Like her predecessor, Wang Huiwu, Xiang Jingyu saw the creation of a strong voice for herself in the feminist press as her first major goal as director of the Communist women's actions. The resolution she had drafted on women's work for the third congress of the Chinese Communist party had emphasized the need to have a new publication that would "guide" and "criticize" the women's movement.[51] Xiang Jingyu chose to implement this element of her resolution not by turning to an independent women's group, as Wang Huiwu had done for *Women's Voice*, but rather by gaining approval from the Nationalist party leaders in charge of the *Republican Daily* newspaper to put out a new supplement entitled *Women's Weekly* (Funü zhoubao). On August 22, 1923, the first issue of this publication appeared, providing Xiang Jingyu with a public platform to air her views to Chinese activists. Echoing Xiang Jingyu's resolution for the third congress, its lead article announced that the role of this new publication was to guide and criticize the women's movement.[52]

Gaining editorial control of this weekly newspaper supplement, which generally contained four to eight pages, represented a real coup for Xiang Jingyu. In one stroke she gained the expertise and distribution networks of a publishing establishment that had been in existence for eight years. Moreover, included in the decision to commence *Women's Weekly* was the provision that *Women's Critic*, which had also been a supplement of the *Republican Daily*, would be shut down.[53]

For two years *Women's Critic* had served as an important medium for male Communists, particularly Mao Dun and Chen Wangdao, to present their views on women's issues and the women's movement. *Women's Critic* had in fact featured many articles that were basically supportive of the Chinese women's rights movement. Wang Yizhi's piece in support of the Shanghai Women's Rights League, for instance, had appeared in that publication. Moreover, Chen Wangdao and Mao Dun had cultivated a few women writers, such as Yang Zhihua, in an effort to develop a definite female voice for their publication. In the second half of 1922, shortly after Yang had joined the Socialist Youth League, she published five articles in *Women's Critic* on topics closely connected to important issues in her personal life at that time, namely, love, morality, divorce, and social contact between men and women.[54] Nonetheless, this weekly supplement of the *Republican Daily* newspaper was controlled by a small group of Communist male feminists who from time to time were inclined to express their reservations and criticisms of the activities of the Communist women's program and the women's rights movement, as Wang Huiwu had experienced. In this respect, *Women's Critic* differed from the other male-feminist and Communist periodicals in Shanghai, such as *Awakening* (Juewu), *Women's Magazine* (Funü zazhi), and *Chinese Youth* (Zhongguo qingnian). *Awakening*, also a supplement of *Republican Daily* under the editorial control of Nationalist/Communist member Shao Lizi, featured many articles on women's issues but rarely served as a sounding board for strong criticisms of specific actions by women's rights groups. Yun Daiying, who was just commencing *Chinese Youth* for the Chinese Communist party, was also a more sympathetic editor to the actions of women's groups than Chen Wangdao and Mao Dun had been. Thus, by shutting down *Women's Critic* and thereby effectively blocking the most likely outlet for criticism of her efforts to influence the Chinese women's movement, Xiang Jingyu asserted herself as the leader of the Chinese Communist women's program.

At the same time, she strengthened her ability to implement one of her goals set forth in the resolution on women at the third congress, namely, that party members should desist from expressions of scorn about the women's rights movement or its leaders and be careful not to drive them away from the revolutionary movement by overstressing the theory of class struggle in a rigid fashion.[55] From its inception in August of 1923 until its demise in January 1926, *Women's Weekly* carried articles on a wide range of topics such as love, sexuality, morality, and consciousness. In this respect it was very similar to *Women's Critic*. The major distinguishing characteristics was Xiang Jingyu's concerted effort to use it as a vehicle to appeal directly to Chinese women's organizations to involve themselves with national affairs. Indeed, the majority of the thirty-some articles that Xiang Jingyu contributed to *Women's Weekly* were dedicated to this purpose. Xiang Jingyu went to great lengths to express support and encouragement for the basic orientation of these women's groups, which she believed promoted "the human rights and civil rights of women."[56] Perhaps her strongest statement in support of the goals of women's suffrage groups was contained in her article about Wang Bihua's efforts in Zhejiang to use the Women's Rights League to press for women's civil rights, particularly the right of women to hold posts in government. On this occasion she wrote:

The women's rights movement is born out of the need to solve the specific problem of the female sex.... Sometimes the problem might appear superficially to be that of a few or a certain group of women, but actually it has general significance. The significance of the women's rights movement is to wipe out the oppression of the female sex, develop equality between men and women, and restore the human rights to which women are entitled.[57]

While writing in support of these women's groups, Xiang Jingyu nevertheless maintained that they could not accomplish their goals unless they became involved in revolutionary politics. She contended that they could not ignore the fact that warlord regimes and imperialist meddling were "wrecking China" and "trampling" on civil rights, seriously impairing all efforts to win equality for women. Without such involvement, she warned, their achievements would all disappear like "sand castles," as had happened in Hunan when the "diehards had offhandedly abolished" women's hard-won right to own property.[58]

Whether Xiang Jingyu cajoled or criticized women's rights groups, she aimed to persuade them to pay more attention to problems affecting the vast majority of Chinese women. In one article, for instance, Xiang Jingyu urged women's rights leaders to emulate the unusual example of Tang Qunying and Zhang Hanying, two Hunanese women involved in the 1911 Revolution. She recounted how Tang Qunying and Zhang Hanying had listened patiently as women poured out their tales of maltreatment by husbands and then "actually acted as women judges who gave out rulings that touched many people ... some of the women of Changsha came to love and respect them and united under their banner."[59] On another occasion, Xiang Jingyu urged that Wang Bihua, a prominent Zhejiang women's suffrage leader, propose laws that would allow women to own property in order to improve women's social status. Through such efforts, Xiang believed, women leaders of the 1920s could give birth to a genuine "mass" (qunzhong) women's movement.[60]

To Xiang Jingyu, the only way to develop a truly "mass" women's movement was to integrate the struggles of feminist groups with those of workers. First and foremost, it was necessary to bring the "miserable state" of women workers to the attention of women's rights advocates.[61] For this purpose, Xiang focused on silk workers, devoting six articles in *Women's Weekly* to this topic in the autumn of 1923. These women had first caught her attention in 1922 by engaging in a major industrial strike, which put forth the demands that their union, the Women's Industrial Society to Promote Virtue (Nüzi gongye jinde hui), be recognized, and that they be given a ten-hour workday, a day off once every two weeks, and improved working conditions.[62] Before long, this strike spread from a few filatures to over forty, despite the limited resources of the women strikers, who usually depended on their day's wages to feed themselves and their families. Their ability to stay out of work for four days was regarded as truly phenomenal. Thus, even though they were unable to win their major demands, they did succeed in getting the leaders of the Women's Industrial Society to Promote Virtue released from jail and winning the right to leave work half an hour early during the oppressively hot summer days. The strike was viewed by Communists as a milestone in Shanghai labor history and prompted male feminists such as Shao Lizi to write extensively about the event.[63] However, in the transition of the leadership of the Communist women's program between Wang Huiwu and Xiang Jingyu, no Communist organizers were able to develop solid links with the strikers that August.

In the autumn of 1923 Xiang Jingyu used her pen to draw the attention of Shanghai literate women to the plight of these silk workers. Although the strike wave of 1922 had subsided, she dedicated herself to devising tactical coalitions that could strengthen the organizational basis of workers' struggles. In her writings, she stressed not only the importance of women workers expanding their own networks and relying more heavily on their own organizations but also the need for women's social action groups to come to the support of women workers, particularly during strikes, when they could provide financial and political assistance. In particular, she suggested that they could appeal to government authorities to release union leaders who had been imprisoned. Xiang exemplified her advice by personally sounding the alarm in *Women's Weekly* when Ninth Sister, a former silk worker who had become a leader of the Women's Industrial Society to Promote Virtue, was detained by the police.[64]

Xiang Jingyu was not always pleased with the response of Chinese women intellectuals and suffrage activists to the plight of women workers. The pages of *Women's Weekly* and other journals carried a number of her articles expressing frustration and criticism. Indeed, Xiang Jingyu did not completely embrace female intellectuals after the third party congress. In fact, from time to time in her writings she expressed her concern for the narrowness of their vision and their passivity. In her most harsh indictment of women's rights groups and suffrage groups during her three-year tenure as head of the Women's Bureau, she described them as made up of the "cream of women intellectuals," who were used to lives of leisure and were totally dependent on the support of men—fathers, husbands, and sons. Moreover, she wondered whether these women's involvement in feminist organizations amounted to anything more than a passing fancy. Of particular concern was the tendency of many of their organizations to easily lapse into dormant periods. On one occasion she lashed out at the merits of trying to establish a representative system of government in China when it was so besieged by despotic, decadent warlord rule. Her caustic remarks on this subject included women's suffrage, which she believed was doomed to failure. "Their efforts will result in the whole bunch of them entering the pigsties in the capital and the provinces where, together with the male pigs, they will preside over the country's catastrophes and the people's calamities."[65]

Citing such examples, several scholars have noted this seeming vacillation in Xiang's stance, interpreting it as either a type of ambiguity that resulted from the dilemmas inherent in the politics of the United Front or from a tension between her Marxist and feminist predilections.[66] However, a close scrutiny of her writings in conjunction with the political events of the day and her political activities reveals that her essays for *Women's Weekly* and other journals were intended to meet the needs of a specific political moment. For instance, her despair about the ability of suffrage groups to obtain civil rights for women was voiced in early 1924, a time when Cao Kun, a thoroughly corrupt president, had brought what was left of representative government in China to an all time low by buying the votes (reportedly at $500 each) to secure his election. At the same time, he imprisoned one of the few upstanding members of the cabinet, the brilliant jurist Luo Wengan, who had originally agreed to serve in the Beijing warlord government in order to upgrade its integrity and moral character.[67] Throughout China at this time, the Cao Kun regime was likened to a "bunch of pigs." Thus, Xiang's pessimistic views on the efforts of women to gain rights in a representative political system that had essentially disintegrated seems quite understandable. At this moment she may well have decided that it was hopeless to continue in this direction. However, as will be discussed at greater length in chapter 5, in late 1924 when she was once again able to see a purpose for pursuing women's rights issues, she did so with tremendous exuberance and dedication.

By the same token, Xiang Jingyu shifted her assessment of Christian social action groups. To begin with, she was quite critical of such organizations, particularly the YWCA, which she labeled as "a tool of foreign capitalism" in July of 1923, soon after she began to lead the Communist Women's Bureau.[68] Four months later, Xiang Jingyu changed her mind. She acknowledged in *Women's Weekly* that the YWCA's commitment to social activism and its organizational capacity were quite impressive, surpassing what she had seen in at least a dozen other women's groups in Shanghai. Now she clearly viewed these social activists as potential partners in any upcoming revolutionary movement. What was most striking about her appeal to these Christian women was that it was embedded in the logic of their religion. Xiang reasoned: "Were Jesus living today, he surely would be leading the oppressed Chinese people to wage intense struggles against the foreign powers and warlords. I very much hope that my sisters of the YWCA will persist in Jesus' true spirit and heroically take part in the National Revolution."[69]

In this case, her views seemed to have changed as a result of her increasing knowledge about the activities of the YWCA in Shanghai. Indeed, the pioneering efforts of its staff, especially Cheng Wanzhen, to draw national and international attention to the deplorable working conditions of Chinese women factory workers dovetailed quite closely with Xiang Jingyu's agenda. What is most notable in this respect is that Xiang's admiration for these Christian women was articulated when many male Communists were pursuing a vigorous anti-Christian movement. A weaker women's leader would not have dared to counter in any way such a major party undertaking.

The National Revolution that Xiang Jingyu foretold to YWCA social activists was still an unrealized goal in 1923. Although the alliance constructed between the Nationalist and Communist parties was predicated on the assumption that such a revolution could be brought to fruition, there were few indications in 1923 that it might actually occur. At this time, Sun Yatsen had just regained a foothold in Guangzhou and was beginning to build a government there. Nonetheless, Xiang Jingyu dedicated herself to the task of setting in motion a National Revolution by assiduously creating an organizational foundation among various sectors of women. Her ultimate aim, as spelled out in the resolution on women's work she drafted for the third congress, was to unite the Chinese women's movement. In this regard, *Women's Weekly* functioned as an important vehicle for creating links between various sectors of women and the revolutionary women's political center that she was simultaneously trying to forge.

Significantly, Xiang Jingyu decided to construct this political center in the heart of the Nationalist party. The first steps in this direction were taken by Communists at the first executive meeting of the third congress, which was convened in Shanghai on November 24, 1923, when it was decided that forty members of the Shanghai Communist organization, including Xiang Jingyu and a core of women Communists, would join the Nationalist party in order to promote the nationalist movement. After the Nationalist party formally moved to establish the Central Women's Department in January 1924, the Shanghai Nationalist organization created a women and youth section under the control of veteran party leader Ye Chucang, who was the chief editor of *Republican Daily* in Shanghai. In April of 1924, the Shanghai Women's Movement Committee of the Nationalist Party was established under its auspices, with Xiang Jingyu named as its head.[70]

The bureaucratic paper trail left by Xiang Jingyu suggests that she was very energetic in her assumption of this post.[71] This committee was to accomplish four tasks: (1) develop contact with women professionals, workers, students, and housewives, (2) stress the importance of disseminating education to the common people, (3) unify all women's groups, and (4) publicize other socialist countries' practices concerning women.[72] To commence, Xiang Jingyu gathered together thirty members to form the Shanghai Women's Movement Committee, which grew in the next half year to more than sixty. Its members included important women in public affairs, such as Wang Liming, the founder of the Chinese Women's Temperance Society (Zhonghua funü jiezhi xiehui), but the core of activists were primarily members of the Communist movement, such as Yang Zhihua, Zhang Jinqiu, He Jinghui, Li Yichun, and Wang Yizhi.[73] This Communist core held open meetings of the Shanghai Women's Movement Committee in order to solidify links with various women's organizations in Shanghai, set up night schools which offered literacy classes to workers, issued indictments against British and Japanese imperialist actions, investigated the conditions of women workers, and gathered information on girls' schools in the region. Indeed, they launched the first systematic attempt to gather information about the full range of women's activities under way in Shanghai.

The effort Xiang Jingyu devoted to *Women's Weekly* and to the Nationalist women's program seems to have left her little time to develop the infrastructure of the Communist Women's Bureau as well, a state of affairs that Peng Shuzhi, one of the leaders of the Shanghai Communist organization, noted in his memoirs.[74] For Xiang Jingyu, the Nationalist women's program had two distinct advantages over the Communist one: legitimacy and resources. The Nationalist program could operate in the open as a legal entity and hold public meetings. In addition, it had access to the party's political and, to a limited extent, fiscal resources, including an office from which to coordinate its various programs.

Xiang Jingyu might have chosen to put more effort into developing the institutional structures of the Communist Women's Bureau if the upsurge in female labor militancy of 1922 had not dissipated. She remained strongly interested in helping China's disinherited, particularly factory workers, but found little opportunity to develop strong ties with working-class women. No doubt her Hunanese origins were an impediment, as she could not communicate directly with most women workers who spoke Shanghaiese or some other regional dialect. But a much more difficult problem resulted from her decision to target women silk workers. From Xiang's perspective, women in the Shanghai filatures possessed the greatest potential for revolutionary action because they were the most oppressed and in 1922 the most militant.[75] Indeed, during the hot summers, these factories, with their boiling vats of water for softening cocoons, seemed like the very epitome of capitalist exploitation: these virtual infernos were without question unfit for human use. It was invariably during these sizzling summer months that strikes occurred. However, Xiang never succeeded in developing roots among the silk workers. In large part this failure was because she was up against a formidable adversary in Mu Zhiying, a leader of the Women's Industrial Society to Promote Virtue, a union that had established sway over the silk workers in the impressive strike of 1922. Despite Xiang's overtures, Mu refused to allow young women Communists to influence the course of strikes of 1923 and 1924 in the plants under her union.[76]

Xiang Jingyu's frustrations with working-class organizing were offset by her accomplishments in developing a foundation for Communist women's work among students and intellectuals both in Shanghai and elsewhere. Miao Boying, for example, became very active in the Beijing Nationalist Women's Department. And Liu Qingyang and Deng Yingchao followed in her stead in women's journalism by assuming the editorship of *Women's Daily* (Funü ribao), which began publication in Tianjin in 1924 and was China's only women's newspaper at that time. Although it was not formally affiliated with a political party, this newspaper was funded by Michael Borodin, the special Comintern adviser to Sun Yatsen, who arrived in China in late 1923 to oversee the consolidation of the alliance between the Nationalist and Communist parties.[77]

Xiang Jingyu thus laid the organizational foundation for the eagerly hoped for mass mobilization of women in the National Revolution. She not only cultivated leaders and strengthened networks but also began to demonstrate the potential value of women's work to leaders of both the Chinese Communist and Nationalist parties. Indeed, she started the first viable women's program in the Nationalist party and thereby encouraged women in Guangzhou at the heart of the Nationalist party to follow in her footsteps. At the same time, she played an important role in shaping the political careers of the first generation of Communist women, a topic that will be explored in the next chapter.

CHAPTER 4

Inside the Party

The histories of revolutionary movements from the Paris Commune to the Sandinista Liberation Front reflect a common practice of according lower political status to female participants than to their male counterparts despite impassioned proclamations by male leaders about the importance of women's emancipation. Many aspects of women's political experiences in the Chinese Communist party during its formative years conform to this worldwide pattern.

Despite the universality of this feature, the inner workings of these parties have remained one of the most obscure areas of their histories. We know little about how the particular individuals participating in these movements came to grips with these conflicting and paradoxical dimensions of party life. Of particular concern are the motivations of and accommodations made by the women who chose to remain inside the party rather than pursue gender issues through other means. These issues are all the more perplexing in the Chinese case because the first generation of women attracted to the Chinese Communist party was an outstanding group of revolutionaries who had been radicalized in the May Fourth Movement and dared to challenge countless expressions of patriarchal social power in their families and schools.

This chapter examines the interior life of the Chinese Communist party from its inception until the May Thirtieth Movement (1925) primarily by focusing on the experiences of the men and women in the Shanghai Communist organization. It reveals the processes through which central aspects of the existing gender system in the larger society were reproduced and reinscribed in the body politic of this party at the

[handwritten marginalia: "Use contradiction of sexuality & equality : patriarchy"]

same time that its founders formulated a radical program on gender transformation that challenged the dominant culture. It also reveals how this contradiction was further mirrored in the fashion in which male Communists conducted their personal lives.

Because women party members rarely committed their thoughts on such problems to paper, the sources are limited. That much of the information is fragmentary and presented from a male perspective inhibits a comprehensive exploration of the connections between the personal and political aspects of women's lives. As a result, these women sometimes seem to sit somewhat stiffly on the pages of party documents. Nonetheless, an exhaustive combing of the relevant materials illuminates much about gender relations inside the party in those years. This chapter begins by looking at the backgrounds and early politicalization processes of the first generation of women Communists and then probes into their experiences once they entered the party.

The First Generation of Women Communists

Between 1921 and May of 1925, Chinese Communist party leaders were successful in recruiting approximately one hundred women into the party.[1] This generation of women in the Communist cosmos, like some early male members of the party, experienced the May Fourth Movement as a great historical event that endowed them with a specific identity. For these women, May Fourth served as a common point of reference in their lives that distinguished them from both previous and subsequent generations of radical women.[2]

While the impact of May Fourth was the most crucial unifying characteristic of this generation of Communist women, an examination of their class origins, education, and politicalization process reveals other salient characteristics about their radicalization. As is common in revolutionary movements in other parts of the world, these early women Communists for the most part came not from the ranks of the dispossessed but from gentry, intellectual, or commercial families, though the economic circumstances of these families varied enormously. Among those from prosperous families were Xiang Jing-yu (discussed in chapter 3), Yang Zhihua, who was the daughter of a silk merchant and small landlord in Zhejiang, and Yang Zilie, whose childhood in an extended multigenerational compound in Hubei was reminiscent of gentry life as portrayed in the novel *Dream of the Red Chamber*. Also from a financially well-off family was Liu Qingyang, whose Muslim (Hui) father rose from poverty to modest prosperity by operating a mutton market in Tianjin and whose brothers became influential in north China newspaper circles. However, the largest group of the first generation of women Communists according to the existing evidence consisted of women from déclassé backgrounds. Illustrative of those déclassé women who came from recently impoverished elite families were Zhong Fuguang, whose father was a destitute Sichuan landlord; Cai Chang, who claimed descent from the illustrious official Zeng Guofan, although she too grew up in straitened circumstances; and Deng Yingchao, whose gentry mother was widowed early and had to work as a teacher to support her children.

A second similar feature about these women Communists was their enrollment in provincially run middle and normal schools. From what we can ascertain, these schools exerted a considerable impact on their early political socialization. They not only removed these women from the direct control of their families but also gave them a new sense of self-worth, a quality that often had been lacking in their mothers' lives. Indeed, in some cases, their mothers had even lacked a name and responded to a variety of role-specific appellations, such as the mother of so and so, or the person in the house. The newfound identity that was acquired in school was instrumental in helping those women who had been raised to be docile and self-effacing to confront the tremendous psychological impediments that stood in the way of their breaking with prescribed gender roles and assuming assertive roles in public life. Freeing them from fairly isolated lives like their mothers', the schools allowed them a unique opportunity to experience a strong sense of community with other young women and exposed them to a host of new ideas. These schools also conditioned women's early political orientation by engendering a feminist and nationalist consciousness, as well as by providing certain participatory skills, particularly during the May Fourth protests.

To be sure, only a small percentage of the women enrolled in these schools responded to the nationalist and feminist ideals that were circulating in these girls' schools in the late 1910s to the extent that they could be deemed May Fourth political activists. Even fewer ultimately joined political parties or independent women's organizations. However, an examination of the backgrounds of those early Communist women for whom biographical information is available, in conjunction with information on Nationalist and women's rights leaders, reveals that these schools were critical to the making of women political activists in the 1920s. Significantly, many of the women who did participate in local May Fourth demonstrations and boycotts of Japanese goods began to rebel against school authorities for upholding traditional values about female decorum. Yang Zilie and five other students at the Hubei Provincial Girls' Normal School in Wuchang bobbed their hair to signal their emancipation from traditional bondage.[3] Wang Yizhi and her schoolmates at the No. 2 Hunan Provincial Girls' Normal School mobilized the student body to abolish the moral ethics course (*xiushen ke*), which extolled the Confucian virtues of female chastity and subservience to male authority.[4]

Their transition from May Fourth activists to Communists was quite similar to that of early male Communists. For some, participation in study groups such as the New Citizen's Study Society, Awakening Society, and the Work-Study Mutual Aid Corps was crucial. For others, the influence of Communist teachers or closer relatives proved decisive. Yang Zilie, Chen Bilan, Xu Quanzhi, Xia Zhixu, and Zhuang Youyi were tutored for a semester by founding members of the Wuhan Communist cell as part of a compromise agreement worked out with the principal of the Hubei Provincial Girls' Normal School after they had been expelled for leading a two-week strike. This instruction not only earned these five rebel leaders a normal school degree but, more important, turned them into ardent Communists (Yang Zilie joined the party in 1921, and the others took out membership soon thereafter).[5]

Similarly, Zhong Fuguang's decision to seek membership in the Chinese Communist party was influenced by Deng Zhongxia, a founding member of the Beijing Communist cell. Zhong first met Deng in the summer of 1921 when she and some classmates from the No. 2 Sichuan Provincial Girls' Normal School in Chongqing attended a lecture he delivered on the status of Chinese women. She was so taken by his message that Chinese women needed to break away from conventional norms and gain an education that she and her friends set up private talks with Deng to discuss the problems they were encountering in their school. Under his guidance they called a student strike to protest the quality of their education and succeeded in forcing the removal of the principal. Zhong Fuguang did not have any further contact with Deng until 1923 when she read in *New Youth* (Xin qingnian) that he had assumed the post of provost of the newly established Shanghai University and she wrote him asking for admission with a complete scholarship. He not only agreed but also played a crucial role in recruiting her into the party after she enrolled.[6]

The importance of the May Fourth Movement as a motivating political force for the first generation of women Communists not only marked them as a distinct group of women in the party but also distinguished them somewhat from early Communist males who were more evenly spread over several student generations. A number of male Communists, such as Chen Duxiu, had gained valuable political experience during the 1911 Revolution. In fact Martin Wilbur, in his study of 102 early Communist leaders, has identified 12 Communist male "elders" who ranged in age between thirty-five and fifty-three in 1927 (most of whom were quite prestigious), whereas I can only identify a few Communist women, such as Chen Junqi (1885–1927), in this age bracket, and they never became important leaders.[7] Among those women who achieved prominent roles in the party, Liu Qingyang (1894–1977), who was thirty-three in 1927, was the only one who was galvanized to participate in political actions by the 1911 Revolution. In her case, she clearly sought to emulate the Hua Mulan model and become a woman warrior.[8]

This discrepancy seems to reflect the difference between the historical pattern of political involvement of men and that of women. Of the relatively small number of women who participated in the 1911 Revolution, most withdrew from politics shortly afterwards, either because of child-rearing responsibilities or because of their disenchantment with political parties after the Nationalists' refusal to support a women's suffrage clause in the provisional constitution of 1912 and its refusal to retain an equal rights plank in the party program of 1912. With the outbreak of student protests in 1919, only a few of these women found their way back into politics, but generally as leaders of women's groups rather than as active members of political parties. Notably Huang Zonghan, the widow of Huang Xing, formed the Shanghai Federation of Women's Circles, and Wang Changguo founded the Hunan Federation of Women's Circles, which stunned the nation in 1921 by actually engineering her election to the Hunan provincial assembly.

Another significant difference between men and women Communists was their motivation for joining the party. The issue of women's emancipation was not a compelling reason for males, even male feminists, to seek membership in the Communist party. While women were influenced by the same Marxist ideological currents that prompted their male counterparts to join the Communist party, gender issues played a much more important role in their decision to become Communists. Particularly instrumental was their perception that the party was a vigorous proponent of women's equality and would provide the possibility of an alternative lifestyle to those resisting conventional gender roles. Because few career opportunities were open to these women and higher education was even more difficult to obtain, they looked to the party as a sanctuary of like-minded people who would support their rejection of an arranged marriage and their determination to create new gender roles.[9]

In short, the party loomed as a viable answer to the taunting question voiced by the prominent writer Lu Xun in his famous lecture at Beijing Normal Women's College when he asked, "What happens after Nora Leaves Home?" In this talk, Lu Xun explained:

Actually, today, if just one Nora left home she might not find herself in difficulties; because such a case, being so exceptional, would enlist a good deal of sympathy and certain people would help her out. To live on the sympathy of others would already mean having no freedom; but if a hundred Noras were to leave home, even that sympathy would diminish; while if a thousand or ten thousand were to leave, they would arouse disgust.[10]

This first generation of women Communists wanted to break free of family constraints and were attracted to the party because it provided a supportive environment in a largely hostile society. Indeed, to these women who were concerned with challenging traditional gender relationships and providing alternative role models, the party appeared more as a subculture than as a political institution. First and foremost, it facilitated their efforts to reject family controls over the marriage process and to define new social arrangements, such as free-choice marriage, which came to include a public declaration of the union by the couple themselves, such as a wedding ceremony, a party, or a formal announcement. Some women explicitly refused to submit to any marriage rituals and entered into consensual unions; others experimented with casual affairs. Wang Yizhi fled from her father's house when the subject of an arranged marriage was raised and entered into a free-choice marriage first with Shi Cuntong and then with Zhang Tailei, both Communists.

The experimentation in social relationships and the redefinition of gender roles in this Communist subculture served to increase these women's sense of dignity and constituted a powerful incentive for their political involvement. To be sure, venturing into politics was a big step, particularly in a country where until quite recently the realm of politics had been strictly a male domain and women had been denied formal access to political roles. Thus the entry of these women into the Chinese Communist party put them at the cutting edge of social change.

Shanghai University was a major attraction to young women who were interested in furthering their education and pursuing political interests. Established as one of the first major collaborative projects of the United Front between the Communist and Nationalist parties, the university was headed by Yu Youren (1879–1964),[11] a veteran member of the Revolutionary Alliance of the early 1900s and a life-long friend of Sun Yatsen. Many of the important posts were filled by Communists, including Deng Zhongxia as provost, Mao Dun as chairman of the literature department, Qu Qiubai as chairman of the sociology department, Cai Hesen as an instructor of historical sociology, Zhang Tailei as a political science teacher, and An Ticheng as an economics professor.[12]

Almost from its very inception in 1923, Shanghai University became a center of political and cultural ferment, as Beijing University did during the May Fourth Movement.[13] This buoyant atmosphere was an important factor in its ability to attract over four hundred students by the spring of 1924, including several dozen women who were eager to make use of the rare opportunity to attend a university.[14] Wang Jianhong and Ding Ling, two women who had left the Shanghai Pingmin Girls' School in despair over the dismal academic standards a year earlier, enrolled in the literature department and were quite pleased by the level of instruction. They were particularly inspired by Mao Dun's lectures on the *Odyssey* and the *Iliad* and Qu Qiubai's introduction to Marxist literary criticism. Zhong Fuguang came from Beijing, where she had spent a year in vain trying to pass the difficult entrance examination to the Beijing Normal Women's College. She immediately enrolled in the sociology department, where the vast majority of women students were concentrated.[15]

The emancipated lifestyle of Communists was most easily practiced in Shanghai, where the vast urban metropolis with its large foreign community, Western industrial, commercial, and educational institutions, and great hustle and bustle tempered the stifling social enforcement of conventional Chinese customs that prevailed in most Chinese cities. At Shanghai University this Communist subculture bloomed. The social defiance and boldness of this generation of Communist women is well illustrated by Yang Zhihua, a female student at Shanghai University who shocked the conservative elites of Shanghai, and perhaps even some of the Nationalist and Communist party leaders, when she published an announcement of her divorce to Shen Jianlong in a daily newspaper in November of 1924.[16] Yang opted for the newspaper announcement because there were no legal procedures for divorce at that time, and she was unwilling to commence a new relationship without some public notification of her decision to leave her husband. For Yang Zhihua, divorce was a legitimate solution not only for arranged marriages but also for ones that had been freely entered into on the basis of love. In an article she published on the subject, Yang asserted that if divorce in either case is not allowed, "the couple essentially will be strange bedfellows, prompting the occurrence of immoral and unnatural behavior."[17]

If people were shocked by the idea of a woman's initiating a divorce, they were equally astounded when Yang Zhihua placed an announcement in the same newspaper a few weeks later announcing her impending marriage to Qu Qiubai, the chairman of the sociology department at Shanghai University. Not only did her remarriage follow quite closely on the heels of her divorce but her second husband had until quite recently been living with Wang Jianhong, another student at Shanghai University, who had died of illness in the fall of 1924.[18] Yang had thus revealed herself in a very public fashion as a radical who was willing to defy social norms. Yet Yang Zhihua was not merely a social heretic. She was also one of the few women in the Communist movement who argued about the need for a new morality and new social conventions to replace the discredited customs of the traditional culture. Unlike many of her contemporaries, she advocated free-choice marriages over consensual unions, and she labeled casual affairs as "barbaric" (*yeman*).[19]

Aware of the strong social criticism that was mounting over the trend towards unchaperoned social contact between the sexes, Yang Zhihua sounded an alarm to her fellow cultural revolutionaries that if this trend degenerated into a pretext for loose sexual morals, it would be impossible to truly reform the feudal custom of refusing to allow young men and women to mingle in public.

Women as Informal Power Holders

Almost from its inception, strong impediments to according women equal political status existed in the party. This pattern was most clearly illustrated in the Shanghai organization, which had the largest number of women members of any urban center after the third party congress (1923). Neither Gao Junman nor Wang Huiwu, for instance, was given formal party membership status after they were asked to head up the women's program. To be sure, they possessed credentials that justified their being selected as women's organizers. Although Gao Junman had never shown a great deal of interest in politics in the 1910s, she was a graduate of the Beijing Normal Women's College and a cultural revolutionary.[20] Wang Huiwu, younger than Gao, had been radicalized during the May Fourth student protests and had published her articles on women's issues in widely read journals. She had also already proved effective as a logistic organizer for the first party congress. Despite their capabilities and their success in beginning the party's women's program, Gao Junman and Wang Hui did not achieve their own status in the party; rather their roles were solely legitimated through their husbands, who were prominent Communist leaders.

Similarly, when Xiang Jingyu arrived in Shanghai from France at the beginning of 1922, there is no record of her having undergone a formal admission procedure. Although party historians assert that Xiang became a member at that time, they have been unable to identify anyone who might have introduced her to the party, whereas it is well known that her husband, Cai Hesen, was formally proposed for membership by Chen Duxiu and Chen Gongpei.[21] Like Gao Junman's and Wang Huiwu's, her "membership" derived from the formal status of her husband. If Xiang Jingyu's membership had been raised at a cell meeting, at least one of the participants would have remembered, particularly in view of the fact that she would have been the first woman suggested for party membership in Shanghai. Even when Chen Duxiu made the decision unilaterally to grant membership status, such as in the case of Li Lisan, his doing so was well known among party members.[22] Thus her membership seems to have been considered as a natural, automatic extension of that of Cai Hesen. Perhaps the fact that Xiang Jingyu was in the last trimester of a pregnancy when she arrived in Shanghai in early 1922 contributed to the casual attitude of party leaders towards her membership. Nonetheless, the differences in admission procedures for Xiang Jingyu and Cai Hesen, particularly when taken into consideration with the nebulous status of Wang Huiwu and Gao Junman, the organizers of the first Communist women's program, point to the early existence of distinctly diverging gender roles at the center of power in the Communist movement.

Less is known about women's status in other cells before the second party congress, but most places had not formally accepted women members by that time. By July of 1922, there were only 4 "official" women members in the Chinese Communist party out of a total membership of 195: they were Xiang Jingyu, Liu Qingyang, Yang Kaihui, and Miao Boying.[23] Liu Qingyang, who is reported by official sources as having joined the Chinese Communist party while in Europe in early 1921, and Yang Kaihui, who enrolled in the Communist party in Changsha later that year, were accepted by organizations that were peripheral to the locus of party power and possibly more influenced by egalitarian principles.[24] However, in both cases the evidence does not exist to clarify if they underwent formal admission processes. Thus, it is entirely possible that their memberships were handled in a similarly casual manner as that of Xiang Jingyu and were considered a natural extension of those of their husbands, Zhang Shenfu and Mao Zedong.[25]

In the case of Miao Boying, the first woman to become a member of the Chinese Communist party, it is clear that her admittance into the Beijing cell at such an early date was somewhat of a fluke. Rather than being admitted individually in her own right, she came in with a group of Socialist Youth League members in November of 1920, soon after the membership of the Beijing party organization had been depleted by a sizable expulsion of anarchists. This situation was described by Zhang Guotao, who wrote: "Five anarchists withdrew amicably from our nucleus. They handed over *Voice of Labor*, which they had edited, to Lo Chang-lung [Luo Zhanglong]. Although we continued to maintain friendly relations with the anarchists, this must be called a serious split. The nucleus went ahead with its work energetically, but there were now only four persons left in it. It looked so weak and isolated that we decided to invite key members of the Socialist Youth League to join. Nine of them immediately came into the nucleus. . . ."[26] Clearly in such circumstances it would have been hypocritical to have specifically excluded her from membership while admitting the male Socialist Youth League members. To do so would have constituted a blatant form of gender discrimination that Li Dazhao, the head of the Beijing Communist organization, could not have abided given his deep ideological commitment to the cause of women's emancipation.

The barrier to female membership in the Shanghai Communist organization was broken by the formal establishment of a Women's Bureau at the second party congress in 1922. Within a very short time, women were accorded formal membership status and were appointed to responsible positions. Wang Yizhi, a student at the Shanghai Pingmin Girls' School, became the first woman to be formally admitted to the Shanghai Communist organization in August 1922.[27] In the same month, Xiang Jingyu was selected as the director of the Communist Women's Bureau. Significantly, the naming of Xiang Jingyu as the head of this bureau marked the first explicit female leadership appointment by the Chinese Communist party.

Before Xiang Jingyu actually committed herself to the role of director of the Women's Bureau, she took steps to develop her stature in the party by emulating male practices. By devoting her time to launching the new Communist theoretical journal *The Weekly Guide* (Xiangdao zhoubao), which was started soon after the second party congress, and contributing twenty-three articles on anti-imperialist themes during its first year, she broke with the conventional gender roles that were emerging in the Shanghai organization. She addressed subjects that were normally expounded on by male writers—the self-proclaimed theoreticians in the party—demonstrating that she could function well in the male-dominated realms of the party. Few other women, however, were willing or able to follow her example.

Once Xiang Jingyu made the decision to send her newborn child back to Hunan and entrust her to the care of her mother-in-law, she became quite assertive in other inner-party matters. Most notably, she took the highly unconventional act of differing with her husband on an important matter under consideration by the party leadership, the issue of forming an alliance with the Nationalist party. In taking this public stance, Xiang Jingyu once again revealed her staunchly independent nature. Cai Hesen had objected vociferously to the idea of this alliance at the congress, arguing that the Nationalist party was not a revolutionary force.[28] Even after the congress agreed to the alliance, Cai reportedly remained aloof from the Nationalist party and often criticized its leaders.[29] Particularly in light of the intensity of his feelings on the subject, Xiang's refusal to show more wifely deference to her husband's opinions demonstrated beyond a doubt that she was a strong-willed woman who could be counted on to make up her own mind on important political issues.

Xiang Jingyu's assertiveness was immediately manifested in her post as director of the Communist Women's Bureau, particularly in her decision to persevere against the largely unarticulated assumptions that Communist men held about sharing power and prestige in the party with women. When Xiang drafted her resolution on the women's movement for the third party congress in 1923, for instance, she strove to combat the deep-seated contempt some male members felt toward the women's movement. She argued that this movement was important politically despite its history of strong divisions and lack of action. She warned her comrades that if the Chinese Communist party were to have any impact on invigorating and influencing these women's groups, Communists could not show disdain toward "madames" (*taitai*), "young misses" (*xiaojie*), and women politicians and should not scare them away by stressing the theory of class struggle.[30] Xiang was also critical of her male comrades for failing to encourage female recruitment, with the result that Communist organizations in places such as Guangzhou had few if any women members. It was only after Xiang agitated for the adoption of a resolution at the fourth party congress (January 1925) placing a special priority on recruiting women that a breakthrough was achieved in at least some of these places.[31]

Nevertheless, her efforts to combat patriarchy in the Chinese Communist party proved largely ineffectual in promoting women in other areas of the party hierarchy, with the result that women found it enormously difficult to assume positions outside the Women's Bureau. By the fourth party congress, the emergence of inequalities of power organized along a gender axis was a permanent reality in the party. It seems significant, in light of the fact that the majority of female recruits came from girls' middle and normal schools, that women commanded so few leadership positions in the Socialist Youth League. Women were also unable to gain official delegate status at the first four party congresses, although at least a few of them were present at the meetings in an informal capacity associated with their relationships to important male Communists.[32] Thus, women could express their opinions, but they did not have a vote.

Perhaps most illustrative of the barriers that women faced in assuming official positions in the political hierarchy were the experiences of Xiang Jingyu herself. For years, a host of hagiographic biographies have claimed that she was an elected official of the Central Committee from 1922 until 1927. The All-China Women's Federation has been particularly interested in promoting this image of Xiang Jingyu in its publications. However, most of the evidence in support of her election as a member or even as an alternate is quite suspect and has not been confirmed by recent studies.[33]

The ambiguity over Xiang Jingyu's status in the party hierarchy stems to a large extent from the fact that she participated fully but had limited institutional status. It is significant that much of the evidence supporting the claim that she was elected to the Central Committee at the second party congress comes from the writings of Li Lisan, Cai Chang, and Zhou Enlai, none of whom were present at that meeting.[34] From the memoirs of various high-ranking Communists who were present, it is clear that Xiang attended Central Committee meetings and was in charge of much of the organizational work related to that body. Luo Zhanglong, who was elected to the Central Committee at the third party congress and was alternate at the fourth party congress, was quite impressed by Xiang Jingyu's political skills and recalled that she managed and arranged all matters concerned with the Central Committee.[35] Thus, while Xiang Jingyu was not an officially elected member of the Central Committee, she served on this body in an unofficial capacity. Wang Huiwu was also remembered for having attended every meeting with her husband, Li Da, though she lacked any official status or decision-making authority.[36] In this way, Xiang Jingyu, Gao Junman, and Wang Huiwu became the first members of this nascent, informal political power structure.

To be sure, informal power pervaded the organization in these years and was not just limited to women. Yet important differences existed between the informal power wielded by male and female leaders. Women were never able to command the status and legitimacy of male leaders in the informal structure, in part because their access to the reins of high authority were totally dependent upon marriage or consensual unions with important Communist leaders. It was an unwritten requirement for advancement. Moreover, if a woman remarried or her spouse lost his high political position, she forfeited her high status. Most of the key women figures in the party were partners of male Communist leaders. The political identities of the female members who functioned at the highest echelon of Communist party politics were shaped to some extent by the realities of their second-class status. Regardless of a woman leader's capabilities and effectiveness, she could rise to only a certain level of leadership within the party before hitting a glass ceiling. Thus, the most important criterion for a woman's high political status in Communist institutions was not her political accomplishments but the political rank of her partner.

Significantly, these patterns of gender hierarchy closely reflected social hierarchies in the patriarchal family. Thus, it was quite common for men to bring women into the party, but it was unusual for women to recruit men. The many single women who joined the party were strongly encouraged to find a spouse among the membership, and at least some women felt that a decision to marry a non-Communist (that is, outside the family) was out of the question.[37] Many men, however, felt no compunction about commencing a relationship with a woman who was unwilling to join the party. Qu Qiubai, for instance, commenced a relationship with Wang Jianhong, who refused to become a party member, though she was willing to participate in party programs. These doings signaled the infusion of a patriarchal gender hierarchy into the Communist organization and subculture.

Patriarchal Preferences

The tolerance by Communist men of such a discrepancy between their writings about women's equality and the reproduction of an unequal power hierarchy in the party seemed to have arisen from the influence of traditional conceptions of power on their political identities. Despite their ardent espousal of the cause of women's emancipation, these early male Communists assumed that they should be the power holders, without realizing their virtual monopoly became a means to define their self-importance through exclusiveness. It seemed only too natural to them that men should hold the reins of power and serve as theoreticians and policymakers while women filled less important roles. By the same token, the apparent unwillingness of at least some of these men to share power in the personal realm undermined the egalitarian basis of the subculture.

Although these patriarchal attitudes remained for the large part unarticulated, occasionally they were vocalized. Peng Shuzhi, for in-

stance, once objected to a woman's wielding formal power on behalf
of the party because her behavior violated his sense of what was
appropriate. He was upset with Chen Duxiu's decision to send Liu
Qingyang to the Comintern's fifth congress in Moscow (1924). She
was much too outspoken and strident for his tastes. Moreover, in his
estimation she was culturally deficient and politically uncouth, definitely the wrong choice as a Communist delegate to an international
Communist meeting, from Peng Shuzhi's point of view. And yet
Liu Qingyang was one of the most articulate, experienced, and well-
educated women in the Communist movement. She had first found
her way into politics by serving as a leader of the May Fourth protest
in Tianjin while a teacher at a well-known women's normal school.
Later she studied in Europe, where she joined the Chinese Communist party in 1921, and upon her return to China she assumed several
positions, including the editorship of a Tianjin women's newspaper.
She was hardly a culturally deficient woman. No doubt if she had not
spoken up at the Comintern meetings, had sat docilely on the train
to and from Moscow, and had only spoken when addressed, Peng
Shuzhi would have tolerated—even welcomed—her presence. As it
was, she harassed him continually by her attempts to engage him in
conversation.[38]

Most male Communists, it seems, retained some traditional expectations of gender roles despite their support for the cause of women's
emancipation. Chen Duxiu, for instance, still recalled, several decades
after the event, the anger he felt towards his first wife, Gao Dazhong,
when she refused to give him her gold bracelet to cover his traveling
expenses to study in Japan. No doubt Chen believed that the importance of his studies more than justified his wife giving up a major
portion of her dowry.[39] Thus, for all his rhetoric about female emancipation, Chen Duxiu seemed in some ways very traditional in his relationships with women.

Such traditional expectations were most clearly revealed in the division of labor within the families of these male Communists. Many
assumed that their wives would perform domestic duties and shoulder
the responsibilities of child raising while they maintained a high level
of political activity. Li Dazhao entered into an arranged marriage with
Zhao Renlan, a self-sacrificing, illiterate woman who attended to their
children and the menial work around the house so that her husband
could devote maximum time to his studies and to his public life as a
party leader and teacher. She made it possible for him to pursue his
ideals while her life was weighed down with household drudgery.

Although he may have indeed loved her dearly, as one biographer maintains, he took little interest in relieving her of some of her household responsibilities so that she might gain time for intellectual development or public activities.[40]

While Li Dazhao failed to subject his family's traditional division of gender roles to a penetrating critique, Chen Duxiu was widely reputed to be a womanizer. He reportedly frequented the red-light district in Beijing (Bada Hutong) and was said to have had numerous affairs.[41] Admittedly, Chen was not the only prominent intellectual of the period known to frequent the brothels. Hu Shi, to cite just one example, found such practices a useful antidote to an incompatible arranged marriage.[42] No doubt many of the claims of Chen's reckless abandon in his sexual practices were exaggerated to facilitate the aims of his political opponents. Even Gao Junman's statement, ten years after their relationship had ended, that Chen had often boasted that he had slept with women from every province except Gansu cannot be taken literally.[43] Nevertheless the evidence of Chen's womanizing seems too strong to dismiss outright, particularly when considered in conjunction with the cognizance that many radicals of that era believed that challenging existing sexual mores was an integral part of their overall endeavor to transform traditional social relations. Indeed, many male Communists during the 1920s experimented extensively with their sexual relationships, even pursuing other comrades' wives.[44]

Zhang Shenfu, a very articulate proponent of women's emancipation who was a founding member of the Beijing Communist organization, offered his biographer, Vera Schwarcz, a penetrating insight into his view of his relationship with Liu Qingyang, the fiery, independent emulator of a woman-warrior whom Peng Shuzhi found a "sheer hell" to be with in Moscow.[45] While Peng Shuzhi failed to tame the shrew, Zhang Shenfu claims to have procured her willing compliance.

It was she, you know, who started the affair on the boat to France. After that she did pretty much what I told her to. She joined the Communist Party upon my recommendation. She cooked pork for me even though she was Moslem.... When we came home from Europe, she lived with my family even though I had another wife at the time. She was more of a concubine at first. But we were above such notions.... I wrote most of her speeches. She could not think very clearly. But she was a fiery, convincing public speaker.[46]

While these patriarchal persuasions and practices no doubt eroded the egalitarian life of the Communist subculture, they were more strongly inscribed in the Communist body politic. Just as male Communists seemed blissfully unaware of the self-serving nature of their radical sexual politics, they seemed equally blind to the influence of traditional notions of power on their political identities. This patriarchal style, in turn, gave sustenance to the perseverance of other traditional notions of power, including those affecting gender relations, and militated against the serious critique of existing power relations in the early party. As a result, a type of court politics somewhat reminiscent of that of the imperial period emerged within the center of the Chinese Communist party. A central characteristic of this type of court politics was the development of an informal power structure for women premised on the notion that women's access to formal decision-making positions was not necessary.

Female Complicity

Although male Communists played a major role in creating a gender hierarchy within the party, women also participated in the defining of their second-class status. In other words, the social expectations of Communist men were critical in shaping these women's political identities, but the self-images of the women themselves were also operative in their decisions to accept secondary political status that clearly distinguished them from their male counterparts.

While Communist ideals about the importance of women's emancipation served as a powerful force in motivating women to join the party, traditional representation of women continued to shape the women's political identities. As a result, Communist women gravitated toward the roles of organizers and managers—roles that seemed compatible with their self-images of their strengths. Many of their duties, which were often taken for granted and not highly valued, can thus be seen as an extension of women's traditional roles as mothers and housekeepers. For instance, Wang Huiwu took logistical responsibility for the first party congress, including the procuring of a site. When the meeting was discovered by Shanghai International Settlement police, she again was commissioned to find a haven for the deliberations, and this time she utilized contacts in her hometown area of Zhejiang. Xiang Jingyu also managed many of the day-to-day details of the Central Committee between 1922 and 1925 because she was seen as more capable than the male members in such matters.[47] By agreeing to do tasks that men were not doing, these women participated in the setting of the historical boundaries of female behavior and experience in the Chinese Communist party. In so doing, they were participating in the construction of gendered political identities that would have a long-range impact in the making of a Communist state.

Women's retention of traditional ideological traits that shaped their political behavior was not just due to historical influences. Most women revolutionaries at that time could not break through the psychological and tangible barriers to their assuming more egalitarian political roles inside the party. They did not seem to question the extent to which they assumed child-rearing responsibilities, which they saw as an extension of their biologically determined reproductive roles. While they looked forward to the day when a socialist state would relieve them of some of their responsibilities through the establishment of day-care centers and canteens, they adhered to the sanctity of *muxing* (maternal instincts) and thus failed to agitate for a redivision of household responsibilities with their husbands.[48]

Because these women Communists assumed a greater role in household affairs, particularly child raising, they had less time to pursue careers in the party, and their self-images as revolutionary women were adversely affected. While Communist men felt relatively little infringement upon their political careers by the addition of children, Communist women had to recast their lives. These female revolutionaries often were able to ameliorate their burden to some extent by the hiring of nannies (*baomu*), yet it was still the female revolutionary who had to oversee these nannies and fill in during their absences. The managing of the household became a major affair in the lives of Communist women. For some it became a real feat if they could still carry on with their political lives after having children. For example, Luo Zhanglong, an early male member of the party, has attributed Yang Kaihui's outstanding ability to juggle the raising of two children with her numerous political tasks to her unusually good health.[49] Yet it is significant that she did not hold any specific positions in the party but served as an all-purpose organizer. The real constraints imposed upon the lives of many of these revolutionary mothers militated against their developing self-assertion and independence in the realm of politics—attributes that were essential to their assumption of leadership roles.

It is significant that those women who became important leaders in the area where they had some legitimacy—the Communist Women's Bureau—either sent their infants off to relatives to raise, such as Xiang Jingyu and Yang Zhihua, or did not have children, such as Deng Yingchao and Liu Qingyang.[50] They were then in a position to devote all their time to developing those values and skills that were necessary for them to feel self-confident as decision makers and authority figures. But even these women did not seem to challenge the gender division of labor in their families or in the party organization.

For most early women Communists, participation in this revolutionary lifestyle constituted an important reason for their attraction to the party. Unlike male Communists, they could not easily turn back once they had broken with social conventions, for their families by and large regarded them as outcasts and were unwilling to have them return. But for most of them, the thought of returning to a conventional lifestyle was highly objectionable. The party became their new social network, their newly constructed extended family. Working for the party offered them a much more public and meaningful life as well as more room for personal development and expression than becoming traditional wives and mothers. Putting up with unequal power relations inside the party seemed a relatively small price to pay in light of their other options.

Plates

Wang Huiwu, first leader of the Chinese Communist women's program. Courtesy of her family.

Miao Boying, the first woman to join the Chinese Communist
party, holding her young son.

Yang Zhihua with her daughter, Qu Duyi, in Moscow in 1929. Courtesy of
Qu Duyi.

Yang Zhihua and Qu Qiubai, who were married in late 1924. Courtesy of Qu Duyi.

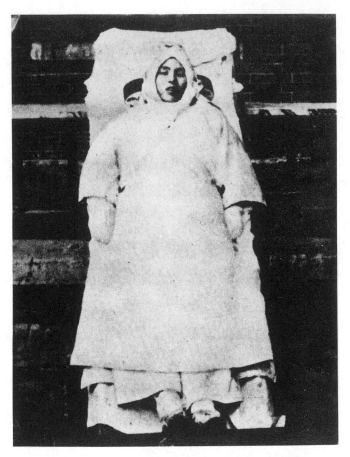

Corpse of Liu Hezhen, the student from Beijing Normal
Women's College who was killed in the March Eighteenth
Incident of 1926.

Gao Tianbo (middle), a woman Communist from Guangdong, with two other women comrades after arriving in Changsha with the Northern Expedition armies in July 1926.

You Xi, a Sichuan woman who enrolled at the Wuhan Military and Political Institute, frequently donned male attire.

Wang Jingyan, a graduate of Sun Yatsen University in
Moscow.

Xiang Jingyu (far right) with other New Citizen's Study Society members in France in 1920.

PART II

The Politics of Gender in the National Revolution, 1925–1927

Introduction to Part Two

The year 1925 was a remarkable one for Chinese women. It started with an unprecedentedly bold bid for active citizenship. A host of urban women's groups coalesced around the demand that women's suffrage be granted in the proposed constitution under consideration by the Duan Qirui warlord government in Beijing. Just as this campaign was reaching a climax, the May Thirtieth Incident occurred, providing a powerful catalyst for the creation of mass women's movements in China. Widespread nationalist indignation at the Western interference in China served to mobilize large numbers of women—students, workers, intellectuals, professionals—into political participation. This revolutionary nationalism was linked explicitly with issues of gender change as a basis for women's participation in the National Revolution.

The southern province of Guangdong, which came to be called the cradle of the revolutionary camp, produced a set of cultural symbols and organizational mobilization principals directed at bringing women into the political process. The province beckoned women from all over the country to join the ranks of the National Revolution and served as the center for the training of a core of able women organizers. This mode of mobilization aimed to challenge traditional norms regulating gender conduct by promoting the formation of new values and beliefs about the role of women in the political, economic, and social arenas of a modern nation-state. Before the end of 1925, myriad women's associations sprang up throughout south and central China, including rural communities, where the issue of emancipation was vastly more complex and the obstacles within the family and society were far greater. Nonetheless, these associations ushered in a heady period for those who had dared to imagine that significant transformations in gender relations might be possible in China during the 1920s. Whether measured by a Chinese or an international yardstick, the extent of women's mobilization in those few years was extraordinary.

Scholars have differed in their assessment of whether more credit should be attributed to Communist organizers or to Nationalist organizers for facilitating and directing this mass upsurge of women in the mid-1920s. Sun Yatsen's Nationalist party enjoyed greater prestige and a wider following, and He Xiangning and other Nationalist women played very important roles in the making of the women's mobilization campaigns. But the nucleus of women radicals who joined the Chinese Communist party in the early 1920s constituted the driving force in the effort to give both organizational leadership to this revolutionary mass movement of women and cogent expression to the importance of women's issues in the Chinese endeavor to create a modern nation-state and to battle foreign imperialism, warlordism, industrial exploitation, and landlordism. At a grassroots level, however, Communist and Nationalist activists generally complemented each other and often looked and sounded very similar to one anther.

The magnitude and forms of women's involvement in the revolutionary movement during this three-year period varied markedly according to the political environment in each locality. To be sure, vast social differences existed between various regions of China that also affected the nature and strength of the women's mobilization campaign. Thus, a revolutionary government in Zhili would not have obtained the same results as a feminist women's organization in Guangdong at this time. In Shanghai, where the May Thirtieth Movement began, the initial wave of protests galvanized women throughout the city to new levels of political activism, but the activism could not be sustained in this treaty port or the surrounding provinces to the extent that was possible where revolutionaries were able to establish their own governments. It was in Guangdong, Hunan, and Hubei that female activism ripped through the political and social fabric of China with compelling intensity and where mass revolutionary politics served as a tool for women to utilize in transforming a patriarchal world.

Regardless of locale, however, we can discern in this revolutionary upsurge two simultaneous and contradictory processes that affected Communist women's efforts to bring about gender transformation in the National Revolution of the 1920s: the power of feminist issues to draw certain constituencies of women into the revolutionary mass movement; and the articulation within the revolutionary coalition and in society at large of traditional gender ideologies in resistance to the women's emancipation campaigns. Indeed, gender issues were at the crux of this explosive effort to create a new nation because they were so central to the redefinitions of the political order, family, morality, and the very meaning of masculinity and femininity. Thus, the revolutionary process encompassed intense contention over the status, roles, and power of women, as well as the very definition of feminism in the new order.

As gender issues became increasingly contentious, they welled up in the various mobilization campaigns and played a role in the breakdown of the collaboration between Communists and Nationalists. The disastrous unraveling of the alliance brought the women's mobilization to a dead halt and unleashed a rash of violence against women activists and a propaganda war over the politicization of gender issues. The crushing of the mass women's movement and the brutalization of women's bodies changed the direction of the new nation-state that came into being at this time. It also reshaped the Chinese Communist women's program as this beleaguered party regrouped its forces in isolated rural areas in order to mount yet another attempt at gaining state power.

Part 2 consists of three chapters that look at Communist, and to a lesser extent Nationalist, efforts to integrate gender issues into the mass revolutionary upsurge in China in the mid-1920s. Chapter 5 examines the impact of the May Thirtieth Incident on the Communist mobilization of women in the cities of Shanghai and Beijing. Chapter 6 is a study of the dynamics of revolution and gender transformation in the province of Guangdong. Chapter 7 discusses the expansion of the women's mobilization campaigns into Hunan, Hubei, and Henan with the launching of the Northern Expedition and the impact of the breakdown of the United Front on these campaigns.

CHAPTER 5

May Thirtieth Revolutionary Upsurge

May Thirtieth will be one of the great dates of Far Eastern history, like the fall of the Bastille in Europe.

Frank Ashton-Gwatkin

Since the May Thirtieth Movement, the women's movement has sprung up like bamboo shoots after a spring rain.

Chen Bilan

When British police in the Shanghai International Settlement opened fired on a large crowd of Chinese demonstrators who had gathered in front of the police station on Nanjing Road on the sultry afternoon of May 30, 1925, they not only perpetrated a tragedy but also set off a series of events that culminated in a spectacular mass mobilization against Western imperialists, which came to be known as the May Thirtieth Movement. By misjudging public reaction to the killing of thirteen students and workers, the International Settlement authorities inadvertently handed Communist and left-wing Nationalist organizers a potent issue to transform a local labor dispute into a nationwide revolutionary movement. Seizing on this extraordinary opportunity almost instantaneously, Shanghai radicals staged an unprecedentedly large-scale public protest by wide sectors of the populace throughout the city and then extended it to other parts of the country. In so doing, they ushered in a period of nationalist revolutionary ferment in China that lasted for almost two years. The significance of May Thirtieth as an important turning point was immediately recognized by both Westerners and Chinese. It marked the true beginning of the National Revolution.

Xiang Jingyu found in the May Thirtieth movement a rare opportunity to build a genuine mass women's movement. Many of the organizational links and the personal contacts she had developed with women's rights groups, student activists, and women workers since assuming the position of director of the Communist Women's Bureau in 1923 and head of the Nationalist party's Women's Movement Committee were utilized for this purpose. The speed with which various women's networks were vitalized in Shanghai and elsewhere was astonishing. For a moment, it appeared possible that Xiang Jingyu might become a truly national women's leader who would oversee the mobilization of women throughout much of China. However, Xiang Jingyu's successes were not sufficient to protect her high political status in the party once her marriage to Cai Hesen began to flounder. By the end of the year she was packed off to Moscow for political study at Sun Yatsen University, only to see from afar the retrenchment of the Communist Women's Bureau into a Shanghai regional office, the unraveling of the close-knit working relations she had constructed between Communist and Nationalist women in Shanghai, and the difficulties encountered by women activists in the north, particularly in Beijing, to consolidate the gains of May Thirtieth. Indeed, the violence meted out to women in that city during the March 18, 1926, massacre revealed the depth of emotional reaction evoked by the widespread participation of women in political movements.

Constructing Female Networks

The story of Xiang Jingyu's efforts to lay the groundwork for a mass revolutionary upsurge of women could begin in several places. One might start, for instance, with her efforts to politicize women students, particularly those in middle schools, who responded with great exuberance to the massacre in Shanghai. Yet another source of female involvement in the revolutionary upsurge of May Thirtieth was the campaign initiated by Xiang Jingyu to promote women's participation in the proposed National Assembly to draw up a constitution. Commenced in November of 1924, the campaign spread to many Chinese cities and culminated in the formation of a large and vibrant new women's organization on the eve of the May Thirtieth protests. The mobilization of women in May of 1925 can also be traced to Xiang Jingyu's attempts to establish night schools as a vehicle to encourage women's involvement in political action in their place of work and in mass street protests. It was through these schools that a core of Communist female recruits, such as Yang Zhihua, first gained valuable knowledge and experiences in organizing women workers. These three areas of pursuit paved the way for significantly greater organized female political involvement in 1925 than during the May Fourth Movement.

Before Xiang Jingyu began to direct either the Communist or the Nationalist party's women's work, Communist cadres assigned to the Socialist Youth League had begun to construct a network in girls' schools around Shanghai as early as the summer of 1922.[1] One of the first schools to be designated for this purpose was the Jingxian Girls' Middle School, located in the county seat of Songjiang, Jiangsu, about thirty miles from Shanghai. A Communist teacher there developed the initial Socialist Youth League tactics for drawing women students into political action.[2] In order to attract students to the school, the radical leaders of this school prevailed upon the sympathetic editors of *Women's Critic* (Funü pinglun) to carry laudatory articles about their innovative curriculum.[3]

In 1924 Xiang Jingyu, in her role as director of the Women's Bureau, decided to broaden this Communist strategy to include students in more conservative schools. Using her editorship of *Women's Weekly* (Funü zhoubao) as a podium, she encouraged students to challenge school authorities, particularly on outdated-curriculum issues. In March of that year she published an article asserting that the majority of women's schools were in a state of crisis. Unless prompt action was taken, she contended, the future educational opportunities of most Chinese women students would be jeopardized. According to her prognosis, women students would be increasingly unable to pass the entrance examinations for institutions of higher learning unless the quality of their secondary education was brought up to the standards of that of their male counterparts.[4]

Xiang Jingyu believed that once women students were made aware of the connection between the crisis in women's education and the larger issue of the social decay of Chinese society, which in her view was "oozing with pus," they would become involved in revolutionary political actions.[5] She therefore devoted some of her attention to encouraging female and normal-school students to drive out incompetent principals and teachers with "archaic ideas and no awareness of modern trends and scientific knowledge." To this end, she used the pages of *Women's Weekly* to report extensively on two major school conflicts that erupted in 1924: the strike at the Second Zhili Provincial Girls' Normal School in Baoding and the more drawn out conflict at Beijing Normal Women's College. In both cases, she portrayed the principals as patrons of patriarchal authority. In Baoding, Principal Yan Shiji was reported to have provoked a massive student strike by arbitrarily expelling six students in order to quell complaints about teacher incompetence (particularly that of the economics teacher), low educational standards, and outdated dress codes. Moreover, Yan had refused to reprimand a teacher for striking a student across the face. In her commentary, Xiang Jingyu related this specific incident to national politics by portraying it as an example of the ways in which warlords meddled in educational affairs. In her view, Yan Shiji was bowing to warlord "patriarchal social forces" that wanted the schools to produce "submissive" and "fearful" women.[6]

Six months later, when a similar conflict erupted at Beijing Women's Normal College, Xiang carried extensive coverage of the dispute in the Shanghai *Women's Weekly*.[7] In this case, a bitter student dispute with Yang Yinyu, the chancellor of the institution, commenced in November 1924 when she summarily expelled three students for returning several months late to the school, rejecting their excuse that the delay was caused by the raging civil war in the south.[8]

Under the editorship of Xiang Jingyu, the *Women's Weekly* coverage of this conflict during the winter and spring of 1925 clearly sided with the students, who were seen as justified in their decision to hold a meeting in January 1925 during which they voted to expel Chancellor Yang because of her intransigence and harsh policies. The students, for their part, tried to get support for their actions by sending a statement to the newspapers, which published it, and to the Ministry of Education, where it was ignored. Ironically they found themselves in combat with a chancellor who was more qualified on paper than most of her contemporaries for this position. Shunning marriage for a professional career, Yang Yinyu had graduated from Tokyo Women's Higher Normal Institute and then had chosen to seek further education by going to New York in 1918 to attend the Teachers' College at Columbia University, where she was awarded a master's degree.[9] Despite these impressive educational credentials, many students found

Chancellor Yang as old-fashioned in her views as principals who had never been abroad. Her bound feet may have predisposed them against her from the start. But much more objectionable to these young modern-minded students was the stress she placed on traditional female virtues. She continually talked about herself as playing the role of mother in a large family of students. From the student perspective, she was a product of a feudal tradition and her use of power was fundamentally patriarchal.[10]

The prominent writer Lu Xun, who was employed as a professor at the Beijing Normal Women's College, sided with the student rebels against the school authorities and used his writings to thoroughly ridicule Yang Yinyu. In his view, she was behaving more like a tyrannical mother-in-law than a loving mother and treating the students more like helpless child-brides than daughters.[11] In yet another essay, Lu Xun took his searing critique a step further by subjecting Yang Yinyu's behavior to a Freudian analysis. He argued that her actions revealed a repressed sexual psychology, resulting from her lack of a normal sex life, that she was taking out on the students. Her strong compulsion to restrict her students stemmed, he believed, from her vicarious need to carry out her own suppressed erotic dreams.[12]

As this conflict continued to stew into May of 1925, it served to radicalize students on that campus on the eve of the May Thirtieth Incident. Yang Yinyu's decision to expel six students on May 7, including Xu Guangping, one of Lu Xun's favorites, provided Xiang Jingyu with a useful case to draw upon in order to heighten political consciousness among women students at other girls' schools in China as well. In so doing, she established a conducive environment for other Communists organizers to create networks among women students on the eve of the May Thirtieth Movement.

Xiang Jingyu left the practical work of actually forging the organizational links to the Socialist Youth League, which carried out its work primarily through the anti-Christian campaign of 1924.[13] This effort to infuse Chinese revolutionary nationalism with a strong dose of anti-Christian sentiment was quite pronounced in the Shanghai region because of the large Western presence and because of the active role of Shanghai University students in promoting the campaign. Such activists often trekked into the neighboring provinces of Jiangsu and Zhejiang, where Christian-run schools were quite numerous.

A brief look at the unfolding of this campaign at Yongjiang Girls' Middle School in Ningbo reveals much about the tactics of male

Communist organizers. Because of its special designation as one of the five original treaty ports specified by the Treaty of Nanking in 1842, Ningbo was the site of numerous Christian schools. During 1924, promoters of this anti-Christian campaign were spotted on a number of occasions entering mission schools in the city to distribute their propaganda and cause a minor disturbance.[14] However, for the most part they worked behind the scenes, contacting students through informal channels. Communist organizer Zhang Qiuren, for instance, came from Shanghai and met with small groups of students in the homes of sympathetic faculty members, who often ran regular political study groups for a select group of their students.[15]

Zhang Qiuren encouraged students to attack the Christian establishment, particularly mission schools, as running dogs of the imperialist powers. Although his message was more or less the standard fare, he was a particularly persuasive organizer for the anti-Christian movement in Ningbo because of his extensive personal experiences there. He regaled his student listeners, including Xu Chengmei, with his own story of conflict as a student in the Chongxin Middle School in Ningbo during the May Fourth era. His firsthand account of the school's opposition to patriotic student protesters and his ultimate expulsion from this Christian-run educational institution proved quite instrumental in convincing many students that these schools were pawns of imperialism cloaked in religious attire.

Zhang Qiuren had a very profound impact on Xu Chengmei. She began to scrutinize her own background in Christian schools, particularly her five years at Shengmo Girls' Middle School, where she had been a student during the May Fourth tumult. It now seemed quite disturbing to her that she had been made to read the Bible repeatedly in those years; it had served as the main textbook in her English classes. Her critique was further facilitated by the political literature that Zhang Qiuren began sending her from Shanghai, items such as *Religion and Revolution*, which was a merciless indictment of religious institutions, Darwin's *On the Origin of Species*, and Marx's *Outline of the Critique of Political Economy*. At the same time, Zhang also sent her copies of *The Weekly Guide* (Xiangdao zhoubao) and *Chinese Youth* (Zhongguo qingnian), journals that contained anti-Christian articles laced with much Communist terminology.[16] Although these Communist publications did not adequately explicate Marxist terminology to the satisfaction of Xu Chengmei, this daily diet of Communist journals was a prelude to her entry into what was then still the

Socialist Youth League, which she joined with two other women students in the fall of 1924.[17]

The admission of these women students into the league strengthened the Communist network that was gradually developing throughout the school system of Ningbo. During the next six months Xu Chengmei and the other women in the league received instructions on organizing skills, which they applied to their continued activities in the anti-Christian movement. Through these efforts, they were able to attract a few more women students from various Ningbo schools, including Yongjiang.[18] Thus, when the May Thirtieth shootings occurred, Xu Chengmei was well positioned to oversee a mobilization drive in the Yongjiang Girls' Middle School.

While Socialist Youth League cadres were busy extending their networks in middle schools, Xiang Jingyu turned her attention to constructing an organizational alliance among women's groups in her capacity as head of the Nationalist Women's Movement Committee in Shanghai.[19] From November 1924 until the May Thirtieth Incident, she devoted most of her time to personally overseeing the development of a mass women's organization. The issue she seized upon to commence this project was provided inadvertently by Sun Yatsen when, in the fall of 1924, he called for the convening of a national convention in Beijing of Chinese leaders from all professions to end militarism and unify the nation peacefully. His omission of women as a group that should be included in this convention prompted Xiang Jingyu to call for their participation, arguing that it was preposterous to think that women's interests could be represented by anyone other than women.[20] In an essay appearing in *Women's Weekly*, she wrote:

Can student unions, trade unions, or commercial organizations represent and raise such issues as the need to protect the rights of mothers, freedom in marriage and divorce, women's right to inherit property, professional equality, equal access to an education, and the rights to pursue other social and political actions? ... If women's organizations are not seated in the National Convention that is to be called to resolve national problems, even if there were some people to raise the specific demands of women, no one would be there to wage the struggle.[21]

Her ability to infuse this issue with a distinctly female perspective struck a particularly responsive chord. Within a short time, Xiang Jingyu was able to mobilize many women's groups and individuals to agitate for female participation in the proposed conference on national issues. She quickly followed up on this positive response by publishing a call for the formation of an organization for this purpose in Shanghai's *Republican Daily* and by instructing members of the Nationalist party's Women's Movement Committee in Shanghai to contact important women leaders throughout the city.[22] Before Sun Yatsen reached Beijing to begin deliberations for this national conference, at least ten women's organizations had responded positively to Xiang Jingyu's invitation to establish what became the Committee to Promote Women's Participation in the National Assembly (Funü guomin huiyi cuchenghui), and many of these organizations published their endorsements in Shanghai newspapers.[23]

Much to Xiang Jingyu's credit, the founding convention of this ad hoc organization of women was a resounding success. More than six hundred people showed up at the meeting hall of the Ningbo native-place association office in Shanghai on the afternoon of December 21, 1924.[24] A measure of Xiang Jingyu's ability to elicit the participation of a broad spectrum of Shanghai women's groups was demonstrated by the acquiescence of Wang Liming, the founder and head of the Chinese Women's Temperance Society (Zhonghua funü jiezhi xiehui), to serve as chairperson.[25] Xiang Jingyu delivered the main address to this gathering, during which she called both for an improvement in women's political and legal rights and for the abrogation of the unequal treaties.[26] This mixture of feminist and anti-imperialist demands henceforth became the hallmark of women's organizations under joint Nationalist-Communist sponsorship.

In February 1925 this campaign was energized when a National Assembly planning session called by Duan Qirui, the chief executive of the warlord government in Beijing, adopted draft regulations that specified in Article 14 that only men would be enfranchised. Through these actions, this body of male politicians essentially construed women as passive subjects rather than mature political citizens in the proposed new state structures. Once again, Xiang Jingyu seized the moment to rally mass public support to condemn Article 14 for its gender-exclusive definition of the Chinese citizenry. She demanded that the word *nanzi* (male) be replaced with the nonexclusive term *guomin* (citizen) to enable women to function as active political agents in the Chinese nation-state. New Committees to Promote Women's Participation in the National Convention sprang up in cities and county towns of Hebei, Henan, Zhejiang, Jiangsu, Jiangxi, Shandong, and Guangdong. In Tianjin, the women's rights leader Deng Yingchao succeeded in drawing more than a hundred people to meetings.[27]

Deng's successes in building this organization became a stepping stone to joining the Chinese Communist party. Recruiting the twenty-year-old Deng Yingchao was an important accomplishment for the Communist women's program because she had become such a prominent women's rights leader in Tianjin since the May Fourth Incident. She had first become known in Tianjin student politics as the youngest founding member of the Awakening Society, which had functioned as a mobilization organization for the May Fourth Movement. Later she distinguished herself as a national women's leader through her involvement in the Zhili Women's Rights League, which was headquartered in Tianjin, and as an editor for *Women's Daily* (Funü ribao), which was published in Tianjin in 1923 and 1924. Although she had many friends who were Communists, including Liu Qingyang and Guo Longzhen, and she married Zhou Enlai, secretary of the European branch of the Chinese Communist Youth Corps, in late 1923 upon his return from Europe, Deng Yingchao had remained on the sidelines of party activities until the campaign for women's participation in the National Assembly persuaded her that Communists were serious about constructing a woman's program.

Tianjin was just one example of the many urban centers in which women brought pressure to bear on Duan Qirui's committee. Ultimately, however, their call for women's civil rights fell on deaf ears. Duan's regime refused to bow to their public pressure. Oddly enough, this failure ultimately proved to be beneficial to the efforts of Nationalist and Communist revolutionaries who wanted to elicit greater female support. This outcome revealed in stark terms that the existing warlord political system would not accommodate women and, therefore, that their interests were best served by the revolutionary camp. Very soon, Xiang Jingyu moved to consolidate the following that had been amassed through this campaign by establishing the All-Women's Association (Quanguo gejie funü lianhehui) in Beijing on April 29, 1925, at a meeting of five hundred people.[28] A few weeks later a chapter of this organization was founded in the southern city of Guangzhou under the slightly different name of the Guangdong Women's Emancipation Association (Guangdong funü jiefang xiehui).[29] Preparations were underway to establish a similar organization in Shanghai when the May Thirtieth massacre occurred. The timely convergence of these two events facilitated the integration of these women's groups into May Thirtieth mobilization networks.

The ease with which Xiang Jingyu was able to rally a mass women's movement highlighted all the more sharply the difficulties she was experiencing in sinking roots into women workers' organizations. Her previous efforts to form solid alliances with local women workers, particularly in the silk and tobacco industries in Shanghai, had proved largely ephemeral. Much of the difficulty stemmed from the male ethos and perspective that permeated the Communist labor outreach. Emily Honig's work on Shanghai women workers presents illuminating evidence to this effect. Deng Zhongxia, for instance, revealed a gross insensitivity to female workers' mores when he casually touched a young woman's arm in a way that would not have been inappropriate in radical student circles.[30] Perhaps because of the importance attributed to the proletariat, Communist men did not allow much space for women to develop their own organizing niche within the Communist labor program. This assertion of male power in this area of Communist work definitely hampered the party's ability to develop strong links with women factory workers, especially as Communist male organizers were known for manifesting a condescending attitude towards women's work. This general disdain for women workers was evidenced in the "Resolution on the Labor Movement" passed at the fourth party congress in January 1925, which portrayed women workers as a hindrance to the development of the labor movement because they were "still trapped under a religious and traditional society."[31] Because male Communist organizers seem to have adopted the biases of male workers regarding women, women workers were reluctant to involve themselves in union efforts under Communist auspices.

In order to reverse this sorry state of affairs, Xiang Jingyu promoted the idea of setting up night schools for workers in her "Resolution on the Women's Movement," which was passed by the third congress in 1923.[32] In so doing, she refashioned the original concept of the Shanghai Pingmin Girls' School, which had attempted to cater to women students from both working-class and elite backgrounds while retaining the notion that women's education had to be conducted separately from men's. This decision to establish working-class schools represented a recognition of the strong sentiments of many working-class families that contact between men and women, particularly unmarried people, should not be permitted. As a May Fourth activist, Xiang Jingyu had been committed to challenging the strict taboos against social contact between men and women, and she had even founded a coeducational school in Hunan, but as a Communist organizer she chose to heed these cultural practices in order to maximize the political reach of her party. Under her guidance as director of the Women's Bureau, twenty of these schools were established in working-class neighborhoods in Shanghai during 1924 and the first half of 1925. By the time of the May Thirtieth Incident, two to three hundred women workers had enrolled in the literacy classes at these schools, of whom approximately forty were eventually recruited into the Chinese Communist party.[33] While the ostensible purpose of these schools was to teach reading and writing skills, the classes served as a means to advance explicit revolutionary ideals on a wide range of topics. The desire of some workers for an education was strong enough that they were willing to listen to the political message of these young intellectuals. In addition, some women Communists, such as Yang Zhihua and Zhang Qinjiu, who had recently been recruited into the party from Shanghai University, gained valuable knowledge and contacts while serving as teachers in these schools. Thus, the roots of women workers' participation in the May Thirtieth protests can be traced to these night schools for women workers.

As the Chinese Communist organizers were beginning to develop ties with some women workers, a bitter strike occurred in February 1925 at the No. 8 Naigai Wata Cotton Mill. A forerunner of the May Thirtieth Movement, the strike was sparked by the firing of forty to fifty male workers on the night shift and their replacement with cheaper female trainees. Thus, the initial spark of the May Thirtieth conflagration was essentially ignited by the gender tensions in the workplace.[34] These antagonisms arising from the sexual division of labor in Shanghai, antagonisms that had often presented radical organizers with greater difficulties than had the influence of gangs or native place and ethnicity, prohibited Communists from initially eliciting the enthusiastic participation of women workers in the February strike.[35] However, once the gender dimensions of this conflict were engulfed by waves of anti-imperialism, the Communist contacts that had already been established with women workers could be utilized. In other words, it was difficult for Communist labor organizers to rally both male and female workers for a labor protest because of the gendered hierarchy in the factories. Women workers were willing, however, to join a protest with male workers that was organized around nationalist aims.

Women in the May Thirtieth Uprising

The tensions that had flared up in the Japanese-owned textile mills in the western section of Shanghai between February and

May of 1925 were greatly exacerbated when guards at the no. 15 mill fatally shot Gu Zhenghong, a worker and Communist party member, for resisting a company lockout. Although the Shanghai Municipal Council banned newspapers from publishing accounts of Gu's death in an effort to maintain order, organized groups of students spread the news through the streets. As feelings rose in the city, the Chinese Communist party succeeded in extending considerable influence over the Shanghai Student Union.[36] In a bid to tap the antiimperialist popular sentiments in the wake of Gu's killing, the Chinese Communist party called a large demonstration for May 30, 1925. When a jittery British officer ordered Sikh and Chinese police to open fire on an unruly crowd of demonstrators who had gathered in front of the Louze police station on Nanjing Road in the International Settlement, they killed thirteen students and workers.

The shooting that day transformed a localized labor issue into a national revolutionary movement. The use of violence in the May Thirtieth Incident altered the consciousness of students in a way that May Fourth had not. As Vera Schwarcz has noted, no one died in the Tiananmen Square protests on May Fourth; the only fatality was a Beijing University student who expired a few days later from overexertion and injuries.[37] No bullet had pierced his body. But when students were felled on the streets of Shanghai in 1925, the Chinese public was both horrified and galvanized. The small dose of violence meted out on May 30 inspired a great burst of nationalistic and revolutionary fervor that large numbers of Chinese experienced in a particularly intense manner.

The May Thirtieth Incident electrified the organizational networks that Xiang Jingyu had established among different sectors of women during the preceding year or two. Major successes were registered among students, professional women, and workers. Indeed, the incident arguably produced more female student activists than any previous Chinese revolutionary upheaval of the twentieth century. Moreover, Communist organizers were able to use this movement to make significant inroads among women workers and to cultivate a number of Communist women labor leaders, including Wang Genying, Zhu Yingru, and Lu Dinghua. Lastly, the All-Women's Association that Xiang Jingyu had created out of the ruins of the promotion committees was transformed by the May Thirtieth tumult into a women's mass mobilization organization that was established under a variety of names (e.g., Guangdong Women's Emancipation Association, Shanghai

All-Women's Association) in both urban and rural areas throughout much of China proper. One indicator of the success of Communist women organizers can be measured by the increase in female members in the Chinese Communist party. By September of 1925, the number of women recruits into the party had risen sharply to around one thousand, ten times what it had been before the May Thirtieth Incident.[38] More important, however, was the much larger number of women who ventured out of the confines of their homes or schools to participate in rallies, distribute leaflets, provide strike support, or simply listen to speeches in public parks and read the mountains of mass propaganda that were generated by this momentous event. In so doing, they were participating in the making of new roles for women in China's public sphere.

That the visible participation of women in the May Thirtieth protests was immediately reflected in literary and art works reveals the dramatic shift that had occurred in the public image of women in Chinese politics. Communist writer Mao Dun, in a piece he dashed off a few days after the event entitled "Tempest—May Thirty-First," portrayed women as ardent agitators who hurled piercing denunciations of imperialism in public forums and militantly surrounded the Shanghai Chamber of Commerce asserting they would rather die than let anyone out of the building until a general strike was agreed upon.[39]

Ye Shengtao, a prominent May Fourth intellectual who taught at revolutionary Shanghai University, used a similar portrayal of women's actions during the May Thirtieth agitations in *Ni Huanzhi*, a novel about an idealistic educator. His fictional account of these revolutionary events also presented the scene of women activists at the Chamber of Commerce. Written in a more moving, impassioned style than Mao Dun's, it nonetheless conveyed this same image of female militancy:

The most effective plan was decided on: to ask the Chamber of Commerce to declare a strike for all the shops and markets. If the Chamber did not consent, then no one would withdraw even if they had to die! Enthusiastic applause signaled their wholehearted approval to this plan. Girl students undertook the task of picketing the building and keeping guard over every single entrance; until their demands were met, they would only allow those involved in the proceedings to enter the building but not to leave it.[40]

Yet Ye Shengtao also imbued his depiction of the determined May

Thirtieth female student agitator with the quality of a secular goddess. Her short hair and simple student attire contrasted sharply with traditional representations of femininity.

Armed British, Sikh, and Chinese police with angry glares stormed into the crowd of demonstrators to disperse them; the road temporarily was quiet. But then a shrill cry cut through the dense humid air: "Down with Imperialism!" Huanzhi quickly looked and saw Miss Yin from the school. She stood in the middle of the road, water dripping from her short hair. She wore a dark blouse and a black skirt that reflected bright drops of water. Her arms were held high and her head was extended toward the sky. She looked like a valiant goddess.[41]

The image of the militant female idol was also conveyed in the writings of Chinese who were unsympathetic to the Communist effort. Wen Yiduo, for instance, who had just returned to China from a period of study in the United States when the May Thirtieth Movement commenced, portrayed women agitators as Mao Dun and Ye Shengtao did. He wrote of one female student whose "piercing yells cut through the crowd, astonishing all listeners; this same young female comrade, he was told, had been to the fore in the demonstrations against the May Thirtieth massacre, marching boldly through the streets with banner aloft, so that awestruck Beijing citizens referred to her as the 'Chinese Joan of Arc.' "[42] The extension of the powerful representation of this vocal May Thirtieth woman into other art forms was later exemplified by the captivating wood-block print made by the Chinese artist Ye Fu.[43]

These fictional portrayals had some basis in reality: women achieved a greater visibility at the center of public mass actions during the May Thirtieth Movement than they had in the past. Some, for instance, did actually participate in the students' effort to press the Chinese Chamber of Commerce into declaring a work stoppage in Shanghai. Indeed, Xiang Jingyu served as one of the representatives who negotiated with the vice-president of the Chamber of Commerce on May 31. When the Shanghai General Labor Union was founded on June 1, the woman Communist Yang Zhihua was elected as one of its leaders. The protesters who flooded the streets and parks of Shanghai included large numbers of women students who disseminated propaganda, and female workers joined the general strike and showed up at the large demonstrations. At the mass rally on June 11 at the Public Recreation Grounds, the strong showing of women textile workers was particularly noted because it was unprecedented. At yet another rally called for June 17 in the working-class district of Zhabei, two thousand women mill workers took part.[44] In addition, the fact that many women's groups, some of them only recently formed, issued statements in the press supporting the general strike and the anti-imperialist boycott conveyed the impression of strong women's mobilization in the May Thirtieth Movement.[45]

Perhaps the greatest effect of the May Thirtieth Incident on the mobilization of women in Shanghai was the impact it had on electrifying and expanding the extensive student networks that had been created in surrounding middle and normal schools over the preceding four years. Until this movement began, these networks remained largely informal and diffuse. For the most part, women students were brought only into small study groups by Communist teachers, where they were slowly familiarized with revolutionary literature. Some joined the Socialist Youth League, but many did not. May Thirtieth served to stimulate and enlarge these networks.

Shanghai University played an important role in this mobilization process. It was transformed from a revolutionary intellectual center into a command post for the student mobilizations, which involved an estimated fifty thousand students in the Shanghai area.[46] This role consisted of both coordinating much of the political action of the May Thirtieth Incident and producing great quantities of revolutionary rhetoric about the event. *Hot Blood Daily* (Rexue Ribao), published at Shanghai University, was one of the more provocative publications dedicated to the cause of transforming May Thirtieth into a large-scale revolutionary movement. Its use of the blood metaphor, which was echoed in many other publications of that period, reinforced the sense of a tragedy that needed to be redressed.[47]

However, what remained undefined in this highly charged political literature was the relationship between the powerful blood imagery and the vocal, assertive female activist. Did their sex provide these young women with immunity, or did their assumption of political roles make them possible targets of violence? The answer to this question lay in the future unfolding of the revolutionary process. Most women student activists at this time seemed to feel little fear of danger. Their immediate attention was focused on rallying as many other students to the cause as possible. To this end, they busily converted their schools into recruitment centers.

One important reason for the increase in female activism in these schools at this time was the inability of authorities to enforce rules and keep national political issues off the campus. By 1925, women students generally faced fewer restrictions in schools than they had during the May Fourth era. The numerous conflicts, termed "student storms" (*xuechao*), in the early 1920s over such issues as hairstyles, curriculum, and rules had altered the environment in schools and given birth to a more heightened political atmosphere than had been the case in 1919. As a result, school authorities were less able to simply lock up the school gates and stop women students from participating in demonstrations.[48] School authorities that resorted to such tactics often encountered tremendous student opposition.

By the same token, by the mid-1920s larger numbers of women students no longer felt compelled to stay out of the public eye. The weakening of the belief that it was improper for unmarried women to be out on the streets without chaperons facilitated the entry of female students into the large-scale street protests. Moreover, at least some girls were quite willing to assume visible roles in collective political actions. This change in gender mores greatly facilitated the expansion of mobilization networks into girls' schools. In Shanghai, May Thirtieth helped Communist organizers penetrate schools that had previously proved resistant, such as Kunfan Girls' Middle School and Wuben Girls' Middle School.[49] Many of these schools had been mapped by women in the Nationalist Women's Movement Committee in Shanghai, which had collected a great deal of information about the various women's educational institutions in the area.[50] As a result, even students in conservative and foreign-run schools were mobilized to participate in the wave of indignation sweeping across the city. Christian girls' schools were no exception. Such religious schools as Biwen Girls' Middle School, Zhongxi Girls' Academy, and Shengma Liye Girls' Middle School were all swept into the turbulence.

Within a short time, these networks were expanded throughout Shanghai and the surrounding region. The female mobilization in Ningbo, as described by Xu Chengmei, illustrated the ways in which these networks tended to function. Almost instantaneously after the May Thirtieth Incident, Qimeng Girls' Middle School became the command center of the network of girls' schools, in large part because of the critical Communist presence there provided by the principal, Yang Meishan, and several teachers.[51] Three girls were particularly active in mobilizing their classmates at Qiming: Feng Yongshu, Yang Liuqing, and Chen Yiseng. It was through Chen Yiseng that they also expanded this network into the Ningbo Girls' Normal School, as her sister, Chen Liuliang, was a student there and was willing to assume leadership of the effort to institute a student strike, organize a boycott of Japanese goods, and disseminate literature on the streets condemning the role of the imperialist powers in China.

Although Xu Chengmei and her classmates were initially quite successful, the school authorities instituted strong measures to suppress the student mobilization. All school gates were locked, and letters were sent to the parents of the student leaders detailing their actions and demanding that they be taken home immediately. When these tactics proved ineffectual, the principal decided to issue diplomas immediately to all graduating activists and then strike their names from the school roll. Among the twenty students who were dispensed with in this manner were four women who had joined the Socialist Youth League, including Xu Chengmei.[52] Similar tactics were used at the Chongde Girls' School in Ningbo, where fifteen female activists were forced out.

Although Xiang Jingyu often served as a model women radical for these students at public gatherings, she was not personally involved with the Communist effort to direct their activities and radicalize and recruit them. However, those, like Xu Chengmei, who did join the Chinese Communist party at this time quickly found themselves working under her guidance as organizers for the Shanghai All-Women's Association, which Xiang Jingyu had established during the May Thirtieth tumult. Indeed, the timing of the May Thirtieth Incident proved to be quite fortuitous in expediting the transformation of a women's rights organization, that is, the Committee to Promote Women's Participation in the National Assembly, into a mass women's movement organization. The founding meeting of the Shanghai All-Women's Association was held on June 5, 1925, with eighty people attending. Although this was a small crowd by May Thirtieth standards, representatives from more than twenty-three women's groups and schools in the city attended.

The press coverage of the founding meeting of the Shanghai All-Women's Association clearly reveals the overwhelming impact of the May Thirtieth Incident on the group's orientation. Both the Communist and Nationalist organizers of the Shanghai group placed most if not all of their stress on anti-imperialist issues. Shen Yibin, the wife of a prominent Nationalist party leader, delivered the keynote speech at the founding meeting in which she urged all members to give their support to the victims of the May Thirtieth massacre.[53] Her remarks reflected the general ambiance of the meeting, which was strongly affected by the events of the previous week. It was difficult for the founding members of this group to articulate any specific planks for the statement of principles regarding women's issues: the goals of the organization were entirely devoted to May Thirtieth anti-imperialist causes. The first set of goals, presented at the meeting by Xiang Jing-yu, concerned redressing the immediate ill effects of the event. They called for the withdrawal of troops from the city and the end of martial law, which had been imposed after the shootings, the release of all Chinese jailed on May 30, and compensation for all the victims: the dead, the injured, and those whose property had been damaged. Another set of goals was concerned with altering the terms of the Western presence in China: abolishing the foreign concessions, making it illegal for foreigners to kill Chinese nationals, and abrogating the unequal treaties.[54] However, once the student protests slackened, the Shanghai All-Women's Association devised a statement of principles that explicitly called for a fundamental transformation of women's rights.[55]

In the next few months, this organizational basis was given a boost from a large influx of women students who were mobilized in the area's middle schools after the May Thirtieth Incident. This influx of students facilitated its growth into a dynamic mass mobilization women's organization with a membership of around five hundred by the middle of 1926.[56] At the same time, a number of student activists were sent out to other cities with the dual task of disseminating the May Thirtieth anti-imperialist message and founding women's organizations to promote women's issues. Zhong Fuguang, a leading activist in the Shanghai All-Women's Association and a member of the Chinese Communist party, went back to her home province of Sichuan to mobilize women; Wang Yizhi, also a Communist party member and a student at Shanghai University, went to Guangzhou where she stayed for more than a year, becoming a leading member of the Guangdong Women's Emancipation Association.

The Expansion of Women's Organizations outside Shanghai

The May Thirtieth Incident provided Xiang Jingyu with the possibility of dramatically extending the influence of the Communist Women's Bureau to other locals outside of the Shanghai region. Indeed, it had originally been conceptualized as an office that would oversee the party's work throughout China, not just at the center of the Communist world. The initial catalysts were the women students, who served not only as agitators to promote the anti-imperialist boycott but also as founders of mass women's movement organizations.

This student mobilization after the incident quickly spread to other cities. Student protests erupted in such faraway places as Beijing, Wuhan, Chongqing, and Guangzhou. The example of Xu Chengmei's becoming a Communist revolutionary as a result of the May Thirtieth nationalistic outburst was not an unusual one. This scenario was repeated in many other localities, drawing large numbers of schoolgirls into the revolutionary tempest. The tempest was particularly intense in Guangzhou because of a violent clash that occurred between Chinese demonstrators and British police near the foreign enclave in Guangzhou. On June 23 a massive throng of protesters expressed their support for those slain in Shanghai by marching around the perimeters of the foreign-controlled Shameen Island. British and French guards fired upon them, killing fifty-two people, including one woman; another one to two hundred were wounded. Because this mishap occurred on Shaji Road, it quickly came to be called the Shaji Incident. It had a profound impact on the politicization of people in this region of China, including large numbers of schoolgirls. Ou Mengjue was one of the women students who became a revolutionary leader as a result of the intense nationalist reaction to this atrocity. From a prosperous entrepreneurial family that lived in Nanhai, she persuaded her father to send her to a private school in Guangzhou, the Kunwei Girls' Middle School, after her graduation from a local primary school. Like Xu Chengmei, she was already attending a study group under the direction of a Communist teacher, Tan Xiasheng, when the May Thirtieth disturbances broke out. Ou Mengjue was able to convince many of her schoolmates to participate en bloc in the planned demonstration around Shameen Island. Her family was shocked to hear of her actions from the school authorities, however, and immediately took steps to prohibit her from attending the rally. Deciding that this was a life and death issue, she escaped from her locked room at home and threw herself into a nearby river. Although a fisherman pulled her out, her parents decided that she would only find another way to commit suicide if they did not relent. She was at the demonstration on June 23 when foreign police sprayed the crowd with bullets. Soon afterwards she joined the Chinese Communist party and, like Xu Chengmei, became involved in the Guangdong Women's Emancipation Association that Communists had recently established. In 1926 she was elected as its chairperson.

Ou Mengjue was not the only student in her study group who would become a prominent Communist women leader as a result of the May Thirtieth/Shaji protests. Equally prestigious was Chen Tiejun (1904–1928), who ultimately became a martyr for the Communist cause.[57] Her father was a businessman who had originally made his fortune in Australia. He resettled in his hometown of Foshan soon after the 1911 Revolution and founded a thriving business. As a result, his daughter was given an excellent education at Kunxian Private Academy. Upon her graduation, her family followed conventional practices and arranged for her marriage. Chen handled this situation in a very unusual manner, however, by proceeding to convince her new family that she be allowed to continue her education. In 1922 she entered the Kunwei Girls' Middle School. At Kunwei, Chen Tiejun encountered a host of nationalist and feminist ideas. She soon decided to terminate her arranged marriage, which she accomplished with the aid of one of her teachers, Tan Xiasheng, who had been instrumental in influencing Ou Mengjue. Tan also persuaded her to undertake a serious study of Marxist texts. She joined other classmates, including Ou Mengjue, in his study group until she gained entrance in the fall of 1924 to Guangdong University. This was a fairly unusual opportunity for a young woman, as there were only a few universities in China that accepted women in the 1920s, and it might well have led her away from the Communist party had it not been for the revolutionary upsurge of 1925. She first served as a mass organizer and then she joined the party in April of 1926. The next month, she was elected to the executive committee of the Guangdong Women's Emancipation Association.

In fact, many of the women students who gravitated toward radical politics joined the Communist-sponsored mass women's group in Guangdong. Founded in early May of 1925, it bore a slightly different name than its Shanghai equivalent, perhaps because it wanted to place greater stress on gender-transformation goals from the very beginning of its existence. In contrast to the declaration of the Shanghai All-Women's Association, which was drafted after the May Thirtieth anti-imperialist upsurge, the Guangdong Women's Emancipation Association's declaration contained more emphasis on gender issues and less on nationalist ones. It called for changing the patriarchal mentality and marriage system, giving women a number of important political rights, facilitating women's access to education and vocational training, and improving conditions in the workplace. In this document, mention was made of imperialists' and warlords' oppressive actions and their links to women's subordination, but such references were kept to a minimum. Similarly, in the declaration for the Beijing Communist mass women's organization, most of the emphasis was placed on the need to eradicate female patriarchal oppression and patriarchal thinking. The declaration of the All Women's Association in Beijing also called on women to realize the importance of building a strong unified organization in order to achieve gender equality. No mention was made of anti-imperialist or antiwarlord goals.[58]

Communist-sponsored women's organizations continued to be established in many localities throughout China in the months after May Thirtieth. Indeed, the impact of this anti-imperialist movement on the proliferation of these groups was quite pronounced. By July, Tianjin Communists had attracted two hundred members to their organization, while Hubei boasted eight hundred members in August 1925. Tangshan, Qingdao, and Wuzhou (Guangxi) also had established women's associations by the autumn of 1925 as a result of the May Thirtieth upsurge. In Hunan, women's associations spread from the capital of Changsha into the surrounding county towns. Yet, the most impressive expansion of these Communist-sponsored women's groups into county towns occurred in Guangdong, where the Nationalists had established a revolutionary government (see Appendix I).

The Removal of Xiang Jingyu

Xiang Jingyu, more than any other single woman Communist, laid the organizational foundations for the Chinese Communist party's advantageous utilization of the upsurge in women's political activism in the wake of the May Thirtieth Incident. However, just in her moment of triumph, she was removed from her position as director of the Women's Bureau and sent to Moscow for further "study." Her status in the Communist party was damaged by objections to her management of her personal life—the deterioration of her relationship with Cai Hesen and her romantic involvement with Peng Shuzhi, a high-ranking Hunanese leader in the party. Thus, despite the centrality of her role in building mass women's movements in the context of the May Thirtieth upsurge, Xiang Jingyu became a casualty of personal politics within the party.

The removal of Xiang Jingyu reflected a weakness of party organization and a failure to sustain good leadership. It revealed in the starkest of terms the traditional underpinnings of the party institutional structure. Attachment to an important male Communist not only served as an unstated requirement for a woman's attainment of a high-level political position but was required for the maintenance of that high status. Ironically, it was precisely Xiang's attempts to combat such patriarchal precedents that brought about her undoing. Xiang Jingyu's sudden departure must have been disconcerting to the Shanghai women who had entered into political participation under her tutelage. It also was disconcerting to Xiang Jingyu, who, at least for a while, wanted to drop out of politics completely. In fact, she announced to a gathering of the Shanghai All-Women's Association that she wanted to return to France and improve her French language skills. Why she did not act upon this aspiration is not clear, but ultimately she ended up at Sun Yatsen University, where she had to endure much criticism for her "bourgeois" ways.

The removal of Xiang Jingyu had serious repercussions both in Shanghai and in the larger Communist movement. Only she had the experience, knowledge, and contacts to extend the influence of the Women's Bureau outside of Shanghai. She was also one of the few women Communists who had the respect of the Nationalist establishment in Shanghai. Much of the success of the women's movement of the United Front, particularly the creation of the Women's Committees for the Promotion of the National Assembly and the founding of the Shanghai All-Women's Association, was largely due to her leadership. Subsequently, the goal of building a unified national mass women's organization proved elusive, and the great damage caused by her departure was revealed. Similarly, the alliance in women's work between Communists and Nationalist suffered as well. Most notably, the Nationalist party decided to suspend funding for *Women's Weekly* once Xiang Jingyu stepped down from its editorship, and it quickly ceased publication.

Yang Zhihua, an outstanding Communist women's leader, was selected to fill Xiang's shoes. Yang's marriage to Qu Qiubai in the fall of 1924 had bought her into the inner circles of Communist politics. A student at Shanghai University, Yang Zhihua had distinguished herself as a women's labor leader during the May Thirtieth tumult, having risen to prominence in the public eye when she was named as a leading member of the Shanghai General Labor Union. Her efforts to cultivate links with the women workers at the B.A.T. (British-American Tobacco) factories yielded very positive results. Large numbers of women workers in the packing department joined the general strike called in June of 1925 and served as propagandists for the cause.[59] The sharp contrast between their participation and that of the female cotton workers revealed the effectiveness of a woman labor organizer of Yang Zhihua's abilities and determination.[60] She clearly took the time to befriend the women working at B.A.T.; she even adopted their style of dress. In Elizabeth Perry's estimation, Yang Zhihua's "altruistic" example inspired many workers to join the cause. Thus, she was uniquely well suited to provide strong leadership to developing a Communist program for women workers. She also had the necessary knowledge and experience to accomplish this goal. However, Yang Zhihua was less able than Xiang Jingyu to take on United Front work. For one thing, her former father-in-law, Shen Xuanlu, who had recently joined the Western Hills Clique of the Nationalist party, used his influence to have his wife installed in the position left vacant by Xiang Jingyu, the chair of the Nationalist Women's Movement Committee in Shanghai. Secondly, a number of Nationalist party women found it objectionable that Yang Zhihua was a divorced woman.[61]

Unable to emulate Xiang's accomplishments as director of the Communist Women's Bureau, Yang Zhihua shaped the position to fit her strengths and achieved significant breakthroughs in the area of labor organizing during her tenure of office. Her initial triumphs during the May Thirtieth Movement bolstered her confidence in her ability to take on the much more difficult problem of gaining some leverage among silk workers, who were quite noticeable in their refusal to honor the general strike in June of 1925. Yang's efforts facilitated the demise of Mu Zhiying's power base among women silk workers in 1926, when women workers decided to remove her as head of their union and launch a major strike in June of 1926.[62] As she did with the B.A.T. women workers in 1925, Yang Zhihua maintained daily contact with these silk workers during this critical labor action. Moreover, her writings about this strike reveal her familiarity with and genuine concern for the difficulties these women strikers faced. She wrote:

We should know more about women's oppression from their families. Those brave and ardent young women workers who energetically supported the strike want to extricate themselves from the bonds of the family and march forward. But in the end they have to go home. I heard that some who returned home after the strike were beaten and humiliated by their parents, brothers, and sisters-in-law. They were refused food. One family said: "You haven't been back for several days. You must have a lover. For all we care, you can die." The parents of another woman gave her a rope and knife and told her to choose. Poor women workers. They don't sleep or eat well during the strike and then they have to go onto a tragic stage. This is the evil of China's patriarchal society and old feudal ethics. You need to realize that the filial kindness and chastity of Oriental civilizations have actually become an auxiliary tool of capitalist oppression.[63]

At the same time that Yang Zhihua was developing Communist ties with women workers, she also promoted the growth of the Shanghai All-Women's Association. By the summer of 1926, the Shanghai All-Women's Association was the major proponent of the plan to unify women's groups. Its organ *Chinese Women* (Zhongguo funü) began carrying articles calling for a national representative congress of women as an important initial step to effect a unification.[64] Among the pieces was one penned by Chen Bilan, an early Communist member who by 1926 was an important leader of the Shanghai All-Women's Association. She argued:

Since the May Thirtieth Movement, the women's movement has sprung up like bamboo shoots after a spring rain. In the course of the fermenting women's movement, and in the course of this continuous struggle, the strength of the women themselves has become quite strong and militant. Now the time has come to take stock and review our strength, like an army seeking victory over the enemy in a war. To achieve this step, we must convene a meeting of representatives of those women's organizations which presently are active. Such a meeting will allow groups to report on recent events in their localities and assess their strength. This, in turn, will allow us to determine the correct policy and tactics for obtaining victory over the enemy. The lack of such a plan thus far has prevented the women's movement from keeping abreast with other movements.[65]

Chen Bilan's judgment that the women's movement had not kept pace with other mass movements provides an indication of how Communists in Shanghai assessed women's organizational progress. Chen's negative appraisal also was echoed in the writings of other female and male Communists, indicating that the low opinion of the their progress was fairly common in the party by 1926. Central Committee member Cai Hesen wrote in March 1926, for instance:

The women's movement has been promoted for many years in China, but in general does not have many successes. Compared to the worker's, peasant, and student movements, which have been advancing by leaps and bounds, the women's movement really is staring helplessly at the vanishing backs of the runners ahead.[66]

In light of the wide mobilization campaigns in the south, this appraisal seems overly pessimistic. Cai Hesen, however, was not a witness to the mobilization of women in Guangdong. In fact he was not in China but in Moscow at the time his article was published. Nevertheless, his statement is indicative of what was at stake in the bid for unification. The successful realization of a national mass women's organization offered the possibility of improving women Communists' image of their mobilization campaign. Success perhaps also offered Communist women the possibility of increased power within their party.

Mobilizing Women Students in Warlord Beijing

Despite Communists' efforts to consolidate the gains of the May Thirtieth upsurge throughout China, by the beginning of 1926 it had become clear that sustaining a women's movement in warlord sectors of the country was quite difficult. Nowhere was this problem more evident than in Beijing. To be sure, the mass demonstrations in Beijing to protest the killings in Shanghai on May 30 had been spectacular, momentarily breaking through the police repression that had been adopted in the city to curb student involvement in political affairs. Hundreds of female students were among the fifty thousand who marched around the city on June 3 and the one hundred thousand people who gathered at the Gate of Heavenly Peace on June 10, including representatives from Wuben Women's University, the First Women's Middle School, the attached middle school of Beijing Normal Women's College, and Beijing Normal Women's College itself.[67]

Student disturbances continued through the next year, particularly at Beijing Normal Women's College, where the conflict with Chancellor Yang Yinyu persisted. Eventually the school stopped functioning, but students refused to obey orders to leave the campus. They continued to be active in radical politics, deciding to joined the six thousand demonstrators who took to the streets on March 18, 1926, to protest the cowardly stance of Chinese warlord regimes toward the foreign powers' Taku Ultimatum. No one was prepared for the violence that Duan Qirui's troops perpetrated that day. Forty-seven protesters were slaughtered in what became known as the March Eighteenth Incident, including six women, a chilling demonstration of the warlord stance on the woman question. It was not purely accidental that one-eighth of those slaughtered by Iron Lion Gate that day were female. In the May Thirtieth and Shaji Incidents combined, only one woman had been killed. It was widely assumed that the soldiers who opened fire at point-blank range in Beijing on March 18 intentionally included a good number of women students among their victims.[68] No longer could women suppose that their gender would protect them from urban political violence; rather, with this massacre their bodies became a turf upon which both the symbolic and actual conflict over social change took place.

For those far away from the site of this atrocity, it was the poignant writings of Lu Xun that captured in the most gripping fashion the savagery of this incident. Sarcastically he recalled that when he had heard the news that some of his students had been killed, he was somewhat skeptical: "I am always ready to think the worst of my fellow-countrymen, but I could neither conceive nor believe that we could stoop to such despicable barbarism." For these students, he underscored, had gone forth "gaily" with a petition never imagining that such a trap had been concocted. Based on the accounts of survivors he reconstructed what had happened when the shooting began:

She [Liu Hezhen] was shot before Government House, shot from behind, and the bullet pierced her lung and heart. A mortal wound, but she did not die immediately. When Miss Zhang Jingshu who was with her tried to lift her up, she was pierced by four shots, one from a pistol, and fell. And when Miss Yang Dequn who was with them tried to lift her up, she was shot too: the bullet entered her left shoulder and came out to the right of her heart, and she also fell. She was able to sit up, but a soldier clubbed her savagely over her head and her breast, and so she died....

Lu Xun was struck by the glaring contrast between the barbarism of the authorities and the valor of the young Chinese women who had been willing to help each other in the face of death that fateful morning. He regarded their attempt "to rescue each other amid a hail of bullets, regardless of their own safety" as a telling sign of "the courage of Chinese women which has persisted through the thousands of years of conspiracies against them and suppression." Moreover, in his estimation they embodied an "indomitable spirit" of young Chinese women in the public sphere that had started to manifest itself in 1925.[69]

This act of violence against women demonstrators changed the nature of women's participation in political activities. This loss of immunity from such violence by virtue of their gender suddenly made their physical beings targets in the social contention over what women's roles should be. It also revealed the grave difficulties of continuing revolutionary mass activities in warlord China, particularly when the prospects for successful mobilizations seemed so much more promising in the south, where by mid-1925, Guangdong was functioning as an acclaimed revolutionary center. As the May Thirtieth strikes and supporting activities petered out in other parts of the country, many activists, including women students, made their way to this southern region of China in order to continue their revolutionary activities under the most favorable conditions possible at that time.

CHAPTER 6

Guangdong Mass Women's Movement

Although the geographical terrain of the revolutionary protests of the mid-1920s was quite extensive and ever expanding, Guangdong emerged as the center of this challenge, in large part because of the success of the Nationalist party in establishing a political base there in 1924. Soon dubbed "the cradle of the Chinese Revolution," Guangdong allowed for the earliest and most concerted attempt to alter existing gender arrangements in this period. Moreover, both the manner in which women's emancipatory issues were infused into the political culture and the patterns of female participation that emerged in Guangdong served as models for revolutionaries when they extended their operations into other southern and central provinces of China.

The social terrain of Guangdong, especially the Pearl River delta, was characterized by its large, powerful, and affluent patrilineages, which perpetuated a strong patriarchal ideology that placed little value on females and generally regarded them as expendable.[1] Yet certain aspects of women's culture, labor participation, and political activism in this province diluted the potency of traditional norms governing female conduct and thereby contributed to the creation of a receptive cultural context for the initiation of this women's mobilization campaign of the mid-1920s. Ono Kazuko's and Rubie Watson's discussions, for instance, of women's ballads, girls' houses, festivals, and sisterhoods reveal the existence of a rich women's expressive culture that facilitated the fostering of ties between women and their articulation of a countervailing social vision of gender relations.[2] If the prevalence of foot binding among the Cantonese-speaking population (the Hakka had never practiced this custom) is taken as a measure of the tenacity of traditional norms regulating female propriety, then it is significant that this custom was definitely on the decline by the early 1920s.[3] According to one foreign sojourner, foot binding was "almost unknown" in the entire province by the 1920s, a claim that is supported by the fact that revolutionaries did not make it into an issue of the women's mobilization campaigns in Guangdong during the National Revolution, whereas in Hubei it became a main focus of revolutionary activity.[4]

By the same token, it is difficult to characterize Guangdong women as "insiders" (*neiren*) entrapped within family compounds without much knowledge of the outside world, for many were involved in agricultural production.[5] Surveys conducted by Chen Han-seng in the 1930s revealed the surprising reality that more than half of the day laborers in the fields throughout the province were women.[6] Indeed, the scene of large numbers of women working in the fields in the East River area seemed quite remarkable to Zhu De, a Communist general, when he passed through with his Nanchang armies in 1927.[7] Of course, it was difficult for many patrilineages to keep women as *neiren* inside the family compound when their men had gone abroad to find work. Indeed, the practice of male out-migration, particularly among the Hakka, to various parts of Southeast Asia, the Pacific Islands, and the West Coast of the United States was quite extensive by the 1920s.[8] If the Hakka stood out in everyday life for their lack of conformity to many prevailing gender practices, they also were well known for their direct onslaught on gender customs during the momentous Taiping Rebellion in the mid–nineteenth century.[9] This revolutionary tradition was subsequently augmented by the strong participation of Guangdong women in the 1911 Revolution and through the bustling activities of a host of women's groups—the most of any province in China—that sprang up in the May Fourth era.[10] The legacy of a century of agitation for gender transformation in this province perpetuated an image of Guangdong women as the leaders of the Chinese women's movement and thus laid a strong foundation for the women's mobilization campaigns of the National Revolution.

The mass mobilization of women in Guangdong during the mid-1920s was pursued through the strikingly innovative and extensive use of cultural symbols, propaganda, and organization that was based to a great extent on practices developed in the Soviet Union after the Bolshevik Revolution.[11] The explicit aim of this intense effort of mass mobilization was to bring women into the political process, usually for the first time, and make them feel like they were an integral part of the new political order that was being created. Secondarily, this mode of mobilization aimed to challenge traditional norms regulating gender conduct by promoting the formation of new values and beliefs about the role of women in the political, economic, and social arenas of a modern nation-state. The Chinese adoption of Soviet mobilization practices reflected the tremendous prestige and special role that was accorded the Soviet Union and representatives of the Moscow-based Third International (Comintern) in the National Revolution. Ever since the issuing of the joint declaration by Sun Yatsen and Soviet diplomat Adolph Joffe in January of 1923, the Soviet Union had provided money, political and military advisers, and arms to the Nationalists in Guangzhou in order to facilitate a revolutionary effort to establish a unified nation-state in China.

While the specific mode of the women's mobilization campaigns that unfolded in Guangdong bore a distinct resemblance to the programs of the Zhenotdel (the women's section of the Soviet Communist party), it would be erroneous to suppose that what transpired in the Guangdong women's mobilization campaigns of the 1920s was a direct transplant of the Russian revolutionary experience. To begin with, the National Revolution was influenced by the upsurge of feminism in China of the 1910s. The cause of women's emancipation influenced many political activists of both the Nationalist and Communist parties and predisposed them to support the development of a large-scale women's mobilization campaign around such May Fourth issues as marriage reform, the abolition of polygamy, concubinage, and prostitution, female employment in the public sector, and far-reaching legal reform that would guarantee women's suffrage and property rights.[12] A close examination of the mobilization programs reveals much about the ways in which these May Fourth concerns were translated into action during the National Revolution as well as about the emergence of social and political constraints on this effort of gender transformation.

The Revolutionary Context for the Women's Mobilization Campaign

The transformation of Guangdong into a revolutionary center in the mid-1920s was brought about by the consolidation of

Nationalist power in the province with the critical support of funding from the Communist Third International.[13] The Nationalist party was reorganized along lines specified by Mikhail Borodin, the Russian Comintern special adviser to Sun Yatsen. The successful Nationalist military campaigns in the eastern and western sections of Guangdong in 1924 and the first part of 1925 created a relatively safe haven for revolutionary discussions and undertakings that was decidedly preferable to other areas of the country, where political control was in the hands of menacing warlords or Westerners.

However innovative and promising social movements initially were in places like Shanghai and Beijing, their expansion was always checked by the warlord or Western authorities. Public discussions and gatherings were subjected to stiff police regulation, and political organizers had to plan actions in a piecemeal fashion from "underground" nooks. Organizers worked under constant threat of police persecution, as was so dramatically demonstrated during the May Thirtieth Incident (1925), when the International Settlement police disputed protesters' access to the streets and closed down institutions involved in the protest, such as Shanghai University.[14]

Ultimately these Shanghai police actions in May of 1925 precipitated a spectacular outpouring of mass nationalist sentiment and gave rise to the emergence of a profound revolutionary consciousness throughout much of urban China. Throngs of students and intellectuals, now confident that a revolution was actually achievable, streamed southward to Guangzhou, which they viewed as the revolutionary capital of the country. This reputation swelled with the calling of a massive Hong Kong seamen's strike in June 1925 involving tens of thousands of workers; the strike proved to be one of the longest general strikes (lasting sixteen months) and boycotts of foreign goods in Chinese history.[15] Moreover, a reenactment of the May Thirtieth tragedy occurred right in Guangzhou when foreign police opened fire on a large group of Chinese demonstrators, causing many causalities and deaths in what came to be called the Shaji Incident. The combined impact of these events activated a large number of Guangdong people to participate in the revolution alongside those from outside the province. In so doing, these new political actors, both mobilizers and mobilized, became involved in the complex process of creating a new nation-state through revolution.

From the early formation of a revolutionary center in Guangzhou, Nationalist and Communist leaders consciously worked to construct a cultural system that would solidify public support for the new order. A new set of political rituals, revolutionary symbols, festivals, and press publications was devised that had an immediate impact on popular life, particularly in Guangzhou. For many people, participation in political life—rallies, parades, public meetings, holidays—became a routine, indeed almost a daily occurrence, prompting Western journalists to refer to the city as "Red Canton" in their dispatches.[16]

Women's emancipatory issues were integrated into this revolutionary political culture and were strongly promoted by the new government as an indication of its commitment to gender reform. Women's issues were inserted into newspapers, journals, theater, and the celebrations of most revolutionary public holidays. The cause of women's emancipation as an abstraction seems to have been widely embraced by all the parties involved in the revolutionary coalition, but the invention of an appropriate revolutionary tradition that would give greater credence to the anticipated women's mass mobilization campaign was left mainly to the Chinese Communists and Comintern advisers.

Much of the specific content of the political culture that was created was appropriated directly from European socialist feminist traditions and then explicitly linked to the goal of achieving a National Revolution.[17] Intertwined with this internationalist political culture were practices and symbols derived from the May Fourth era. In such a charged environment, for instance, fashion became a political statement. Many of the urban women who assumed visible roles in the political arena expressed their revolutionary modernity through their hairstyles. As in the 1911 Revolution when men cut their long queues as a sign of their defiance of the Manchu rulers, women in the National Revolution appropriated the May Fourth practice of bobbing their hair to symbolize their emancipation from the traditional codes for women. In Guangzhou it became the most important way for a young woman to signify that she was an active participant in the grand effort to construct a new order.

Many new festivals that promoted women's emancipation had a decidedly internationalist tone. Thousands of people streamed into the parks in Guangzhou every May 1 to celebrate the socialist labor day. They called for a variety of changes in working conditions for women, including the granting of paid maternity leave to women and equal pay for men and women performing the same job. Although Chinese radicals, particularly Communists in Shanghai, had previously held small gatherings to celebrate socialist labor day, this was the first time that it was widely observed as a public occasion in a Chinese city. Similarly, for the celebrations in recognition of the Bolshevik Revolution, official addresses and speeches expounded on the great changes that Russian women had experienced under Soviet rule. Most important, the Nationalist government, following the practice of Western socialist parties, incorporated International Women's Day into its calendar of rituals, a holiday that was originally created at the suggestion of Clara Zetkin at the International Conference of Socialist Women in Copenhagen in 1910.[18]

The first Women's Day celebration in Guangzhou was held on March 8, 1924. More than three thousand people participated in this inaugural celebration, which called for gender equality in wages, educational opportunities, and the law, as well as for the elimination of concubines, prostitutes, child-brides, and girl bond servants. During the next few years the slogans became more radical and included calls to end the arranged-marriage system, permit divorce, and oppose capitalist exploitation of women. The size of the gatherings grew substantially over time as well: by 1926, the numbers of people attending the March 8 festivities in Guangzhou expanded to more than ten thousand; by 1927, they were estimated around twenty-five thousand. For those city dwellers unable to attend the rallies, the significance of this occasion was impressed upon them through articles in the press and the circulation of pamphlets on buses and in the streets.[19]

Indicative of the role that male political leaders initially played in defining the rituals and symbols for promoting the ideals of women's emancipation in the National Revolution, Liao Zhongkai was the featured speaker at the first March 8 rally, in 1924. Significantly, while he was invited to proclaim the significance of this holiday, the soon-to-be-appointed female head of the Nationalist Central Women's Department, Zeng Xing, stood by his side on the podium.[20] No doubt his tremendous political stature as Sun Yatsen's plenipotentiary and as governor of Guangdong, coupled with his reputation as an eloquent speech maker, lent great legitimacy to this women's festival. But over the next few years, as the power and prestige of the Nationalist Central Women's Department grew, women leaders came to dominate the proceedings.

No changes appeared to have occurred in subsequent years in the internationalist tone of these celebrations, however. The recollections of Vera Vladimirovna Vishnyakova-Akimova, who as a twenty-one-year-old Russian woman had participated in the 1926 Women's Day celebration in Guangzhou, provide a vivid account of the celebration. In response to a request by the Nationalist Central Women's Department, she and some other Russian women staged an amateur performance for the occasion, which began with their singing the Internationale. Then they put on a skit that portrayed women of the world looking to the Soviet Union as a beacon of inspiration. Vishnyakova-Akimova recalled how they all dressed up in international costumes to symbolize the many different countries of the world.

[We] surrounded Soviet Russia—the wife of the adviser Rogachev in a sarafan and a kokoshnik (a type of old Russian woman's headdress) holding a red banner. I was made up as a Chinese woman—dressed in pajamas embroidered with dragons and shod in ancient satin men's slippers on high wooden soles. My head swam in a jet-black wig, parted in the middle, with a bang and long braids, fastened from both sides near the ears; the hairdo was not in the least Chinese. I portrayed awakened China and stretched out my hands towards Soviet Russia. No matter how surprising it may seem, the Chinese recognized themselves in me and applauded deafeningly.[21]

The internationalism of the symbolic framework that was constructed in Guangdong was also reflected in the tribute paid to the memory of Rosa Luxemburg, a famous woman leader of the German socialist party who was brutally murdered during the ill-fated Communist uprising in Berlin in 1919. Not only Communist but also Nationalist journals and newspapers carried articles every January on the anniversary of Rosa Luxemburg's death. Official ceremonies were held to honor her memory as well. She came to represent revolutionary virtue, commitment, and self-sacrifice. Biographers portrayed her as a woman who dedicated her entire life's work to the cause of revolution, who was willing to go through with a fictitious marriage in order to obtain German citizenship and thereby continue her revolutionary activities in Germany, and who ultimately died for her convictions.

By 1927, Rosa Luxemburg's visual image by itself was used to represent the ideal of women's emancipation. Her photograph was featured in many publications, particularly around March 8.[22] In the rural areas her picture was hung in public places, for example in the office of the Huaxian Peasant Association at its opening ceremony, as a model of a woman revolutionary, alongside those of Sun Yatsen, Lenin, Marx, Engels, and Liebknecht.[23] Over time, new meaning was given to the image of Rosa Luxemburg: she came to epitomize militancy as well. When local conflicts intensified and became violent, hundreds, perhaps thousands, of women took up arms for the peasant associations and fought in Rosa Luxemburg battalions.[24]

In hindsight it seems curious that the revolutionary government made no significant effort to invent a more Chinese female revolutionary tradition, one featuring Qiu Jin, for example, who in more recent epochs has come to be venerated by both Nationalists and Communists as the second most important revolutionary of the 1911 Revolution after Sun Yatsen.[25] Like Rosa Luxemburg, she too had been a dedicated woman revolutionary who had defied the old regime and died for her ideals. In some ways she would have been an even more appropriate symbol of female militancy in the Chinese revolution than Rosa Luxemburg because she had consciously identified with the image of a woman warrior. Known for her fondness of donning male attire, riding a horse, brandishing a sword, learning how to make bombs, excelling in marksmanship, and downing large quantities of wine, she viewed herself as following in the footsteps of illustrious male heroes in Chinese history and historical fiction, such as Jing Ke, celebrated for making an attempt on the life of the first emperor of China, Liu Bei and Cao Cao, famous rival heroes in the romanticized Three Kingdoms period (ca. 220–280), and Li Shimin, a founder and great sovereign of the Tang dynasty of the first half of the seventh century.[26]

The revolutionary leaders in Guangzhou did not show much interest in reviving the memory of Qiu Jin and infusing her image with political symbolism. Although the Nationalist Central Women's Department did make a feeble attempt to gather some information about Qiu Jin, and her name was mentioned in passing in the local Nationalist newspaper, *Guangzhou Republican Daily* (Guangzhou minguo ribao), nothing more came of these efforts.[27] This lack of interest in making Qiu Jin into a revolutionary symbol may well have stemmed from a lingering animosity of Nationalist party members for the Restoration Society, a loose-knit revolutionary organization that had collaborated with Sun Yatsen's Revolutionary Alliance before the 1911 Revolution but had later became involved in a contentious factional struggle with Sun's group. Although Qiu Jin had joined the Revolutionary Alliance in Tokyo in 1905, upon her return to Zhejiang she became a member of the Restoration Society as well and conducted her revolutionary activities on its behalf. Once animosities between the Restoration Society and the Revolutionary Alliance came to a head in 1912, Qiu Jin's reputation among Sun Yatsen's clique was tainted.[28]

Qiu Jin's close women friends believed that Sun Yatsen acted on this animosity when he refused to support the construction of a grand mausoleum to honor Qiu Jin's contributions to the overthrow of the Qing imperial government. Not long after the 1911 Revolution, Qiu Jin's friends had arranged to have her remains brought back from Hunan, where they had been interred at the site of her husband's family graveyard, a fate they knew would have been quite objectionable to Qiu Jin because of her unhappy marriage. They planned to construct a magnificent mausoleum complete with an elaborate epitaph on her revolutionary activities written in the elegant calligraphy of one of her best friends. Just when construction was to begin, however, the recently installed president of the new republic, Yuan Shikai, objected to this project on the grounds that it would eclipse the nearby shrine for Yue Fei, the eminent general of the Song dynasty. Qiu Jin's friends believed they would have mustered enough local elite support to override Yuan's objection had it not been for Sun Yatsen's personal intercession in the dispute.[29]

If Sun Yatsen decided in favor of maintaining male dominance in the realm of symbolism in the 1910s, his own image was increasingly being used in the mid-1920s to imbue the National Revolution and the state-making endeavor with a distinctly male identity. In fact, Sun Yatsen became a more powerful figure in the public eye and in his party after his death than he was during his life. The tremendous force of his memory as a national symbol was first demonstrated at his funeral in March of 1925, when thousands upon thousands of people poured out along the procession route from Beijing to the Western Hills to commemorate him, despite the strong opposition of the warlord government to any sort of public demonstration. At that moment, Nationalist leaders recognized the tremendous potential political value of a purposeful and well-designed effort to enshrine the memory of Sun Yatsen as widely as possible in public consciousness.[30]

Although the glorification of Sun Yatsen through these means occurred throughout China, Guangdong became the center of this endeavor. His picture was hung everywhere in the city and even appeared on the currency. Streets, buildings, and parks increasingly bore his name, and Guangdong University in Guangzhou had its name changed to Sun Yatsen University in 1926. In March of that year the revolutionary government in Guangdong held province-wide commemorations to mark the first anniversary of his death in order to foster the notion that Sun Yatsen was the incarnation of Chinese nationalism. Thus, within a short time, this not terribly successful politician was converted into the overarching symbol of the nation, the embodiment of nationalism, the father of the revolution. That the nationalist revolutionary ideology of the mid-1920s in Guangdong was so strongly imbued with a male identity militated against the creation of a full-fledged comparable mother of the revolution from either the international socialist tradition, Rosa Luxemburg, or from the annals of Chinese revolutionary history, Qiu Jin.

The Organizational Infrastructure for the Women's Campaigns

The Nationalist party established a Central Women's Department early in 1924 to oversee the women's mobilization drive for the National Revolution. Although no specific tasks initially were assigned to this department, the proclamation of the first party congress in January 1924 articulated the department's general purpose and pledged to advance the principle of gender equality in the law, economy, education, and society as well as to promote the development of women's rights.[31] While party members found the basic sentiment of this statement acceptable, the actual impetus for incorporating a gender plank in the party's proclamation and for creating a women's department came from Mikhail Borodin, the chief Comintern adviser assigned to the Nationalist party. After his arrival in Guangzhou in the autumn of 1923, he had devoted his efforts to drafting a new Nationalist constitution and a reorganization plan for the party along the lines of the Russian Communist party.[32]

The person most responsible for giving explicit meaning to this women's emancipation declaration and organization was He Xiangning, the veteran woman party member who assumed the post of director of the Central Women's Department in August of 1924. She held tremendous stature in the Nationalist party in her own right as the first women to join the Revolutionary Alliance in 1905 and as a member of Sun Yatsen's inner circle in the 1920s. Her legitimacy among Nationalist leaders was further enhanced by her marriage to Liao Zhongkai, one of the most powerful political figures in the Nationalist party and the Guangdong revolutionary government at that time. Moreover, this appointment seemed entirely appropriate because of her long-standing interest in women's rights issues.[33] Indeed, she demonstrated her potential as a future pioneer of the Chinese women's movement even as a child. Inspired by the model of Hakka women warriors in the Taiping Rebellion, she took the extremely unusual action for the daughter of a prosperous business-man in the 1880s of refusing to have her feet bound.[34] This strength of character was again manifested when she was in Japan as a young married woman and decided to join the Revolutionary Alliance with-out consulting her husband. When Liao Zhongkai returned from Hong Kong, she persuaded him to become a member as well. For many years thereafter, however, she maintained a fairly low profile in politics. By accepting this appointment as director of the Central Women's Department in 1924, He Xiangning for the first time in her political career stepped from the wings of her party onto center stage.

During the three years that He Xiangning headed this department, it succeeded in overseeing the social mobilization of large numbers of women for the National Revolution. To this end, it not only expanded its organizational networks and developed a core of its own organizers but also coordinated the work of several mass mobilization organiza-tions, particularly the Communist-run Women's Emancipation Asso-ciations and the peasant associations, which were also involved in arousing specific constituencies of women for the cause. In Guang-dong alone, Comintern advisers estimated that approximately 113,000 women were mobilized (25,000 workers, 80,000 peasants, 8,000 in the Women's Emancipation Associations).[35] According to Nationalist party records at that time, 1.6 million women joined the ranks of the Nationalist Revolution, which included 350,000 women workers, 150,000 peasant women, and 600,000 women students and "ordinary women" (*putong funü*) nationwide.[36]

These spectacular figures were no doubt inflated. More important, they mask the immense difficulties that He Xiangning faced as she tried to breathe life into the Nationalist Central Women's Department in August of 1924. Her two predecessors in this position, Zeng Xing and Liao Bingjun, had failed to make the department operational.[37] Although they were highly respected members of the Nationalist party, they were plagued by inadequate financial support. Even though the Nationalist party had agreed to established the Central Women's Department at the first party congress, it failed to commit any funds to its operations. At least some influential members of the Nationalist party, it seems, regarded the prospect of a full-scale women's mobilization under the auspices of the Central Women's Department with disdain and preferred to have the department hold receptions for various women's groups and issue a few press releases.

This lack of financial support from the Nationalist party ultimately proved so frustrating that He Xiangning took the highly usual step of mentioning it in her official report to the second party congress in January 1926.[38] But she did not want to wait for this party convention to begin the programmatic development of the women's mobilization campaign. Instead she prevailed upon Mikhail Borodin (through his wife, Fanya) to provide the Nationalist Central Women's Department with an operating budget from certain discretionary funds under his control.[39]

Another serious problem that He Xiangning faced was unifying her staff, which was divided along generational, political, linguistic, and geographical lines. These differences became more pronounced over time as newcomers were added to what originally had been a rather close-knit group. The earliest members were Guangdong women who had been active in provincial women's groups, such as Wu Zhimei of the Guangdong Federation of Women's Circles, or in one of Sun Yatsen's previous political parties, like He Xiangning and Zeng Xing, who joined Sun Yatsen's Revolutionary Alliance soon after it was founded in Japan in the early 1900s. Some members of He Xiangning's staff were in their late thirties or forties by the time of the National Revolution; she herself was forty-six in 1924, when she was appointed director of the department. The original core of activists spoke Cantonese and could not communicate in standard Mandarin, relying instead on a mandarinized version of Cantonese to communicate with those who came from the north.[40]

The main influx of newcomers came after the May Thirtieth Movement of 1925, when the belief that a revolutionary effort might actually succeed became more pervasive and credible. It was at this time that the Chinese Communist party sent a group of its women leaders down to Guangzhou. The group included two high-ranking Communist women, Deng Yingchao and Cai Chang, who were assigned to work at the department. Politicized during the May Fourth period, both were considerably younger than many of the Guangdong women who were part of He Xiangning's original staff. Deng Yingchao was well known in women's circles for her articles in the *Women's Daily* and as a founding member of the May Fourth Awakening Society in Tianjin, the Tianjin Women's Rights League, and the Tianjin Committee to

Promote Women's Participation in the National Assembly. Cai Chang had become politicized through her involvement in the New Citizen's Study Society in Changsha during the May Fourth era, but she had very little stature in Chinese women's circles in 1925 because she had only recently returned from five years abroad, where she had studied in France and then in Moscow at the University of the Toilers of the East.

Although Cai Chang technically held the higher-ranking position, as she was a secretary in the Central Women's Department while Deng Yingchao was the secretary of the Guangdong Provincial Women's Department,[41] Deng Yingchao immediately assumed a more visible role in the Nationalist cosmos. Believing that the Guangdong masses could build the revolution in their province under proper political guidance and then serve as the "revolutionary vanguard" for the entire nation, she traveled up and down the province tirelessly organizing municipal and county party women's departments and eliciting women's support for the National Revolution.[42] She was particularly vigorous in promoting women's activities in Shantou, where she was the keynote speaker for the March 8 rally in 1926, reportedly attended by more than one thousand people.[43] She also published extensively in *The Voice of Women* (Funü zhi sheng), the main organ of the Central Women's Department. She was selected as a delegate to the second party congress in 1926, delivered a detailed speech on the state of the women's movement, and was elected by the congress to serve as alternate member of the Nationalists' Central Executive Committee.[44]

When Deng Yingchao spoke of "our party" in her speeches and articles, there was no doubt that she was referring to the Nationalist party. In every article she urged women to support the Nationalist party because it was leading the revolution and because through its women's department it represented the interests of women.[45] Although she usually refrained from invoking the memory of Sun Yatsen, she did bolster her nationalist message with a strong explanation of the importance of rallying against Western imperialism, which she portrayed as posing a constant threat to Chinese sovereign rights, as had been so blatantly evidenced in the Shaji Incident.[46]

At the same time, Deng Yingchao did not conceal her Communist convictions. She frequently denounced capitalism and called for its overthrow in her articles for Central Women's Department publications. Moreover, she often promoted the Communist-sponsored

Guangdong Women's Emancipation Association as the ideal mass organization, with two-thirds of its members of worker or peasant background, and as the "core organization of the Guangdong women's movement."[47] Like most Communists of her day, Deng Yingchao placed great stock in the importance of organization, especially national and provincial organizations. Thus, her identification of the Guangdong Women's Emancipation Association as the "core" group signified her aspiration that it would serve as the main force working with the Central Women's Department to unify the many disparate independent women's groups of the province.

Neither Deng Yingchao's nor Cai Chang's actions with the Nationalist women's department were directed by the Communist Women's Bureau in Shanghai. Indeed, the general tensions that existed between Shanghai and Guangzhou in the Communist movement made it difficult for the women's program to establish a working relationship. Moreover, the Communist party never established a solid women's program in Guangdong as it did elsewhere. As a result, the Communist women cadres sent into Guangdong to work operated in a fairly autonomous fashion.

The effect of extremely energetic young Communist women like Deng Yingchao on the development of the Central Women's Department and the simultaneous expansion of these mass women's organizations throughout the province in the second half of 1925 tilted the entire political climate in Guangdong women's circles toward the left. The increasing numbers of younger, more radical women who had became active in the revolutionary movement often found themselves discontented with the moderate pace and policies of the more senior, established women leaders of Guangdong, including He Xiangning. These young women wanted to politicize gender issues and try to involve women in the National Revolution on this basis.[48] To them, this meant stressing the potentially divisive issues of free-choice marriage, the right to divorce, and the abolition of concubinage and polygamy.

He Xiangning's principal concern in this situation was to prevent the growth of deep divisions in her staff. To this end, she stressed the importance of promoting women's issues in the context of the wider struggle to win the Nationalist Revolution. She did not oppose the more feminist actions of radical women, and she even opted to adopt their boyish bobbed hairstyle.[49] But she chose to focus her attention on developing programs that were designed to promote women's practical interests in the new order, such as drafting legal codes in the new state to protect women, developing a cadre school, urging the government to hire women, opening up literacy schools, hosting teas for various women's groups that supported the National Revolution, setting up the People's Drama Society, and organizing women's Red Cross units that would be needed to care for the wounded and work in hospitals once the National Revolutionary Army launched the Northern Expedition in the summer of 1926.[50] Thus, even though she was willing to sponsor a resolution at the second party congress in January of 1926 that explicitly stated that the party had to deal with gender oppression if it wanted large numbers of women to support the revolution,[51] most of her speeches and publications stressed the great importance of women's becoming involved in the revolutionary effort for nationalist reasons.[52]

These views were consistent with He Xiangning's early views on women's emancipation. Moreover, by constructing a moderate role for herself, He Xiangning was able to retain sufficient support from Nationalist leaders for her program. In so doing, she succeeded in building a strong organization with a staff that was able to develop its own agenda, one that embodied two different approaches to mobilizing women and was under the control of women. While the differences between these two women's mobilization strategies were quite striking—one aimed to activate women primarily through programs designed to overcome women's subordination, the other through programs that essentially stressed nationalist issues—they managed to coexist with relatively few tensions and often proved mutually supportive. No doubt He Xiangning's style of leadership facilitated this compatibility.

The Guangdong Women's Emancipation Association

The nationalist mission of the revolution was reflected in the programs and propaganda of the Guangdong Women's Emancipation Association (Guangdong funü jiefang xiehui), the principal nongovernmental women's group involved in the mobilization campaigns. Founded in early May of 1925, it benefited from the strong outpouring of nationalist sentiments generated by the May Thirtieth and Shaji Incidents, and within a short time it had attracted several thousand members throughout the province. Its first director, Xia Songyun, from the outset stressed nationalist priorities as a basis for female participation in the association. At times she seemed to conflate women's emancipation and nationalism by arguing that women's emancipation could occur only through the consummation of a nationalist revolution.[53]

The intense nationalism that was exhibited in the mobilization activities of this organization in Guangzhou and its environs was matched by a vehement articulation of gender issues. Although this type of mass women's organization was promoted by the Chinese Communist party in many provinces during the National Revolution, only in Guangdong and the neighboring province of Guangxi was the word *jiefang* (emancipation) inserted in its title, and this word signaled the group's strong May Fourth orientation on women's matters.[54] The founding declaration of the Guangdong Women's Emancipation Association placed much emphasis on such May Fourth issues as marriage reform, women's access to education, and women's legal rights of inheritance and suffrage.[55] During the next two years, branch organizations of the Guangdong Women's Emancipation Association were established in approximately twenty-seven counties in the province and spilled over into the neighboring province of Guangxi. They stirred up a great deal of contention through their zealous promotion of marriage reform and their willingness to give strong support to women contesting arranged marriages, for which they earned the derisive epithet of "divorce and remarriage bureaus" or even "high class brothels."[56]

This organization attracted five thousand women from a wide cross section of the population during its two years of existence.[57] The founders were primarily young women students from secondary schools like the Kunwei Girls' Middle School in Guangzhou. A distinguishing characteristic from the outset, however, was the participation of women workers from the "red" telephone-operators union, such as Ma Xiaofen, who was selected to be on the first executive committee.[58] When the Hong Kong seamen's strike was called a few weeks after the May Thirtieth Incident, it provided a working-class focus for the mobilization program of the Women's Emancipation Association. Seizing on the fact that over ten thousand women workers and family members were involved directly or indirectly in the strike, these women activists took to the street to present plays dramatizing the plight of these Hong Kong workers who had dared to resist imperialist pressures. They also organized bands of women students from the various girls' schools to go around to all the shops asking for contributions for the strike support fund.[59] Later, they set up a part-time school, which attracted over forty students and incorporated revolutionary ideas in its academic curriculum.[60]

Although successful, these experiences of raising money or offering classes to women workers were ancillary to the main tasks of working-class organizing. Activists of the Women's Emancipation Association, aided by Communist labor organizers and Central Women's Department personnel, were pleased to see that more than four thousand women weavers, two thousand garment workers, and three thousand women working in match factories were willing to form unions.[61] But according to Communist reports, women workers in Guangzhou, particularly in the textile mills, were suspicious of Communist organizers' pushing them into unions that were dominated by men and ultimately represented only male interests in most conflicts or negotiations with the management. In one instance, union leaders succeeded in getting much greater wage hikes for male workers than for women and throughout paid little attention to the issues that women workers were raising. Moreover, in any conflict between male and female workers, the union leadership decided in favor of the men, with the result that women workers often felt that they would be better off without a union.[62]

These problems were compounded by the disdain of many male Communist labor organizers in Guangzhou for the very idea of organizing women or working with the women's movement. Where the work force was predominantly female, such as in match production and certain clothing trades, efforts to build unions were more successful. But labor organizers for the Chinese Communist party and Women's Emancipation Association seemed unable to organize the female silk workers in Shunde.[63] No doubt these organizers found it disappointing that the radical marriage practices pursued by some of these women silk workers—delayed transfer marriage, compensation marriage, and sworn spinsterhood[64]—did not predispose them to supporting the revolution. According to Robert Eng, this seeming paradox is explained by the fact that the silk workers of Shunde were under the tight control of the patrilineages of the surrounding villages. While outside labor agitators were thwarted because they posed a distinct threat to the economic power of the patrilineages, unconventional marriage practices were not considered particularly threatening to patriarchal power because the women were still economically tied to their natal families.[65]

Also difficult, but more rewarding, was the effort of the Women's Emancipation Association to mobilize rural women for the National Revolution. Motivated by a shared commitment to create a new type of society for women in both the urban and rural areas, the young, urban women activists in Guangzhou recognized quite early that they needed to address the plight of women in rural areas. To what extent their gaze may have been steered in that direction by Communist party officials is unclear, but certainly the successes of Peng Pai in his organizing of peasant associations in Haifeng and Lufeng counties were well known throughout Guangdong by this time.

A short time after the founding of the Guangzhou Women's Emancipation Association, its women leaders launched their rural strategy by sending letters to potential organizers in the rural areas encouraging them to consider starting up branch associations. Then traveling performers were dispatched to such counties as Meixian, Chaoan, Jieyang, and Denghai in order to attract the interest of illiterate peasant women. The next March, Women's Emancipation Association activists designed an International Women's Day program that they sent out to various counties.[66] Such activities contributed to the establishment of more than twenty-two branches of the Guangdong Women's Emancipation Association outside of Guangzhou between June of 1925 and 1926 as well as to their expansion into neighboring Guangxi. The first branch was founded in Haifeng by six women students, for which they earned a reputation as the "six famous stars" in June of 1925.[67] By the end of the year, branches were established in Chaoguan, Meixian, Qiongya, Renhua, Shantou, Shaoguan, Xinhui, and Shunde, and in the next six months another thirteen became operational.[68]

One of most perplexing problems facing women activists involved in rural communities was identifying an organizational base. They found it quite difficult to situate associations in rural communities because of the shortage of public space available to women. Unlike the cities, where the women's mobilization campaigns of the National Revolution could readily utilize the resources developed by previous women's groups, there was no recent history of public action by women in most of these rural communities. Deciding that local girls' schools were the preferred site if at all possible, teams of Women's Emancipation Association activists set out to investigate local conditions. Tan Zhushan made a study of Huizhou and found that school authorities of the only girls' normal school in that county were quite hostile to May Fourth notions of female emancipation and ardently stuck to their belief in the need to develop women into good wives and mothers.[69] Tan found this particularly unfortunate because this school contained the largest number of women students in the area, and few female students could be found in the county-run elementary school. Without access to a progressive girls' school, Tan clearly despaired about the possibility of the Huizhou Women's Emancipation Association's extending its influence into the surrounding towns, such as Huishu. To her this rural terrain appeared as a bastion of "backwardness" in which communities "stubbornly resisted" ideas about social change and women were too uneducated to understand what the revolution was offering them.[70]

Women organizers sometimes found that a change in administration of a local school could radically alter their ability to reach young women in a community. In Meixian, for instance, Deng Yingchao was able to use her stature as an official in the Nationalist Central Women's Department to have a Shanghai woman who had graduated from Xinan University appointed principal of the Meixian county-run girls' normal school. This action, coupled with the simultaneous removal of a problematic Nationalist official in the local Nationalist women's department, allowed for the rapid development of the Meixian Women's Emancipation Association. Within a short time it became one of the most active branches in the province and even published its own journal, *Meixian Women* (Meixian funü).[71] Once women activists were able to gain a foothold, they could be quite effective in implementing their programs of action.

The most active women's associations outside of the Guangzhou environs were located in Hakka communities and in areas with high levels of out-migration or with large minority populations, such as Hainan Island. At a grassroots level, these women's associations made little mention of nationalist issues; rather, feminist programs were emphasized. The women's associations worked to promote women's education, free bond servants, and encourage women to participate in political activities. But these women's associations were often totally consumed by marriage issues. Clearly women's petitions to escape arranged or abusive marriages were extremely contentious in their communities because the petitions struck at the heart of social life, the marriage contract. If women had the right to determine their own marriages, they were asserting an authority over their own lives that was quite threatening to the patriarchal order. By all accounts these marriage cases taken up by the Women's Emancipation Associations, often with the help of the Nationalist Central Women's Department, caused tremendous strife in local communities. Sometimes women who were granted divorces had to be extricated from their communities with the support of the women's associations and the Nationalist women's departments. In at least one case, a woman was sent all the way to Moscow to attend Sun Yatsen University in order to remove her from a vengeful husband.

Nonetheless, many women's associations were effective in altering conditions for women in their communities. Cai Biheng, for instance, a sixteen-year-old school student in Guiping, Guangxi, was pulled into the revolutionary activities through the influence of her Communist brother. She took on the position of director of the Guiping women's association and within one year had freed seventy bond servants, child-brides, and prostitutes from their exploitative situations and provided them with literacy and job training classes. At the same time, these freed women became politically involved in establishing a new order in this Guangxi community.[72]

Gender Issues in Peng Pai's
Peasant Movement

The Nationalist Revolution's mobilization of women was also conducted through the peasant associations, which ultimately attracted by far the largest sector of women in the revolutionary forces of Guangdong. At the peak of revolutionary fervor in mid-1926, as many as eighty thousand women reportedly were involved in the provincial peasant associations, more than fifteen times the membership of the women's associations. Admittedly, this number was inflated by the common practice of automatically extending peasant association membership to the wives of male recruits. Nevertheless, an examination of female activism in the Guangdong peasant associations indicates that more women were willing to involve themselves in the National Revolution on the basis of community and class issues than feminist issues. In this way, the gender orientation of the peasant associations' programs contrasted sharply with those of the women's associations.

Peng Pai, the foremost Communist organizer of the Chinese peasantry in Guangdong, placed much emphasis on involving women in the revolutionary movement. Unlike male Communist working-class organizers, Peng Pai made a concerted effort to activate women in the organizations he oversaw. In this respect, he stood out as one of the most dedicated of the male Guangdong Communist leadership to the proposition of encouraging female participation in the peasant associations. After he rose to a leadership position in Guangdong in 1924, he was influential in implementing this policy as a grassroots organizer of peasant associations, as the commanding figure in the Nationalist Peasant Department, as director of the Chinese Communist Peasants' Committee, as a leading figure in the Guangdong Peasant Association, and as a teacher and director of the Peasant Movement Training Institute.

As a grassroots peasant organizer in Guangning, Haifeng, and Fengshun counties, Peng Pai encouraged and even personally recruited women into the cause. When necessary, he was willing to take the time to provide peasant women with explanations of the most basic political vocabulary, such as the meaning of "organize" (zuzhi), a term that stumped Li Jianshen when she first heard Peng speak out on the importance of establishing a peasant association in her village of Baixi. His patient coaching and encouragement were instrumental in Li's decision to assume leadership positions both in her village's peasant association and in the district peasant associations.[73]

In 1924 Peng Pai was a leading figure in the intense and violent conflict to establish a peasant association in Guangning, an out-of-the-way county in the West River region of the province, that was infamous among radical organizers for its "feudal" practices, including higher-than-normal tenancy rates and, in some places, virtual serfdom.[74] Although Guangning was not the type of place where high levels of female participation would be expected, Peng Pai worked with the local student leaders to build a peasant association that claimed the largest female membership in the province—thirty thousand.[75] A significant number of these women were quite active in the building of this peasant association, both in behind-the-scenes supportive activities, such as preparing glutinous rice cakes decorated with the ideograph "revolution" (geming) for a large meeting of more than five thousand members, and at the center of public occasions, such as the presentation of petitions to the county magistrate. When fighting broke out in February of 1925 against landlord militias, women worked behind the lines of battle and even participated in the fighting.[76]

Peng initially supported the spread of the women's associations in the rural areas. When women students and workers from the Nanfang Weaving Factory established the first women's association in the province outside of Guangzhou in June of 1925, Peng Pai honored the occasion by delivering the inaugural address at its founding meeting.[77] The peasant association in Haifeng, where Peng Pai turned his attention again in early 1925, also reported a significant number of women members, perhaps as many as seventeen hundred.[78]

Ultimately Peng created a peasant organization of unique resilience in Haifeng, one that succeeded in establishing its own soviet government after the collapse of the alliance between the Nationalist and Communist parties in 1927. Significantly, in this time of great crisis, more opportunities opened up for women in leadership and the militia. A few women were elected to important positions in the soviet government, and thousands of women took up arms to fight for the existence of the peasant soviet. Gender issues also came to the fore, with the women's association advocating the abolition of girl bond servants and brothels. At the same time the peasant association found that 30 percent of the cases being brought to the arbitration department concerned marriage issues, including the sale of wives by their husbands.[79]

Peng Pai's support of women's issues and activism in the peasant movement was often qualified, however, by the practical realities of rural society. As early as 1922, when the glow of May Fourth feminism was still quite bright in the Communist party, Peng Pai encountered a potentially thorny problem for his fledgling peasant association when a six-year-old child-bride drowned in a latrine in Chishan, a village in his native Haifeng county. The family she was living with was accused of having contributed to her death by beating her so severely that she lost her balance and fell into the privy. As the girl had been living in the home of a peasant association member, Peng was concerned that any proof of wrongdoing might have a negative impact on his fledgling organization. When thirty or so of the girl's relatives arrived in Chishan to press the issue, Peng Pai refused to open the casket and prove that the girl had not been beaten. Rather, he assembled the entire peasant association and through his officious manner and the militancy of his group intimidated the accusers into finally dropping the charges. Afterwards Peng commented revealingly that this incident showed that "powerless men will be tricked" and thus served as living proof of the value of a united peasant association.[80]

Thereafter, Peng Pai exercised caution when dealing with gender issues in the peasant movement. He showed little interest, for instance, in encouraging female enrollment in the Peasant Movement Training Institute, which was established in July of 1924 as the main means for extending the reach of the revolution into many rural communities in Guangdong.[81] While many Communists were involved with this school, including Mao Zedong, it was Peng who served as director of the first class and thereafter exerted the most profound and consistent influence over the shaping of the school and the orientation of the curriculum. During its three years of operation, only 30 or so of the 996 graduates of the institute were women.[82] The only female teacher on the staff was Li Yichun, a Hunanese Communist who was in charge of the singing classes. It was probably difficult to encourage household heads to send female members of their families to attend what was essentially a male-dominated school. Nonetheless, Peng Pai's influence over the peasant associations was sufficiently powerful to elicit a higher number of female applicants if he had been so inclined.

From the little that is known about these thirty female students, most were selected by their peasant associations and upon graduation went back to their localities. With a few exceptions, they were not inclined to promote feminist issues. The women with a clear interest in overcoming women's social subordination were not assigned to work in peasant associations but rather were sent directly into the women's associations or into the Nationalist Women's Department, particularly if they manifested any strong interest in gender transformation issues. Gao Tianbo, a member of the first class, found herself assigned to the Guangzhou Women's Emancipation Association, and Zhong Zhujun (1903–1929) primarily worked as a women's association activist after graduation, setting up a branch in Suiqi county.[83] Such practices suggest the intention to restrict feminist influences from the peasant associations.

Even more telling than the small number of women students at the institute and the types of assignments received by the handful of women graduates was the lack of emphasis on women's issues in the curriculum. In fact, Peng Pai specifically instructed all his male students to desist from spreading May Fourth notions about freedom and equality and to never fall in love with a peasant woman.[84] Peng's main concern was to avoid any criticism of the arranged-marriage system as it was practiced in rural localities. Moreover, his position was shared by other Communists involved in peasant work, who encouraged young male peasant association members to go along with parentally arranged marriages unless the woman was physically defective and discouraged them from divorcing their wives. The most latitude a May Fourth–oriented organizer could have on this issue was to encourage peasant men to put off agreeing to a parentally arranged marriage until they had met someone of their own choosing.[85]

Yet, as Peng Pai was only too well aware from his travels through rural Guangdong, for most male peasants the issue was not finding a wife of one's liking but being able to afford a wife. In many localities where Peng Pai organized associations, 50 percent of the male members were not married. And many of those who were able to marry were able to do so only by arranging for a young girl from a poverty-stricken family to be raised in their homes, with the result that the wives were often ten to twenty years younger than the husbands. From Peng's perspective, these child-bride marriages stood as yet another sign of peasant oppression.[86]

Peng Pai could easily empathize with the misfortune of peasant men going through life without a wife, and he even was saddened by the idea that they would ask to have wooden plaques placed on their graves with the names of fictitious wives in a last bid for conventionality. Yet he rarely seemed to consider peasant adversities from the point of view of poor women or child-brides.[87] Peng Pai's perspective on these issues was consistent with the identity of the peasant associations that was being constructed. Peasant association publications, for instance, were directed at a male audience. The infrequent images of women that were published in these journals tended to portray women as possessions of men. One cartoon featured a landlord using his beautiful wife to bribe leaders of peasant associations.[88] Indeed, it appears that these associations were intentionally imbued with a male identity in order to solidify their legitimacy in the community and increase their acceptability among skeptical, conservative local notables. To this end, Communist peasant organizers decided in 1925 to coin the slogan "The Nationalist party is the father, and the peasant association is the son."[89]

In his leadership of the peasant movement, Peng Pai also seems to have steered clear of organizing peasant associations in localities where women dominated agricultural work. Such was the case in Meixian, for instance, which had experienced heavy out-migration of its male population for many years.[90] Although Peng Pai was in charge of the Chaomei regional board that oversaw the Meixian region, no peasant organizer was sent out to that county, despite the protests of women activists in the area who complained that the peasant association leaders were not interested in helping them form an organization because of the preponderance of women peasants.[91] Perhaps Peng Pai was concerned that an existing women's association in the county that was as dedicated to the proposition of gender transformation as the one in Meixian would be a constant thorn in the side of a peasant association, or that the peasant association would develop programs that were not in harmony with those of other associations in the province.

These expedient measures eventually altered the ideas and work styles of the radical leaders themselves, many of whom fancied themselves as quite progressive. Peng Pai is a case in point. Whereas in his early days as a peasant organizer he had sought out the opinions of association members about his policies, as his reputation grew he increasingly adopted a patriarchal leadership style and assumed his reports and orders would be accepted without questions or objections. As he toured the countryside, throngs of peasants would hail him as "the Emperor."[92] Even in Guangzhou, he was known as "the King of the Hailufeng peasants."[93]

Peng Pai's relationship with his wife became increasingly patriarchal over time as well. The scion of a wealthy landlord Hakka family, he agreed to an arranged marriage but then made a serious attempt to convert their relationship into a more modern marriage. In 1912, for instance, he convinced Cai Suping, his new wife, to unbind her feet, and he often was seen strolling through the town of Haifeng holding her hand. When he went to Japan to pursue his education, he continually encouraged her in his letters to study, with the result that she acquired a certain degree of literacy. Later, he encouraged her involvement in the peasant associations as a women organizer, and she seemed to share many of his activities.

This modern marriage was transformed in December of 1926 when Peng Pai invited Xu Bing, a student he had met in the Communist party office in Shantou, to move into his home where Cai Suping was also residing. When Xu Bing accompanied Peng Pai on his trips to Guangzhou and Wuhan, they appeared as a couple in public; but in the rural community where he lived, he cohabited with the two women. Peng Pai may well have reasoned that it was more humane to allow Cai Suping to remain in his household than to subject her to the painful humiliation of a divorce. Moreover, he most likely would have objected to the allegation that he had essentially turned Xu Bing into a concubine. However, Xu must have been seen that way by his peasant following, particularly after both women gave birth to children over the course of the next year or two.[94] In any event, this behavior was exceedingly unusual for a high-ranking Chinese Communist leader, and it directly contradicted strongly articulated principles in the Communist movement against polygamy and concubinage.

CHAPTER 7

On the Verge of Revolutionary Gender Transformations

Between July 1926 and July 1927 the victories of the National Revolutionary Army expedited an unprecedented social mobilization of women in southern and central China, particularly in the two provinces of Hunan and Hubei. Many features of the social mobilization replicated the experiences in Guangdong. Feminist issues were linked closely with nationalist ones, although women's interests for the most part were not instrumentalized by nationalist imperatives. The symbolic framework extolling the ideal of women's emancipation created by the new revolutionary government established in Wuhan also closely imitated the Guangdong model. Moreover, the different strategies of the women's associations and the peasant associations for mobilizing women that had emerged in Guangdong were continued here. What was most distinctive in this phase of the National Revolution was the Wuhan government's stronger emphasis on transforming gender relations as it went about the complex process of building a nation-state through revolution. During the short life of the Wuhan revolutionary government, one can discern certain distinct similarities between its effort to redefine gender relations and those policies adopted by the post-1949 Communist state.

With the expansion of the revolutionary terrain, every effort to improve women's rights and end forms of gender oppression met resistance. In much of Hubei and Henan, secret societies, local elites, and militarists responded quite harshly to the women organizers who sought to promote gender equality. As frequent instances of brutality toward women served to signal deep-seated opposition to the revolutionary government, gender issues became increasingly contentious and were used to distinguish revolutionaries from their opposition. At the same time, rumors about bizarre sexual practices of the Wuhan government circulated as a means to discredit it and bring about its demise.

Women in the Northern Expedition

In early July 1926, revolutionary armies marched north out of Guangdong in what became known as the Northern Expedition. The expedition's purpose was to defeat more than thirty-four warlord forces in order to unify China under one Nationalist government. In a major offensive against the warlords, this fighting force marched along three routes from Guangdong: up the Xiang River and Canton-Wuhan Railway towards Changsha, up the Gan River into Jiangxi, and along the east coast into Fujian. Reminiscent of the Taiping offensive some seventy-five years earlier, the Northern Expedition facilitated the extension of the Guangdong mass women's movement into southern and central China.

The Northern Expedition was primarily a male endeavor, with women constituting a relatively minor segment in the overall military operation. In this respect, it differed markedly from the 1911 Revolution, where women had formed battalions and were actively engaged in combat.[1] As the National Revolutionary Army rolled out of Guangdong, however, women were involved in a variety of auxiliary teams. They worked in front of and behind the lines as spies, propagandists, nurses, carriers, and grassroots organizers. That those assigned to the political or medical teams of the National Revolutionary armies were dressed in military uniforms gave them the appearance of soldiers, though women rarely were involved in direct combat.[2] The Nationalist Central Women's Department organized a small group of thirteen women into a medical and propaganda corps (*jiuhu xuanquandui*), which set forth with the Fourth Army and moved into Hunan. The head of the medical section for this army was Gao Tianbo, one of the first female participants of the Guangdong Communist organization and the Peasant Movement Training Institute. During the Northern Expedition, she earned special recognition for her heroic

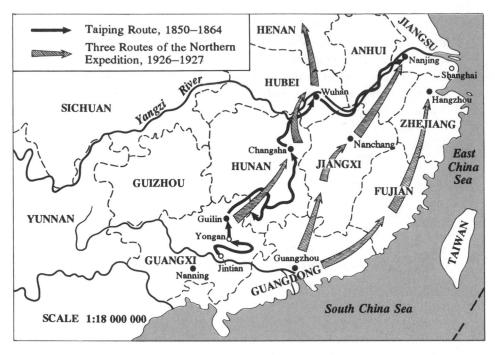

3. The Northern Expedition/Taiping Route

deed of pulling a wounded soldier off the battlefield while dodging bullets.[3] General Li Zongren boasted that his army included the largest contingent of women. The women's propaganda team attached to his Guangxi regiment consisted of more than one hundred students who had been organized by the Guangxi Nationalist Women's Department. Under the leadership of Guo Dejie, General Li's wife, these women worked on the front lines, whereas other armies reportedly did not permit their female personnel to hazard such risks.[4]

As the Northern Expedition mounted its three-pronged offensive in Jiangxi, Fujian, and Hunan, it spurred the formation of numerous women's associations. Within a few months of its entry into Jiangxi, practically every county and town in the province reported the establishment of a women's association, and in Hunan, women's associations had been founded in fourteen counties by May 1926 and during the next year expanded to approximately another forty counties.[5] The Hengyang Women's Association was said to be one of the largest in Hunan, with more than three thousand members.[6] The Liling

Women's Association also became quite active; it announced that a total of fifty branches had been set up in the county with a membership of more than six thousand by the end of 1926.[7] When the National Revolutionary Army entered Hubei, female organizers claimed they had been able to establish thirty-eight women's associations by March of 1927 with a total estimated membership of more than ten thousand. A few months later, it was reported that the number had risen to over sixty associations and the membership had tripled.[8]

To be sure, the numbers reported in the press and the periodicals were exaggerated.[9] In the exuberance of the revolutionary upsurge, a specific purpose of the mass propaganda was to convey the sense of massive popular receptivity to the programs of the revolutionary forces. No doubt many associations existed more on paper than in fact. Nonetheless, between mid-1926 and mid-1927 a significant number of women joined these mobilization organizations, and a good portion of these women actively participated in political affairs in their communities as long as the political conditions remained conducive.

Mapping the expansion and development of these women's associations presents many difficult questions. What were the main reasons for the proliferation of these organizations? Who took responsibility for setting them up? What was the main message that they disseminated? To what extent, if any, did they present a vision of a new gender order? To whom did the new values appeal most strongly? The available evidence is only partially satisfactory; many mysteries remain. Little is known, for instance, about the extent to which women outside towns were drawn into political participation. However, even with these limitations, certain patterns that provide some clues emerge from contemporary sources.

Hakka women may well have played an important part in the proliferation of these women's associations in south China, particularly Guangdong, Guangxi, Jiangxi, and Hunan. Although General Li did not specify the ethnicity of the women who joined the women's propaganda team of his Guangxi regiment, their normal, that is unbound, feet suggest that they may have come from the Guangxi Hakka villages, most of which had been established by migrants from Guangdong more than a hundred years previously.[10] Only scattered references exist in the historical literature to Hakka participation in the National Revolution. Some mention is made of the Hakka women who carried the supplies for the National Revolutionary Army in Fujian when male carriers refused to cooperate. Subsequently these

Hakka women carriers became involved in establishing women's associations in Fujian.[11]

Tracing the role of the Hakka in China's twentieth-century revolutionary process is quite difficult because the contemporary materials rarely reveal the relevant ethnic issues. Arguing on the basis of linguistic evidence, Mary S. Erbaugh has suggested that Hakka participation in the Chinese revolution was greater than previously recognized.[12] The four Hunan counties of Liuyang, Liling, Pingjiang, and Leiyang, where large concentrations of Hakka were located, were centers of the Hunan women's mobilization campaign of the mid-1920s. Viewed from this perspective, the Hakka women in Guangdong, Guangxi, Jiangxi, and Hunan may well have played a critical role in kindling this large-scale women's mobilization for the National Revolution, as they had for the Taiping Rebellion in the mid–nineteenth century. Moreover, those communities located along the route that the Taiping armies had traveled some seventy-five years earlier were the most receptive to the vision of women's emancipation put forth by the political organizers of the Northern Expedition. Thus, it appears that the revolutionary successes in rousing support for gender transformation were at least partially due to enduring influences of the Taiping egalitarian gender ideology on peasant politics.

In contrast to this somewhat nebulous impact of Taiping rebels and Hakka activists, the role of Communist, Nationalist, and student activists in setting up and developing these women's associations is much easier to discern. Some Communist and Nationalist women organizers traveled with the Northern Expedition; others had been recruited locally and were galvanized into action when the troops passed through their communities. They were aided by a host of enthusiastic female students and recent graduates who had been politicized by their teachers. The extent of school girl participation was not surprising given the extensive public school system and the intense nationalist political culture that existed in Hunan.

The leadership roles commanded by Communist women were illustrated by Cai Chang, who served as head of a propaganda team for one of the armies. This prominent Communist women's leader traveled with the revolutionary armies from Guangzhou to Nanchang, where she set up a short-term leadership training class for women. As a result of this effort, women's emancipation associations (*funü jiefang xiehui*) were soon established in Nanchang (December 2, 1926), Shangnao, Yiyang, Huangfeng, and Guixi. Huang Yi, a

Communist who had been appointed director of the Nationalist Women's Department in Hunan, was able to organize fifty propaganda teams and fourteen first aid teams, which included large numbers of women, many of whom had bound feet. Moreover, when the National Revolutionary Armies crossed from Guangdong into Hunan in the summer of 1926, she oversaw the effort to enlist large numbers of women volunteers to cook for the troops and work in makeshift field hospitals.[13] When Guo Dejie, the head of the Guangxi army's women's propaganda team, reached the Hunanese provincial capital at the end of July 1926, she devoted much effort to encouraging women to join the revolutionary forces through her speeches and extolling the general significance of the National Revolution in altering women's oppression.[14] Her words of encouragement did not fall on deaf ears: many Hunanese Communist female recruits, including Jiang Guoren from Ningxiang county, Zhang Qiong of Changsha, and Shao Zhenxiong of Liuyang, immediately joined the special auxiliary units of the Northern Expedition designed to accommodate female participants.[15]

The strength of the Hunanese women's support for the Northern Expedition forces and for the establishment of women's associations to some extent reflected the organizational strength of the Hunan Communist party, which even before the May Thirtieth Movement had recruited more women than any other single provincial organization.[16] Some Hunanese women Communists who had become active elsewhere were sent back to Hunan in the mid-1920s to build the infrastructure for mobilizing women for the National Revolution. Most notably, Miao Boying returned from Beijing in early 1925 to assume the position of the head of the Hunan Communist Women's Committee. She had gained a wealth of experience in Beijing joining the Chinese Communist party in 1920, particularly in organizing the student protest at the Beijing Normal Women's College. Once she returned to Hunan, much progress was made in the year or so between the May Thirtieth Incident and the arrival of the Northern Expedition in expanding and strengthening the organizational basis for a women's mobilization campaign.

After the Northern Expedition arrived in Changsha, many graduates of women's middle and normal schools went to the countryside to organize women's associations. Probing into the ideological messages and programs that these women's associations generated reveals a distinct shift from the inception of these groups to their maturity.

Their main function initially was providing support for the National Revolutionary armies, including supplying tea, food, medical aid, and towels and repairing shoes and tattered uniforms.[17] Communist and Nationalist political organizers attached to the armies went out into the various communities to encourage women to form women's associations, which at first were expected primarily to provide support for the troops. While supporting the military served as the raison d'être for establishing women's associations and facilitated local acceptance of their right to exist as organizations, the purpose of their work quickly shifted to defining women's roles in the new order. Political activists encouraged women to become involved in the public domain, unbind their feet, cut their long locks of hair, seek marriages of their own choosing, terminate bad marriages, and work within their communities to promote literacy and to end the practices of taking child-brides, female indentured labor, concubinage, polygamy, and prostitution.[18] In short, the associations shifted in a relatively short time from primarily serving nationalist aims to promoting women's issues. The Liling Women's Association, for instance, which published its own publications and reported fifty branches throughout the county and a membership of more than six thousand by the end of 1926, fashioned an ideological message that was heavily tinged with May Fourth feminist concepts. Much stress was laid on the oppressive nature of the patriarchal family system, which was blamed for inhibiting the development of women's individual personhood (ren'ge), an important May Fourth concept, and for perpetuating the practice of polygamy.[19]

Throughout the course of the Northern Expedition, women's issues were used to distinguish revolutionaries from reactionaries. The propaganda teams of the National Revolutionary Army distributed much literature distinguishing their treatment of women from that of the warlords, who were portrayed in Nationalist pamphlets as ardent foes of the cause of women's emancipation. Much space was devoted in the leaflets and booklets to the worst atrocities that warlord troops committed against women. Specific examples of warlord crimes against women, such as the tragic murder of a seventeen-year-old girl, were often cited.[20] The accounts sometimes were quite graphic—one depicted a lactating mother being raped and having her nipples torn off—in order to drive home the point that warlord regimes held women in such disdain that they would not abide the prospect of citizenship or greater public roles for women.

The general portrayal conveyed in the revolutionary propaganda was that warlord troops often committed acts of random violence against women in order to terrorize them and force them to seek the safe haven of their homes. In contrast, the revolutionary soldiers of the Northern Expedition were presented as defenders of women who wanted to create public roles for women in their communities and end female exploitation.[21] In fact, the soldiers of the Northern Expedition were exposed to an intensive educational barrage that was intended to fundamentally alter their notions of military conduct and thus facilitate their efforts to uphold this image. This indoctrination was carried out not only in classrooms but also through extemporaneous lectures and cultural performances.[22]

The revolutionary portrayal of warlord atrocities was not unfounded. Indeed, warlord forces did commit violent acts against women as a public demonstration of their support for the maintenance of patriarchal social power. One of the most visible displays of warlord defiance to the call for women's emancipation was made by Liu Yuchun, one of warlord Wu Peifu's generals, who had managed to hole up behind the massive walls of Wuchang city and wage a strong resistance to the Northern Expedition when it arrived at the Yangzi. At the same time, he also mounted an effort to quash popular resistance within Wuchang by rounding up and killing a number of local activists, including Chen Dingyi, a female student leader from the First Provincial Normal School. Her severed head hung above one of the main gates to the city for three days in late August as a public symbol of the warlord's stance on female activism and gender reform.[23]

Revolutionary Wuhan

Well before the Hunan women's mobilization campaign was underway, the National Revolutionary Army had moved on to the sprawling Yangzi River tri-cities of Hankou, Hanyang, and Wuchang. Two of these cities fell relatively easily in September 1926, but the battle for Wuchang dragged on for forty days. During the forty days that the National Revolutionary Army was held at bay, many people inside the walls of Wuchang starved. Eventually warlord resistance weakened, and on October 10, the fifteenth anniversary of the uprising in Wuchang that had begun the historic 1911 Revolution, the city gates were thrown open and the victorious National Revolutionary Army marched in.

The reputation of these revolutionary forces as promoters of women's equality had preceded them. Among the people who poured out onto the streets to celebrate the victory after long months of working underground were the hundred or so members of the Communist-sponsored mass women's group, the Hubei Women's Association. Xu Quanzhi, Yuan Puzhi, and Yuan Mu, all Communist members, held up a big banner welcoming the troops on behalf of the organization on October 10.[24] The next day a large group of women came together in the offices of the Hubei Women's Association and ceremoniously cut off their long locks of hair in celebration of the new political order.[25] This public display inaugurated a very busy week for the Hubei Women's Association, during which many young women rushed to join and pushed the number of members over the one thousand mark.[26] This kind of female mobilization grew throughout the autumn, predicated on the belief that the new revolutionary government would institute sweeping changes for women.

At the same time the very existence of this mobilized force served as an incentive to the revolutionary government to attend to women's issues. When the first contingent of Nationalist government officials arrived in Wuchang from Guangzhou on December 12, 1926, they were greeted with a poster pasted to the city wall that expressed the hopes of many Hubei women that the new government would grant women economic, political, and legal equality with men. It also called upon Hubei women to resist the urge to sit back and expect the government to do their bidding. They needed to take advantage of the new political freedoms to press for their rights by participating in mass organizations. In conclusion the poster urged: "Fellow women of Hubei! This is our chance to seek freedom and equality. A thousand times over, we don't want to lose this opportunity."[27]

On January 1, 1927, the revolutionary government issued a decree proclaiming the establishment of Wuhan as the new capital of the national government of China. In the big celebration held that day, musicians, drummers, and dragon dancers performed amidst anti-imperialist banners and continual bursts of firecrackers, creating a carnival-like effect. The gaiety that reigned in the streets, however, masked the political tension that prevailed behind the scenes. The new government leaders decided to keep the news of a brewing political conflict with Chiang Kaishek, who was in charge of the eastern flank of the National Revolutionary Army, from spreading among the Wuhan populace.[28] Members of the Nationalist Central Committee who had supported the decision to transfer the Nationalist capital from Guangzhou to Wuhan were made only too well aware of the displeasure of Chiang Kaishek at this plan when they passed through his stronghold in Nanchang on their way to Wuhan.[29] Indeed, the contrast between remote, medieval-looking Nanchang, which Chiang Kaishek chose as his temporary military headquarters, and the large, industrialized, metropolitan city of Wuhan situated on the Yangzi River, where left-wing Nationalists and Communists established their capital, reflected their different positions on the importance of linking political revolution and social revolution.

This split in the revolutionary camp freed the revolutionary Wuhan government from the constraints imposed by the right wing of their party and enabled it to pursue more radical gender-transformatory policies. The great opportunity and challenge presented by this situation attracted many of the most talented women revolutionaries in the Chinese Communist and Nationalist parties. Soong Qingling, the young widow of Sun Yatsen, came into the political limelight in a much bolder and more assertive fashion in Wuhan than she had ever done previously. She brought to this revolutionary regime the legacy of Sun Yatsen, her high prestige and influence in the Nationalist party, fluent English, which she had learned during her college days in Georgia, and a strong commitment to social change, including women's emancipation. Her decision to become more involved in politics at this time was based more on conviction than on ambition. She was an extremely shy person who did not enjoy public presentations. No doubt her heavy Shanghai (Pudong) accent contributed to her self-consciousness.[30] When the new government was installed, she was one of the speakers who addressed the large crowd of more than three hundred thousand who had turned out that evening. Only her close friends, however, seemed to have been aware of the personal struggle she had to wage in order to become a political leader of the Nationalist revolutionary government in Wuhan. Her general reputation, in fact, was that of a formidable person. Many Westerners commonly referred to her as "China's Joan of Arc" and depicted her as a leader of a Chinese women's battalion. Quite a few erroneously believed that she had even led troops into battle.[31]

Soong Qingling was immediately selected to serve on the highest governmental bodies of this revolutionary order: she not only was a member of the Central Committee but also was elected to a select committee of five that held supreme authority over both state and party matters.[32] Thus, more than any other woman leader in Wuhan, Soong Qingling emerged as the most important role model for young women seeking to emancipate themselves from traditional habits and ideas. During her first weeks in Wuhan, scores of women students sought her advice on how they might facilitate the efforts of the Nationalist party to create "new women" who were in step with the times, politically knowledgeable, and independent.[33]

Aside from setting an example for young women seeking to alter gender roles in the new political order, Soong Qingling took an active interest in promoting women's emancipation, particularly through her establishment of a Party Training Class for Women (Funü dangwu xunlian ban) on February 2, 1927. However, the main leader of the Nationalist women's program in Wuhan was He Xiangning, who had come from Guangzhou to continue in her post as director of the Nationalist Central Women's Department. He Xiangning, now a much more able head of the Nationalist women's department with two years of valuable experience in Guangdong leading the revolutionary women's movement to her credit, made the long trek from Guangzhou to join the Wuhan revolutionaries. She brought along some remarkable young women to strengthen the staff of the Central Women's Department.[34] While the basic operation of her department remained faithful to the Guangzhou experience, in this more radicalized political environment, He Xiangning allowed the strength of the leftists to be augmented.

The political environment created by Soong Qingling and He Xiangning provided a tremendous opportunity for radical women to promote gender transformation in the revolutionary order. Local Communist women assumed important positions in the Nationalist Central and Provincial Women's Departments and the Hubei mass women's organizations. In addition, an impressive array of Communist women traveled from afar to promote the revolutionary cause in Wuhan; some joined He Xiangning's staff while others were assigned to Communist party or women's mass movement organizations. Cai Chang, leaving Deng Yingchao behind in Guangzhou, arrived in Wuhan with the National Revolutionary Army and assumed the position of general secretary of the Hubei Women's Committee of the Chinese Communist party.[35] Wang Yizhi vacated her post in Guangzhou as editor of the Guangdong Women's Emancipation Association publication, *Light* (Guangming), and made her way into Wuhan. Liu Qingyang, who had sought refuge with Li Dazhao and at least nineteen other Communists from the anti-Communist warlord zealot Zhang Zuolin in the Soviet Embassy in Beijing, managed to slip past the guards stationed around the compound and travel to Wuhan, where she assumed a position in the Nationalist Central Women's Department. Zhong Fuguang and Yang Zilie took a boat down the Yangzi from Shanghai, and Xiang Jingyu came back from Moscow.[36] In short, some of the strongest Communist women's leaders were brought into Wuhan to build the women's mobilization campaign for the National Revolution.

Unlike Guangzhou, Wuhan quickly attracted a large contingent of Westerners who were supportive of the revolutionary aims of the new order. An English newspaper, *The People's Tribune*, was established under the editorial control of William and Rayna Prohme, two American journalists. Millie Bennett, Anna Louise Strong, and Vincent Sheean were among a few of the sympathetic journalists who began sending dispatches from this revolutionary capital in an effort to proclaim its significance to the world.[37] Vincent Sheean wrote about those days as truly unusual: "For a few months in 1927, a little more than half of the year, Hankou [one of the three cities that constituted Wuhan] concentrated, symbolized and upheld the hope for a revolution of the world."[38]

Contemporary observers, such as Herbert Owen Chapman, were generous in their words of admiration for the steps taken to change women's legal and social status in the new order. In Chapman's estimation, the promotion of the women's movement would, in all likelihood, be seen in years to come as the National Revolution's greatest achievement.[39] Indeed, the revolutionary government, which was very much in the international limelight, placed a great deal of emphasis on transforming key aspects of China's gender system. Critical to this effort was the transformation of the marriage system. Some measures were indirect, such as the prohibition issued by the Wuhan Police Department against holding expensive weddings, which were said to cost wealthy families at least ten thousand *yuan* and poor people two or three thousand.[40] At the same time, the Wuhan government extended to women unprecedented legal guarantees in marriage, such as the right to pick their own husbands, petition for divorce, and obtain alimony in those cases where the husband initiated divorce proceedings. In addition, the right of inheritance was extended to women, and the sale of women was prohibited, as was their maltreatment, a provision that was particularly applied to daughters-in-law and maids. One innovation in gender reform that had no precedent in Guang dong was the provision that women be allowed to serve as jurors in all cases involving women defendants.[41]

The Nationalist Central Women's Department, the Hubei Nationalist Women's Department, and the Hubei Women's Association all assumed a quasi-judicial role in enforcing these regulations.[42] Although the Central Women's Department was a Nationalist party institution, its operations were seen as closely intertwined with the nascent state. In effect, the party and the state functioned as one political unit. In this very politicized environment, mass mobilization organizations such as the Hubei Women's Association were involved in the operations of the state. In matters of law, for instance, the association took cases to court and also issued its own decisions, particularly on divorce cases heard in its informal hearings.[43] Its involvement in this governmental process reflected the pattern of state making that was emerging in China in this revolutionary upsurge.

Ultimately the Hubei Women's Association, under Communist sponsorship, became a powerful mass organization, with its membership growing from the original eleven in July of 1925 to reportedly as many as sixty thousand by May of 1927, and to seventy thousand by July.[44] To a large extent, its rapid growth stemmed from the linkage of a feminist agenda to the revolutionary nationalism that was sweeping through this province in the wake of the Northern Expedition. While its main goal was ending female oppression, attention was given to the overall nationalist goals of the revolution. At every important meeting, a portrait of Sun Yatsen was hung at the front of the room, and participants were expected to show their respect by bowing three times in front of this likeness before the main issues of the agenda were discussed. At the First Women's Congress of Hubei held in March 1927, Sun Yatsen's last will and testament was read as well.[45]

The newfound prestige of the Wuhan Women's Association was reflected in its main offices, where ten secretaries, dressed in pink and white attire, could be found overseeing the work of the organization. Divided among six departments, the secretaries had a monthly budget of approximately fifty dollars in gold to pay for rent, servants, handbills, and food. Only the recording secretary was paid a wage; the rest volunteered their time.[46] Often this staff would mobilize large numbers of women, at the behest of the leaders of the Hubei Women's Association, to demand government action. Soon after He Xiangning arrived with the second contingent of Nationalist leaders from Guangzhou in early January 1927, for instance, a large meeting was held to welcome her. In front of the several thousand women in attendance, a member of the executive board requested that the government enact a law prohibiting foot binding. Then at a large meeting in March, the Hubei Women's Association once again passed a resolution calling for the unbinding of feet. This public pressure was sufficient to prompt the Hubei provincial government to issue a regulation against foot binding on March 12, 1927.[47]

The actions taken by the Hubei Women's Association to publicize and compel compliance with the anti–foot binding regulation also revealed much about the political roles of mass mobilization organizations in this revolutionary order. Cultural workers, such as performing singers and actors, were relied upon to disseminate the new regulation. In Huangguang county, for instance, a male vocalist performed a popular song, "Unbind Feet" (Fangzu ge), that claimed foot binding made women dependent on men, thereby contributing to men's inclination to abuse women. It was no wonder that husbands often beat and cursed their wives, the song maintained, but men would desist from such abusive treatment if women would unbind their feet and go to work.[48] Such cultural productions were backed up with more heavy-handed methods of forcing families to comply with the new regulation. Families persisting in binding their daughters' feet were visited by a contingent of women, criticized, and sometimes heavily fined (twenty *yuan*).[49] Those women who did unbind their feet were given a government-issued card that bore the inscription "No one will marry a woman with bound feet." Finally, this agitation compelled the Wuhan government to issue another order in early May requiring all women under the age of thirty to unbind their feet by May 16, 1927. Reportedly the compliance rate was quite high—90 percent.[50]

The assumption of quasi-government functions by mass organizations became even more pronounced in March of 1927, when the Hubei Women's Association convened the First Women's Representative Meeting of Hubei Province with more than one hundred delegates and another five hundred participants in attendance.[51] On the first day the chairperson characterized the organization as a backup force for the government that would also provide guidance in government affairs. During the next ten days, a number of resolutions were passed, which functioned as basic laws. Indeed, one observer has characterized certain measures adopted by this body as constituting a "Bill of Rights" for women.[52]

Another prominent feature of the political order in Wuhan was the establishment of a variety of institutions to train women to assume new political roles. This practice had begun in Guangzhou, where the most significant undertaking of this type had been a Women's Movement Training Institute (Funü yundong jiangxisuo), which had been established to develop grassroots women organizers just before He Xiangning left for Wuhan in the autumn of 1926. One hundred women, ten of whom were Communists, were enrolled in a six-month course, which included instruction in leading mass movements based on the Soviet model.[53] After moving to Wuhan, the Nationalist Central Women's Department decided to commence a similar undertaking in Wuhan under the name of the Party Training Class for Women (Funü dangwu xunlianban), which was headed by Soong Qingling. Many Communists were invited to join the staff, including two men, Zhang Tailei and Yun Daiying, and Fanya Borodin, wife of the Comintern adviser to the Nationalist party. It commenced operation on January 1, 1927, with a class of 103 women ranging from eighteen to forty years of age. Students were instructed in mass movement leadership techniques, provided with a background in world revolutionary history, and familiarized with all the new laws concerning women's status and rights. After three months of course work, the graduates were sent out to propagate the revolution, with a large group assigned to accompany the Second Northern Expeditionary Force sent into Henan.[54]

The most famous of the training programs for women in Wuhan was the one at the Wuhan Central Military and Political Institute. Admitting women to the Nationalist-run institute represented a significant departure from the practices of the Whampoa Academy in Guangzhou. Whampoa constituted the densest concentration of male power in the new revolutionary order. In creating this "modern" military institution, Chiang Kaishek had chosen to totally exclude women. In so doing, he deviated from the tradition established in 1911, when female battalions had participated in the revolution. He also departed from the Soviet revolutionary experience, where women had played an important role in the Red Army, with as many as eighty thousand women serving in combat and auxiliary roles, fifty-five of whom had been awarded the Order of the Red Banner.[55] Because the newly created institute in Wuhan, though technically a branch of Whampoa, was in fact outside the control of Chiang and other conservative Nationalists, the influences of the Russian and Chinese revolutionary experience regarding women prevailed. As soon as the news was circulated that women would be admitted, the institute was flooded with applicants, and the fact that most of the applicants put down on their application that they wanted to carry on the tradition of Hua Mulan indicated the strength of this woman warrior tradition in galvanizing women for the National Revolution.[56] After some indecision about what the exact size of the class should be, 195 women were permitted to enroll in the class that matriculated in January 1927.[57]

As in the case of the Peasant Movement Training Institute, the Wuhan Central Military and Political Institute attempted to achieve some geographical diversity in the female student body. However, many of its female recruits appear to have come from Hubei, Hunan, and Sichuan, the most famous of whom was Xie Bingying. Most of them had graduated from middle or normal schools, which had provided them with sufficient education to pass the institute's stiff entrance examination.[58]

Although much of the training at the institute—such as shouting out anti-imperialist slogans and delivering speeches in public, marching through the streets singing revolutionary songs, and soliciting support at the gates of factories—was modeled on the idealized notion of the May Thirtieth female revolutionary, the female students in this program deviated significantly from this model by creating a new revolutionary persona: the Amazon. Dressed in gray cotton uniforms, caps, and high boots, they carried guns, trained with male soldiers, rode horses, and endured hardships. They consciously sought to duplicate male actions and demeanor as much as possible. Above all, they shunned romantic attachments, which they labeled as selfish and unrevolutionary.[59] For at least some of these women recruits, virginity was preferable to marriage, which in their eyes was often a form of enslavement.[60]

This unisex model for female revolutionaries contrasted sharply with the model of the quintessential May Fourth emancipated woman, who incorporated sexual liberation into her overall political stance. Although this unisex paragon was based on historical precedent—for example, the legendary Hua Mulan and Qiu Jin, who was known for male attire and horseback riding—it also was shaped by the new roles that women revolutionaries in the mid-1920s were assuming. While May Fourth women revolutionaries were situated in urban areas, mostly foreign treaty ports where Western influences were quite pronounced, the female recruits at the Wuhan Central Military and Political Institute were trained to work in the rural areas, where traditional norms of female conduct and decorum prevailed. The very act of dispatching a mixed group of women and men to a farming community was shocking to local sensitivities. No doubt it was believed that any indication that these men and women might be engaging in illicit sexual relations would be quite damaging to their cause. Just the fact that these women had short hair and natural, unbound feet already made them seem quite different from the norm. They were often seen as freak curiosities in rural communities.[61]

The experiences of You Xi and Xie Bingying, two of the most famous recruits at the Wuhan Central Military and Political Institute, indicate that the women soldiers felt this unisex model often expanded their social space of operations and thereby facilitated their ability to command respect and issue directives in rural communities. Indeed, it offered them a convenient way to break out of a very socially constricted gender role. Perhaps for this reason, the custom adopted by both You Xi and Xie Bingying of donning male attire when out of uniform was also adhered to by other Communist women organizers, even those not attached to the military.[62] Perhaps their practice of cross-dressing was inspired by Qiu Jin, who had done the same twenty years earlier. Once when Xie Bingying wore a foreign male suit in Xinti, Hubei, she was suddenly accosted by a group of young prostitutes who mistook her for a man. Xie Bingying was filled with a great sense of sadness and consternation that such beautiful young women had to engage in such a degrading occupation in order to earn a minimum daily wage.[63]

Expansion of the Women's Associations in Hubei and Henan

Women's associations experienced dramatic growth throughout the province of Hubei in late 1926 and the first half of 1927. In addition efforts were made to cultivate them in Henan as well, though with less success. The greatest successes were claimed to have occurred in Hubei, where by March of 1927 the mass women's associations boasted a total membership of ten thousand with chapters in thirty-eight counties.[64] In some counties, multiple branches were established, as in Suixian, where one woman who was a member of both the Nationalist and Communist parties ran a short-term training program for sixty local women, who then were sent out to set up branches of the Suixian Women's Association in the small towns around the county. In all these women founded twenty branches with a total membership of 1,300 by March of 1927.[65] By June, the total number of women's association members in Hubei was said to number more than sixty thousand when women workers were included.[66]

The graduates of the Wuhan Central Military and Political Institute assigned to the army played an important role in facilitating the extension and growth of the county women's associations in Hubei and Henan. Wherever the troops went, women propagandists would immediately gather together local women and try to persuade them that such an organization could be used as a leverage against oppressive family practices. When such an organization already existed, the women cadres would determine how it was faring and try to provide direction and encouragement. When women's association activists were extremely radical in imposing their will, particularly in compulsory haircutting and unbinding of feet, the army women encouraged a more moderate stance. They proposed that attention be devoted to preventing foot binding and that hairstyles should remain purely a matter of personal choice.[67]

When local women's associations were demoralized, as they were when warlord troops reoccupied an area after a women's association had been active and its leadership visible, then the army propagandists tried to impart a note of encouragement. Arriving in the southern Hubei town of Xianning, Xie Bingying found the makings of a strong women's association that had been disheartened by the vicissitudes of the war. She was surprised that such an out-of-the-way place had a women's association with more than two thousand members. Moreover, the chairwoman was only seventeen years old. As a sign of their commitment to the new order, three-fourths of the members had bobbed their hair. Xie's discussions with the local members revealed the difficulties of pushing for gender reform in an area that was constantly under threat from warlord armies. One member of the Xianning Women's Association, Zhang Jingyun, who had unbound feet and bobbed hair, recounted how some of the old women in Xianning had turned her over to the warlord soldiers when they swept through the area. Ultimately everyone else in her prison cell had been shot, but the district magistrate had spared her because she was still a child. Even after the warlord soldiers were forced to withdraw, the impact of their presence was still felt. Women were unwilling to circulate literature, hold demonstrations, or shout slogans in public.[68]

Arriving in Puqi, just fifty kilometers to the north, Xie Bingying learned that the women's association there was much more active than the one in Xianning, even though it too had suffered serious destruction from rampaging warlord troops. Although Xie Bingying did not account for such a variance in spirit between the two associations in her diary, it appears that the association in Puqi had managed to maintain better community relations, with the result that conservative elderly women and patriarchal heads of households were not inclined to identify its leaders to hostile forces. Thus, even though some warlord soldiers told the women with bobbed hair in Puqi that their haircuts were "counter-revolutionary," none of these "counter-revolutionary" women were thrown in jail or executed.[69]

Most women's associations, however, found it difficult to maintain harmonious community relations and pursue policies intended to radically overhaul gender relations. They directly attacked the androcentric kinship system by advocating free-choice marriages, the right of divorce, and the termination of ill-treatment of maids, concubines, and wives. In cases of wife beating, harsh punishments, often involving some form of public humiliation, were inflicted on the perpetrator.[70] If necessary, these associations would even challenge the power of the village head. In one village in Huangmei county, the women's association took action against a local despot whose power was bolstered by his strong kinship ties; all the families in the village bore the same surname he did. This merging of kinship and political power facilitated his ability to arrange for the sale of more than seventy widows in that community before the revolutionaries took power. They immediately punished him and removed him from his post.[71]

In the spring of 1927, Wuhan was rife with stories of compulsory haircutting by rural women's association zealots, sometimes with tragic consequences. Some women felt so humiliated at losing their long hair that they committed suicide.[72] One reason efforts by the Wuhan revolutionary government to dampen this haircutting binge proved so futile in rural areas was because organizers had imbued short hair with such symbolic import. Long hair was characterized as an unsanitary, inconvenient "feudal tail," whereas bobbed hair was living proof of one's success in breaking with the traditional "feudal" culture. It was said to embody the essence of "modern civilization" and became known as the "civilized hairstyle" (*wenmingtou*).[73]

By the same token, the campaigns to unbind feet also became excessive because of the social significance of the issue. That older women still hobbled around on their tightly bound feet was not of such concern to the revolutionaries as how the practice was viewed in the community. Female middle school graduates wanted to change forever the notion that small, bound feet were beautiful by instilling the idea that such a practice was barbaric and a national humiliation. As Xie Bingying wrote in her diary, "The bound feet here [in southern Hubei] are insufferable."[74] "I believe that foot binding is really a great misfortune of our sex, and I cannot help regarding it as a great disgrace that even today in the period of emancipation of women there are those of our sex who are still willing to be 18th century slaves."[75] Her use of the word "willing" revealed her belief that many women still wanted to have small bound feet. During the military campaigns that took the women's army corps deep into rural China, she was surprised to find women with two inch feet, an inch smaller than the ideally sized "golden lily" foot she believed was prescribed in standard texts on female propriety. Moreover, many women with bound feet performed taxing jobs. Xie Bingying wrote about watching a group of maids and old women who turned the pedals of the draining wheel with their small feet. The onlookers applauded in amazement at the speed of these women "with their small feet rapidly treading and catching the pedals of the wheel."[76] Thus, while National Revolutionary armies and warlord troops fought on the battlefield for ultimate control of political power, the mass women's mobilization campaign was waging a struggle over the power to alter the cultural meanings of and social practices related to womanhood in China.

For most rural communities, the most controversial actions of local women's associations concerned divorce. Numerous stories circulated about the social conflict provoked in one locality after a women's association had granted a divorce to a woman. In this case, as had also happened in Guangdong, the revolutionary peasant association sided with the divorced husband, with the result that the two mass organizations of the revolutionary coalition came into conflict.[77]

If a women's association was forced to back down in such a situation, it often lost the support of its membership.[78] If it persisted, it essentially went to war with an important ally in the revolutionary movement. As a result, the Communist leadership preferred to have women peasants join the peasant associations rather than the women's associations. This policy was followed in a number of communities. For instance, in Xianning ten thousand women were members of the peasant association, whereas only two thousand belonged to the women's association.[79]

Things Fall Apart

As the numbers of mobilized women continued to grow, particularly in Hunan and Hubei, the campaign began to show signs of eroding patriarchal notions embraced by many male Communist revolutionaries about excluding women from political positions. In Hunan, Shao Zhenxiong became the first woman to become a Communist county head.[80] The number of women who were official delegates to the fifth party congress of the Chinese Communist party when it convened in Wuhan in May of 1927 was significantly greater than ever before. In all, four women were accorded official delegate status: Yang Zhihua and Wang Genying from Shanghai, Ou Mengjue from Guangzhou, and Zhang Jinbao from Hubei. In addition, Yang Zhihua was confirmed as director of the Women's Bureau, a post she had filled after Xiang Jingyu's departure to Moscow, and was also elected as the only woman on the Central Committee.[81] In this respect, at least, the massive social mobilization of women in the National Revolution based on grassroots activism and a feminist agenda possessed the capacity to effectively counter traditional modes of behavior and thinking at the core of the political system under construction. However, this revolutionary momentum could not be sustained. Some signs of its demise were evinced in the backlash to the women's mass movements, which was sometimes as strong as the original impulse for change. On some occasions, men became quite violent.[82] Even men who were part of the revolutionary coalition were known to voice their opposition. A demonstration of husbands protesting the prolonged absence of their wives from their homes reportedly occurred in Wuhan. Sometimes women activists also took steps to curtail their aims. For instance, women students demonstrating at a rally on March 8, 1927, in Changsha refused to chant the slogan "Women should have the freedom to decide on their own marriages and to sue for divorce" purely because they feared this demand would spark a strong negative reaction. This instance of self-censorship was all the more telling because these students ardently believed women should have this right, and they were unwilling to allow their parents to assume decision-making power over their own marital affairs.[83]

These problems did not critically impair the momentum of the large-scale women's mobilization campaigns. However damaging revolutionary excesses, backlash, and malicious rumors were to the women's mobilization campaign, they did not bring about its demise. Rather, its undoing was caused by the shattering of the political alliance that had sustained its dramatic growth in the mid-1920s. Indications of impending doom appeared in March 1927, when Chiang Kaishek's army brutally suppressed Communist unions in Hangzhou and Chongqing. The critical turning point came early on the morning of April 12, when Shanghai gangsters, at Chiang's behest, crushed the Shanghai General Labor Union and initiated a massacre of workers and labor organizers.[84]

The Wuhan government was stunned by the Shanghai betrayal, but it still decided to launch a military campaign into Henan, termed the Second Northern Expedition, in mid-April. In sharp contrast to that in Hubei, the development of a women's mobilization campaign in Henan was much more difficult. Notably, the Taiping troops of the mid–nineteenth century marched from Wuhan eastward along the Yangzi River to Nanjing, totally bypassing Henan. From the perspective of one 1920s observer, it was amazing that the women's movement even reached Henan, which in his estimation was "drugged by old customs" and "unresponsive to popular opinion."[85] The Guangdong Women's Emancipation Association publication characterized the province as one of the worst places in all of China for women. Devoid of any major industry and dominated by peasant production and a "peasant mentality," with only a few small handicraft industries in the capital of Kaifeng, it offered few opportunities for women to obtain an education or a wage-paying job, with the consequence that most women worked in the home and had to submit to strong family controls, including the binding of their feet.[86] Even though the revolutionary government gained military and political control of Henan, it lacked a social environment receptive to the growth of a vigorous women's mobilization campaign like those in Guangdong, Jiangxi, Hunan, and Hubei. Indeed, the campaigns of warlord Feng Yuxiang's troops to stop women from binding their feet had been largely unsuccessful in Henan.

Even in such a conservative environment, however, a few Communists managed to situate themselves in the First Provincial Women's Middle School. A geology teacher was able to influence one young girl from Xinyang, in the southern part of the province, into participating in the May Thirtieth protests. After her graduation, she enrolled in the Wuhan Central Military and Political Institute and joined the Chinese Communist party in April of 1927.[87]

Before the arrival of the National Revolutionary Army in the spring of 1926, Communist efforts to build a women's organization in Kaifeng met with mixed results. While the founding meeting of the Henan Women's Association (Henan nüjie lianhehui) on January 1, 1926, was attended by one thousand people, the principal of the provincial women's vocational school walked out of the meeting in anger because the first speaker was a man. She went back to her school and forbade her students to join the organization. Thus, even though the association had a hundred or so members (20 percent workers, 20 percent students, 30 percent elementary teachers, and 30 percent unemployed middle school graduates), as well as some outstanding women leaders, including Zhou Xiaopei from Xiuwu, Henan, who had graduated from the Beijing Normal Women's College, this inauspicious beginning proved quite demoralizing, and the association failed to flourish.[88]

The launching of a military campaign into Henan in the spring of 1927 created the possibility for expanding the women's movement into this unfavorable social terrain. Many women students of the Wuhan Central Military and Political Institute, including Xie Bingying, were assigned to this operation. The women army propagandists, however, encountered a host of difficulties, particularly from the Red Spear Society. In Xinyang, southern Henan, this secret society spread rumors to the effect that the National Revolutionary Army "shared wives" and thus constituted a danger to the community. It also orchestrated the murdering of some members of the propaganda team. In Xindian, the Red Spear Society shut down the offices of the local women's association because it had attracted more than three hundred members through its training program, its promotion of unbinding women's feet, and its emancipation of child-brides.[89]

The Henan women's associations also experienced a good deal of internal factionalism. Particularly noteworthy was the Xinyang situation. Once women's association leaders in this city overcame the problems caused by the Red Spear Society and managed to attract two hundred members, they found that the Liulin Women's Association, which had been set up by the Henan Women's Congress, had decided to move to Xinyang and operate there as well. Having two organizations operating in Xinyang under exactly the same name produced quite a bit of confusion and tension. Finally a work team sent in to resolve the issue convinced the two organizations to slightly change their names.[90]

After a few months of struggling to establish branches of the Henan Women's Association in various counties, only two thousand members had been recruited, much fewer than in Guangdong, Hunan, and Hubei.[91] Even more disappointing was the Wuhan government's decision to withdraw the women propagandists accompanying the troops because their very presence had aroused such opposition among the local populace.[92]

As its women's campaign bogged down in Henan and the conflict with Chiang Kaishek intensified, the revolutionary Wuhan government was engulfed by a nasty rumor campaign. The most damaging accusations were sexual insinuations. One common story was that the women who traveled with the army only wore the scantiest of clothing.[93] The most vicious rumor alleged that a group of women was planning to parade through the streets of Wuhan stark naked on May 1 in order to celebrate their newfound freedoms and independence. Before long, this story was picked up by the foreign correspondents and reported in *Time* magazine (April 25, 1927) as a substantiated fact.[94] The revolutionary authorities went to great pains to suppress this rumor, charging three people with the crime of fabricating and spreading malicious slander. After their arrest they were paraded through the streets in order to humiliate them for this crime.[95] Nonetheless, such rumors effectively damaged the legitimacy and influence of the Wuhan government both in China and abroad.

Throughout May and June 1926, the lone woman in the top echelon of the Wuhan government remained steadfast in her support for the continuation of the revolution, including the transformation of China's women. Soong Qingling persevered in this stance even when her friends and her brother tried to convince her to leave Wuhan and distance herself from its policies.[96] She did not, however, have enough influence to counteract the immense damage inflicted by M. N. Roy, one of the Comintern advisers to the Wuhan government, whom Mao Zedong later labeled a "dunce" when he showed Wang Jingwei a telegram from Stalin ordering an all-out effort to arouse a mass uprising of peasants and workers.[97] The prominent Wang Jingwei, who had recently returned from abroad to become head of the Wuhan government, immediately concluded that the Communists could no longer be trusted as a reliable partner in a political alliance. On July 14 he summarily announced their expulsion from the Nationalist party.

Soong Qingling reportedly made a desperate last-ditch effort to salvage the situation by proposing that the revolutionary armies return to Guangdong, the historic heartland of the revolution, rather than unite with Chiang Kaishek. None of the other Nationalist leaders in the Wuhan government was willing to support such an action.[98] Soong Qingling then issued a statement condemning Chiang's usurpation of power in which she asserted, "Revolution in China is inevitable.... My disheartenment is only for the path into which some of those who had been leading the revolution have strayed."[99] She vanished from Wuhan and went to Moscow in a dramatic statement of her sentiments on the new Nationalist government that was to be installed in Nanjing under Chiang Kaishek. He Xiangning, the next most important Nationalist woman leader in Wuhan, quietly slipped out to the mountain resort of Lushan. Few were prepared for this rapid change in events or for the new political era that was ushered in by this tragedy. One of Xie Bingying's last diary entries reflected the shock and consternation of a whole generation of young women:

Why should we be demobilized? Our hopes, our ideals, are they finished after such a short appearance? ... So we are to leave the school tomorrow. Tomorrow is the time when we shall go into hell, for going back to our old-fashioned homes is as bad as going to hell.[100]

Women were not spared from the political violence unleashed by the bloody breakup of the coalition between Communists and Nationalists. Before He Xiangning left Wuhan and went into retreat on Lushan Mountain, the killing of women activists began in the city. Protected by her deceased husband's stature among Nationalists, she watched from afar in horror while the Communist members of her women's department staff were hunted down and executed. Though the female casualties were considerably fewer than the male casualties, intense political symbolism was associated with the women's deaths.

Women's bodies were subject to mutilation as a statement against female activism, which had come to be viewed as a disturbing indicator of a world turned upside down. When the Nationalist Commander Xia Douyin, for instance, ordered his troops to put down the peasant associations in Hubei, they reportedly "cut open the breasts of the women comrades, pierced their bodies perpendicularly with iron wires, and paraded them naked through the streets."[101]

Cai Chang estimated in her discussions with Helen Snow that the Nationalist troops killed more than one thousand Communist women organizers and leaders during the first year of the White Terror.[102] No one has ever attempted to count the total number of women participants who lost their lives in the backlash that occurred throughout much of China, though the random accounts of specific incidents indicate that the number was not insignificant. In Hubei, for instance, five hundred women reportedly were slain in the spring of 1927.[103] Some suspected women radicals were shot down in the streets such as occurred in the well-known massacre in Horse Square in Changsha. Others were arrested and summarily executed. Understandably, the vast majority of women activists, including Liu Qingyang and Xu Chengmei, dropped out of politics at this time. Inactivity normally brought immunity from arrest and prosecution.

Some women radicals went underground and continued to organize resistance in the cities against the Nationalist authorities in the hope of rekindling the revolutionary movement that had promised so much. But before long, many were turned in by informants and executed. In March of 1928 the Guangdong revolutionary Chen Tiejun was arrested together with her comrade-in-arms Zhou Wenyong. Before their execution, they were granted their last wish, to hold their own public marriage ceremony. In many ways their dramatic declaration of mutual affection signaled the end of a period in which it was possible to conceptualize the linking of romantic love and revolution. Yet for those who might still have nurtured some hope for the return of the heyday of the 1920s mass women's movements, the public execution of Xiang Jingyu in Wuhan on May 1, 1928, served as a final testimonial. The Nationalist party's official announcement of her execution described in detail the events of that day, including what she wore, and then briefly sketched the major events in her life, including her sexual liaisons. In the party's view, the most important aspect of the revolutionary woman's career was the wanton destruction of her marriage.[104]

Conclusion and Consequences

The Chinese revolution of the mid-1920s encompassed the most comprehensive effort to alter gender relations and end women's subordination of all of China's twentieth-century revolutions. Although women activists in the 1911 Revolution drew some attention to the cause of women's emancipation, and the 1949 Revolution touted this issue, it was in the 1920s that radicals seized upon revolutionary action as a means to consciously refashion China's gender order. They believed that emancipating women should constitute an essential component of their revolutionary endeavor to create a modern Chinese nation-state. To this end, they strove to make a radical break with the past and reconstitute gender relations by employing new political practices—mass propaganda, revolutionary cultural symbols, and mass mobilization campaigns. As a result, the 1920s proved to be the most significant era of the century for politicizing women's issues.

My account has examined this historical process primarily through the prism of the Chinese Communist party both because of the critical role Communists played in integrating women's emancipatory issues into the rhetoric, festivals, calendar, and political mobilization in the revolutionary upsurge of the 1920s and because of the importance of this party in shaping women's roles in the Chinese polity, economy, culture, and society once it came to power. Indeed, it is a contention of this work that some essential features of women's relationship to the Chinese Communist polity and state were fashioned in this formative period of the party.

Feminist goals were accorded an unusual prominence and respect in the mass propaganda and social mobilization programs of the nascent Chinese Communist party, in large part because its founding coincided with a period of extraordinary political and social ferment in China, including the burgeoning of feminism. This feminist orientation was first reflected in the writings of the party's founders, who were overwhelmingly male. Deeply influenced by the feminism of the May Fourth era, they shared a set of expectations about the importance of women's equality in developing a new political and social order. Indeed, the cluster of men in the party who were dedicated to the prospect of women's emancipation constituted a special breed in the world of international Communism, and these men helped to create a greater compatibility between Marxism and feminism in the Chinese Communist party during its first phase (1920–1927) than generally existed elsewhere in the international socialist movement.

To be sure, some Chinese Communists were attentive to the tensions between Marxism and feminism that were articulated in Western communist and socialist parties. Most notably, the famous writer Mao Dun stood out among the Shanghai male feminists as a sharp critic of certain contemporary feminist positions and practices. Yet, at the same time, he was also known as a tough critic of traditional "feudal" gender practices, often delivering searing attacks in his writings against the old morality, which he branded an evil poison. Like many others of his generation, he strove to forge a new modern morality that based marriage on love.

Perhaps because Mao Dun and those of his persuasion were such dedicated advocates of the cause of women's emancipation, their skepticism about the merits of the suffrage issue and about their party's association with women's rights organizations did not seriously impair the development of a feminist-oriented Communist women's program. Their attack on liaisons with independent women's groups was also effectively countered by other male feminists in the party, particularly Chen Duxiu and Li Dazhao. Chen Duxiu represented those Chinese Communists for whom May Fourth antifamily issues were integrated into an overall socialist feminist stance. He believed that the "woman question" would be solved with the advent of socialism, yet he did not allow this stance to become a justification for ignoring the issue of women's emancipation during the revolutionary process or for simply reducing it to a form of class exploitation. He not only continued to discuss women's issues in his writings but also provided the political leadership for Communist efforts to forge links with the independent women's movement. Li Dazhao clearly articulated the logic of nationalist anti-imperialism in his rationale for supporting women's rights initiatives. At a time when China was beleaguered by marauding warlords and truculent imperialist forces, he argued that the independent women's movement was essentially revolutionary because it agitated for full civil rights for women, and he believed that they should be brought into the political realm in the name of national interest. Thus, unlike the nationalism in many Western countries of the late nineteenth and early twentieth centuries, which served to confine women to the private sphere and exclude them from citizenship, Chinese nationalism in the early 1920s construed women's relationship to the state in much more egalitarian terms.

Although nationalist influences served to ameliorate the tensions between Marxism and feminism in the early Chinese Communist party, its feminist leanings were countered by patriarchal precedents. Thus, much more detrimental to the Communist effort to transform gender relations in this period than tensions between Marxism and feminism was the incorporation of traditional hierarchical gender patterns into the Chinese Communist polity. We can discern the beginnings of the process to construct a male-dominated authority structure in the party through the efforts of male Communist leaders to produce mass propaganda on women's emancipation. Their domination of ideological formulations of women's issues in the first years of the party enabled Communist male leaders not only to set the terms of debate but also to assume the right to speak on behalf of women. Their domination of the ideology was indicative of the gendered nature of the political organization that they then constructed. Women Communists had little opportunity in the first years of the Communist organization to assume important decision-making positions in the power structures of the party except in the Women's Bureau. Moreover, a woman's marriage to an important personage in the party was often an unstated criterion for her obtaining a high position in the Women's Bureau or elsewhere. In many cases, in fact, women Communists were able to wield greater power through their informal roles as partners of male leaders than through formal positions in the power structure. Thus, while male Communists wholeheartedly supported the notion that women should participate in politics, they were reluctant to name women to powerful positions in the new polity. In so doing, they reproduced and reinscribed certain cardinal features of the prevailing hierarchical gender norms of the larger society within their own political organization.

In contrast to most scholarly treatments of the Chinese Communist party during the 1920s, which have simply excluded or marginalized women from the focus of their studies, this book moves Communist women onto center stage. It examines the motivations and actions of women who were attracted to a Communist party that was often contradictory in its gender politics. Thus, the May Fourth generation of women Communists was arguably more committed than any of the later generations of female recruits to the cause of women's emancipation. From their entry into the Communist polity, these women were not silenced by the male domination of ideological formulations of women's issues. Rather, they instinctively realized the importance of making their first order of business the creation of their own organs of mass propaganda. They did not merely parrot men's voices but through their writings often asserted a female perspective on a number of issues. They stressed the importance of criticizing a variety of expressions of male power rather than viewing women's oppression primarily in systemic terms. Whereas many male feminists discussed female exploitation in a detached, depersonalized manner, women in the Chinese Communist movement manifested their heartfelt concern and empathy for the most downtrodden of their compatriots. Sometimes the issues they took up differed from those of male Communists as well. Women activists immediately saw the significance of the right of abortion to women's emancipation, for instance. Most important, the women of the Chinese Communist party stressed the importance of female political activism in obtaining women's emancipation and the need for women to represent themselves in national political bodies.

The pattern of female agency displayed by these radical women in conjunction with their resistance to societal forms of women's oppression stands in stark contrast to their acceptance of the creation of a hierarchical gendered power structure within the Communist polity. Indeed, one wonders how they could have put up with such unequal roles within the party. No doubt part of the answer lies in the fact that they had created their own space, culture, and lives within this political organization. But their agency was counterbalanced by their compliance to subtle forms of patriarchal controls within the Communist body politic. In this respect, these women colluded with and gave sustenance to the continuation of patriarchal patterns within the Communist polity.

This complex dynamic of agency and compliance was well illustrated by Xiang Jingyu, who emerged as the most outstanding Communist leader among this first generation of women recruits. In attempting to locate the actual role of Xiang Jingyu beneath heaps of hagiographic literature that has portrayed her as the archetype of a Communist woman revolutionary of the 1920s, much attention has been given to the complexities of her personal and political life. The primary documents and periodical literature from this period make clear that she was the most outstanding Communist woman leader of this era and that her most significant contribution was to build the foundation for women's work in the United Front with the Nationalist party. To be sure, Xiang Jingyu was persistent in her efforts to create strong links with the female proletariat, particularly women silk workers, but her efforts yielded only the most paltry of results. Xiang Jingyu's labor organizers encountered a number of obstacles stemming from lack of knowledge, experience, access to female workers, and competence with the local dialects. However, the most significant impediment to constructing party links to female workers stemmed from patriarchal tensions between male and female workers. As a result of prejudicial treatment by male workers, many women workers in Shanghai were not readily amenable to organizers from a party that primarily represented male workers in industrial conflicts. Although subsequent Communist women labor organizers were able to overcome many of these restraints, she herself was frustrated in her bid to become a woman's labor leader.

The process of developing a Communist women's program compelled Xiang Jingyu to confront the inherent tensions in socialist movements between class and gender priorities. Her ultimate accommodation with "bourgeois" feminism was made largely in the context of the Communists' fashioning of a political alliance with the Nationalist party in 1923. The evidence available on this controversial party decision reveals that she was a strong supporter of this decision. Xiang Jingyu's endorsement of this United Front policy reflected not only her political orientation at that time but also the importance of nationalism and Sun Yatsen's party in her political development.

Ultimately, however, it was Xiang Jingyu's transactions with the patriarchal facets of party life that proved more perplexing than her predicament over feminist issues. More than any other Communist woman of the May Fourth generation, Xiang Jingyu attempted to combat some of the most blatant patriarchal practices that affected women's work in the party through her position as director of the Women's Bureau. In the party resolutions on the women's movement, she demanded an end to the condescending views expressed by male Communists about women's rights organizations. She also insisted that male labor organizers counter the disdainful expressions and disrespectful behaviors of male workers towards their female counterparts. When it became apparent that certain Communist organizations, such as the one in Guangzhou, were not willing to accord women membership status, Xiang Jingyu argued for a reversal of such practices.

While Xiang Jingyu displayed great clarity about the dangers posed by patriarchal practices to the party's revolutionary program, there is no indication that her words had any effect. At the same time, she was privy to the discussions at the highest levels of party politics, but she was rarely if ever accorded official status in the male-dominated power structure. Her willingness to accept these terms for her political participation represented a form of compliance with traditional norms. Ironically, it was precisely such traditional gender precedents that ultimately undermined Xiang Jingyu's standing in the party. Her abrupt removal from the Women's Bureau in 1925 exposed at once the patriarchal underpinnings of both the institutional power structures of the party and the Communist subculture. Once her marriage to an important Communist leader was in serious jeopardy, the basis for her high-level position in the political hierarchy eroded. Moreover, the egalitarian life of the Communist subculture was brought into question when her right to experiment with a new relationship was not upheld, indicating that Communist males, if they were so inclined, could assert more authority in personal affairs than women.

The paradoxical and contradictory nature of Chinese Communist gender politics was further manifested in the revolutionary upheaval of the mid-1920s. The combined effect of the Nationalist party's establishment of a revolutionary territorial stronghold in the southern province of Guangdong and the mushrooming of the May Thirtieth mass protests in much of urban China ushered in a profoundly revolutionary environment, which proved conducive to the prospering of certain feminist ideals and programs. First and foremost, revolutionaries politicized gender issues in a way that fundamentally altered China's political culture. Secondly, the large-scale mobilization of women that occurred in much of southern China challenged patriarchal social power and endeavored to reconstitute gender relations in a more equitable form. However, at the same time that a radical program to transform the dominant culture was pursued, we can discern the infusion of traditional organizing principles into many facets of the revolutionary movement.

The women's mobilization campaign in south China was initially fueled by a combination of nationalism and feminism. Coordinated under the auspices of the Nationalist Central Women's Department run by He Xiangning, the campaign elicited the participation of a broad array of women's groups and individuals. Although frustrated in the endeavor to forge these disparate groups into one national women's organization, it nonetheless not only activated urban women but also reached far into the countryside. In this endeavor, the role of Communist women organizers was critical. Benefiting from the crucial opportunities made available by the collaboration with the Nationalist party, including legitimacy, funds, access to resources, and valuable contacts, Communist women activists were able to spearhead the establishment of grassroots women's organizations throughout much of south and central China, some of which were quite successful in attracting large memberships on the basis of feminist and nationalist issues.

The Nationalist party also benefited from the collaboration with the Communists in the domain of the mass women's movement. Although it had propagated feminist issues and attracted several outstanding women revolutionaries, such as Qiu Jin, in the early part of the century, when it operated under the name of the Revolutionary Alliance, its image had been sorely tarnished immediately after the 1911 Revolution by its support of the provisional constitution issued on March 11, 1912, which neither allowed women to be elected to office nor enfranchised them. Even when activists of the Women's Suffrage Alliance burst into the legislative hall in Nanjing and staged a mildly disruptive protest in order to force lawmakers to consider the adoption of a women's rights amendment that had earlier been summarily dismissed, male Republican power holders responded with moral shock to their disturbance and refused to reverse themselves. Their refusal to grant women full citizenship rights in the republic—even before Yuan Shikai's imperial aspirations and the subsequent dynamics of warlord politics had made a complete mockery of the new state—starkly revealed the hypocrisy of a party that had espoused the cause of women's emancipation before the revolution.[1] Shortly afterwards, Sun Yatsen's party added greater insult to this injury by entirely dropping the women's rights plank from its party constitution.[2]

The Nationalist party was able to distance itself a bit from this discredited historical record with the creation of a women's department in January of 1924. Initiated by the Comintern, it provided a mechanism for women in the Nationalist party, such as He Xiangning, to articulate a feminist program and coordinate a large-scale women's mobilization. The male leaders in her party, in collaboration with Communists, were willing to signal a radical break with tradition in the cultural sphere by extolling at least symbolically the ideal of women's emancipation in many of the festivals, publications, and theatrical productions in the new revolutionary order. However, without the financial backing of the Comintern through Mikhail Borodin, it is unlikely that the Nationalist Central Women's Department could have sustained the level of vitality necessary for a campaign of that magnitude. Although it is beyond the scope of this book to explore in depth the magnitude of patriarchal prejudices in the Nationalist party, the picture that emerges from even a limited probe is that Nationalist party feminists had to contend with many problems in the polity similar to those of their Communist counterparts.

What does emerge in this study is the infusion of patriarchal premises into the revolutionary nationalism of the 1920s. The process was greatly facilitated by the death of Sun Yatsen in March 1925, which was seized upon by Nationalist party leaders to consolidate mass support for the revolutionary endeavor. The deliberate effort to transform Sun Yatsen into a father-demigod imbued a strong male identity into the revolutionary nationalist consciousness of the day. In such an environment, the efforts of the Nationalist Central Women's Department and the grassroots women's associations to create a broad symbolic framework for the cause of women's emancipation were hampered, with the result that they relied heavily on foreign representations of female revolutionaries rather than Chinese models. And such models existed. It is likely that these images were so strongly embedded in Chinese women's consciousness that they in fact operated in attracting large numbers of women from various backgrounds to join the revolutionary movement. Had they been visibly incorporated into the revolutionary pantheon, a much more explicit link to this women's revolutionary tradition would have been constructed and even more women would have been emboldened to challenge the paternalistic and patriarchal power structures during the course of the National Revolution.

Nonetheless nationalist and feminist issues continued to be intertwined in this revolutionary effort, but in ways that failed to incorporate women's interests into nationalist imperatives. Indeed, He Xiangning's choice to wrap her Central Women's Department programs in a heavy nationalist cloak, an action that was clearly echoed by the Guangzhou Women's Emancipation Association's anti-imperialist proclamations, may well have protected the feminist components of her program from strong criticisms by the more conservative members of her party as well as created an environment in which younger, more radical women could operate. What is striking about the rural women's associations is that nationalist issues often were much less strongly articulated than feminist ones. Indeed, the mass propaganda produced by these organizations usually revealed a distinctly May Fourth rendition of women's emancipation issues.

The feminist-oriented women's mobilization campaign achieved impressive results. In areas where revolutionary forces were able to gain political control, such as in Guangdong, Guangxi, Hunan, and Hubei, activists often were able to establish grassroots women's associations that vigorously challenged patriarchal power. It was in Guangdong, where the revolutionary forces held power for the longest period of time, that women's associations were able to undertake the most sustained effort to alter traditional and highly hierarchical gender arrangements. The launching of the Northern Expedition in mid-1926 and the establishment of a revolutionary government in Wuhan temporarily expanded the terrain for feminist mobilization. The strength of the response in certain communities suggests that the Taiping's egalitarian gender ideology may have left lingering traces in peasant politics that were triggered by this revolutionary upsurge.

The fundamental problem for Communist-sponsored rural women's associations was their encounters with direct expressions of male power, particularly over the knotty issue of women's right to seek a divorce. When unhappy wives responded to the revolutionary feminist propaganda and sought the support of these women's organizations in their bid to leave abusive, coercive arranged marriages, intense conflicts often resulted and involved not only the immediately families but also the local elites. Although the female plaintiffs were often able to mobilize enough support to leave their marriages, such controversies often resulted in the marginalization of the women's associations in these communities, with peasant families barring their female members from participating in future political action programs.

Peng Pai and other peasant association leaders shared many of the assumptions of feminist leaders about the oppressive aspects of traditional gender practices, but they possessed a sober vision of the practical limits of feminist programs in rural areas. They felt compelled to invent a set of cultural symbols and a political action program that reflected male perspectives and male interests. As a result, the peasant associations mobilized women in ways that prudently avoided any suggestion that male peasants might lose power over the female members of their families. The much higher membership figures for female recruits in the Guangdong peasant associations suggests that this program provided a basis for female participation in the revolution that was more acceptable to peasant families than that of the women's associations. Moreover, these women no doubt gained many firsthand experiences in the political domain as a result of their participation that enabled them to develop their potential as full citizens in their communities. Yet, the practical decision of Peng Pai and other peasant association leaders to conform with rural patriarchal practices not only facilitated the domination of traditional gender-organizing principles in their institutions but also affected their leadership styles and social relationships.

The revolutionary government established in Wuhan on January 1, 1927, extended unprecedented citizenship rights to women and encouraged their active agency in the new order through participation in women's mass movement organizations. Indeed, it was mass movements and mass propaganda that were the main state mechanisms employed in Wuhan to bring about women's emancipation from traditional forms of oppression and customs and to define their status in the new society. A distinguishing feature of the women's mass movements at this time was the role they assumed in formulating women's legal rights in the public and private domains. It was in this political setting that the unisex revolutionary woman model was constructed as well, facilitating the social acceptance of women as public figures. The experiences in Hubei revealed the extent to which a feminist agenda could be pursued in the context of fervent nationalism and powerful patriarchal social institutions.

Throughout this explosive process of revolutionary upsurge, gender issues were the hub of contention, in large part because they were central to the creation of the political, cultural, and social constructs of the Chinese nation-state. Throughout the revolutionary upsurge of the 1920s, intense conflict ensued over women's place in the new order, particularly over their status in the family and in their communities. These tensions and strife caused numerous setbacks for women in specific localities. Often the very issue of women's emancipation came to symbolize the difference between revolutionaries and reactionaries. When the women's mass mobilization effort was engulfed by a vicious rumor campaign, its legitimacy and influence were somewhat tarnished. Nevertheless, the women's mobilization campaign was brought to a halt not by these problems but rather by the disastrous unraveling of the political alliance between the Communists and the Nationalists that had initially spawned it.

Impact of the 1927 Debacle

From the vantage point of the late twentieth century, we can see that the outcome of the feminist political mobilization during the National Revolution was not revolutionary. No significant changes were effected in Chinese social structures that permitted a dramatic improvement in women's status in either the public or the private domain. In the changed political climate ushered in with the civil war between Nationalist and Communists, both parties imposed constraints on women's active agency, particularly through the instruments of mass movements dedicated to radically changing the gender system. After 1927, feminist programs lost their political backing as neither party was willing to repeat the full-scale assault on patriarchal social controls over women that had occurred in the 1920s.

After the breakdown in the United Front in 1927 the new Nationalist government that was established in Nanjing closed down its women's department and worked quickly to distance itself from the radical policies of the "Communist bandits." In the political environment of the White Terror initiated by the Nanjing regime, Nationalists found the charge of sexual immorality an extremely effective weapon for discrediting Communist organizers, especially women. Radical women activists were portrayed as sexually promiscuous and a danger to the moral order. In the worst situations, such as the Horse Square Incident in Changsha in 1927, women were reportedly hunted down and killed as Communist radicals for the sole provocation of having bobbed hair. When Xiang Jingyu was publicly executed in Wuhan on May 1, 1928, the official statement that appeared in Nationalist newspapers emphasized her sexual conduct and the breakup of her marriage, insinuating that the most important facet of her political career had been her sexual behavior.

If the Nationalists and sundry warlord regimes viewed this ritualistic killing of women as a necessary means to restore social order, the prominent writer Lu Xun saw it as a sign of utter madness. In one of several articles he devoted to this topic, he scathingly commented on a newspaper account he had read about a particularly large turnout in Changsha for the execution of three women revolutionaries, aged fourteen, sixteen, and twenty-four.

I felt I could see ... the three headless female corpses at the Teacher's Association. They must have been stripped to the waist at least, too—or perhaps I am guessing wrongly because I am so corrupt. And then all those "citizens," one contingent heading south, another north, jostling and shouting.... I could fill in the details too, the rapt attention on some faces, the satisfaction on others.[3]

The fact that large crowds of "citizens" seemed to derive such pleasure from the sight of women being crucified, having their breasts amputated and the remaining part of their bodies mutilated beyond recognition, underscored for Lu Xun the sexually perverse nature and moral degeneration of the Chinese national character.

Deeds that seemed so morally reprehensible to Lu Xun seemed morally justifiable and even necessary to the new state authorities who were intent upon restoring social order. Yet, the appalling instances of violence against women would have been unthinkable without the previous large-scale mass mobilization of women. Female activism came to be viewed as a disturbing indicator of a world turned upside down. The White Terror inflicted on these women served to repress the women's mass movement and to vividly demonstrate the penalty for political participation. In so doing, it showed implicit recognition that a critical aspect of their power to challenge traditional gender arrangements resided in their ability to be active in the public sphere and organize a women's movement.

To be sure, women political radicals were not the only ones to feel the impact of the Nationalist party's new state morality. Zhang Jingsheng, a professor of philosophy at Beijing University, for instance, was arrested in 1928 by the Nationalist authorities on charges of "disseminating sex education and inciting youth" through the publication of his book *Sex Histories* (Xingshi).[4] Indeed, his propagation of unorthodox views, largely inspired by Emile Durkheim, had also incurred the staunch opposition of some influential scholars like Pan Guangdan, Zhou Jianren, Zhou Zuoren, and Zhang Xichen, who objected to the ways in which his ideas crossed the boundaries of acceptable social discourse on this topic. But much more significant to the creation of a state morality were the actions taken by the Nationalist government against Zhang Jingsheng, which effectively shut down the public discussion of the meaning of sexuality.[5]

Thus, one important outcome of the National Revolution was that it gave impetus to the redefining of women's social roles. In an effort to project a sense of stability and control during a turbulent period, the new government in Nanjing wedded nationalism to the cultivation of traditional values. Chiang Kaishek and his new wife, Soong Meiling, the younger sister of Soong Qingling, personally promoted this neotraditional state culture through the New Life Movement, which was officially launched in 1934.[6] They argued that for the sake of the social regeneration of the country, women had a special responsibility to the nation to cultivate the virtues of chastity, domesticity, and respectability. Women were explicitly enjoined against allowing themselves to be unwittingly guided by feminist ideas. In some provinces, the promoters of the campaign invoked state power to interfere in the personal lives of women in myriad minute ways, including issuing regulations about the required number of inches their skirt hemlines should fall below their knees.[7] Another key facet of this morality was its emphasis on the imposition of the sexual restraint on women. In such an environment, women were construed primarily as mothers for the country, and their sexual lives existed purely for functional reproductive purposes, not pleasure.

The massive demonstration of support for changing gender relations manifested in the revolution did not go totally unheeded by the Nanjing government, however. The feminist ideals that had been successfully integrated into the political culture during the 1920s found expression in the promulgation of the new Nationalist legal codes. Veteran Nationalist party leader Hu Hanmin, who was in charge of the project to draft the government's civil code, saw to it that women were granted unprecedented rights under this law. For the first time in Chinese history, women were entitled to suffrage, inheritance, and divorce rights. Promulgated in 1929 and 1930, this civil code was considered the embodiment of the revolutionary spirit of the Nationalist party's commitment to gender equality. Indeed, certain portions of the law, such as the granting of suffrage, were advanced by comparative standards. In the 1930s, for instance, most Catholic European countries still refused to extend suffrage to their female nationals. However, a close examination of the law reveals many contradictory sections, which resulted in part from the fact that its 1,223 articles were heavily influenced by very different types of legal precedents, including the Qing and Yuan Shikai provisional legal systems and Western and Japanese laws. Some of the provisions regarding marriage, such as the ban on concubinage and arranged marriage, were in fact directly contradicted in other portions of the law that had been formulated as a part of the provisional codes of the Qing reformers or Yuan Shikai. Little is known about the extent to which these laws on marriage reform were actually implemented in various localities. But the suffrage extended to women was without doubt granted only on paper, since the Nationalist government declared the establishment of a "training period" for citizens, male and female, in which the populace would be educated about their full civil rights.[8]

As Communists retreated from the cities into the remote hinterlands of China and established small soviet states, they too enacted laws to guarantee women's rights. The first marriage regulations drafted in the Chinese Soviet Republic of Jiangxi in 1931 were quite radical and more straightforward than the Nationalist provisions. They codified the principle of free-choice marriages and the right to divorce. They also proscribed polygamy, the sale of women into marriage, the practice of foster daughters-in-law (*tongyangxi*), and child marriages. Communists working underground in Shanghai hailed these new laws as a continuation of the feminist policies of the 1920s. The Communist writer Hu Yepin, who had married Ding Ling, wrote a short story, "Living Together," that presented a romanticized version of how couples of the Jiangxi soviet could decide on their own marriages and divorces amicably with little social interference from their families.[9] Yet Hu Yepin did not, in fact, know whether Jiangxi women could divorce their husbands as easily as they did in his stories.

Indeed, little is known about the implementation of this law, and it seems doubtful that it was uniformly enforced throughout the soviet districts.[10]

Much more indicative of the Communist party's stance on the feminist policies of the 1920s was the resolution on women's issues it passed at its sixth congress, which was convened in Moscow in June 1928. This document contained an explicit denunciation of the "bourgeois feminist" women's program of the previous eight years and specifically noted that it had been a mistake to allow the establishment of independent women's associations.[11] It thus facilitated a clear departure from the feminist program and the subsequent adoption of an orthodox Communist position on the primacy of economic class oppression over gender exploitation.

In the same year, the Communist writer Mao Dun came to a similar conclusion. In response to the carnage and despair ushered in by the breakdown of the United Front, he dropped out of the party, fled to Japan, and began writing fiction as a way to come to terms with the tragedy of the Chinese revolution. His first three novels, which were dashed off in rapid succession and later published as a trilogy entitled *Eclipse*, can be read as a postmortem on the Communist attempt to implement May Fourth feminist ideals through its women's program. A vivid account of the events of the Northern Expedition, the trilogy contained gory scenes detailing the brutal deaths of women's association activists at the hands of counterrevolutionary thugs and rampaging soldiers. The message of this fictional account of the revolutionary efforts to emancipate women was quite clear: they had been naive and misguided. Significantly, it was for this trilogy that he first assumed the pen name Mao Dun, meaning "contradiction."

Thus, even before Chinese Communist leaders shifted from a standard proletarian model of revolution to one based on the countryside, they pronounced judgment on the feminist policies of the party's formative phase. No doubt, once it became clear that Communists could no longer operate effectively in the cities, the need to avoid antagonizing male peasants served as a further incentive to discard policies designed to challenge patriarchal controls over women and bring about full-scale gender transformation. In such an environment, it was preferable to encourage women to participate in the public sphere of work and strive to become labor heroines as the chief means to achieve emancipation. Once women were able to achieve economic independence, it was argued, they would be able to emancipate themselves from patriarchy. With the establishment of the

Jiangxi Soviet, the Chinese Communist party became more conservative socially, even somewhat puritanical in the 1930s.[12] This trend became even more pronounced with the shift of the main Communist base area to Yan'an in the north. Indeed, when Ding Ling settled there in the late 1930s, she was horrified by the lack of a feminist women's program and published a sharp critique of the treatment of women cadres in the party newspaper on March 8, 1942, International Women's Day. Her words fell on deaf ears, however, and she was strongly chastised for her inappropriate emphasis on the need to address gender discrimination. Moreover, she was told that her feminism was both detrimental to the party's prestige and obsolete, as "full sexual equality had already been established" in Yan'an.[13]

This response penetratingly revealed not only the gap that had occurred between Communist rhetoric and practice on women's issues, but the estrangement between Communists and the independent women's movement. Indeed, after the 1920s Communists increasingly came to view feminism and its proponents as critical weapons in the arsenal of Western hegemony. Such a turn of events raises the question of whether feminist-minded Chinese women radicals had been misguided in their original decision to link their commitment to women's emancipation to nationalist and socialist agendas in the revolutionary upsurge of the 1920s. Indeed, one could easily conclude that the union of feminism to a socialist-nationalist revolutionary movement was basically an ephemeral relationship without significant benefit to the goal of fundamental gender transformation. However, such a conclusion fails to take into account the sustenance that May Fourth feminism received from Chinese nationalism and communism. Moreover, this union that had been forged in the specific historical context of the demise of the Chinese empire and the intensification of Western world hegemony did not totally disappear from the world of Chinese Communism in the fallout of 1927. Women's emancipatory issues continued to be linked both explicitly and implicitly to the modernizing agenda throughout the rest of the century. After the Communist state was established in 1949, a significant core of Communists continued their efforts to end gender oppression. The campaigns in the early 1950s to end arranged marriages, for instance, revealed the enduring legacy of the feminist phase of the Chinese Communist movement. After 1949 the party kept alive much of the language and rituals of women's emancipation, providing a legitimate basis within the Communist state for anyone with the determination and savvy to utilize them.

Communist-Sponsored Mass Women's Organizations

Name of Organization	Date Founded	Size	Journal
Quanguo gejie funü lianhehui (Beijing)	5/12/1925	250 (at founding)	
Guangdong funü jiefang xiehui (Guangzhou)	5/1925	1,000	*Guangming*; later *Funü shenghuo*
Other chapters in Guangdong			
Haifeng	6/1925	20+	
Xunde	9/1925	50+	
Shaoguang	10/1925	200+	
Xinhui	11/1925	30	
Meixian	12/1925	200+	
Qiongya	12/1925	200+	
Shantou	12/1925	200+	
Huizhou		50	
Yingde		400	
Qujiang		—	
Leizhou		—	
Shishi		100	
Shanghai gejie funü lianhehui		500	*Zhongguo funü*
Other chapters in Shanghai			
Nanshi			
Yangshupu			
Tianjin gejie funü lianhehui	7/1925	200	
Hubei funü xiehui	8/1925	800	*Hubei funü*
Other chapters in Hubei			
Huanggang		10,000	

(continued)

Name of Organizations	Date	Size	Journal
Xiaogan			
Huangpi			
Huangmei			
Mianyang	3/1925		
Tianmen	12/1926		
Zhongxiang	1/1927		
Xianning	1/1927	2,000	
+38 others			
Hunan nüjie lianhehui			*Funü xianfeng*
Other chapters in Hunan (1925–1927)			
Xiangnan			
Hengyang			
Leiyang		300	
Liuyang			
Tangduanxiang			
Xiangtan			
Liling			
Lingxiang			
Baoging			
Tangshan nüjie xiehui	1925		*Tangshan funü*
Qingdao nüjie lianhehui	1925	70+	
Wuzhou funü lianhehui (Guangxi)	10/1925		
Guilin jiefang xiehui			
Henan nüjie lianhehui	1/1926	100+	
Nanjiang gejie funü lianhehui	5/1926	30	
Wujiang funü lianhehui (Jiangsu)	5/1926		
Wenzhou nüjie lianhehui (Zhejiang)	5/1926	100	
Suzhou funü lianhehui	6/1926		
Ningbo gejie funü lianhehui	7/1926	100	
Anqing funü lianhehui (Anhui)	1926		

This chart was compiled from several Communist and Nationalist sources, particularly *Zhongguo funü* [Chinese Women], *Guangming* [Light], *Funü zhi sheng* [The Voice of Women], and *Minguo ribao*, Wuhan. It seems curious that no groups were reported to have been established in Sichuan. Further investigation into local newspapers and gazetteers is necessary to determine whether this was in fact the case.

Biographical Directory

Cai Chang (1900–1990). Cai was born in Xiangxiang, Hunan. Her father's family traced its lineage back to the prominent nineteenth-century Hunanese scholar-official Zeng Guofan, but her father did little for the family and her mother, Ge Jianhao, eventually left him. Cai Chang graduated from the progressive Zhounan Girls' School in 1916. She was a member of the New Citizen's Study Society and a participant in the work-study movement, traveling to France in 1919 together with her brother Cai Hesen, her mother, and a large contingent of Hunanese, including Xiang Jingyu. In France she worked in several factories and joined the Chinese Communist organization established in Europe in 1923. In 1924 she went to Moscow with her Hunanese husband, Li Fuchun, whom she had married in 1922, for further study. Returning to China in August 1925, she worked in the mass women's movement in Guangdong, working with He Xiangning's Nationalist Central Women's Department and serving as secretary of the Guangdong Communist party women's committee, and then in Wuhan during the National Revolution. After the failure of 1927, she was appointed a member of the party's Central Women's Committee and attended the sixth party congress in Moscow in June 1928. In 1931 she entered the Jiangxi Communist base area and later participated in the Long March. In 1945 she was a delegate to the seventh party congress and from then on held high-ranking positions in the party hierarchy, including Central Committee member and chairperson of the All-China Women's Federation.

Cai Hesen (1895–1931). Cai was born in Shanghai. The older brother of Cai Chang, he was a student of the prominent Changsha educator Yang Changji while he attended the First Provincial Normal School along with Mao Zedong. In April of 1918 he helped to found the New Citizen's Study Society. An important leader of the Hunanese work-study contingent, he went to France in 1920 where he participated in the formation of the Diligent Work Frugal Study Association (Qin-gong jianxue lijinhui). In 1921 he joined the European branch of the Chinese Communist party and was very active in Communist activities until he was deported from France after the Lyons Incident in 1921. Returning to Shanghai, he became the chief editor of *The Weekly Guide*, which was made an official organ of the Central Committee of the Chinese Communist party in 1922. He published a book entitled *A History of Social Evolution* (Shehui jinhuashi), which advanced many Marxist theories on the historical development of society. He was a leader of the May Thirtieth Movement and was selected to be a delegate at every party congress from the second to the sixth (1922–1928). For most of his career in the Communist party, he held a number of top positions on the Central Committee and the Politburo. He also served as director of the Central Propaganda Bureau and as acting secretary of the Central Committee. He was very entangled in the factional disputes that racked the party after 1927 until he was arrested while doing underground work in Hong Kong in 1931. He was executed at the age of thirty-six in Guangzhou by the Nationalist authorities, leaving four children, two from his five-year marriage to Xiang Jingyu and two from his five-year marriage to Li Yichun.

Chen Duxiu (1879–1942). Chen was a leader of the May Fourth Movement and the first secretary-general of the Chinese Communist party. Born into a prosperous official family in Anhui in 1879, he studied the classics and attempted to pass the civil examinations. After failing the provincial-level exams, in 1897 he went to study in Japan where he participated in radical societies. In 1915 he founded *New Youth*, which was later viewed as having ushered in the May Fourth era. In 1920 he became a Marxist and founded the Shanghai Communist organization and is credited as one of the cofounders of the Chinese Communist party. From the first to the fifth party congress, he served as a member of the Central Committee and secretary-general. After 1927, he was blamed for the erroneous United Front policy and was forced to step down from his position as secretary-general. In November 1929 he lost his party membership and was branded a Trotskyite.

Chen Wangdao (1891–1977). Chen was a translator of *The Communist Manifesto* and a founding member of the Shanghai Communist organization. He established the Communist publications *Labor World* (Laodongjie) and *Communist Party* (Gongchandang), was an editor of *New Youth* and *Awakening*, and was chief editor of *Women's Critic*. He was well known for publicizing the October Revolution in Russia and promoting women's emancipation. An early advocate of the use of punctuation for vernacular Chinese, he also became well known for his editing of the first Chinese work that presented a systematic account of the art of rhetoric and for founding the China Linguistic Society (Zhongguo yuwen xuehui). After 1949, he served as minister of culture for a short time and then was appointed as president of Fudan University. He was vice-director of the Chinese Democratic League and was a chief editor of *Cihai*.

Deng Yingchao (1904–1992). Deng was one of the most important Communist women's leaders. Originally named Deng Wenshu, she was born in Nanning, Guangxi. Her father died when she was a young child, and she was raised by her mother, who earned a living through teaching. In 1919 Deng Yingchao became the youngest founding member of the Awakening Society, for which she organized a public speaking group. She became a prominent women's rights leader in Tianjin through her leadership role in the founding of the Tianjin Women's Patriotic Society in 1919 and the Zhili chapter of the Women's Rights League, which had its headquarters in Tianjin, in October 1922. She also served as an editor of *Women's Star* (Nüxing) and *Women's Daily*. In 1923 she married Zhou Enlai, whom she had met during the May Fourth Movement in Tianjin, and in 1924 she joined the Socialist Youth League. After participating in the nationwide campaign to promote women's participation in the National Assembly, she joined the Chinese Communist party in early 1925. In August she went to Guangzhou, where she served as a staff member of He Xiangning's Nationalist Central Women's Department. In 1932 she held various posts in the Jiangxi soviet, and in 1934 she joined the Long March. After 1949 she served as vice-head of the All-China Women's Federation and held numerous other positions, including chairperson of the Sixth Political Consultative Conference.

Ding Ling (1904–1986). Ding was a well-known writer who was born in Hunan to a gentry family. Her father died early, freeing her mother, Yu Manzhen, to seek an education in Changde, where she was a classmate of Xiang Jingyu. Under her guidance, Ding Ling attended the No. 2 Provincial Girls' Normal School in Taoyuan and the Zhounan Girls' School and Yueyun Middle School in Changsha. In 1921, at the age of seventeen, she went to Shanghai, together with Wang Jianhong and Wang Yizhi and enrolled in the Communist-run Shanghai Pingmin Girls' School and then in Shanghai University. Then she went to Beijing, where she lived with the aspiring poet Hu Yepin. She first made a name for herself as a writer with the publication of "Miss Sophie's Diary" in 1927. In 1930 she joined the League of Left Wing Writers. She joined the Chinese Communist party in 1932, a year after Hu Yepin was executed by the Nationalists along with twenty-two other Communists who had been arrested at a secret party meeting. In 1936 she went to Yan'an and worked as a writer. When she used her pen to criticize the Communist party's treatment of women cadres and the party's women's program for bowing under to nationalist and party imperatives, she was soundly criticized. In 1948 she wrote a novel, *The Sun Shines over the Sangan River* (Taiyang zhao zai Sangan heshang), which was hailed as a model of socialist realism and awarded the Stalin Prize for Literature in 1951. In the 1950s she served as chief editor of several journals until she was branded as an antirightist in 1957 and sent to a remote area of Heilongjiang. In the late 1970s she came back to Beijing, where she lived the last years of her life with a certain amount of comfort and prestige.

He Xiangning (1878–1972). He Xiangning was a feminist anti-Manchu revolutionary who headed the Nationalist Central Women's Department in the mid-1920s. She was born in Hong Kong on June 27, 1878, and grew up in a middle-class family in Hong Kong. Inspired by the Taiping women rebels, she refused to have her feet bound as a child. She married an overseas Chinese, San Francisco–born Liao Zhongkai, and in 1902 sold her bridal trousseau to accompany him to Japan, where she enrolled in the Tokyo Women's Art School. She took the unusual step of joining Sun Yatsen's Revolutionary Alliance in Tokyo in 1905 before her husband, who was away in Hong Kong, did so. After he returned to Tokyo in September of that year, she convinced him to join, and from then on he overshadowed her in his power and influence in Sun's revolutionary organizations. After the failure of the 1913 Second Revolution, she and Liao lived in exile in Japan for several years, maintaining close relations with Sun Yatsen. When the revolutionaries regained control of Guangdong in 1924, Liao became one of the most powerful officials in the Nationalist party revolutionary government, and He Xiangning was appointed to the directorship of the Central Women's Department in 1924. Although Liao was assassinated by right-wing elements in the Nationalist party in August 1925, she continued to be an active leader of the Central Women's Department until the United Front with the Chinese Communist party collapsed in mid-1927. During the next twenty years she remained aloof from politics and spent time abroad. After 1949 He Xiangning served in a number of official posts, including honorary chairperson of the All-China Women's Federation. She died in 1972 at the age of ninety-five.

Huang Zonghan (1876–1944). Huang was an anti-Manchu revolutionary. Originally named Xu Peixuan (she later assumed the name Xu Zonghan), she was born in Singapore to a wealthy tea merchant family from Zhongshan, Guangdong, and was educated in Shanghai. She married at the age of eighteen and gave birth to two children. Her first husband, who came from a Qing scholar-official family, died young, and she became involved in Christian medical services, working with the famous Chinese woman doctor Zhang Zhujun. In 1907 she joined the Revolutionary Alliance and worked underground in Guangdong, where she participated in two failed uprisings. Through such activities she met Huang Xing and became his revolutionary companion, giving birth to several of his children. She adopted Huang's surname and continued to use it after his death in 1916. She participated in founding the Shanghai Federation of Women's Circles in 1919 and served as its first chairperson. Later in the 1920s she became involved in a children's home in Nanjing, where she lived until the outbreak of the Sino-Japanese War in 1937. She spent the last years of her life traveling to the United States and Europe to raise funds for China's war effort.

Li Da (1890–1966). Li was a Marxist theoretician and president of Wuhan University. From Hubei, he studied in Japan. He joined the Shanghai Communist organization at its inception in 1920, working closely with Chen Duxiu to lay the foundation of the political organization. His main interest was in developing mass propaganda for the party, which led him to establish the first underground Communist press, Renmin Chubanshe, in September 1921. He published many articles on women's issues and also translated a number of articles by Yamakawa Kikuei that presented a classical Marxist approach to the "woman question." He came to know Wang Huiwu, a May Fourth feminist from Zhejiang and a cousin of the writer Mao Dun, when she rented a room in Chen Duxiu's home and before long they decided to marry. He was named as the principal of the Shanghai Pingmin Girls' School, although Wang Huiwu in fact ran the school. He lost his position on the Central Committee at the second congress in July 1922 and left Shanghai at the end of the year for Changsha, where he worked with Mao Zedong to establish *New Times* (Xin shidai). Sometime in the mid-1920s he left the Communist party, but he did not lose his interest in Marxism and became a well-known theoretician in the 1930s. He became a professor at Sun Yatsen University in Guangzhou, Shanghai's Law and Politics University, and Beiping University Law and Commerce Institute. In 1935 he published "An Outline for Sociology" (Shehuixue dagang). After 1949 he was appointed as president of Hunan University and then of Wuhan University, where he worked from 1952 until the outbreak of the Cultural Revolution in 1966.

Li Dazhao (1889–1927). Li was an important intellectual leader in the May Fourth Movement and one of the founders of the Chinese Communist party. Born to a poor peasant family in Luoting, Hebei, Li Dazhao acquired a modern education with great difficulty. He spent four years in Japan studying political economy, where he became known for his skills as a writer and editor. In 1918 he was appointed librarian at Beijing University, where he established a political study group that came to be called the Marxist Research Society. It attracted many young radicals, including Mao Zedong and Qu Qiubai. He was also known for his essays on the Russian revolution and Marxism that were published in *New Youth* and other May Fourth periodicals. In 1920 he set up a Communist organization in Beijing and was widely recognized as a cofounder, along with Chen Duxiu, of the Chinese Communist party. He served as a member of the Central Committee for the second through the fourth party congresses. He took refuge in the Soviet Embassy in Beijing from the zealous anti-Communist warlord Zhang Zuolin, who in early April decided to ignore the diplomatic immunity of a foreign embassy and ordered his troops to arrest all the Chinese who were hiding there. On April 28, 1927, Li Dazhao was hung along with nineteen others.

Li Yichun (1899–1984). Li was a Hunanese woman Communist. Probably a student at the Zhounan Girls' School in Changsha, she went to Shanghai with her husband, Li Lisan, who had participated in the work-study movement in France until he was deported along with Cai Hesen after the Lyons Incident in 1921. She then became a prominent Communist labor organizer in the Hunan Anyuan strike. In 1923 she began to study at Shanghai University and to participate in party activities. She joined the Chinese Communist party in 1925 and went to Guangzhou, where she taught the singing classes at the Peasant Movement Training Institute. In 1926 while she was in Moscow, she left Li Lisan to marry Cai Hesen, with whom she had two children. In 1937 she taught at Lu Xun Normal School in Yan'an. After 1949 she worked in the field of education and the production of theoretical works.

Liu Qingyang (1894–1977). Liu was born into a prosperous Tianjin Muslim family. Her father ran a butcher (mutton) shop, and her brothers later became influential in north China newspaper circles. Galvanized by the 1911 Revolution during her student days, she sought to emulate the Hua Mulan woman-warrior model. During the May Fourth Movement, she surfaced as a student leader in Tianjin. She was a member of the Awakening Society and the New Citizen's Study Society, which she was encouraged to join by Cai Hesen when he was in Beijing in 1918, even though she was not from Hunan. In 1920 she went to France and participated in the founding of the Communist party nucleus. She joined the European Communist organization in January 1921 and is considered to be the second woman member. Around that time she also married Zhang Shenfu, a Communist intellectual who was greatly influenced by Bertrand Russell's trip to China in 1920. Returning to China in 1923, she became active in Tianjin where she joined the Nationalist party and became an editor of *Women's Daily*. In 1924 the party sent her to the Comintern's fifth congress in Moscow as one of its official representatives. She participated in the campaign to promote women's participation in the National Convention in early 1925 and joined the staff of He Xiangning's Central Women's Department in Wuhan in 1927. After the 1927 debacle, she withdrew from politics and started a family. Prior to the Chinese Communist victory in 1949, she divorced

Zhang Shenfu and declared her support for the new government. She held a number of prominent positions after 1949, including the deputy directorship of the All-China Women's Federation. In 1961 she was readmitted to the Chinese Communist party.

Liu Yaxiong (1901–1988). Liu was from a well-to-do Shanxi family. She attended the Provincial Girls' Normal School in Taiyuan, and then in 1923 she entered Beijing Normal Women's College, where she subsequently became a student leader in the protracted conflict that developed with the notorious principal Yang Yinyu. In 1926 she joined the Chinese Communist party, and shortly afterwards she went to study in Moscow's Sun Yatsen University. She was married to Chen Yuandao for two years before he was executed by Nationalist authorities in 1933. During the war against Japan she established a guerrilla detachment in southeast Shanxi. After 1949 she was appointed vice-head of the communications bureau.

Lu Xun (1881–1936). Lu was China's most brilliant and renowned short story writer of the twentieth century. His prolific works offered searing critiques of Chinese traditional culture and the mentality of Chinese. Among his most famous short essays are "The True Story of Ah Q" and "Madman's Diary." He also criticized Chinese notions of chastity and what he saw as Chinese sadism.

Mao Dun (1896–1981). Mao Dun is the pen name for the well-known leftist writer Shen Yanbing. Born in Tongxiang county, Zhejiang, he attended a middle school in Hangzhou and later studied literature at the National University in Beijing. Because of financial difficulties, he had to terminate his studies in 1916 and take a job as a proofreader at Commercial Press in Shanghai. In 1920 he founded the Literary Research Society (Wenxue yanjiu hui). Joining the Shanghai Communist organization in August 1921, he taught at the party-run Shanghai Pingmin Girls' School, which his cousin Wang Huiwu had established, and at Shanghai University. He was well known in literary circles for his prolific essays, his translations, and his editorship of *Xiaoshuo yuebao* (Short story monthly) and *Women's Weekly* from 1921 to 1923. In 1926 he went to Guangzhou to work in the political department of the revolutionary government, and after the revolutionary armies captured Wuhan, he traveled there to become an editor of the newly established *Republican Daily* in that city. After the debacle of 1927, he assumed the pen name Mao Dun, which signified "contradiction," and began to write fiction. He traveled to Japan in July 1928, severing his connection with the Chinese Communist party, and did not return until April 1930. Among his most well-known pieces were "Spring Silk Worms" and the novel *Midnight*, which helped to establish his reputation as one of China's leading realist writers in the republican era. After 1949 he served as head of the Writers' Association and then became minister of culture. He later also served as chief editor of *People's Literature* (Renmin wenxue).

Miao Boying (1899–1929). Miao was the first woman to join the Chinese Communist party. Born in Changsha, Hunan, she attended the First Girls' Normal School from 1916 to 1919, when she successfully passed the entrance examination to the prestigious Beijing Normal Women's College. Through Li Dazhao and Deng Zhongxia, she became involved in the Work-Study Mutual Aid Corps. She was admitted to the Beijing Communist organization in November of 1920, which was also the year she began publishing articles on women, including "Family and Women," which appeared in *Research on Women*. In the summer of 1922 she became a founding member of the Women's Rights League and traveled to a number of other cities to promote its expansion. Along with her husband, He Mengxiong, she was sent back to Hunan in 1924, where she became the secretary of the Hunan Communist women's committee. She died of illness caused by the difficult living circumstances she experienced as a Communist organizer during the White Terror.

Ou Mengjue (1906–). Ou came from a relatively well-off family in Nanhai, Guangdong. Upon her graduation from a local elementary school, her father sent her to Kunwei Girls' Middle School, an expensive private school in Guangzhou, with the expectation that her education would facilitate the expansion of his business. There she came under the influence of a Communist teacher along with her classmate Chen Tiejun. During the May Thirtieth Movement and the local protests over the Shaji Incident a few weeks later, they both became radicalized and in 1926 joined the Chinese Communist party. She was director of Guangdong Women's Emancipation Association and was an official delegate to the fifth congress of the Chinese Communist party, convened in Wuhan in May 1927. In 1930 she became a teacher at a girls' middle school. In the 1930s and 1940s she was arrested a number of times by the Nationalist authorities and the Japanese for her political activities. In 1940 she went to the Communist base area in Yan'an. After 1949 she held many positions in the Guangdong provincial government, was a member of the standing committee of the All-China Women's Federation, and served as secretary of the Guangdong provincial committee.

Peng Pai (1896–1929). Peng was a Communist pioneer in organizing the peasantry. The scion of a wealthy landlord Hakka family, he went to Japan to further his education. Although he was influenced by the May Fourth Movement, he agreed to an arranged marriage. However, he then made a serious attempt to convert his relationship with his new wife, Cai Suping, into a modern marriage. He convinced her to unbind her feet and urged her to become literate. He began to organize Guangdong peasant associations in 1922. After joining the Chinese Communist party in 1924, he held prominent positions in the Nationalist Peasant Department and assumed the directorship of the first and fifth classes of the Peasant Movement Training Institute. He was elected to the Central Committee of the Chinese Communist party at the sixth party congress. He was arrested in 1929 and executed.

Peng Shuzhi (1895–1983). From Hunan, Peng joined the Chinese Communist party in 1921 and edited party publications such as *The Weekly Guide* and *New Youth*. At the fourth and fifth party congresses, he was elected to the Central Committee. In 1929 he sided with Chen Duxiu and was ejected from the party. Later he went abroad and lived much of the remainder of his life in France.

Qiu Jin (1875–1907). Qiu was an anti-Manchu feminist revolutionary. She left an unhappy marriage and went to study in Japan, where she joined the Revolutionary Alliance. Returning to her native province of Zhejiang, she founded a girls' school and plotted an unsuccessful uprising against the Qing imperial government. She was quickly apprehended and executed by Manchu authorities.

Qu Qiubai (1899–1935). Qu grew up in Changzhou and came to Beijing, where he enrolled in the Russian Language Institute and participated in Li Dazhao's Marxist study group. He went to Moscow in 1920 and joined the Chinese Communist party there in 1922. He was the first Chinese to write extensively about the situation in Russia, sending back a host of pieces for the *Morning News* in Beijing. He also translated the Communist Internationale into Chinese. After his return to China, he taught at Shanghai University and was elected to the Central Committee of the party at its third and fourth congresses. After the death of Wang Jianhong, a student he had met and fallen in love with at Shanghai University, he married Yang Zhihua in November 1924 in the house of Shao Lizi. When Chen Duxiu was dismissed as secretary-general of the party in 1927, Qu Qiubai assumed the post. He was captured by the Nationalists when their troops took control of the Communist Jiangxi Soviet, and executed.

Shao Lizi (1882–1967). Shao joined the Revolutionary Alliance in 1908 and participated in the 1911 Revolution. In 1912 he established *Democracy* (Minzhu bao). In 1919 he joined the Nationalist party and became the chief editor of *Awakening*, a supplement of the party's main organ, the *Republican Daily*. He held dual membership in the Chinese Communist party for a short time in the mid-1920s, but resigned his Communist membership in late 1924 or 1925 while retaining his Nationalist affiliation. He wrote prolifically on women's issues, served as vice-president of Shanghai University, and became a director of the political department of Whampoa Academy in Guangzhou.

Soong Qingling (1893–1981). Soong was the middle daughter of the prominent businessman Charlie Soong. She became the wife of Sun Yatsen in 1914. After his death in 1925, she supported the Nationalist party's alliance with the Chinese Communist party, attending the second party congress in January 1926 and then assuming a leadership position in the Wuhan left-wing government that was established in late 1926. After the collapse of this government in July 1927, she went to Moscow and traveled in Europe. She was very disheartened to learn that her younger sister had decided to marry Chiang Kaishek. Soong Qingling worked in the industrial cooperative movement in the 1930s and 1940s and stayed in China after 1949, where she held a number of prominent government positions.

Sun Yatsen (1866–1925). Sun is generally viewed as the father of the Chinese republican revolution. He first earned a reputation as a revolutionary in his efforts to overthrow the Qing imperial government. For this purpose, he founded the Revolutionary Alliance in 1905. As leader of the Nationalist party in the 1910s and early 1920s, he struggled to combat warlordism and unite China. In 1923 he agreed to form an alliance with the Chinese Communist party and accepted aid and advisers from the Soviet Union. When he passed away in March 1925, the leadership of his party passed to Chiang Kaishek.

Wang Huiwu (1898–). Wang was born in Jiaxing, Zhejiang, to an impoverished school teacher and his illiterate wife. Wang Huiwu was educated at the Jiaxing Women's Normal School and the Hujun Academy for Girls. A May Fourth student activist, she established herself as a effective proponent of women's emancipation through her publication of articles in *Young China* in 1920. Moving to Shanghai, she rented a room in the house of Chen Duxiu, where she met and fell in love with Li Da. She oversaw the development of the first Communist women's program in Shanghai in 1921 and 1922, taking prime responsibility for running the Shanghai Pingmin Girls' School and editing *Funü sheng* (Women's Voice). She left Shanghai with Li Da in late 1922 for Hunan. Later they were divorced. After 1949 she worked for the Legal Committee of the Central Government.

Wang Yizhi (1901–1991). Wang was born in Zhijiang, Hunan, into a scholar-bureaucrat family. Her father went to study in Japan for many years just after her birth. When he decided upon his return to take a concubine, his wife left him. Wang was raised by her mother and sent to the Second Provincial Girls' Normal School in Taoyuan. Upon graduation she taught at the school founded by Xiang Jingyu in Xupu and then went to Shanghai with her former classmates Ding Ling and Wang Jianhong, where she enrolled at the Shanghai Pingmin Girls' School. She married Shi Cuntong, one of the founding members of the party, in 1922, and became the first woman to go through a formal admission process for entry into the Shanghai Communist organization in 1922. In 1925 she left Shi Cuntong and married Zhang Tailei. She went with him to Guangdong and became the editor of *Light*, the journal of the Guangdong Women's Emancipation Association, and later traveled to Wuhan. After Zhang Tailei was killed in the Canton Commune Uprising, she entered Communist underground work in Shanghai until her contact was arrested. She ceased party work for several years and then with her husband, Gong Yibin, went to Chongqing during World War II to work for the Chinese Communist party. After 1949 she was appointed principal of No. 101 Middle School in

Beijing and built it into one of the city's most prestigious schools until it was ravaged by the Cultural Revolution.

Xiang Jingyu (1895–1928). Xiang was born in Xupu, Hunan, to a merchant family. The ninth daughter, she was well educated, graduating from Zhounan Girls' School in 1915. She ran her own girls' school in Xupu for a few years before being swept up in the May Fourth activities in Changsha. She joined the New Citizen's Society and organized women to travel to France to participate in the work-study movement. Leaving for France in December 1919, she married Cai Hesen and became involved in radical politics. After Cai Hesen was expelled from France for his involvement in student protests, she returned to Shanghai in late 1921 and joined the Chinese Communist party. At the second party congress in July 1922 she was named director of the Women's Bureau and devoted herself full time to party work, sending her two children back to Hunan to the care of her mother-in-law, Ge Jianhao. She joined the Nationalist party in 1924 and served as the head of its Women's Movement Committee and editor of its publication *Women's Weekly*. In the fall of 1925 she was sent to Moscow to study and separated from Cai Hesen. Returning to China in 1927, she stayed in Wuhan after the collapse of the left-wing government, where she edited *Yangzi News*. She was arrested in March 1928 and executed on May 1, 1928, in Wuhan at the age of thirty-three.

Yang Zhihua (1900–1973). Yang was born in Xiaoshan, Zhejiang, into a landlord family. In 1917 she entered the Hangzhou Girls' Normal School and participated in the May Fourth protests in 1919. After graduation, she entered into a marriage her parents had arranged with Shen Jianlong, the son of Shen Xuanlu, a member of the Nationalist party. Shen Xuanlu greatly influenced his daughter-in-law by involving her in *Weekly Review*, a Nationalist journal he had established in Shanghai, and in an experimental peasant school he founded near the family homestead in Yaqian. In 1924 she joined the Chinese Communist party, divorced her husband, and married Qu Qiubai, whom she had met while a student at Shanghai University. In October 1925 she became acting director of the Women's Bureau when Xiang Jingyu was removed and was officially confirmed in this position at the fifth congress in May 1927. She also served as editor of *Chinese Women*, the organ of the Shanghai All-Women's Association. Much of the next fifteen years was spent in the Soviet Union. On her way back to China in 1941 she was arrested in Xinjiang and imprisoned for the remainder of the war years. Afterwards she went to Yan'an and then settled in Beijing with the establishment of the People's Republic of China. She was appointed minister of the Women's Bureau of the All-China Workers Union and director of the International Section of the All-China Women's Federation.

Zhong Fuguang (1903–). Zhong came from an impoverished landlord family in Jiangjin, Sichuan. She was educated at the Second Provincial Girls' Normal Institute, where she was exposed to Communist influences. With the encouragement of a Beijing Communist organizer, Deng Zhongxia, she and some classmates launched a successful student movement in their school to remove the principal. She enrolled in Shanghai University in 1923 and the next year joined the Chinese Communist party. She served primarily as a women's activist in Shanghai until late 1926, where her most responsible post was as head of the Shanghai All-Women's Association, and then she went to Wuhan with her husband, Shi Cuntong, to become an instructor for the women students at the Wuhan Central Military and Political Institute. After 1927 she worked as a translator, educator, and editor. After 1949 she held successive posts as vice-secretary of the Labor Academy and of the Beijing Economics Academy.

Notes

Introduction

1. For a discussion of the relevant source materials, particularly those made available through the efforts of the All-China Women's Federation, see Gilmartin, "Recent Developments in Research about Women in the PRC," pp. 57–64.

2. For an illuminating discussion of gender, see Scott, "Gender: A Useful Category of Historical Analysis," pp. 1053–75.

3. Actually for most of the period, this body was known as the Central Executive Committee. It was at the fifth party congress in 1927 that the name Central Committee was formally adopted, and this name has continued to be used up to the present time.

4. By "traditional" I am referring to a set of prevailing cultural and social practices and norms existing in the late nineteenth and early twentieth centuries. The use of this word is not intended to imply that Chinese social customs remained static for centuries. In the view of May Fourth iconoclasts, these traditional customs were feudal.

5. According to one theorist, most modern social-change movements have involved tremendous contention over definitions of culture, particularly gender constructs. Moghadam, "Revolution, Culture, and Gender."

6. Teng, "Introduction, A Decade of Challenge," pp. 1–14.

7. Since the early 1970s, when the first studies on Chinese women's topics appeared, there has been a proliferation of excellent feminist scholarship, as evidenced by the articles recently published in Gilmartin, et al., *Engendering China: Women, Culture, and the State*. While acknowledging the contribution of many scholars in developing gender studies in the China field, I will cite just the pioneering monographs related to a gender analysis of the Chinese Communist party's march to power (1921–1949). They are Croll, *Feminism and Socialism in China*; Davin, *Woman-Work*; Johnson, *Women, the Family, and*

Peasant Revolution in China; Stranahan, *Yan'an Women and the Communist Party*; and Stacey, *Patriarchy and Socialist Revolution in China*.

8. See, for instance, Hartmann and Bridges, "The Unhappy Marriage of Marxism and Feminism," pp. 1–33; Quataert, *Reluctant Feminists*; Stites, *The Women's Liberation Movement in Russia*; and Vogel, "Questions on the Woman Question," pp. 39–59.

9. See, for instance, Leith, "Chinese Women in the Early Communist Movement," pp. 47–71; Witke, "Woman as Politician in China of the 1920s," pp. 33–43; Croll, *Feminism and Socialism in China*; and Johnson, *Women, the Family, and Peasant Revolution in China*, in particular chap. 3.

10. For discussions of these German and Russian variants of socialist feminism, see Quataert, *Reluctant Feminists*, and Clements, *Bolshevik Feminist*.

11. Catherine Gipoulon is the only scholar who has drawn attention to the feminist leanings of Xiang Jingyu. Gipoulon's work is based primarily on a collection of Xiang's writings and two biographies that were published in the early 1980s. Using these same materials, Andrea McElderry offers a somewhat different interpretation of Xiang Jingyu, revealing the extent to which the release of these new materials in the early post-Mao period still left many questions unanswered in the effort to untangle Xiang's ideas and life from the mounds of hagiographic literature created after her martyrdom in 1928. As I was fortunate to conduct my dissertation research in China and subsequently was also able to make use of evidence located in archives in Taiwan and Russia, my study is more comprehensive. Gipoulon, "Integrating the Feminist and Worker's Movement," pp. 29–41; Gipoulon, "Xiang Jingyu ou les ambiguïtés d'une carrière entre communisme et féminisme," pp. 101–31; and McElderry, "Woman Revolutionary: Xiang Jingyu," pp. 95–122.

12. Hobsbawm, *Nations and Nationalism Since 1780*, pp. 136, 148.

13. See especially Mohanty, Russo, and Torres, *Third World Women and the Politics of Feminism*; hooks, *Feminist Theory*; Jayawardena, *Feminism and Nationalism in the Third World*; and Kandiyoti, "Identity and Its Discontents: Women and the Nation."

14. Mohanty, "Cartographies of Struggle," pp. 3–4, 10.

15. Cott, *The Grounding of Modern Feminism*, pp. 3–10.

16. A small segment of the feminist women's movement of the 1920s to which some Communists did object was the *nüxing zhuyi* (literally the "ism" of females) movement. Tani Barlow has delved into the subtle differences between *nüxing* and *funü* (both translated as "woman") and argued that *nüxing* denoted a sexual biological essentialist woman, whereas *funü* was part of a nationalist discourse. To some Communist political radicals of the era, however, the difference was expressed in more concrete terms. For Mao Dun, a prominent Communist essayist and editor of the 1920s, women who identified themselves as *nüxing* feminists were unwilling to work with men or to allow their cause of eliminating women's oppression to be linked to political movements with other goals. (In this work, I have chosen to refer to the writer Shen Yanbing by his most famous pen name, Mao Dun.) Barlow, "Theorizing Woman," 132–60; and [Shen Yan] Bing [Mao Dun], "Suowei nüxing zhuyi de liang jiduanpai," pp. 1–2.

17. By "patriarchy" I mean a preindustrial social formation in which power is vested in the senior male members of a kinship, and property, residence, and descent proceed through the male lines. Although junior males and children were also subjected to patriarchal domination, women were subjected to a distinct form of subordination, including their restriction from access to public life.

18. For a discussion of the Nationalists' policy on women see Diamond, "Women Under Kuomintang Rule," especially pp. 8–18.

Part 1

1. The most comprehensive examination of the shortcomings of various socialist and communist parties in dealing with women's issues can be found in Kruks, Rapp, and Young, eds., *Promissory Notes*.

2. Hartmann and Bridges, "The Unhappy Marriage of Marxism and Feminism," pp. 1–33.

3. This feminist position is discussed more fully by Molyneaux, "Mobilization without Emancipation," p. 229.

4. Hunt, *Politics, Culture, and Class in the French Revolution*, p. 10.

5. Despite the claims of Zhang Shenfu, most scholars have concluded that the cell in Paris was not established until after the first party congress. See, for instance, van de Ven, *From Friend to Comrade*, p. 76.

Chapter 1

1. For pertinent discussions of the relationship of nationalism to the early Chinese Communist party as well as nationalism's general revolutionary impact on the political discourse of early-twentieth-century China, see Dirlik, *Anarchism in the Chinese Revolution*, chap. 2; Lin, *The Crisis of Chinese Consciousness*, pp. 59–62; and Meisner, *Li Ta-chao and the Origins of Chinese Marxism*.

2. Of the fifty-three members in the party at the time of the first congress in July 1921, all but two were men. Dirlik, *The Origins of Chinese Communism*, p. 156.

3. For a more in-depth treatment of these nationalist concerns framed within a modernist discourse, see Duara, "Knowledge and Power in the Discourse of Modernity," pp. 67–83; and Dirlik, *Anarchism in the Chinese Revolution*, chap. 2.

4. Many of the gender issues raised in the late nineteenth century had been discussed during the Ming (1368–1644) and Qing (1644–1911) dynasties by Chinese scholars, some of the most well known of whom were Li Ruzhen, Lu Kun, Mao Qiling, Yu Zhengxie, Yuan Mei, and Zhang Xuecheng. For a survey of the Western literature on this topic, see Ropp, "Women in Late Imperial China," pp. 347–83.

For a discussion of the modernist discourse in which nationalist thinkers around the turn of the century began to consider transforming the social status of Chinese women, see Beahan, "The Women's Movement and Nationalism in Late Ch'ing China," pp. 86–153.

5. For a discussion of Liang's ideas on women's emancipation, see Collins, "The New Woman," pp. 239–42.

There were other formulations linking the improvement in women's status and nationalism. Ren Baoluo, a contemporary of Liang, put this idea of the need for women's emancipation in slightly different terms when he wrote that the reason the country was deteriorating was that women were treated so badly. Like many adherents of the Confucian persuasion, he believed that the foundation of the country was the family, but in addition he stressed that the foundation of the family was Chinese women. While Ren's reasoning differed from that of Liang, his argument still boiled down to the fact that women had to receive better treatment if the nation was to survive. See his article in Li and Zhang, eds., *Jindai Zhongguo nüquan yundong shiliao, 1842–1911*, 1:415.

6. Zarrow, "He Zhen and Anarcho-Feminism in China," p. 799.

7. The appearance of modern Chinese feminism was more or less contemporaneous with the formation of an industrial working class and the development of formal political parties. Its origins as a social and political ideology had two distinct sources: indigenous and Western feminist intellectual currents. Many Western scholars have attributed great explanatory power to the primary role of Western influences in giving rise to modern Chinese feminism. However, they may have been unduly swayed by a general ethnocentric Western paradigm that views the major events in modern Chinese history as reactive to the Western impact. The vitality and intensity of modern Chinese feminism in the first decades of the twentieth century, particularly in the May Fourth Movement (1917–1921), perhaps can be better understood in historical terms by tracing its main origins to the appearance of indigenous feminist strains in both popular and elite culture from the Ming dynasty (1368–1644). Although further research is needed to substantiate such an interpretation, the work by Paul Ropp and others has been quite illuminating. For a discussion of early feminist strains in Chinese history, see Ropp, "The Seeds of Change"; Handlin, "Lü K'un's New Audience"; and Beahan, "The Women's Movement and Nationalism in Late Ch'ing China," pp. 11–32.

8. The specific content of Qiu Jin's and He Zhen's feminism is discussed in Rankin, "The Emergence of Women at the End of the Ch'ing"; and in Zarrow, "He Zhen and Anarcho-Feminism in China."

9. On the discussion of women's issues in this period, see Witke, "Transformation of Attitudes towards Women during the May Fourth Era of Modern China."

10. For a list and description of these periodicals, see Chow, *Research Guide to the May Fourth Movement*; and *Wusi shiqi qikan jieshao*.

11. For a fuller theoretical discussion of this process, see Duara, "Knowledge and Power in the Discourse of Modernity," p. 68.

12. The claim that Liu Bannong, who served on the editorial committee of *New Youth* magazine, invented the female ideograph for "ta" is widely accepted. However, some ambiguities still remain as to exactly when this happened. According to one author, Sima Changfeng, Bannong first used this ideograph in a poem written on September 4, 1920. An examination of several

pieces in *Funü zashi,* however, reveals that one article and two short stories published in its pages before that date used this ideograph. See Changfeng, *Xin Zhongguo wenxue shi,* pp. 89–91; [Shen] Yanbing, "Nüzi de juewu"; Shen Zemin, "Nüzi de juewu"; and Wang Jianhong, "Duyao."

13. Chen Dongyuan, *Zhongguo funü shenghuo shi,* pp. 336–37.

14. Cini, "Le 'Problème des femmes' dans *La nouvelle jeunesse,* 1915–1922," pp. 135–47.

15. Zhang Songnian [Zhang Shenfu], "Nüzi jiefang da budang," pp. 9–13. A full discussion of this essay can be found in Schwarcz, *Time for Telling Truth Is Running Out,* pp. 62–63. Her translation of the title of this article has been adopted in this text.

16. Schwarcz, *The Chinese Enlightenment,* pp. 114–16.

17. Examples of some recent scholarship on male discussions of women's issues in the Ming and Qing dynasties include Carlitz, "The Social Uses of Female Virtue in Late Ming Editions of *Lienü zhuan,*" pp. 117–48; Mann, "'Fuxue' [Women's Learning] by Zhang Xuecheng (1738–1801)," pp. 40–62; and McMahon, "A Case for Confucian Sexuality," pp. 32–55.

18. Chen Duxiu, "Kongzi zhi dao yu xiandai shenghuo," pp. 99–105.

19. Lin Yü-sheng, *The Crisis of Chinese Consciousness,* p. 67.

20. Yun, "Jiehun wenti zhi yanjiu"; and Yun, "Bo yang Xiaochun 'fei ertong gongyu,'" pp. 195–99, 321–26.

21. Witke, "Mao Tse-Tung, Women, and Suicide," pp. 7–31.

22. See, for instance, Mai, "Wo duiyu Zhao nüshi zisha de ganxiang."

23. Research on Miss Zhao's suicide was conducted by Charles Eric Rosenblum in Changsha and presented in a senior thesis entitled "The Last Lie nü, the First Feminist," pp. 1–6, 25–28.

24. Ibid., pp. 69–70.

25. Ibid., p. 104.

26. For a few examples of their writings in the May Fourth era, see Zhonghua quanguo funü lianhehui funü yundong lishi yanjiushi, *Wusi shiqi funü wenti wenxuan,* pp. 15–20, 32–34, 35–48, 64–67, and 78–79.

27. Deng Enming, "Jinan nüxiao de gaikuang," pp. 296–300.

28. For a discussion of women's issues in *New Tide,* see Schwarcz, *The Chinese Enlightenment,* pp. 114–16. For a list of articles in these publications, see *Wusi shiqi qikan jieshao,* 1:469–501, 755–67.

29. Strand, *Rickshaw Beijing,* p. 146.

30. van de Ven, *From Friend to Comrade,* p. 70. His citation for this information was "Beijing gongchanzhuyi xiaozu de baogao" [Report of the Beijing communist organization]. In Zhongyang Dang'anguan, ed., *Zhongguo Gongchandang di yici daibiao dahui dang'an ziliao,* p. 21.

31. Li Dazhao, for instance, published his articles "Geguo de funü canzheng yundong" and "Lixiang de jiating" in *Yishibao* on February 19, 1921, and December 19, 1921, respectively, under the pseudonym Shou Chang. Then under the same pseudonym he published "Xiandai de nüquan yundong" in the Shanghai *Minguo ribao* supplement *Funü pinglun.*

32. For a discussion of the activities of radicals in Shanghai in the early twentieth century see Rankin, *Early Chinese Revolutionaries.*

33. *New Youth* was founded on September 15, 1915, under the editorship

of Chen Duxiu. *Awakening* and *Women's Critic* were supplements of the Nationalist newspaper *Republican Daily* (Minguo ribao). *Awakening* was established on June 16, 1919, and edited by Shao Lizi; *Women's Critic* and *Women's Magazine* are discussed later in this chapter.

34. The first partial translation of Engels's work appeared in *Tianyi bao* [Natural justice] in 1907. During the May Fourth era, Yun Daiying translated sections of this work in *Dongfang zazhi* [Eastern miscellany]. The date of 1929 for the first complete translation of this work is given by Laszlo Ladany, *The Communist Party of China and Marxism*, p. 4. For a discussion of the overlap between the ideas of August Bebel and Friedrich Engels, see Meyer, "Marxism and the Women's Movement," pp. 96–99.

35. [Li] Hanjun, "Nüzi zenyang cai neng dedao jingli duli?" pp. 3–4.

36. Xiaofeng [Chen Wangdao], "Hun zhidu zui'e de beigan," p. 562; Chen Wangdao, "Xi Shangzhen nüshi zai shangbao guanli shangdiao shijian," pp. 1–2; [Shen Yan] Bing [Mao Dun], "Nüxing de zijue," p. 4; Pei Wei [Mao Dun], "Lian'ai yu zhenjie de guanxi"; Heming [Li Da], "Gaodi hui nannü shejiao de xinxiang yuan," pp. 3–4; [Shao] Lizi, "Nannü shejiao yu jiu lijiao"; [Shao] Lizi, "Jiushi hunzhi wenti de beiju"; Shen Zemin, "Sanjiao lian'ai de wenti"; [Shen] Xuanlu, "Taolun nannü tongxiao wenti"; [Xiao] Chunü, "Qudi nüxuesheng lihun wenti"; [Li] Hanjun, "Nannü shejiao yinggai zenyang jiejue?"

37. The name of Beijing Normal Women's College changed a number of times during the first decades of the twentieth century. For purposes of clarity, only one name is used in this text. For a discussion of of the development of this educational institution, including the various names it held in these years, see Yen-chu Sun, "Chinese National Higher Education for Women in the Context of Social Reform, 1919–1929: A Case Study."

"Regret for the Past" depicts the death of a "new woman" named Shijun who had left her family and moved in with her lover, only to find herself without any means of support once the romance failed. Lu Xun was the most eminent May Fourth writer to advocate women's economic independence. Other important writers who advocated this notion included Hu Shi, a Western-educated intellectual who was the most prominent promoter of pragmatism in China; Chen Youqin, an eminent scholar of classical literature; Gao Xian, a graduate of Tokyo University who worked at Commercial Press; Li Xiaofeng, a founder of the New Tide Society in Beijing who published extensively under the pseudonym of Y. D. in Shanghai feminist periodicals; and Wu Yu, the leading intellectual iconoclast critic of feudalism. See, for example, Hu Shi, "Nüzi wenti de kaiduan," p. 126; Chen Youqin, "Nüzi jingji duli zhi jichu," p. 55; Gao Xian, "Lian'ai duli," pp. 56–71; and Y. D. [Li Xiaofeng)] "Zhiye yu funü," pp. 8–11.

38. Shen Zemin, "Nüzi jinri de diwei," pp. 1–2.

39. Dirlik, *The Origins of Chinese Communism*, pp. 151–52, 209–16.

40. [Shi] Cuntong, "'Wuru nüzi renge' de jieshi"; [Shi] Cuntong, "Jiejue hunyin wenti de yijian"; [Shao] Lizi and [Shi] Cuntong, "'Feichu hunzhi' taolun zhong de liangfengxin"; and [Shao] Lizi and [Shi] Cuntong, "Feichu hunzhi wenti de taolun."

41. Dirlik, *The Origins of Chinese Communism*, p. 179.

42. For example, see Chen Duxiu, "Esu pian," 25–36.

43. For some of these important articles on women's issues, see Chen Duxiu, "Shanghai Housheng fang shachang Hunan nügong wenti"; Chen Duxiu, [Shen] Xuanlu and Chen Gongbo, "Lifa gonghui chengli yanshuoci"; Chen Duxiu, "Women weishenma yao tichang laodong yundong yu funü yundong"; Chen Duxiu, "Zhu Shanghai sisha nügong xiehui chenggong"; and Chen Duxiu, "Shanghai sichang nügong dabagong."

44. Such ideas can be found in the following essays: Chen Duxiu, "Funü wenti yu shehui zhuyi"; Chen Duxiu, "Pingmin jiaoyu"; and Chen Duxiu, "Shehui zhuyi duiyu jiaoyu he funü erfangmian de guanxi."

45. See, for instance, Quataert, *Reluctant Feminists*; and Stites, *The Women's Liberation Movement in Russia.*

46. Such ideas were expressed in several articles and official Communist documents disseminated under Chen's name. See, for instance, Chen Duxiu, "Funü wenti yu shehui zhuyi," pp. 80–83; and Chen Duxiu, "Zhongguo Gongchandang zhongyangju tonggao."

47. Shou Chang [Li Dazhao], "Xiandai de nüquan yundong," p. 2.

48. Geertz, "Ideology as a Cultural System," p. 218.

49. Wang Guangyuan, ed., *Chen Duxiu nianpu,* p. 40.

50. Feigon, *Chen Duxiu,* p. 53.

51. Chen Gongbo, "Chen Gongbo huiyi Zhongguo Gongchandang de chengli," 2:412–31.

52. Tang Dongqing, "Tang Dongqing de huiyi," 2:458.

53. Interestingly, Shi Pingmei was opposed to Gao Junyu's declaration of divorce because she was not willing, for the sake of her own happiness, to destroy another woman's happiness by breaking up a marriage. Hu Ping, "Gao Junyu yu Shi Pingmei," p. 26.

54. Chang Kuo-t'ao, *The Rise of the Chinese Communist Party,* 1:156–57.

55. An informative discussion of the recognition of the political uses of propaganda in late imperial and republican China can be found in Lee and Nathan, "The Beginnings of Mass Culture," pp. 360–68.

56. Liang Qichao quoted in Lee and Nathan, "The Beginnings of Mass Culture," p. 367.

57. Link, *Mandarin Ducks and Butterflies,* pp. 99–104; Liu Jucai, *Zhongguo jindai funü yundong shi,* pp. 109–16, 482.

58. For a brief account of the founding of the Guangzhou Communist nucleus, see Dirlik, *The Origins of Chinese Communism,* p. 212.

59. Link, *Mandarin Ducks and Butterflies,* p. 251.

60. For an analysis of the content and role of this magazine, see Nivard, "Histoire d'une revue feminine chinoise: *Funü zazhi* 1915–1931."

61. For a list of the twenty-three journals that were started between June 1919 and the end of 1920, see Zhonghua quanguo funü lianhehui, ed., *Zhongguo funü yundong shi,* pp. 115–16.

62. A partial version of *The Communist Manifesto* had first been published in 1906, according to Ladany, *The Communist Party of China and Marxism,* p. 4.

63. Jacqueline Nivard reports that most writers and readers for *Funü zazhi*

were also male. Nivard, "Histoire d'une revue feminine chinoise." One point of controversy about this journal surrounds the interpretation of the role of Hu Binxia, the senior female editor of *The Women's Magazine* from 1916 to 1919. Jacqueline Nivard has put forward the position that Hu Binxia was a figurehead editor and that many of the essays published under her name were in fact written by others. This view has been contested by Weili Ye, who argues that Hu was a quite visible and capable editor of this journal. Nivard, "Histoire d'une revue feminine chinoise," pp. 58–59; Weili Ye, "Crossing the Cultures." A brief discussion of Hu Binxia's life and writings can be found in Weili Ye, "'Nü Liuxuesheng,'" pp. 330–33. Figures on the circulations of these periodicals can be found in Nivard, "Histoire d'une revue feminine chinoise," p. 65; Lai, *Qishi nianlai Zhongguo baoye shi*, p. 95.

64. Link, *Mandarin Ducks*, p. 250; Nivard, "Histoire d'une revue féminine chinoise," p. 71.

65. The original article provoking the controversy was [Shen] Zemin, "Duiyu 'feichang yundong' shuo jijuhua," pp. 3–4. In addition to Han Ying's responses, which are discussed below, Yi Yi nüshi also submitted a strong criticism of the essay entitled "Wo duiyu lun nüzi diwei liangze tongxin de ganxiang," p. 1.

66. Han Ying, "Tongxin: Nüzi xianjin de diwei zenyang, p. 4; Han Ying, "Han Ying nüshi gei Zemin xiansheng de yuanxin ji fuxin," 1–2. I have been unable to ascertain the identity of Ms. Han Ying. The use of the name Han Ying may well have been intended to serve as a conscious identification with the famous women's rights activist of the 1911 era, Zhang Hanying (1872–1916), who was a member of the Revolutionary Alliance in Tokyo, organized a women's army unit in 1911, and participated in the doomed campaign to petition the new parliament in Nanjing to grant women equality in the new republic.

67. Shen Zemin, "Nüzi jinri de diwei," pp. 1–2.

68. I am grateful to Weili Ye for pointing out this contrast in these two special issues on divorce to me.

69. In fact, Chen Wangdao and Shen Yanbing [Mao Dun] published under many pseudonyms for this publication in order to mask the fact that they were the main writers for *Women's Critic* during its first few months. Writing under a pseudonym was common practice for the most prolific writers of the day, both Communist and non-Communist. Zhou Jianren, the brother of the eminent writer Lu Xun, disguised his prolific contributions to the women's journals of Shanghai by adopting at least five pen names.

Chapter 2

1. Chen Duxiu, "Funü wenti yu shehui zhuyi," pp 80–83. In order to maximize the distribution of this speech, it was also published in Shanghai in *Juewu*, February 14, 1921.

2. Accounts of Chen Duxiu's conversion to Marxism and his role in founding the party can be found in Dirlik, *The Origins of Chinese Commu-*

nism, pp. 160–61, 188–89, 195–201; Feigon, *Chen Duxiu*, pp. 137–65; and van de Ven, *From Friend to Comrade*, especially pp. 16–27, 61–62, 89.

3. Information about Wang Huiwu was obtained from the following sources: Wang Huiwi, interview; Wang Huiwu's writings in the 1920s; and Wang Huiwu, letter to author, spring 1988.

4. The Shanghai and Guangdong Federations of Women's Circles were established in 1919. The Zhejiang group was established in 1920, and the Hunan organization, in early 1921. For a discussion of these groups' leadership and activities, see Tan Sheying, *Zhongguo funü yundong shi*; and Liang Zhanmei, *Zhongguo funü douzheng shihua*.

5. Wu Zhimei achieved national prominence for her role in developing the Guangdong Federation of Women's Circles. She encountered much hostility not only for voting against the admission of concubines as members but also for her controversial decision to engage the group in suffrage activities. Despite these stressful moments, which were widely covered in the national press, this organization grew into the largest and most influential women's association in China during the early 1920s. Shanghai *Minguo ribao*, January 31, 1920 and January 1, 1920.

6. The scholarly literature is unclear about the exact number of women elected to the Hunan provincial assembly. According to one reputable source, Wu Jiaying, Wang Changguo, and Zhou Tianpu were successful in bids for seats in this elected body. Other sources just list Wang Changguo and/or Wu Jiaying. One reason for this confusion seems to be that at least seven women were also elected to county assemblies. Tan Sheying, *Zhongguo funü yundong shi*, p. 108; and Zhonghua quanguo funü lianhehui, ed., *Zhongguo funü yundong shi*, p. 126.

Seven hundred women reportedly demonstrated in Guangzhou on March 29, 1921, for the purpose of pressuring legislators considering a draft provincial constitution that contained an article granting women certain civil rights, including the right to be elected to office. On May 16, 1921, two thousand women demonstrated in Changsha against efforts in the provincial legislature to block suffrage for women. Zhonghua quanguo funü lianhehui, ed., *Zhongguo funü yundong shi*, pp. 125–26.

7. *Dagongbao*, April 25–27, 1921.

8. [Shen Yan] Bing [Mao Dun], "Gao Zhejiang yaoqiu shengxian jiaru san tiaojian de nüzi," pp. 2–3.

9. See, for instance, [Shen Yan] Bing [Mao Dun], "Suowei nüxing zhuyi de liang jiduanpai," p. 1; and [Shen Yan] Bing [Mao Dun], "Ailunkai xuesuo de taolun," p. 4.

10. Chen Duxiu, "Shanghai Housheng fang shachang Hunan nügong wenti."

11. "Gonghui xiaoxi," p. 4.

12. "Laodongjie xiaoxi," p. 3; "Gonghui xiaoxi," p. 4.

13. Ceng and Zhou, "Miao Boying," p. 132; and Schwarcz, *Time for Telling Truth Is Running Out*, p. 74.

14. Li Weihan's recollection that approximately twenty women joined the New Citizen's Study Society at this time is a slight exaggeration. My exam-

ination of the membership list revealed only fourteen women. This list can be found in Zhongguo geming bowuguan, ed., *Xinmin xuehui ziliao*, p. 405. Li Weihan's figure is cited by Levine, *The Found Generation*, p. 51.

15. Levine, *The Found Generation*, pp. 58–59.

16. This residence, ironically, had formerly been occupied by Dai Jitao, a leading member of the Nationalist party and a prominent socialist in Shanghai radical circles. Dirlik, *The Origins of Chinese Communism*, 161; Chang Kuo-t'ao, *The Rise of the Chinese Communist Party*, p. 98; and Wang Huiwu, interview.

17. This information about Gao Junman and Wang Huiwu comes from the following sources: Feigon, *Chen Duxiu*, p. 53; Wang Huiwu, interview; and Wang Huiwu, letter to author, spring 1988.

18. These women were members of a generation that was redefining the term "marriage" from a family-controlled institution to a relationship decided upon by the individuals directly involved. In many ways these relationships could be considered consensual unions. However, this generation used the word *jiehun* (marriage) to characterize these relationships in order to rebut the notion that they were out-of-wedlock relationships. The term "common-law marriage" is not very appropriate to use in this case either, as there was no state regulation of marriages in the 1920s. Only in the 1930s did the government begin to require the registration of marriages, and compliance has been only gradually achieved. Indeed, even in the 1990s, the government has had to exert much effort to insure that couples register their marriages.

19. For a detailed description of the Young China Study Society, see van de Ven, *From Friend to Comrade*, pp. 47–50; and Zhang Yunhou, et al, eds., *Wusi shiqi de shetuan*.

20. Wang Huiwu, "Zhongguo funü wenti," pp. 6–10.

21. Ibid., pp. 8–9.

22. He Ming (pseud.), "Shehui zhuyi de funü guan," pp. 1–2 and 2–3.

23. According to Wang Huiwu's letter of 1988, she and Li Da had a small wedding party. Thus, in many ways, she was his wife. However, in general, this word is quite problematic for a number of reasons. Many people who entered into a free-choice marriage opted to hold a party, as it made this radical custom a bit more socially acceptable. However, many people who did not hold some type of party in the early 1920s later considered that they were in fact "married" and readily refer to their common-law spouse as a husband or wife. Some members of Wang Huiwu's family, who lived much closer to Shanghai than Li Da's family, did attend the party. Wang Huiwu, letter to author, spring 1988.

24. [Shen] Yanbing, [Mao Dun] "Du *Shaonian Zhongguo* funü hao," pp. 1–4.

25. [Shen] Yanbing [Mao Dun], "Funü jingji duli taolun," p. 1.

26. Chang Kuo-t'ao, *The Rise of the Chinese Communist Party*, 1:149.

27. Xu Zhizhen, "Guanyu Yuyangli liuhao de huodong qingkuang," 2:59.

28. Zhang Guotao, "Huiyi Zhongguo Gongchandang 'yida' qianhou," 2:181.

29. Chen Duxiu and Li Da apparently approved the revised declaration and constitution of the reorganized Federation of Women's Circles. This

contention is made in the footnote accompanying the reprinting of the Federation of Women's Circles Declaration and Constitution in *Zhongguo funü yundong lishi ziliao*, p. 11.

30. Wang Huiwu, interview. Huang Zonghan (1876–1944) was originally named Xu Peixuan and later assumed the name Xu Zonghan. She was educated in Shanghai. She married at the age of eighteen and gave birth to two children. She adopted the surname Huang sometime after she became the revolutionary partner of Huang Xing, an important leader of the Revolutionary Alliance and close associate of Sun Yatsen. After Huang Xing's death in 1916, she continued to use the name of Huang Zonghan, perhaps because of the great prestige she derived from her association with Huang Xing's reputation as a leader of the 1911 Revolution. I have chosen to refer to her as Huang Zonghan in this work because she used that name at the time she chaired the Federation of Women's Circles in Shanghai. However, most biographers refer to her by her maiden name, Xu Zonghan.

31. Huang Xing's first wife was Liao Danru (1873–1939). The daughter of a scholar, she was reportedly illiterate and had bound feet. She was the mother of five of Huang's children, three sons and two daughters. Huang Zonghan also had two children during her five years of marriage to Huang Xing. Both women gave birth to children within a few months of each other. Mao Zhuqing, interview; Boorman and Howard, eds., *Biographical Dictionary of Republican China*, s.v. "Huang Xing."

32. An obituary for Li Guo, the chairwoman, was published in *Minguo ribao* (Shanghai), June 28, 1920, p. 10. The main source for the information that dissension existed among the editors is Tan Sheying, *Zhongguo funü yundong shi*, p. 95. According to Mao Zhuqing, a scholar of Revolutionary Alliance veteran Huang Xing, contact between Communist leaders in Shanghai and Huang Zonghan was initially established by Li Shucheng, the older brother of Communist Party member Li Hanjun. Li Shucheng was a Nationalist party member who served as a secretary for Huang Xing. Mao Zhuqing, interview.

33. The declaration and constitution of the group, which was renamed the Chinese Federation of Women's Circles of Shanghai (Shanghai Zhonghua nüjie lianhehui) was published in *Xin qingnian* 9, no. 5 (September 1, 1921): back cover.

34. "Zhongguo Gongchandang zhongyangju tonggao," p. 1.

35. Chen Tanqiu, "Funü yundong," pp. 5–7.

36. Xia Zhiyu, "Huiyi Li Hanjun laoshi," pp. 176–78; Yuan Puzhi, "Hubei shengwei taolunguo Li Hanjun huifu dangji de wenti," p. 183.

37. Information on Wang Jianhong comes from interviews with Wang Huiwu and Ding Ling. According to Ding Ling, who was a close friend of Wang Jianhong, Wang's ability to break with conventional gender roles was also greatly facilitated by her stepmother, who had little interest in restricting her activities. Wang Jianhong's father was Wang Boshan, a Sichuanese with strong Buddhist beliefs and close connections with the Nationalist party. He later became a member of the Western Hills Clique and became a good friend of Xie Chi, a powerful member of the right-wing faction of the Nationalists. Wang Huiwu, interview; and Ding Ling, interview.

38. The class terminology used in this article is based not on Marxism but on the language of the French Revolution. The terms "third" and "fourth class" might well be better rendered into English as "third estate" and "fourth estate." I.C.E., "Duiyu zhengzai gaige zhong de nüjie lianhehui xianyi," p. 1.

39. One important activist they attracted was Dai Yuben. For information on her, see Yuben, "Liubie Shanghai nüjie lianhehui," pp. 3–4; Zhongguo geming bowuguan, ed., *Xinmin xuehui ziliao*, p. 606; and Wang Huiwu, interview.

40. Xu Ruo, "Duiyu muqian funü yundong shuo jijuhua," p. 1.

41. [Wang] Huiwu, "Dui bagong nügongren shuo de hua," p. 3.

42. [Wang] Jianhong, "Jiezhi shengyu yu baochi lian'ai," pp. 1–2.

43. Ibid.

44. [Wang] Huiwu, "Wo duiyu chan'er xianzhi de yijian," p. 2.

45. For an account of the debate in the Social Democratic party in Germany, see Quataert, *Reluctant Feminists*, pp. 95–98.

46. [Shen Yan] Bing [Mao Dun], " 'Shengyu jiezhi' de shengjia," pp. 2–3.

47. Wang Huiwu, "Ru pingmin nüxiao shangke yixingqi zhi ganxiang," p. 3.

48. Wang Huiwu, "Zuzhi gongzuobu de wo jian," p. 1. An account of the Work-Study Mutual-Aid Corps can be found in Levine, *The Found Generation*, pp. 46–47.

49. Li Da, "Pingmin nüxue shi dao xin shehui de diyibu," pp. 2–3.

50. Chen Duxiu, "Pingmin jiaoyu," p. 1.

51. Chow Tse-tsung, *The May Fourth Movement*, pp. 93, 187.

52. Guo Chang [Shi Cuntong], "Wo duiyu pingmin nüxue de xiwang," p. 3.

53. The names of the teachers from the school have been compiled by Wang Huiwu, "Ru pingmin nüxiao shangke yixingqi zhi ganxiang," p. 3; Wang Huiwu and "Gexuexiao xiaoxi huizhi," p. 11.

54. Levine, *The Found Generation*, p. 47.

55. Pan, "Yige nüzi yin beipuo hun tuoli jiating," p. 4.

56. Wang Huiwu, interview.

57. Wang Yizhi, interview.

58. Snow, *Women in Modern China*, p. 204.

59. "Pudong nügong bagong de jieju," p. 2.

60. Ding Ling, interview. These views were also contained in some of her writings from the 1930s.

61. Snow, *Women in Modern China*, pp. 204–5; Ding Ling, interview.

62. Dirlik, *The Origins of Chinese Communism*, p. 219.

63. Zarrow, "He Zhen and Anarcho-Feminism in China," pp. 796–813.

64. See, for instance, "Chen Duxiu yu Ou Shengbai taolun wuzhengfu zhuyi de xin," 2:98–118. This debate between Chen Duxiu and Ou Shengbai has been summarized along with the general polemics between anarchists and Communists in Dirlik, *The Origins of Chinese Communism*, pp. 234–39.

65. For purposes of clarity, this office is called the Communist Women's Bureau in this book. However, the resolutions on women's issues passed at the second congress of the Chinese Communist party established a *funübu*

(women's bureau), and at the third congress (1923) the party established a "women's committee" (*funü weiyuanwei*). By the time of the fourth congress, which was convened in January 1925, the resolution on women's work referred to this office as the *funübu*. By 1926, official party documents were calling this office the *Zhongyang funübu* or Central Women's Bureau. Although no discussion of the evolution of the name of this office exists in the Communist party materials I studied, it is my assumption that its final name was influenced by the Nationalist party's counterpart office, which was created in 1924 at its first congress and called a *Zhongyang funübu* (which for purposes of clarity is translated as Central Women's Department in this book). *Zhongguo funü yundong lishi ziliao*, pp. 30, 68, 172, 280, 475.

66. *Zhongguo funü yundong lishi ziliao*, pp. 29–30.

67. Ch'en Kung-po [Chen Gongbo], *The Communist Movement in China*, p. 129.

68. *Zhongguo funü yundong lishi ziliao*, pp. 29–30.

69. Advertisement in *Juewu*, October 2, 1922, p. 3.

70. Wang Yizhi, interview. This assertion has been confirmed by my research on the subject, which is discussed more fully in chapter 4.

71. Feigon, *Chen Duxiu*, pp. 53, 85.

Chapter 3

1. In this respect, Xiang Jingyu was following in the footsteps of the anti-Manchu feminist revolutionary, Qiu Jin, who founded a small girls' school in Zhejiang when she returned to China from Japan in 1906. However, Qiu Jin was thirty-one years old at that time, whereas Xiang Jingyu was only twenty-one years old when she established her school. This action revealed Xiang's unusual strength of character and leadership qualities compared to those of other women Communists of her generation.

2. The biographical information on Xiang Jingyu was obtained from Dai, *Xiang Jingyu zhuan*; and Gu, "Xiang Jingyu."

3. The most comprehensive analysis of this issue is provided by Lewis, *Prologue to the Chinese Revolution*, pp. 1–2, 197–98.

4. The assertion that Xiang Ruiling was of Tujia minority extraction is made by Gu Ci in his article on Xiang Jingyu. It is based on research of local Xupu historians. Gu, "Xiang Jingyu," 6:58.

5. Esherick, *Reform and Revolution in China*, p. 37.

6. See, for instance, Esherick, *Reform and Revolution in China*, pp. 36–37; and Yang Shiji, *Xinhai geming qianhou Hunan shishi*, pp. 61–64. The account of this incident in this book is based primarily on these sources plus Dai Xugong's account.

7. This information, which has been recounted by Dai Xugong, was originally supplied by Xiang Xianlian, the fifth son of Xiang Ruiling. Cai Bo, son of Cai Hesen and Xiang Jingyu, interview.

Roxane Witke has noted how pervasive this "Mulan complex" was at the turn of the century among young Chinese women who sought to reject domestic female roles and emulate male careers. Examples of other women of Xiang's generation with political aspirations who embraced the Hua Mulan model include Wei Yu-hsiu and Liu Qingyang. This subject is discussed by Witke, "Transformation of Attitudes towards Women," pp. 45–49; and McElderry, "Woman Revolutionary," p. 96.

8. Dai Xugong and Gu Ci both portray Xiang Xianyue as having the most impact of all her siblings. Little attention is given in these biographies to the influence of her other brothers. Dai, *Xiang Jingyu zhuan*, pp. 4–6; and Gu, "Xiang Jingyu," pp. 58–59.

9. This information on Xiang Xianyue's impact on Xiang Jingyu on the eve of the 1911 Revolution comes from Gu, "Xiang Jingyu," p. 59.

Minbao was the organ of the Revolutionary Alliance, and *Xinmin congbao* was a journal founded in Japan in 1902 by Liang Qichao in order to advocate the constitutional monarchy.

10. Spence, *The Gate of Heavenly Peace*, p. 125.

11. Gu, "Xiang Jingyu," p. 61.

12. The account of the rationale behind her change of names can be found in Gu, "Xiang Jingyu," p. 61.

13. Xu Rihui, *Xiang Jingyu wenji*, p. 2.

14. Gu, "Xiang Jingyu," p. 65.

15. Dai, *Xiang Jingyu zhuan*, p. 27.

16. Gu, "Xiang Jingyu," p. 65.

17. McDonald, *The Urban Origins of Rural Revolution*, p. 94.

18. The New Citizen's Society was originally an elitist organization of twelve men which was very selective in its membership criteria and did not allow women to join until after the May Fourth Incident, at which time it admitted Xiang Jingyu and Tao Yi. By the end of 1919 at least four other women had joined, and in the following few years, fourteen more were inducted. They included Cai Chang, Li Qinwen, Zhou Dunxiang, Wei Yunchang, Lao Junzhan, and Xu Ying.

According to Dai Xugong, Xiang Jingyu's first distinct involvement with the New Citizen's Society was in the autumn of 1918, when she went to Beijing and attended French classes and other training sessions set up by the Franco-Chinese Society to prepare Hunanese students to go to France. At that time at least fifty other Hunanese were in Beijing for the same purpose, including Mao Zedong and Cai Hesen. Zhongguo geming bowuguan, *Xinmin xuehui ziliao*, pp. 3, 7. Dai, *Xiang Jingyu zhuan*, p. 33. Part of Dai's evidence for Xiang's activities in Beijing comes from a letter she wrote her family in January 1918.

19. Levine, *The Found Generation*, p. 142; Zhongguo geming bowuguan, *Xinmin xuehui ziliao*, p. 127.

20. Levine, *The Found Generation*, pp. 41, 49, 143; and John Kong-Cheong Leung, "The Chinese Work-Study Movement: The Social and Political Experience of Chinese Students and Student-Workers in France, 1913–1925," pp. 349, 331.

21. Scalapino, "The Evolution of a Young Revolutionary," pp. 49–56.

22. Levine, *The Found Generation*, p. 141.

23. The main evidence for Xiang Jingyu's trip to Beijing is provided by Dai Xugong, who based his account on a letter Xiang wrote to her family in January 1919 in which she mentioned how much she enjoyed her French classes and that she was interested in the part-time work project. Dai, *Xiang Jingyu zhuan*, p. 33; *Jinian Xiang Jingyu tongzhi yinyong jiuyi wushi zhounian*, p. 8; Dai, *Xiang Jingyu zhuan*, p. 164.

24. Dai, *Xiang Jingyu zhuan*, p. 39.

25. Snow, *Women in Modern China*, p. 236.

26. Levine, *The Found Generation*, p. 142.

27. Dai, *Xiang Jingyu zhuan*, p. 51.

28. Xiang Jingyu, "Nüzi jiefang yu gaizao de shangque," pp. 30–37, especially 33–34.

29. Wang Yizhi, "Xiang Jingyu tongzhi," p. 25.

30. Some sources indicate that Xiang Jingyu was selected to direct the Women's Bureau at the second congress, but others indicate that this happened at a session of the Central Committee soon after the congress. See Zhonghua quanguo funü lianhehui, ed., *Zhongguo funü yundong shi*, p. 147; and Gu, "Xiang Jingyu," p. 58.

31. Dai, *Xiang Jingyu zhuan*, p. 78.

32. Ibid., p. 81.

33. Started right after the second congress, this journal was intended to carry theoretical articles. Much effort was required to develop it into a major publication of the party. According to Ren Wuxiong, a historian working at the site of the first party congress in Shanghai, in an interview on February 2, 1983, the initial circulation was around one thousand. By 1925 it had reached seven thousand, and by 1927 it reportedly had climbed to fifty thousand. The last two figures were supplied by Harrison, *The Long March to Power*, p. 66.

34. Dai and Yao, "'Zhenyu' wei Xiang Jingyu biminghao," pp. 313–18.

35. Zhenyu, "Guohui duiyu zaizhi Zhongguo de jiuguo xie yue gu he taidu?"

36. The women leaders of the Women's Suffrage Association were Wang Xiaoying, Wan Pu, and Shi Shuqing. Two good sources on these developments are Liang Zhanmei, *Zhongguo funü douzheng shihua*, pp. 85–86; and Gao Shan, "Zhongguo de nüquan yundong," 2:110.

37. Zhou Min, interview.

38. The events of this meeting were reported in "Nüquan yundong de gefangmian," p. 3.

39. "Shanghai nüquan yundong tongmenghui qingyuanshu," pp. 63–64.

40. [Wang] Yizhi, "Zimeimei kuailai gan nüquan yundong ba," p. 1.

41. Ibid.

42. Chen Wangdao, "Kanle nüquan yundong tongmenghui xuanyan yihou," p. 1.

43. [Gao] Junyu, "Nüquan yundong zhe yingdang zhidao de," p. 65.

44. Li Dazhao, "Li Dazhao jun jiangyan nüquan yundong," pp. 143–45.

45. See, for instance, [Deng] Yingchao, "Zhang Sijing zhuan," pp. 155–61.

46. Both her biographers and her son attribute the authorship of this res-

olution to Xiang Jingyu. Moreover, Xu Rihui's compilation of her writings also notes that this document was drafted by her. Xu Rihui, *Xiang Jingyu wenji*, p. 216.

47. Cai Hesen, "Xiang Jingyu tongzhi zhuan," p. 2.

48. After Xiang Jingyu was removed from her post as director of the Communist Women's Bureau in mid-1925, Cai Hesen published an article in a party publication that was quite critical of the women's mobilization campaign. H. S. [Cai Hesen], "Funü yundong," pp. 453–56.

49. Harrison, *The Long March to Power*, pp. 37–38.

50. Representative examples of Chinese sources that stress Xiang Jingyu's strong support of the United Front policy include Gu, "Xiang Jingyu," p. 75; Xu Meikun, "Canjia Zhonggong 'Sanda,'" p. 44.

51. *Zhongguo funü yundong lishi ziliao*, p. 69.

52. "Funü zhoubao fakan ci," in *Wusi shiqi qikan jieshao*, 2:556–58.

53. This decision was announced in the first issue of *Women's Weekly* along with the information that another Shanghai women's journal, *Contemporary Women* (Xiandai funü), would also be discontinued. *Contemporary Women* was published by the Society on Research into the Woman Question (Funü wenti yanjiuhui), which had been founded in Shanghai in the early 1920s by a group of prominent intellectuals, mostly male, including Lu Xun's brothers Zhou Zuoren and Zhou Jianren; Xia Mianzun, who was a close friend of Li Shutong, the pioneer of modern music and drama in China; and Mao Dun. A list of the founding members was published in *Funü pinglun*, no. 52 (August 2, 1922): 4. For an account of the decision to discontinue these two publications as a part of the effort to launch *Funü zhoubao*, see "Funü zhoubao fakan ci," in *Wusi shiqi qikan jieshao*, 2:556–58.

54. See, for instance, Yang Zhihua nüshi, "Shejiao he lian'ai," p. 1; "Jiu lunli dixia de kelian ren," p. 4; and "Lilun wenti de wojian," p. 1.

55. Xu Rihui, *Xiang Jingyu wenji*, pp. 216–7.

56. Ibid., p. 125.

57. Ibid., p. 103.

58. Ibid., pp. 125, 111, 105.

59. Ibid., p. 130.

60. Ibid., p. 104.

61. [Xiang] Jingyu, "Shanghai nüquan yundong hui jinhou ying zhuyi de sanjianshi," pp. 1–2.

62. "Shanghai sichang nügong quanti bagong," *Chenbao*, August 9, 1922.

63. See, for instance, Shao Lizi, "Shanghai sichang nügong bagongji."

64. [Xiang] Jingyu, "Sichang nügong tuanjieqilai," p. 135; [Xiang] Jingyu, "Shanghai funü tuanti jiang lianhe yuanzhu sichang nügong," pp. 114–16; and [Xiang] Jingyu, "Jiu guniang fanle hezui!"

65. Xu Rihui, *Xiang Jingyu wenji*, pp. 90, 136–37.

66. McElderry, "Woman Revolutionary: Xiang Jingyu," pp. 112–13; and Gipoulon, "Xiang Jingyu ou les ambiguités d'une carrière entre communisme et féminisme," pp. 101–2.

67. Spence, *The Gate of Heavenly Peace*, p. 219.

68. [Xiang] Jingyu, "Zhongguo zuijin funü yundong," p. 92.

69. [Xiang] Jingyu, "Duiyu Nüqingnianhui quanguo dahui de ganxiang," p. 110.

70. Zhonghua quanguo funü lianhehui, *Zhongguo funü yundong shi*, p. 158; "Funü yundong xin zhuzhi," *Minguo ribao*, Shanghai, April 1, 1924. The figure of forty Communists in Shanghai joining the Nationalists at this time was given by Gu, "Xiang Jingyu," p. 76.

71. The files in the Nationalist Party Archives at Yangmingshan contain numerous directives signed by Xiang Jingyu, a daily sign-in list indicating that the members of this committee regularly came to this office, and a batch of materials gathered by various women's investigation teams looking into women's institutions in Shanghai. For instance, a serious attempt was made to collect the names and information on every girls' school in the city. Nationalist Party Archives, Taibei, files 435/262; 435/105; 435/110.

72. Tan Sheying, *Zhongguo funü yundong shi*, p. 144.

73. Zhonghua quanguo funü lianhehui, *Zhongguo funü yundong shi*, pp. 159–60; Liu Qingyang, "Qingyang de baogao," p. 192; Liu Wang Liming, *Zhongguo funü yundong*, pp. 2–3; and Wang Yizhi, interview.

74. Claude Cadart and Cheng Yingxiang, *L'Envol du Communisme en Chine*, p. 470.

75. See, for instance Xiang Jingyu, "Gao sichang laoku nütongbao"; and "Sichang nügong tuanjieqilai," *Funü zhoubao*, no. 14 (November 21, 1923).

76. Xiang Jingyu's decision to target silk workers was quite natural in light of the situation. They were quite militant, and had she been able to win over Mu Zhiying, it would have been a great coup. However, Elizabeth Perry has persuasively argued that the aristocracy of the labor force generally is more likely to respond to calls to strike over economic issues. Those at the bottom of the labor hierarchy, such as silk workers, seem to regard strikes as a luxury they can rarely afford. Thus, had Xiang concentrated her efforts from the start on the B.A.T. factories instead, she might have been able to cultivate a core of women members from the working class. Perry, *Shanghai on Strike*, p. 243.

77. The most complete set of extant copies of *The Women's Daily* can be found at the Nationalist Party Archives in Taiwan.

Chapter 4

1. This number is an approximation based on the total membership at the fourth party congress in January of 1925, which stood at 994. Generally female membership was running at around 10 percent of the total membership. We do have more precise figures for the third party Congress, when there were 37 women members, and in December of 1926, there were 1,892. Wang Jianying, ed., *Zhongguo Gongchandang zuzhishi ziliao huibian*, pp. 8, 17, 30, 33.

Of the twenty-eight women whose provincial origins can be identified, it seems significant that ten came from Hunan, more than from many other single province. The strong representation of Hunanese women in this group is yet one more indication of the conspicuous role that this province played in Chinese revolutionary history. In probing into the reasons why such a high percentage of early women Communists came from Hunan, strong explanatory power has been attributed to the special features of the province's political and economic environment, that were true for men as well. See for instance Lewis, *Prologue to the Chinese Revolution*.

2. For a fuller discussion of the historical process that produced this May Fourth generation of radicals and of some of the theoretical literature on the forging of generational differences, see Levine, *The Found Generation*, pp. 13–22.

3. Yang Zilie, *Zhang Guotao furen huiyilu*, p. 86.

4. Wang Yizhi, "Wusi shidai de yige nüzhong," p. 518.

5. Yang Zilie, *Zhang Guotao furen huiyilu*, pp. 7, 86, 90.

6. Zhong Fuguang, interviews.

7. Wilbur, "The Influence of the Past," p. 47.

8. Schwarcz, *Time for Telling Truth Is Running Out*, p. 70.

9. Based on interviews (1981–1983) with a number of women Communists, including Wang Yizhi, Wang Huiwu, Ding Ling, Ou Mengjue, and Zhong Fuguang, as well as on a survey of various memoirs.

10. Lu Xun, *Lu Xun: Selected Works*, 2:85–92.

11. Yu Youren was born in Sanyuan, Shaanxi, the son of a destitute farmer. He managed to gain a good education in local schools and passed the examination for the *juren* degree in 1904. Influenced by the rising anti-Manchu sentiment, he became a political dissident and published heavily in *Subao*, a revolutionary Shanghai journal. He met Sun Yatsen in Japan in 1906 and became an active member of the Revolutionary Alliance. After the 1911 Revolution, he served briefly as vice-minister of communications in the new Nanking government and then worked in publications until 1918. He served as the commander in chief of the National Pacification Army in the northwest for several years and then returned to Shanghai, where he resumed his friendship with Sun Yatsen and soon accepted the post of president of Shanghai University.

12. It was Li Dazhao who suggested to Yu Youren that Deng Zhongxia assume the important post of provost when he made a special trip to Shanghai in the spring of 1923. Thereafter, Deng brought in most of the other Communist teachers. Huang, Zhang, and Shi, "Shanghai daxue shilüe," pp. 104–5.

13. Spence, *The Gate of Heavenly Peace*, p. 147. One reason why Shanghai University developed so quickly is that it was converted from a previously existing school, the Southeast Special Higher Normal School (Dongnan gaodeng zhuanke shifan xuexiao) rather than created from a vacuum. For a history of the origins of the school and the process of its conversion, see Huang, Zhang, and Shi, "Shanghai daxue shilüe"; and Yeh Wen-hsin, *The Alienated Academy*, pp. 129–68.

14. Huang, Zhang, and Shi, "Shanghai daxue shilüe," p. 106.

15. Zhong Fuguang, interview.

16. Interviews with Qu Duyi and Li Xiaoyun, daughter and granddaughter

of Yang Zhihua. Unfortunately I could not find either the divorce or sub-sequent wedding announcement in *Minguo ribao* because that particular issue was not included in the volumes of the newspaper reprinted in 1981. Yang Zilie asserted in her memoirs that some Nationalist party members found Yang Zhihua's divorce and remarriage scandalous. Yang Zilie, *Zhang Guotao furen huiyilu*, p. 136.

17. Yang Zhihua, "Lilun wenti de wojian," p. 1.

18. Throughout her life, Ding Ling maintained that Wang Jianhong's death was due in large part to her sadness over the dissolution of her rela-tionship with Qu Qiubai caused by the interference of Yang Zhihua. As a re-sult, tremendous animosity existed between Ding Ling and Yang Zhihua for the rest of their lives. Some intimation of Ding Ling's feelings can be found in her article "Wo suo renshide Qu Qiubai tongzhi."

19. Yang Zhihua nüshi, "Shejiao he lian'ai," p. 1.

20. Feigon, *Chen Duxiu*, p. 53.

21. Cai Bo, interview; Dai, *Xiang Jingyu zhuan*, p. 75.

22. Cai Bo, interview.

23. Wang Jianying, *Zhongguo Gongchandang zuzhishi ziliao huibian*, p. 8.

24. Official sources agree that Liu Qingyang joined the Chinese Commu-nist party in 1921, becoming the second woman to do so. *Huaxia funü mingren cidian*, p. 276.

25. Schwarcz, *Time for Telling Truth Is Running Out*, p. 65.

26. Chang Kuo-t'ao, *The Rise of the Chinese Communist Party*, 1:113.

27. Wang Yizhi, interview.

28. Saich, *The Origins of the First United Front in China*, 1:180.

29. Gu, "Xiang Jingyu," p. 75; and Cadart and Yingxiang, *L'Envol du Communisme*, p. 365.

30. *Zhongguo funü yundong lishi ziliao*, pp. 68–69.

31. Ibid., pp. 279–81.

32. There is a great deal of ambiguity about Xiang Jingyu's status at these congresses. Her son, Cai Bo, reported that party historians are divided on this question. The most authoritative scholars, however, do not list her as a dele-gate. See, for instance, the list provided in Guangdong geming lishi bowu-guan, ed., *Zhongguo 'Sanda' ziliao*, p. 99. In Wang Jianying's study, her name was included among thirty some participants with the explanation that nine-teen had voting rights, ten had speaking rights, and ten were guests or had no formal status. Presumably Xiang Jingyu was in the latter category. Wang Jian-ying, ed., *Zhongguo Gongchandang zuzhishi ziliao huibian*, p. 17.

33. Wang Jianying, ed., *Zhongguo Gongchandang zuzhishi ziliao huibian*, p. 18; Guangdong geming lishi bowuguan, ed., *Zhongguo 'Sanda' ziliao*, p. 99; and Saich, *The Origins of the First United Front in China*, pp. 642–43.

34. Dai Xugong, "Zhongguo funü yundong de xianqu," p. 28; Cai Chang, "Mianhuai Xiang Jingyu tongzhi," p. 2.

35. Luo Zhanglong, "Luo Zhanglong tan Zhonggong 'Sanda' de qianhou qingkuang," p. 181.

36. Bao Huiseng, "Laoyuyangli," p. 32.

37. Wang Yizhi, interview.

38. Cadart and Yingxiang, *L'Envol du Communisme*, pp. 367–68. I am indebted to Vera Schwarcz for alerting me to this citation.

39. Wang Guangyuan, *Chen Duxiu nianpu*, pp. 6–23.

40. Zhao Zhang'an, et al., *Lao gemingjia de lian'ai, hunyin he jiating shenghuo*, pp. 30–36.

41. For example, Pu Qingquan, "Wo suo zhidao de Chen Duxiu," p. 369; Li Da, "Zhongguo Gongchandang chengli shiji de sixiang douzheng qingkuang," p. 53; Wang Huiwu, "Jiandang chuqi de yixie qingkuang," pp. 76–77.

42. Spence, *The Search for Modern China*, p. 316.

43. Feigon, *Chen Duxiu*, p. 53.

44. Zheng, "Wei aiqing er douzheng," pp. 81–87.

45. Schwarcz, *Time for Telling Truth Is Running Out*, p. 75.

46. Ibid., p. 65.

47. Luo Zhanglong, "Luo Zhanglong tan Zhonggong 'Sanda' de qianhou qingkuang," p. 181.

48. Wang Yizhi, interview.

49. Luo Zhanglong, "Luo Zhanglong tan Zhonggong 'Sanda' de qianhou qingkuang," pp. 180–81.

50. Although Deng Yingchao experienced one difficult pregnancy in 1927, she never had any children. Liu Qingyang started a family after she withdrew from politics in 1927; she was already in her midthirties.

Chapter 5

1. Throughout this text I refer to the youth organization of the Chinese Communist party as the Socialist Youth League, although in fact the name was changed in January 1925 to the Communist Youth League.

2. The Communist network at this school was begun by Hou Shaoqiu (1896–1927), who was a student at Nanyang Gongxue Zhongyuan during the May Fourth era. Later he became secretary of the Shanghai Student Association and then accepted a teaching post at Jingxian Girls' Middle School. Using the middle school as a base, he played a critical role in the development of the Chinese Communist party network in Shanghai schools. He was later joined at Jingxian by Wu Shuwu, the wife of Chen Wangdao. Xue and Tang, "Hou Shaoqiu," pp. 103–15.

3. [Shao] Lizi, "Songjiang Jingxian zhongxue de jingshen," p. 4.

4. Xiang Jingyu, "Zhongdeng yisheng nüxuesheng de dushu wenti."

5. Ibid.

6. Xiang Jingyu, "Zhili di'er nüshi xuechao zai nüzi jiaoyu gexin yundong shang de jiazhi," pp. 2–3.

7. [Xiang] Jingyu, "Duiyu genben gaige Beijing nüzi shifan daxue de yijian bing zhi Beijing nüzi shifan daxue quanti tongxue"; and [Xiang] Jingyu, "Duiyu Beijing nüshi daxue chao de ganyan."

8. Yen-chu Sun, "Chinese National Higher Education for Women in the Context of Social Reform," pp. 118, 133.

9. Ibid., p. 125.

10. Chen Shuyu, *Lu Xun yu nüshida xuesheng yundong*, p. 19.

11. Lu Xun, *Lu Xun: Selected Works*, 2:160.

12. Lung-kee Sun, "The Fin de Siecle Lu Xun," pp. 81–82. Sun cites Lu Xun, "Guafu zhuyi," 1:262–69; and "Nü xiaozhang de nannü de meng," 7:291.

13. For a discussion of the anti-Christian movement in Chinese schools, see Wasserstrom, *Student Protests in Twentieth-Century China*, pp. 46–49; and Ka-che Yip, *Religion, Nationalism, and Chinese Students*.

14. Lutz, *Chinese Politics and Christian Missions*, p. 139.

15. In the case of Yongjiang Girls' Middle School in Ningbo, for instance, the Communist teacher Yang Shoushi was very effective in reaching students. Xu Chengmei, interview.

16. Although she could not recall it in 1983, it is also likely that Xu Chengmei received copies of *Fei Jidujiao* (The Non-Christian), the main journal of the anti-Christian movement of 1924. It was coedited by two students in the sociology department of Shanghai University, and it featured articles by many Communists, including Cai Hesen. Wasserstrom, *Student Protests in Twentieth-Century China*, p. 48.

17. Xu Chengmei joined the Socialist Youth League along with Li Xiuqing and Zhang Saiying. In the fall of 1924, she was proposed for membership in the league by Zhang Qiuren and Pan Nianzhi, who also frequently attended the study sessions at Yang Shoushi's home. Zhang Saiying also went by the name of Zhang Yezhou. Xu Chengmei, interview.

18. Xu Chengmei specifically recalled the entry into the league of Fan Meiquan (also known as Fan Ying), Hu Zhiduo, Zou Huishan, Fan Boli, and Li Rongfang.

19. This committee was established in April of 1924 under the auspices of the Nationalist Women and Youth Department in Shanghai. *Minguo ribao*, Shanghai, April 1, 1924, p. 10.

20. [Xiang] Jingyu, "Minguo huiyi yu funü."

21. Ibid.

22. These women included Kang Tongbi, a daughter of Kang Youwei; Zhu Jianxia, the principal of Qinye Girls' Normal School and chairperson of the Shanghai Women's Rights League; and Xiong Dihua, chairperson of the Shanghai Women's Suffrage Association. *Minguo ribao*, Shanghai, November 28, 1924, p. 3; December 8, 1924, p. 10.

23. *Minguo ribao*, Shanghai, November 30, 1924, p. 3; December 4, 1924; December 9, 1924.

24. *Minguo ribao*, Shanghai, December 22, 1924; *Shenbao*, Shanghai, December 22, 1924.

25. Wang Liming founded the Chinese Women's Temperance Society soon after her return from a period of study in the United States. She was also involved with the Shanghai Women's Suffrage Association and a board member of the Shanghai YWCA. Following the practice of a number of Chinese women of her generation who had been educated in the West, she opted to take her husband's surname when she married and thereafter she was called Liu Wang Liming. Her work on the women's movement was published in 1933 under that name.

26. Xiang Jingyu, "Zai Shanghai nüjie guomin huiyi cuchenghui chengli dahuishang de jianghua."

27. *Minguo ribao*, Shanghai, July 20, 1925.

28. *Funü zhoubao*, no. 86 (May 10, 1925), p. 4; *Jingbao*, April 30, 1925.

29. In fact, Communist organizers used at least four variations of the name of this women's organization: *gejie funü lianhehui, funü lianhehui, funü jiefang xiehui*, and *funü xiehui*. The reasons for these variations seem to be connected to the predilections of the local organizers.

30. Honig, *Sisters and Strangers*, pp. 207–8.

31. "Duiyu zhigong yundong zhi jueyi," 1:291.

32. Xu Rihui, *Xiang Jingyu wenji*, p. 216–17. These views are also discussed in [Xiang] Jingyu, "Cong pingmin jiaoyu zhong huafen nüzi pingmin jiaoyu de wo jian," pp. 145–47.

33. They included Yang Longying, Lu Dinghua, Liu Yuegui, Liu Guibao, Wang Genying, Song Sanmei, and Lu Xiaomei. Dai, *Xiang Jingyu zhuan*, p. 97.

34. Most accounts of the strikes in the Japanese textile mills beginning in February 1925 do not closely examine the nature of the initial conflict. The most complete account is provided by Ono Kazuko, who relied upon Japanese sources, particularly Udaka Yasushi, *Shina rōdō mondai*. Ono, *Chinese Women in a Century of Revolution, 1850–1950*, p. 131.

35. Honig, *Sisters and Strangers*, pp. 203–9. For a discussion of the difficulties that radical organizers encountered from gangs, see Elizabeth Perry, *Shanghai on Strike*, pp. 74, 86–87, 109.

36. Rigby, *The May Thirtieth Movement*, pp. 29–30, 119.

37. Schwarcz, *The Chinese Enlightenment*, p. 148.

38. Jiang Jiaoshou, interview.

39. Shen Yanbing, "Baofengyu—Wuyue sanshiyi ri," 1:743–46.

40. Ye, *Ni Huanzhi*, p. 233.

41. Ibid., p. 232.

42. Spence, *The Gate of Heavenly Peace*, p. 190.

43. Ibid., p. 191.

44. Ono, *Chinese Women in a Century of Revolution, 1850–1950*, pp. 133–34.

45. Statements were published by the Nationalist party's Women's Movement Committee, the Shanghai University Women Students' Federation, the Shanghai All-Women's Federation, the Shanghai Women's Rights League, the Women's Committee for the Promotion of a National Assembly, and the Women's Political Association.

46. A discussion of the central role played by Shanghai University can be found in Wasserstrom, *Student Protests in Twentieth-Century China*, pp. 48–49, chap. 4. The estimate of fifty thousand students was provided by Rigby, *The May Thirtieth Movement*, p. 36. Throughout the spring of 1925, Shanghai Municipal Police were aware of the increased political role that the university was assuming. Shao Lizi, its acting president and a member of both the Chinese Communist party and Nationalist party, was arrested in February 1925 and opted to leave town soon afterwards. A few days after Shanghai was

engulfed with massive demonstrations and widespread strikes following the massacre on May 30, the foreign-run police force shut down Shanghai University and stationed American troops there to insure that its premises would no longer be used for directing and inflaming the public response. Radical organizers were able to circumvent the police actions by relocating Shanghai University to a working-class section of the city outside of the foreign enclaves and foreign police jurisdiction.

47. For a very insightful discussion of the imagery of blood that permeated the radical literature of this period, see Schwarcz, *The Chinese Enlightenment*, pp. 145, 153–57. For an elaboration on the proliferation of the imagery of blood in periodicals of this period as well as an interpretation of the dual meanings of *rexue* (hot blood) in the texts of the May Thirtieth period, see Wasserstrom, *Student Protests in Twentieth-Century China*, pp. 110–17.

48. During the May Fourth protests, even at the center of the tumult, women students faced many obstacles to participation in demonstrations. Kong Wenzhen, a member of the most distinguished Confucius-Kong family, had to crawl out under the locked gates of the Beijing Normal Women's College in order to join in the demonstrations. Kong, interview.

49. Jiang Jiaoshou, interview.

50. Nationalist Party Archives, Yangmingshan, file 446/22.

51. These teachers were Pan Nianshi, Jiang Benqing, Shi Yubai, Zhou Tianlu, and Zhao Jimeng. Xu Chengmei, *Fuyun shi ziliao.*

52. The other women students who joined the Chinese Communist party at this time were Zou Huishan, Fan Boli, and Li Rongfang. Xu Chengmei, "Huiyi wusa yundong," 22–34.

53. Shen Yibin was married to Xu Qian (1871–1940), who would assume a high position in the Wuhan government under Wang Jingwei in late 1926 and the first part of 1927. For further information on Shen Yibin and Xu Qian, see Boorman and Howard, eds., *Biographical Dictionary of Republican China*, 2:118–22.

54. *Shenbao*, June 6, 1925.

55. *Zhongguo funü*, no. 1 (December 30, 1925).

56. *Shenbao*, June 6, 1926; *Minyuo ribuo*, Shanghai, June 9, 1925.

57. "Da geming shiqi."

58. *Funü zhoubao*, no. 88 (May 5, 1924).

59. Perry, *Shanghai On Strike*, pp. 149–51.

60. Honig, *Sisters and Strangers*, pp. 203–6.

61. Yang Zilie, *Zhang Guotao furen huiyili*, p. 127.

62. *Shenbao*, June 27, 1926.

63. [Yang Zhihua], "Yijiu erliu nian Shanghai sichang nügong yundong zhong zhi ganxiang," p. 7.

64. See, for instance, the article by Qi, "Quanguo funü daibiao dahui de zhongyao," p. 1.

65. [Chen] Bilan, "Zhaoji quanguo funü daibiao zhi dahui zhongyao yiyi," pp. 1–3.

66. H. S. [Cai Hesen], "Funü yundong," p. 453.

67. Zhongguo quanguo funü lianhehui, ed., *Zhongguo funü yundong shi*, p. 194; Strand, *Rickshaw Beijing*, p. 183.

68. Wang Yaquan, interview.

69. Lu Xun, *Lu Xun: Selected Works*, 2:269–70, 272.

Chapter 6

1. For a fuller discussion of the expendability of women in traditional China as well as a conceptualization of lineages as a type of patricorporation, see Gates, "The Commoditization of Chinese Women," pp. 799–832.

2. Ono, *Chinese Women in a Century of Revolution, 1850–1950*, pp. 1–4; and Watson, "Girls' Houses and Working Women," pp. 24–44.

3. Foot binding was always less common in Guangdong than in the north. The Hakka are a Han people who were not indigenous to the region and have been treated as an ethnic minority by the Cantonese-speaking population (known locally as Punti) ever since they migrated south from central China many centuries ago.

4. Franke, *Roving through Southern China*, p. 227.

5. For a full consideration of this issue, see Watson, "Girls' Houses and Working Women."

6. Chen Han-seng, *Agrarian Problems in Southernmost China*, p. 104.

7. Smedley, *The Great Road*, p. 206.

8. For a discussion of the history of out-migration from Guangdong, see Ta Chen, *Emigrant Communities in South China*, pp. 263–71.

9. Hakka women from this province joined with their Guangxi neighbors to fight in the women's army, a force of more than ten thousand that was known for its ferocity in combat and for striking fear into the hearts of imperial (male) troops. Once the Taiping became successful on the battlefield, they initiated a series of radical gender policies, including issuing marriage licenses, giving women work in the public domain, discouraging arranged marriages, and prohibiting foot binding, polygamy, prostitution, and adultery. For an extensive discussion of the new gender codes of the Taiping Rebellion, see Ono, *Chinese Women in a Century of Revolution, 1850–1950*, pp. 5–22.

10. During the 1911 Revolution, women from this province formed their own battalions and fought in the revolutionary battles. Shortly thereafter, thirteen women entered the Guangdong Provincial Assembly. In the May Fourth era, Guangdong produced the most vigorous and path-breaking independent women's movement, which by the time of the National Revolution included approximately sixty different groups. For more complete discussion of the women's movement in Guangdong, see Tan Sheying, *Zhongguo funü yundong shi*, p. 106..

11. For a discussion of Bolshevik mobilization techniques in the 1920s, see Kenez, *The Birth of the Propaganda State*.

12. For a discussion of feminist ideals of the May Fourth era, see Witke, "Transformation of Attitudes towards Women during the May Fourth Era of Modern China," pp. 77–330; and Croll, *Feminism and Socialism in China*,

chap. 4. For a discussion of the impact of May Fourth ideas on Nationalist and Communist activists, see Lu Fangshang, *Geming zhi zaiqi*; and Gilmartin, "Gender in the Formation of the Chinese Communist Body Politic, 1920–1925," pp. 299–329.

13. For a discussion of the extent of Russian financing of the National Revolution, see Wilbur, *The Nationalist Revolution in China, 1923–1928*, pp. 40–42.

14. For an excellent discussion of the restrictions on public meetings and discourse in Beijing in this period, see Strand, *Rickshaw Beijing*.

15. For a discussion of this strike, see Chesneaux, *The Chinese Labor Movement, 1919–1927*, pp. 290–318.

16. Chesneaux, le Barbier, and Bergère, *China*, p. 157.

17. For a discussion of the socialist-feminist tradition, see Quataert, *Reluctant Feminists*; Stites, *The Women's Liberation Movement in Russia*; and Farnsworth, "Communist Feminism."

Communists pledged their general commitment to nationalism as an important immediate goal for China in a number of important documents, including the Sun-Joffe Declaration of 1923, the resolutions of the third party congress of the Chinese Communist party, and the resolutions of the Nationalist party congress in 1924.

18. Even though Clara Zetkin is credited with establishing this holiday among socialists in 1910, the exact date for celebrating International Women's Day differed in Europe and the United States for more than a decade. A specific date was finally set in 1922, when Lenin proclaimed it on March 8 in honor of the women workers whose demonstration had precipitated the Bolshevik Revolution. For an account of the reasons and variations in the celebration of this festival among socialists, see Boxer and Quataert, *Connecting Spheres*, pp. 199, 252.

19. "Guoji funü ri yu Zhongguo funü jiefang." Slogans of March 8 are found in Pi, *Zhongguo funü yundong*, p. 51. The number of participants at the March 8, 1926, celebrations was provided by [Yang] Zhihua, "Zhongguo sanba yundong shi," p. 23. The source for the number of people attending the March 8, 1927, rally is Croll, *Feminism and Socialism in China*, p. 124, citing as her source, I. Dean, "The Women's Movement in China," *Chinese Recorder* 58, no. 10 (1927): 658. General information on the festival can be found in Wenshi ziliao yanjiu weiyuanhui, ed., *Guangzhou wenshi ziliao*, no. 30.

20. "Guomindang de zuzhi," p. 2.

21. Vishnyakova-Akimova, *Two Years in Revolutionary China, 1925–1927*, pp. 208–9.

22. No text was deemed necessary, for instance, by the editors of *Funü shenghuo*, a publication of the Guangdong Women's Emancipation Association, when they ran Rosa Luxemburg's picture on the cover of their March 1, 1927, issue (no. 5) commemorating International Women's Day.

23. Wenshi ziliao yanjiu weiyuanhui, ed., *Guangdong wenshi ziliao*, no. 30, p. 243. Karl Liebknecht was a prominent leader of the German Spartakus League who was arrested along with Rosa Luxemburg on January 15, 1919, and killed soon after. For a detailed account of his political role and his violent

death, see Frölich, *Rosa Luxemburg*, pp. 297–300.

24. Wenshi ziliao yanjiu weiyuanhui, ed., *Guangdong wenshi ziliao*, no. 30, p. 101.

25. Gipoulon, *Qiu Jin, Pierres de l'oiseau Jingwei*, p. 9. In addition to the rhetorical emphasis placed on Qiu Jin in both the Nationalist and Communist press, her home in Shaoxing has been turned into a museum with much material highlighting her revolutionary activities.

26. Rankin, *Early Chinese Revolutionaries*, pp. 40–46; and Rankin, "The Emergence of Women at the End of the Ch'ing," p. 52.

27. *Minguo ribao*, Quangzhou, March 8, 1927.

28. Qiu Jin's decision to join the Restoration Society was most likely made for pragmatic reasons and was not a veiled criticism of Sun Yatsen. However, her involvement with Xu Xilin, a Restoration Society member who was well known for his repudiation of Sun Yatsen, in an uprising against the Manchu imperial government laid the basis for later assertions that she may have shared his feelings about Sun Yatsen. For a fuller discussion of Qiu Jin's political affiliations and the rivalry between the Restoration Society and the Revolutionary Alliance, see Rankin, *Early Chinese Revolutionaries*, pp. 108–12, 154–55, 210–11.

29. Qiu, *Qiu Jin zhuan*, p. 155.

30. Wilbur, *Sun Yatsen*, p. 280.

31. This pledge was embedded in the "First Party Congress Proclamation," which has been reprinted in *Shuangqing wenji*, 2:461.

32. For a discussion of Borodin's role in reorganizing the Nationalist party, see Wilbur, *Sun Yatsen*, pp. 8–9.

33. The assertion that she was the first woman to join the Revolutionary Alliance is made in her article "When I Learned How to Cook," pp. 133–43. It is also contained in the permanent exhibition of the Memorial Hall for Liao Zhongkai and He Xiangning (located at the site of the Peasant-Worker School in Guangzhou). Other women who joined at about the same time were Tang Chunying, Qiu Jin, Wu Yanan, Wu Ruonan, Lin Zongsu, Zhang Hanying, Zhang Zhaohan, and Liao Bingjun. Ultimately fifty-nine women joined this organization. Liu Jucai, *Zhongguo jindai funü yundong shi*, p. 283.

For an early example of He Xiangning's writings about the relationship of women's emancipation and nationalism, see He, "Jinggao wo tongbao dimei," p. 1.

34. He Xiangning [Ho Hsiang-ning], "When I Learned How to Cook," pp. 133–43.

35. Comintern Archives, collection 507, file 105, p. 87.

36. "Funü yundong xuzhi," p. 160. These figures are to some extent impressionistic, as was the slightly smaller number of 1.5 million women that He Xiangning gave in an interview with an American reporter, Anna Louise Strong, in 1927. Nevertheless, they are indicative of the massive number of women who were mobilized for the revolution. Strong, *China's Millions*, p. 115.

37. Zeng Xing was the first woman selected to be head of the Central Women's Department of the Nationalist party. At that time, she was the

principal of the Zhixin School in Guangzhou and also was a veteran member of the Tongmenghui who had studied in France and actually fought in the 1911 Revolution. When she resigned as head of the department in August, Liao Bingjun, a cousin of Liao Zhongkai, was selected, but in a very short time she too resigned. Zhonghua quanguo funü lianhehui, ed., *Zhongguo funü yundong shi*, pp. 159–60.

38. He, "Zhongguo Guomindang di'erci quanguo daibiao dahui zhongyang funübu funü yundong baogao," p. 503.

39. Comintern Archives, collection 507, list 2, file 69, p. 45.

40. Lu Jingqing, interview.

41. Zhonghua quanguo funü lianhehui, ed., *Zhongguo funü yundong shi*, p. 200.

42. [Deng] Yingchao, "Minguo shisi nian de funü yundong," pp. 6–12.

43. Zhonghua quanguo funü lianhehui, ed., *Zhongguo funü yundong shi*, p. 201.

44. For the complete text of Deng Yingchao's speech to the Congress, see "Deng Yingchao guanyu funü yundong de baogao," pp. 508–11.

45. See, for instance, [Deng] Yingchao, "Minguo shisi nian de funü yundong," p. 9.

46. Ibid.

47. Ibid., pp. 6–12.

48. Croll, *Feminism and Socialism in China*, pp. 124–25.

49. Snow, *Women in Modern China*, p. 99.

50. For a discussion of He Xiangning's role in establishing the People's Drama Society, see Wenshi ziliao yanjiu weiyuanhui, ed., *Guangdong wenshi ziliao*, no. 34, pp. 197–98.

51. "Di'erci guan Guomindang daibiao dahui funü yundong jueyi an," *Zhengzhi zhoubao*, pp. 105–9.

52. See, for instance, He, "Guomin geming shi funü weiyi de shenglu," pp. 285–86.

53. Xia, "Funü yundong he guomin geming," pp. 14–16.

54. The term *funü jiefang* came to be preferred during the May Fourth era over *nüquan* (women's rights), which had been widely used in the 1911 Revolution period. The former term signified a belief that much more was necessary for women to achieve emancipation from social constraints than just certain rights. In 1919 and 1920, various male feminists further publicized this term when they debated whether women could actually be liberated. See, for instance, Hu Shi, "Nüzi wenti de kaiduan"; Zhang Songnian [Zhang Shenfu], "Nüzi jiefang da budang."

The Guangxi mass women's associations in the Nationalist Revolution were closely connected with those in Guangdong. Hence, the decision to adopt the same name of the organization. This linkage was also made in the Communist Women's Bureau, which oversaw the women's movements in these two provinces as if they were one closely interconnected unit.

55. "Guangdong funü jiefang xiehui xuanyan ji gangling," pp. 395–97.

56. Galbiati, *P'eng P'ai*, p. 198.

57. "Zhonggong zhongyang funü weiyuanhui gongzuo baogao," p. 697.

58. Guangdong funü yundong lishi ziliao bianzuan weiyuanhui, ed., *Guangdong funü yundong shiliao, 1924–1927*, p. 171.

59. Ibid., p. 321.

60. Ibid. Later the program was formalized, the name of the school was changed to Laodong funü xuexiao, and Chen Tiejun became its head teacher.

61. "Deng Yingchao guanyu funü yundong de baogao," p. 510.

62. "Zhonggong zhongyang funü weiyuanhui gongzuo baogao," pp. 696–700.

63. Guangdong funü yundong lishi ziliao bianzuan weiyuanhui, ed., *Guangdong funü yundong shiliao*, p. 327.

64. For studies of these marriage practices, see Stockard, *Daughters of the Canton Delta*; Topley, "Marriage Resistance in Rural Kwangtung," pp. 67–88; and Watson, "Girls' Houses and Working Women," pp. 25–44.

65. Eng, "Luddism and Labor Protest Among Silk Artisans and Workers in Jiangnan and Guangdong, 1860–1930," p. 92.

66. Guangdong funü yundong lishi ziliao bianzuan weiyuanhui, ed., *Guangdong funü yundong shiliao*, pp. 173, 316.

67. They were Zhang Wei, Peng Keng, Chen Xin, Zhang Xing, Gao Yu, and Fang Shaoqiong. Ibid., p. 315.

68. The establishment of these associations was traced through the periodical literature, such as *Guangming, Funü zhi sheng, Guangzhou minguo ribao*, and clippings from various newspapers that were found in files at the Nationalist Party Archives at Yangmingshan, particularly files 447/47 and 474/47. This list is similar, but not identical, to that provided in Guangdong funü yundong lishi ziliao bianzuan weiyuanhui, ed., *Guangdong funü yundong shiliao*, pp. 195, 209.

69. Tan Zhushan, "Huishu funü de wenhua yu shenghuo diaocha," pp. 3–8.

70. Ibid.

71. I was not able to locate this journal while in Guangdong, but several articles have been republished in Guangdong funü yundong lishi ziliao bianzuan weiyuanhui, ed., *Guangdong funü yundong shiliao*, pp. 233, 235.

Ultimately the reaction against this organization was so strong that the local magistrate was able to install a more conservative administration under Cheng Zhixing. When students protested, the police were sent in to quell them.

72. *Huaxia funü mingren cidian*, p. 1075.

73. Liao Wang Editing Bureau, *Hongjun nüyingxiong zhuan*, pp. 55–56.

74. For a full account of social conditions and the struggle to establish a peasant association in Guangning in the mid-1920s, see Hofheinz, *The Broken Wave*, pp. 179–213.

75. "Zhonggong zhongyang funü weiyuanhui gongzuo baogao," p. 700.

76. Guangdong funü yundong lishi ziliao bianzuan weiyuanhui, ed., *Guangdong funü yundong shiliao*, pp. 330–31.

77. *Peng Pai zhuan*, p. 9; Hofheinz, *The Broken Wave*, p. 143; Galbiati, *P'eng P'ai*, p. 225.

78. Croll, *Feminism and Socialism*, p. 126.

79. P'eng P'ai, "Seeds of Peasant Revolution: Report on the Haifeng

Peasant Movement," p. 39. For a discussion of the female bond servant issue, see ibid., p. 310.

80. *Peng Pai wenji*, p. 119.

81. For a fuller discussion of Peng's role as director and teacher at the Peasant Movement Training Institute, see Galbiati, *P'eng P'ai*, pp. 240-48; and Hofheinz, *The Broken Wave*, pp. 85-86.

82. Hofheinz, *The Broken Wave*, p. 79.

83. Zhonghua quanguo funü lianhehui, ed., *Zhonghua nü yinglie*, p. 49.

84. *Peng Pai wenji*, p. 196.

85. Ibid.

86. Ibid., p. 98.

87. Ibid.

88. *Litou zhoubao*, nos. 17-18, p. 37.

89. Hofheinz, *The Broken Wave*, p. 97.

90. For instance, just in the one Southeast Asian colony of British Malaysia, Meixian immigrants numbered 218,139 in 1921 and 318,739 in 1931. Ta Chen, *Emigrant Communities in South China*, p. 269.

91. *Minguo ribao*, Guangzhou, August 25, 1926, p. 5.

92. *Peng Pai yanjiu shiliao*, pp. 33-34, 227-28.

93. Vishnyakova-Akimova, *Two Years in Revolutionary China*, p. 163.

94. Galbiati, *P'eng P'ai*, p. 205; *Peng Pai wenji*, p 329.

Chapter 7

1. For a discussion of women's military roles during the 1911 Revolution, see Ono, *Chinese Women in a Century of Revolution*, pp. 73-76.

2. According to Strong, *China's Millions*, p. 115, women did not take part in the fighting. However, other sources indicate that they did. See, for instance, Lo, *China's Revolution from the Inside*, p. 263.

3. *Huaxia funü mingren cidian*, p. 887.

4. Li Tsung-jen, *The Memoirs of Li Tsung-jen*, p. 167.

5. "Zuijin Hunan zhi zhengzhi qingkuang he dangwu qingkuang," pp. 11-14: Zhonghua quanguo funü lianhehui, ed., *Zhongguo funü yundong shi*, p. 217-18, 220.

6. "Zhonggong zhongyang funü weiyuanhui gongzuo baogao," p. 700.

7. "Women's Liberation in the Hunan Peasant Association," p. 40.

8. Hubeisheng funü lianhehui, eds., "Hubeisheng funü xiehui de zuzhi he huodong qingkuang," p. 13.

9. Although my citations are taken from contemporary sources, they were compiled uncritically from the numerous scattered accounts that appeared in the press and periodicals of that era. At this point in time, it is impossible to accurately assess the numbers of people involved in this mobilization campaign.

10. Erbaugh, "The Secret History of the Hakkas," p. 947.

11. Jordan, *The Northern Expedition*, pp. 204-5, 250.

12. Erbaugh, "The Secret History of the Hakkas," pp. 954-55.

13. Zhonghua quanquo funü lianhehui, ed., *Zhongguo funü yundong shi*, p. 216.

14. *Dagongbao*, August 1, 1926. It is noteworthy that her remarks on the subject of women's exclusion from combat roles in the National Revolutionary Army were a bit defensive, indicating that women were critical of this practice.

15. Jiang Guoren (1896–1985) was influenced as a student by Xu Deli before she joined the National Revolutionary Army. An educator, she participated in many Communist-sponsored activities, but she did not join the Chinese Communist party until 1945. Shao Zhenxiong (1905–1927), who had earlier been a member of the New Citizen's Study Society, joined the Chinese Communist party in 1925. For biographical accounts of Jiang, Shao, and Zhang Qiong (1901–1981), see *Huaxia funü mingren cidian*, pp. 528, 640, 805.

16. Among the most well known Hunanese women who joined the Chinese Communist party in its first years of existence were Xiang Jingyu, Yang Kaihui, Miao Boying, Xu Wenxuan, Zhang Qiong, and Mao Zejian. Zhonghua quanguo funü lianhehui, ed., *Zhongguo funü yundong shi*, p. 153. On the political culture of Hunan, see Lewis, *Prologue to the Chinese Revolution*.

17. Zhonghua quanguo funü lianhehui, ed., *Zhongguo funü yundong shi*, p. 217.

18. "Beifazhong gongzuo jingguo," pp. 796–98; *Funü yu fengxi junfa*, pp. 1–10; Strong, *China's Millions*, pp. 113, 115.

19. Pamphlet put out by the Liling Women's Association, 1927. I am indebted to Delia Davin for this source, which she acquired from the Revolutionary History Museum in Beijing.

20. *Funü yu fengxi junfa*, p. 18

21. Ibid., p. 4.

22. Jordan, *The Northern Expedition*, p. 234.

23. Lan, "Huiyi Hubeisheng funü xiehui jiqi huodong pianduan," p. 31.

24. Zhonghua quanguo funü lianhehui, ed., *Zhongguo funü yundong shi*, p. 217.

25. Lan, "Huiyi Hubeisheng funü xiehui jiqi huodong pianduan," p. 32.

26. Ibid., p. 33.

27. Lo, *China's Revolution*, pp. 265–66.

28. Vishnyakova-Akimova, *Two Years in Revolutionary China*, p. 274.

29. For a firsthand account of the experiences of the second contingent of Nationalist leaders in Nanchang, see ibid., pp. 261–74.

30. According to Israel Epstein, Song Qingling could not write in Chinese very well either. She preferred to write in English. Epstein, interview.

31. Seagrave, *The Soong Dynasty*, p. 238.

32. Epstein, *Woman in World History*, p. 163.

33. Lo, *China's Revolution*, p. 263.

34. They included Lu Jingqing, a graduate of the Beijing Normal Women's College, and Ren Xiali and Liu Tiansu, two graduates of the Women's Movement Institute in Guangzhou. For some sources on this newly recon-

stituted Central Women's Department, see Lu Jingqing, "Zai He Xiangning xiansheng shenbian," p. 202; and Liu Tiansu, "Liangshi cimu," pp. 172–88.

35. Zhonghua quanquo funü lianhehui, ed., *Zhongguo funü yundong shi*, p. 217.

36. Xiang Jingyu did not come to Wuhan until late April of 1927. Her participation in the Nationalist Central Women's Department was confirmed by Lu Jingqing in "Zai He Xiangning xiansheng shenbian" and in her interview.

37. Bennett, *On Her Own*; Strong, *China's Millions*; and Sheean, *Personal History*.

38. Sheean, *Personal History*, p. 217.

39. Chapman, *The Chinese Revolution, 1926–7*, p. 86.

40. *Minguo ribao*, Wuhan, March 7, 1927, p. 4.

41. Lo, *China's Revolution*, pp. 270–74.

42. Statements by Li Zheshi, the head of the Hubei Nationalist Women's Department and also a member of the Chinese Communist party, according to Lan, "Huiyi Hubeisheng funü xiehui jiqi huodong pianduan," p. 25.

43. Strong, *China's Millions*, p. 117; Croll, *Feminism and Socialism in China*, p. 136.

44. Xian, "Hubei quansheng funü yundong," p. 173. All these figures are impressionistic, but even if the figures are inflated quite a bit, there is no doubt that the women's associations in Hubei were much more vigorous and large than those in Shanghai or the northern regions of the country.

45. *Minguo ribao*, Wuhan, March 9, 1927.

46. Strong, *China's Millions*, p. 114.

47. Hubeisheng funü lianhehui, eds. "Hubeisheng funü xiehui de zuzhi he huodong qingkuang," p. 16. The proceedings of this meeting were also published in the *Minguo ribao*, Wuhan, January 16, 1927, and reprinted in *Zhongguo funü yundong lishi ziliao*, pp. 773–74.

48. Hubeisheng funü lianhehui, eds., "Hubeisheng funü xiehui de zuzhi he huodong qingkuang," pp. 12–13.

49. Ibid., p. 12.

50. *Minguo ribao*, Wuhan, May 28, 1927. Actual compliance was estimated by one source to be only 50 percent in Hankou and around 10 percent in the rural areas. Xian, "Hubei quansheng funü yundong," p. 189.

51. For a comprehensive discussion of the meeting, see Hubeisheng funü lianhehui, eds., "Hubeisheng funü xiehui de zuzhi he huodong qingkuang," pp. 9–13.

52. "Hubeisheng diyici funü daibiao dahui kaimu shengkuang," p. 766. Xian, "Hubei quansheng funü yundong," p. 174. Lo, *China's Revolution*, pp. 270–72.

53. Zhonghua quanguo funü lianhehui, ed., *Zhongguo funü yundong shi*, p. 234.

54. Ibid., pp. 235–36.

55. Stites, "The Russian Revolution and Women," p. 252.

56. Zhou Jianfei, "Dageming shiqi de Wuhan junfenxiao," p. 97.

57. "Zhongyang junzi zhengzhi xuexiao Wuhan fenxiao choubei jingguo gailue," p. 416.

58. Entries from her diary were first published in serial form in a newspaper and then as a book, *Congjun riji* (War diary), which also came out simultaneously in an English translation by Lin Yutang in 1928 as *Letters of a Chinese Amazon and War-time Essays*. Some selections from her diary also appeared under the title *Autobiography of a Chinese Girl*. In 1936 she published *Yige nübing de zijuan* (Autobiography of a woman soldier), which more recently bears the title *Girl Rebel*. Unfortunately these sources represent only a portion of what she originally committed to paper. In the confusion of those times, some of her notes were lost. During the Sino-Japanese War, Xie Bingying once again became involved in mobilizing women to help out with the wounded at the front. She went to Taiwan after the war where she became a professor of Chinese literature at Taiwan University.

59. Xie Bingying, *Autobiography of a Chinese Girl*, p. 100.

60. Lin Yutang, *Letters of a Chinese Amazon*, p. 41.

61. Ibid., p. 29.

62. For instance, Wang Jingyan (1905–1928) from Jiangxi was known for wearing men's clothes.

63. Lin Yutang, *Letters of a Chinese Amazon*, p. 42.

64. Ibid., p. 10.

65. Luo Fanggu, "Dageming shiqi Suixian de funü yundong," pp. 148–51.

66. The number of 32,486 is claimed for women's associations in twenty-three counties. Hubeisheng funü lianhehui, eds., "Hubeisheng funü xiehui de zuzhi he huodong qingkuang," p. 13. In addition, more than 30,000 women workers in Hubei were said to have joined the Communist-sponsored women's associations in Hubei. *Zhongguo funü yundong lishi ziliao*, pp. 696–700.

67. Strong, *China's Millions*, p. 124.

68. Lin Yutang, *Letters of a Chinese Amazon*, pp. 12–20.

69. Ibid., pp. 21–22.

70. For some examples of this type of case, see Hubeisheng funü lianhehui, eds., "Hubeisheng funü xiehui de zuzhi he huodong qingkuang," p. 16.

71. Ibid., p. 15.

72. Ibid., p. 125.

73. Luo Fanggu, "Dageming shiqi Suixian de funü yundong," p. 152.

74. Lin Yutang, *Letters of a Chinese Amazon*, p. 29.

75. Ibid., p. 38.

76. Ibid.

77. An example of such a case in the central Yangzi valley is provided by Croll, *Feminism and Socialism in China*, p. 245.

78. For a fuller discussion of this issue, see Lo, *China's Revolution*, pp. 244–45.

79. Hubeisheng funü lianhehui, eds., "Hubeisheng funü xiehui de zuzhi he huodong qingkuang," p. 13.

80. *Huaxia funü mingren cidian*, p. 640.

81. In addition, Wang Yazhong was selected as an alternate to the Central Committee. Notable by her absence in a top-ranking position was Xiang Jingyu, particularly because Cai Hesen featured prominently in the leadership of

this fifth party congress. Wang Jianying, *Zhongguo Gongchandang zuzhishi ziliao huibian*, pp. 59–60.

82. For examples of violent responses, see Croll, *Feminism and Socialism in China*, p. 245.

83. Ying, "Nüxuesheng weishenma buhan 'jiehun lihun juedui ziyou' de kouhao?" pp. 2–3.

84. For an excellent account of these events, see Perry, *Shanghai on Strike*, pp. 88–92.

85. Lo, *China's Revolution*, p. 259.

86. You Yi, "Henan funü zhuangkuang," pp. 18–21.

87. Hu Hua, ed., *Zhonggong dangshi renwu zhuan*, 39:239–41.

88. Su Qing nüshi, "Henan xin," *Zhongguo funü*, no. 9, p. 6. For a short account of Zhou Xiaopei, see *Huaxia funü mingren cidian*, p. 711.

89. *Zhongguo funü yundong lishi ziliao*, p. 796–97.

90. "Beifazhong gongzuo jingguo," pp. 797–98.

91. Strong, *China's Millions*, p. 115.

92. Ibid., p. 116.

93. Ibid., p. 106.

94. Seagrave, *The Soong Dynasty*, p. 232.

95. Lan, "Huiyi Hubeisheng funü xiehui jiqi huodong pianduan," pp. 30–36. According to Lan, these three culprits were women, whereas another article identifies Yi Fengchu as a man. Xian, "Hubei quansheng funü yundong," p. 189.

96. Seagrave, *The Soong Dynasty*, p. 244.

97. Hsu, *The Rise of Modern China*, p. 624.

98. Strong, *China's Millions*, p. 219.

99. Seagrave, *The Soong Dynasty*, p. 248.

100. Xie Bingying as quoted in Croll, *Feminism and Socialism in China*, pp. 149–50.

101. Zai Yizen, "Difficulties and Recent Tactics of the Hubei Peasant Movement," *Minguo ribao*, Wuhan June 12–13, 1927, as quoted in Isaacs, *The Tragedy of the Chinese Revolution*, p. 227.

102. Snow, *Women in Modern China*, p. 241.

103. *People's Tribune*, July 7, 1927, as cited in Harold R. Isaacs, *The Tragedy of the Chinese Revolution*, p. 227.

104. *Zhongyang ribao* (Central Daily), Shanghai, May 7, 1928, p. 5.

Conclusion and Consequences

1. For a full discussion on this confrontation on the floor of the legislature, see Collins, "The New Women," pp. 382–86.

2. Spence, *Gate of Heavenly Peace*, p. 123.

3. Lu Xun, *Lu Xun: Selected Works*, 3:46.

4. Leary, "Intellectual Orthodoxy, the Economy of Knowledge, and Debate Over Zhang Jingsheng's Sex Histories," pp. 110.

5. This episode soured Zhang Jingsheng on intellectual life in China. He

went back to his hometown in Raoping, Guangdong, where he worked as a local official and lived until his death in 1970. Interestingly, the Red Guards never realized his identity, so he was totally unscathed by the Cultural Revolution. *Xingshi* is still banned in China, but it is rumored to be housed in the rare book room at the Beijing Municipal Library.

6. For a discussion of this movement and other aspects of the Nationalist women's policy, see Diamond, "Women Under Kuomintang Rule: Variations on the Feminine Mystique," especially pp. 8–18.

7. Spence, *The Search for Modern China*, p. 416, citing Michael Lestz and Cheng Pei-kai, "Facism in China, 1925–1938: A Documentary Study," unpublished manuscript, pp. 372–73.

8. Fan Mingxin, *Zhongguo jindai fazhi shi*, p. 204.

9. Spence, *Gate of Heavenly Peace*, p. 267.

10. Davin, *Woman-Work*, p. 29; and Johnson, *Women, the Family, and Peasant Revolution in China*, p. 55.

11. "Sixth CCP Congress Resolution on the Women's Movement," pp. 229–32.

12. For an interesting discussion of some manifestations of these puritanical trends, see Davin, *Woman-Work*, p. 30.

13. Davin, *Women-Work*, p. 36.

Glossary

Bao Tianxiao 包天笑
Beijing nüzi shifan 北京女子師範
Biwen nüzhong 裨文女中
Bowen nüshu 博文女塾
Cai Biheng 蔡碧珩
Cai Chang 蔡暢
Cai Hesen 蔡和森
Cai Suping 蔡素萍
Cao Cao 曹操
Cao Kun 曹琨
Chen bao 晨報
Chen Bilan 陳碧蘭
Chen Duxiu 陳獨秀
Chen Gongbo 陳公博
Chen Gongpei 陳公培
Chen Jiongming 陳炯明
Chen Junqi 陳君起
Chen Tanqiu 陳潭秋
Chen Tiejun 陳鐵軍
Chen Wangdao 陳望道
Chen Yiseng 陳逸僧
Cheng Wanzhen 陳婉珍
Dagongbao 大公報
Dai Xugong 戴緒恭
Dai Yuben 戴毓本
Deng Yingchao 鄧穎超
Deng Zhongxia 鄧中夏
Ding Ling 丁玲
Dongfang zazhi 東方雜誌

Duan Qirui 段祺瑞
Fan Boli 范博理
Fan Meiquan (also 范美泉 (樊英)
known as Fan
Ying)
Fan Shoukang 范壽康
Fangzu 放足
Feng Yongshu 馮永叔
Feng Yuxiang 馮御香
Funü dangwu 婦女黨務
xunlianban 訓練班
Funü guomin 婦女國民會議
huiyi cucheng- 促進會
hui
Funü jiefang xie 婦女解放協會
hui
Funü pinglun 婦女評論
Funü sheng 婦女聲
Funü shibao 婦女時報
Funü weiyuanhui 婦女委員會
Funü wenti 婦女問題
Funü wenti yan- 婦女問題
jiuhui 研究會
Funü yundong 婦女運動
Funü zazhi 婦女雜誌
Funü zhisheng 婦女之聲
Gao Junman (also 高君曼
known as Gao (高君梅)
Junmei)

Gao Junyu	高君宇	Li Dazhao	李大釗
Gao Tianbo	高恬波	Li Guo	李果
Gao Yuhan	高語罕	Li Hanjun	李漢俊
Gaoji changliao	高級娼寮	Li Lisan	李立三
Gu Ci	谷茨	Li Rongfang	李榮芳
Gu Zhenghong	顧正紅	Li Shimin	李世民
Guangdong funü	廣東婦女解放	Li Shucheng	李書城
jiefang xiehui	協會	Li Xiaofeng	李曉峰
Guangdong nüjie	廣東女界聯合會	Li Xiuqing	李秀清
lianhehui		Li Xixian	李希賢
Guangdong nü-	廣東女權動	Li Yichun	李一純
quan yundong	大同盟	Li Zongren	李宗仁
datongmeng		Liang Qichao	梁啟超
Guangming	光明	Liao Bingjun	廖冰筠
Guanxi gejie	廣西各界婦女	Liao Zhongkai	廖仲愷
funü lianhehui	聯合會	*Lienü zhuan*	烈女傳
Guilin jiefang xie-	桂林解放協會	Liu Bannong	劉半農
hui		Liu Bei	劉備
Guo Chang	國昌	Liu Guibao	劉桂寶
(pseud. of Shi		Liu Hezhen	劉和珍
Cuntong)		Liu Qingyang	劉清揚
Guo Dejie	郭德潔	Liu Renjing	劉仁靜
Guomin huiyi	國民會議	Liu Tiansu	劉天素
He Xiangning	何香凝	Liu Yaxiong	劉亞雄
He Zizhen	賀子珍	Liu Yuchun	劉玉春
Hou Shaoqiu	侯紹裘	Liu Yuegui	劉月桂
Hu Shi	胡適	Lu Dinghua	陸定華
Hu Zhiduo	胡之多	Lu Jingqing	陸晶清
Hua Mulan	花木蘭	Lu Liang	盧亮
Huang Shaolan	黃紹蘭	Lu Xiaomei	陸小妹
Huang Xing	黃興	Lu Xun	魯迅
Huang Yi	黃頤	Luo Wengan	羅文干
Huang Zonghan	黃宗漢	Luo Zhanglong	羅章龍
(also known	（徐宗漢）	Mao Dun (pseud.	茅盾
as Xu Zong-		of Shen Yan-	（沈雁冰）
han)		bing)	
Hubei funü xiehui	湖北婦女協會	Mao Zedong	毛澤東
Jiang Benqing	江本青	Miao Boying	繆伯英
Jing Ke	荊珂	*Minguo ribao*	民國日報
Juewu	覺悟	Mu Zhiying	穆志英
Kang Tongbi	康同璧	Nanjing gejie funü	南京各界
Kang Tongwei	康同慰	lianhehui	婦女聯合會
Kang Youwei	康有為	Nüquan yundong	女權運動
Ke Qingshi	柯慶施	Nüquan yundong	女權運動
Kunwei nüzi	坤維女子中學	tongmenghui	同盟會
zhongxue		*Nüxue bao*	女學報
Laodong yu funü	勞動與婦女	Nüzi canzheng	女子參政
Li Da	李達	xiejinhui	協進會

Ou Mengjue	區夢覺	Tan Zhushan	譚竹山
Pan Nianzhi	潘念之	Tao Yi	陶毅
Pan Yun	潘筠	Tian Han	田漢
Peng Keng	彭鏗	Tianjin gejie funü	天津各界
Peng Pai	彭湃	lianhehui	婦女聯合會
Peng Shuzhi	彭述之	*Tianyi bao*	天義報
Pi Yishu	皮以書	Tongmenghui	同盟會
Pingmin jiaoyu	平民教育	Tujia	土家
Qian Xijun	錢希君	Wan Pu	萬璞
Qiming nüzhong	啟明女中	Wang Bihua	王碧華
Qiu Jin	秋瑾	Wang Changguo	王昌國
Qu Qiubai	瞿秋白	Wang Genying	王根英
Quanguo gejie	全國各界婦女	Wang Huiwu	王會悟
funü lianhehui	聯合會	Wang Jianhong	王劍虹
Shanghai gejie	上海各界	Wang Liming	王立明
funü lianhehui	聯合會	Wang Xiaoying	王孝英
Shanghai pingmin	上海平民女	Wang Yizhi	王一知
nüxuexiao	學校	Wen Yiduo	聞一多
Shanghai sisha nü-	上海絲紗	Wenmingtou	文明頭
gong xiehui	女工協會	Widow Xiao	蕭寡婦
Shao Lizi	邵力子	Wu Jiaying	吳家瑛
Shaonian zhong-	少年中國	Wu Peifu	吳佩孚
guo		Wu Shuwu	吳庶五
Shen Jianlong	沈劍龍	Wu Xianzhen	伍獻貞
Shen Xuanlu (also	沈玄廬	Wu Yu	吳虞
known as Shen	（沈定一）	Wu Zhimei	伍智梅
Dingyi)		(Chapter 1)	
Shen Yanbing	沈雁冰	Wu Zhimei	伍芝棡
Shen Yibin	沈儀彬	(Chapter 6)	
Shen Zemin	沈澤民	Wuchan jieji	無產階級
Shi Cuntong (also	施存統	Xia Zhixu	夏之栩
known as Shi	（施復亮）	Xiang Jingyu	向警予
Fuliang)		Xiang Junxian	向俊賢
Shi Pingmei	石評梅	Xiang Ruiling	向瑞齡
Shi Shuqing	石淑卿	Xiang Xianyue	向仙鉞
Shi Yubai	石羽白	Xianqi liangmu	賢妻良母
Shishi xinbao	時事新報	Xiaojie	小姐
Songjiang	松江	Xiaonü	孝女
Song Sanmei	宋三妹	Xiaoshan	肖山
Soong Qingling	宋慶齡	Xie Bingying	謝冰瑩
Sun Yatsen (also	孫逸仙	Xiling pai	西陵派
known as Sun	（孫中山）	*Xin chao*	新潮
Zhongshan)		Xin funü	新婦女
Suzhou funü lian-	蘇州婦女	*Xin qingnian*	新青年
hehui	聯合會	*Xingqi pinglun*	星期評論
Taitai	太太	*Xinmin congbao*	新民叢報
Tan Pingshan	譚平山	Xinmin xuehui	新民學會
Tan Xiasheng	譚夏聲	Xiong Dihua	熊棣華

Xiushen	修身	Yun Daiying	惲代英
Xu Bing	許冰	Zeng Guofan	曾國藩
Xu Chengmei	徐誠美	Zeng Xing	曾醒
(also known as	（徐鏡平）	Zhang Guotao	張國燾
Xu Jingping)		Zhang Hanying	張漢英
Xu Qian	徐謙	Zhang Huaide	張懷德
Xu Quanzhi	徐全直	Zhang Qiuren	張秋人
Yang Changji	楊昌濟	Zhang Renrui	張人瑞
Yang Dequn	楊德群	Zhang Saiying	張賽英
Yang Kaihui	楊開慧	Zhang Shenfu	張申府
Yang Liuqing	楊柳青	Zhang Shoubai	張守白
Yang Meishan	楊眉山	Zhang Tailei	張太雷
Yang Shoushi	楊守實	Zhang Zhujun	張竹君
Yang Yinyu	楊蔭榆	Zhao Jimeng	趙濟孟
Yang Zhihua	楊之華	Zhao nüshi	趙女士
Yaqian	衙前	Zhenyu	振宇
Ye Chucang	葉楚滄	Zhong Fuguang	鍾復光
Ye Shengtao	葉聖陶	Zhong Zhujun	鍾竹筠
Yeman	野蠻	Zhonghua funü	中華婦女
Yiban funü yun-	一般婦女運動	jiezhi xiehui	節制協會
dong		Zhou Changshou	周昌壽
Yishibao	益世報	Zhou Enlai	周恩來
You Xi	游曦	Zhou Fuhai	周佛海
Yu	虞	Zhou Min	周敏
Yu Manzhen	余曼貞	Zhou Wenyong	周文雍
Yu Youren	于右任	Zhou Xiaopei	周筱沛
yuan	元	Zhu De	朱德
Yuan Puzhi	袁溥之	Zhu Jianfan	朱劍凡
Yuan Shikai	袁世凱	Zhu Jianxia	朱劍霞
Yue Fei	岳飛	Zhu Yingru	朱英如
Yueyun zhongxue	岳雲中學	Zou Huishan	鄒慧珊

Bibliography

Bao Huiseng. "Laoyuyangli." *Dangshi ziliao* [Materials on party history], no. 1 (1980): 32.

Barlow, Tani. "Theorizing Women: Funü, Guojia, Jiating [Chinese Women, State, and Family]." *Genders*, no. 10 (Spring 1991): 132–60.

Beahan, Charlotte. "The Women's Movement and Nationalism in Late Ch'ing China." Ph.D. diss., Columbia University, 1976.

"Beifazhong gongzuo jingguo" [Course of work on the Northern Expedition]. *Minguo ribao*, Wuhan, June 19, 1927. Reprinted in *Zhongguo funü yundong lishi ziliao, 1921–1927*, pp. 796–98.

Bennett, Milly. *On Her Own: Journalistic Adventures from San Francisco to the Chinese Revolution, 1917–1927*. Edited and Annotated by A. Tom Grunfeld. Armonk, N.Y.: M. E. Sharpe, 1993.

Boorman, Howard L., and Richard C. Howard, eds. *Biographical Dictionary of Republican China*. 5 vols. New York: Columbia University Press, 1967–1971.

Boxer, Marilyn J., and Jean H. Quataert. *Connecting Spheres: Women in the Western World, 1500 to the Present*. New York: Oxford University Press, 1987.

Cadart, Claude, and Cheng Yingxiang. *L'Envol du Communisme en Chine: Mémoires de Peng Shuzhi* [The origins of communism in China: The memoirs of Peng Shuzhi]. Paris: Gallimard, 1983.

Cai Chang. "Mianhuai Xiang Jingyu tongzhi" [Recalling Comrade Xiang Jingyu]. *Jinian Xiang Jingyu tongzhi yingyong jiuyi wushi zhounian* [In memory of the fiftieth anniversary of the death of Comrade Xiang Jingyu]. Beijing: Renmin chubanshe, 1978.

Cai Hesen. "Xiang Jingyu tongzhi zhuan" [Biography of Comrade Xiang Jingyu]. 1928. In *Jindaishi yanjiu* [Studies in modern history], no. 4 (1982): 1–3.

Carlitz, Katherine. "The Social Uses of Female Virtue in Late Ming Editions of *Lienü zhuan*." *Late Imperial China* 12, no. 2 (December 1991): 117–48.

Ceng Changqiu and Zhou Jianchun. "Miao Boying." In *Zhonggong dangshi renwu zhuan* [Biographies of personages in Chinese Communist party history], edited by Hu Hua, pp. 132–46. Xi'an: Shaanxi Renmin Chubanshe, 1985.

Chang, Kuo-t'ao. *The Rise of the Chinese Communist Party, 1921–1927*. 2 vols. Lawrence: University Press of Kansas, 1971.

Chapman, Herbert Owen. *The Chinese Revolution, 1926–7: A Record of the Period under Communist Control as Seen from the Nationalist Capital, Hankow*. London: Constable & Co., 1928.

[Chen] Bilan. "Zhaoji quanguo funü daibiao zhi dahui zhongyao yiyi" [The significance of convening the national women's representative conference]. *Zhongguo funü*, nos. 16–17 (June 30, 1926): 1.

Chen Dongyuan. *Zhongguo funü shenghuo shi* [A history of the life of Chinese women]. Taibei: Taiwan Shangwu Yinshuguan, 1975.

Chen Duxiu. "Esu pian" [An essay on an evil custom]. *Anhui subao* 3 (May 15, 1904). Reprinted in Chen Tu-hsui, *Chen Duxiu wenzhang xuanbian* [Selected articles of Chen Duxiu], edited by Lin Maosheng, et al., pp. 25–36. Shanghai: Sanlian Shudian, 1984.

———. "Funü wenti yu shehui zhuyi" [The woman question and socialism]. *Guangdong chunbao* [Guangdong masses], January 31, 1921. Reprinted in Zhonghua quanguo funü lianhehui funü yundong lishi yanjiushi, ed., *Wusi shiqi funü wenti wenxuan*, pp. 80–83.

———. "Kongzi zhi dao yu xiandai shenghuo" [The Confucian doctrine and modern life]. *Xin qingnian* [New youth] 2, no. 4 (December 1, 1916). Reprinted in Zhonghua quanguo funü lianhehui funü yundong lishi yanjiushi, ed., *Wusi shiqi funü wenti wenxuan*, pp. 99–105.

———. "Pingmin jiaoyu" [Universal education]. *Funü sheng* [Women's voice], no. 6 (March 5, 1922): 1.

———. "Shanghai Housheng fang shachang Hunan nügong wenti" [The issue of Hunanese women workers in the Shanghai Housheng textile factory]. *Xin qingnian* 7, no. 6 (May 1, 1920).

———. "Shanghai sichang nügong dabagong" [The general strike by Shanghai women silk workers]. *Xiangdao zhoubao*, no. 70 (June 18–25, 1924).

———. "Shehui zhuyi duiyu jiaoyu he funü erfangmian de guanxi" [The relationship of socialism to the two issues of education and women]. *Juewu*, April 23, 1922.

———. "Women weishenma yao tichang laodong yundong yu funü yundong" [Why do we promote the labor movement and the women's movement?]. *Laodong yu funü*, no. 2 (February 20, 1921): 1.

———. "Zhongguo Gongchandang zhongyangju tonggao" [Circular of the Chinese Communist party's Central Bureau]. In *Zhongguo funü yundong lishi ziliao, 1921–1927*, p. 1.

———. "Zhu Shanghai sisha nügong xiehui chenggong" [To the success of the Shanghai women's silk and textile union]. *Xiangdao zhoubao*, no. 52 (January 20, 1924).

Chen Duxiu, [Shen] Xuanlu, and Chen Gongbo. "Lifa gonghui chengli yanshuoci" [An address to the inaugural conference of the hairdressers' union]. *Laodong yu funü*, no. 1 (Febuary 13, 1921).

"Chen Duxiu yu Ou Shengbai taolun wuzhengfu zhuyi de xin" [Letters between Chen Duxiu and Ou Shengbai discussing anarchism]. In *Zhonggong dangshi cankao ziliao*, 2:98–118.

Chen Gongbo. "Chen Gongbo huiyi Zhongguo Gongchandang de chengli" [Reminiscences of Chen Gongbo about the founding of the CCP]. *'Yida' qianhou*, 2:412–31.

Chen Han-seng. *Agrarian Problems in Southernmost China*. Shanghai: Kelley & Walsh, Limited, 1936.

Ch'en, Kung-po [Chen Gongbo]. *The Communist Movement in China*. New York: Octagon Books, 1966.

Chen Shuyu. *Lu Xun yu nüshida xueshenq yundong* [Lu Xun and the student movement at Beijing Normal Women's College]. Beijing: Renmin chubanshe, 1982.

Chen, Ta. *Emigrant Communities in South China: A Study of Overseas Migration and Its Influence on Standards of Living and Social Change*. New York: Institute of Pacific Relations, 1940.

Chen Tanqiu. "Funü yundong" [The women's movement]. *Wuhan xingqi pinglun* [Wuhan weekly review], no. 3 (November 19, 1921). Reprinted in *Zhongguo funü yundong lishi ziliao, 1921–1927*, pp. 5–7.

Chen Wangdao. "Kanle nüquan yundong tongmenghui xuanyan yihou" [After reading the proclamations of the Women's Rights League]. *Funu pinglun*, no. 63 (October 16, 1922): 1.

———. "Xi Shangzhen nüshi zai shangbao guanli shangdiao shijian" [The event of Ms. Xi Shangzhen's suicide in the office of the Commercial Press]. *Funü pinglun*, no. 59 (September 20, 1922): 1–2.

Chen Youqin. "Nüzi jingji duli zhi jichu" [The basis of women's economic independence]. *Funü zazhi* 10, no. 1 (1924): 51–58.

Chesneaux, Jean. *The Chinese Labor Movement, 1919–1927*. Stanford: Stanford University Press, 1968.

Chesneaux, Jean, Françoise le Barbier, and Marie-Claire Bergère. *China: From the 1911 Revolution to Liberation*. Translated by Paul Auster and Lydia Davis. New York: Pantheon Books, 1977.

Chow Tse-tsung. *The May Fourth Movement: Intellectual Revolution in Modern China*. Stanford: Stanford University Press, 1960.

———. *Research Guide to the May Fourth Movement: Intellectual Revolution in Modern China, 1915–1924*. Cambridge: Harvard University Press, 1963.

Cini, Francesca. "Le 'Problème des femmes' dans *La nouvelle jeunesse*, 1915–1922" [The "woman question" in *New Youth*, 1915–1922]. *Etudes Chinoises* 12 (spring, autumn 1986): 133–56.

Clements, Barbara Evans. *Bolshevik Feminist: The Life of Aleksandra Kollontai*. Bloomington: Indiana University Press, 1979.

Clifford, Nicholas R. *The Spoilt Children of Empire: Westerners in Shanghai and the Chinese Revolution of the 1920s*. Middlebury, Vermont: Middlebury College Press, 1991.

Collins, Leslie. "The New Women: A Psychohistorical Study of the Chinese

Feminist Movement from 1990 to present." Ph.D. diss., Yale University, 1976.

Comintern Archives. Collection 507 (Women's International Secretariat). Russian Centre for Preservation and Study of Records of Modern History.

Cott, Nancy F. *The Grounding of Modern Feminism*. New Haven: Yale University Press, 1987.

Croll, Elisabeth. *Feminism and Socialism in China*. New York: Schocken Books, 1978.

"Da geming shiqi: Guangzhou funü yundong pianduan." In Wenshi ziliao yanjiu weiyuanhui, ed., *Guangzhou wenshi ziliao*, vol. 30.

Dagongbao [Public Interest]. Changsha, 1917–1927.

Dai Xugong. *Xiang Jingyu zhuan* [A biography of Xiang Jingyu]. Beijing: Renmin Chubanshe, 1981.

————. "Zhongguo funü yundong de xianqu" [A pioneer in the Chinese women's movement]. *Zhonghua nü yinglie* (Chinese female heroines). Beijing: Renmin Chubanshe, 1981.

Dai Xugong and Yao Weidou. "'Zhenyu' wei Xiang Jingyu biminghao" ['Zhenyu' is a pseudonym of Xiang Jingyu], *Jindaishi yanjiu*, no. 4 (1982): 313–18.

Davin, Delia. *Woman-Work: Women and the Party in Revolutionary China*. Oxford: Oxford University Press, 1976.

Deng Enming. "Jinan nüxiao de gaikuang." *Lixin* [Encouraging the new] 1, no. 3 (January 15, 1921). Reprinted in Zhonghua quanguo funü lianhehui funü yundong lishi yanjiushi, comp., *Wusi shiqi funü wenti wenxuan*, pp. 296–300.

[Deng] Yingchao. "Minguo shisi nian de funü yundong" [The women's movement in 1925]. *Funü zhi sheng huikan*, n.d. (approximately early 1926), pp. 6–12.

————. "Zhang Sijing zhuan" [Biography of Zhang Sijing]. *Nüquan yundong tongmenghui Zhili zhibu tekan* [Special issue of the Zhili Women's Rights League], March 23, 1923. Reprinted in Zhonghua quanguo funü lianhehui funü yundong lishi yanjiushi, comp., *Zhongguo funü yundong lishi ziliao*, pp. 155–61.

"Deng Yingchao guanyu funü yundong de baogao" [Deng Yingchao's report on the women's movement]. *Guangdongsheng di'erci dangyuan daibiao dahui rikan* [Second Guangdong provincial party congress daily], no. 5 (December 29, 1926). Reprinted in *Zhongguo funü yundong lishi ziliao, 1921–1927*, pp. 508–11.

Diamond, Norma. "Women Under Kuomintang Rule: Variations on the Feminine Mystique." *Modern China* 1, no. 1 (January 1975): 3–45.

"Di'erci quan Guomindang daibiao dahui funü yundong jueyi an." *Zhengzhi zhoubao*, nos. 6–7. Reprinted in Guangdong funü yundong lishi ziliao bianzuan weiyuanhui, ed., *Guangdong funü yundong shiliao, 1924–1927*, pp. 105–9.

Ding Ling. "Wo suo renshide Qu Qiubai tongzhi" [The comrade Qu Qiu Bai I know]. *Wenhui zengkan* 2 (1980): 4–9.

Dirlik, Arif. *Anarchism in the Chinese Revolution.* Berkeley: University of California Press, 1991.

——. *The Origins of Chinese Communism.* New York: Oxford University Press, 1989.

Duara, Prasenjit. "Knowledge and Power in the Discourse of Modernity: The Campaigns against Popular Religion in Early Twentieth-Century China." *Journal of Asian Studies* 50, no. 1 (February 1991): 67–83.

"Duiyu zhigong yundong zhi jueyi" [Resolution on the labor movement]. In *Zhonggong dangshi cankao ziliao,* 1:291.

Eng, Robert Y. "Luddism and Labor Protest Among Silk Artisans and Workers in Jiangnan and Guangdong, 1860–1930." *Late Imperial China* 11, no. 2 (December 1990): 92.

Engels, Friedrich. *Origin of the Family, Private Property, and the State.* New York: International Publishers, 1972.

Epstein, Israel. *Woman in World History: Soong Ching Ling (Mme. Sun Yat-sen).* Beijing: New World Press, 1993.

Erbaugh, Mary S. "The Secret History of the Hakkas: The Chinese Revolution as a Hakka Enterprise." *China Quarterly,* no. 132 (December 1992): 937–68.

Esherick, Joseph. *Reform and Revolution in China: The 1911 Revolution in Hunan and Hubei.* Berkeley: University of California Press, 1976.

Fan Mingxin. *Zhongguo jindai fazhi shi* [A history of China's modern legal system]. Xian: Shaanxi Renmin Chubanshe, 1988.

Farnsworth, Beatrice. "Communist Feminism: Its Synthesis and Demise." In *Women, War and Revolution,* edited by Carol R. Berkin and Clara M. Lovett. New York: Holmes & Meier, 1980.

Feigon, Lee. *Chen Duxiu: Founder of the Chinese Communist Party.* Princeton: Princeton University Press, 1983.

"First Party Congress Proclamation." Reprinted in *Shuangqing Wenji,* 2:461. Beijing: Remin Chubanshe, 1985.

Franck, Harry Alverson. *Roving through Southern China.* New York: The Century Co., 1925.

Frölich, Paul. *Rosa Luxemburg: Her Life and Work.* New York: Monthly Review Press, 1972.

Funü pinglun [Women's critic]. Supplement of *Minguo ribao* [Republican daily]. Shanghai, 1921–1923.

Funü sheng [Women's voice]. Shanghai, 1921–1922.

Funü yu fengxi junfa. [Women and the Fengtian warlords]. Guomin geming-junzong silingbu zhengzhibu, 1927.

"Funü yundong xuzhi" [Information on the women's movement]. In Zhonghua quanguo funü lianhehui, ed., *Zhongguo funü yundong shi,* p. 160.

Funü zazhi [Women's magazine]. Shanghai, 1915–1931.

Funü zhi sheng [The voice of women]. Guangzhou, 1925–1927.

Funü zhoubao [Women's weekly]. Supplement of *Minguo ribao.* Shanghai, 1923–1926.

Galbiati, Fernando. *P'eng P'ai and the Hai-lu-feng Soviet*. Stanford: Stanford University Press, 1985.

[Gao] Junyu. "Nüquan yundong zhe yingdang zhidao de" [What those in the women's rights movement ought to know]. *Xiangdao zhou bao*, no. 8 (November 1922): 65.

Gao Shan. "Zhongguo de nüquan yundong" [The Chinese women's rights movement]. In *Funü yundong* [The women's movement]. Shanghai, 1923.

Gao Xian. "Lian'ai duli" [Independent love]. 1925. In *Zhongguo funü wenti taolunji* [Collection of discussions on the Chinese woman question], edited by Mei Sheng, 4:56–71. Shanghai: Xin Wenhua Chubanshe, 1934.

Gates, Hill. "The Commoditization of Chinese Women." *Signs* 44, no. 4 (1989): 799–832.

Geertz, Clifford. "Ideology as a Cultural System." In *The Interpretation of Cultures*, edited by Clifford Geertz. New York: Basic Books, 1973.

Gilmartin, Christina. "Gender in the Formation of the Chinese Communist Body Politic, 1920–1925." *Modern China* 19, no. 3 (July 1993): 299–329.

———. "Recent Developments in Research about Women in the PRC," *Republican China* 10, no. 1b (November 1984): 57–64.

Gilmartin, Christina, et al., eds. *Engendering China: Women, Culture, and the State*. Cambridge: Harvard University Press, 1994.

Gipoulon, Catherine. "Integrating the Feminist and Worker's Movement: The Case of Xiang Jungyu." *Republican China* 10, 1a (November 1984): 29–41.

———. *Qiu Jin, Pierres de l'oiseau Jingwei: Femme et révolutionnaire en Chine au XIX siècle*. Paris: des femmes, 1976.

———. "Xiang Jingyu ou les ambiguités d'une carrière entre communisme et féminisme." *Etudes Chinoises* 12 (spring/autumn 1986): 101–31.

"Gonghui xiaoxi" [Union news]. *Laodong zhoukan*, no. 14 (November 19, 1921): 4.

Gu Ci. "Xiang Jingyu." In *Zhongguo dangshi renwu zhuan* [Biographies of personages in Chinese Communist party history], edited by Hu Hua, 6:58–90. Xi'an: Shaanxi Renmin Chubanshe, 1982.

"Guangdong funü jiefang xiehui xuanyan ji gangling" [Proclamation and program of the Guangdong Women's Emancipation Association]. In *Zhongguo funü yundong lishi ziliao, 1921–1927*, pp. 395–97.

Guangdong funü yundong lishi ziliao bianzuan weiyuanhui, ed. *Guangdong funü yundong shiliao, 1924–1927*. Guangzhou: Hongqi, 1983.

Guangdong geming lishi bowuguan [Guangdong Museum of Revolutionary History], comp. *Zhongguo 'Sanda' ziliao* [Materials on the third congress of the Chinese Communist party]. Guangdong: Guangdong Renmin Chubanshe, 1985.

Guangming [Light]. Guangzhou, 1926–1927.

Guo Chang [Shi Cuntong]. "Wo duiyu Pingmin Nüxue de xiwang" [My hopes for the Pingmin Girls' School]. *Funü sheng*, no. 6 (March 6, 1922): 3.

"Guoji funü ri yu Zhongguo funü jiefang" [International women's day and Chinese women's emancipation]. *Minguo ribao*, Guangzhou, March 9, 1927, p. 2 of the supplement. Nationalist Party Archives, Yangmingshan, Taiwan.

"Guomindang de zuzhi" [The organization of the Nationalist party]. *Funü ribao* [Women's daily], Tianjin, March 1, 1924, p. 2.

Han Ying. "Han ying nüshi Zemin xiansheng de yuanxin ji fuxin" [The original letter Miss Han Ying wrote Mr. Zemin and his response]. *Funü pinglun*, no. 26 (February 1, 1922): 1–2.

————. "Tongxin: Nüzi xianjin de diwei zenyang" [Letter: What is the present status of contemporary women?]. *Funü pinglun*, no. 24 (January 11, 1922): 4.

Handlin, Joanna F. "Lü K'un's New Audience: The Influence of Women's Literacy on Sixteenth-Century Thought." In *Women in Chinese Society*, edited by Margery Wolfe and Roxane Witke. Stanford: Stanford University Press, 1975.

Harrison, James Pinckney. *The Long March to Power: A History of the Chinese Communist Party, 1921–1972*. New York: Praeger Publishers, 1972.

Hartmann, Heidi, and Amy Bridges. "The Unhappy Marriage of Marxism and Feminism." *Capital and Class*, no. 8 (summer 1979): 1–33.

He Guzhi. *Xiang Jingyu zhuan* [Biography of Xiang Jingyu]. Shanghai: Shanghai Renmin Chubanshe, 1990.

He Ming. See Li Da.

He Xiangning. "Guomin geming shi funü weiyi de shenglu" [National revolution is women's only way out]. *Funü zhisheng huikan*, May 31, 1926. Reprinted in *Zhongguo funü yundong lishi ziliao, 1921–1927*, pp. 285–86.

————. "Jinggao wo tongbao dimei" [A warning to my fellow sisters]. *Jiangsu*, no. 4 (June 1903): 1.

————. "Zhongguo Guomindang di'erci quanguo daibiao dahui zhongyang funübu funü yundong baogao" [Report of the Women's Department on the women's movement for the second congress of the Chinese Nationalist party]. In *Zhongguo funü yundong lishi ziliao, 1921–1927*, pp. 502–4.

He Xiangning [Ho Hsiang-ning]. "When I Learned How to Cook." In *Chinese Women through Chinese Eyes*, by Li Yu-ning. Armonk, New York: M. E. Sharpe, 1992.

Hobsbawm, E. J. *Nations and Nationalism Since 1780: Programme, Myth, Reality*. Cambridge, England, and New York: Cambridge University Press, 1990.

Hofheinz, Roy, Jr. *The Broken Wave: The Chinese Communist Peasant Movement, 1922–1928*. Cambridge: Harvard University Press, 1977.

Honig, Emily. *Sisters and Strangers: Women in the Shanghai Cotton Mills, 1919–1949*. Stanford: Stanford University Press, 1986.

hooks, bell. *Feminist Theory From Margin to Center*. Boston: South End Press, 1984.

H. S. [Cai Hesen]. "Funü yundong" [The women's movement]. *Zhongguo qingnian* 107 (March 13, 1926): 453–56.

Hsieh, Ping-ying. *Autobiography of a Chinese Girl*. Translated by Tsui Chi. New York: Routledge & K. Paul, 1943. Reprint, New York: Pandora, 1986.

Hsu, Immanuel. *The Rise of Modern China*. New York: Oxford University Press, 1970.

Hu Hua, ed. *Zhonggong dangshi renwu zhuan* [Biographies of personages in

the Chinese Communist party]. Vols. 1–55. Xian: Shaanxi Renmin Chubanshe, 1980–.

Hu Ping. "Gao Junyu yu Shi Pingmei" [Gao Junyu and Shi Pingmei]. *Taiyuan wenshi ziliao* [Taiyuan historical materials] 5 (December 1985): 25–34.

Hu Shi. "Nüzi wenti de kaiduan" [The starting point of the woman question]. *Funü zazhi* 8, no. 1 (1922): 125–28.

Huang Meizhen, Zhang Yun, and Shi Yuanhua. "Shanghai daxue shilüe" [A brief history of Shanghai University]. *Fudan daxue xuebao* [Fudan University Journal], no. 2 (1981): 104–9.

Huaxia funü mingren cidian [A dictionary of famous Chinese women]. Beijing: Huaxia Chubanshe, 1988.

"Hubeisheng diyici funü daibiao dahui kaimu shengkuang" [The grand occasion of the opening of the first women's representative meeting of Hubei province]. *Hankou minguo ribao*, March 9, 1927. Reprinted in *Zhongguo funü yundong shi ziliao, 1921–1927*, p. 766.

Hubeisheng funü lianhehui [Research Group of the Hubei Women's Association], eds. "Hubeisheng funü xiehui de zuzhi he huodong qingkuang" [The organization and activities of the Hubei Women's Association]. *Hubei funyun shi ziliao*, no. 1, (n.d.): 1–19.

Hunt, Lynn. *Politics, Culture, and Class in the French Revolution*. Berkeley: University of California Press, 1984.

I.C.E. "Duiyu zhengzai gaige zhong de nüjie lianhehui xianyi" [A suggestion for reforming the Federation of Women's Circles]. *Funü pinglun*, no. 16 (November 16, 1921): 1.

Isaacs, Harold R. *The Tragedy of the Chinese Revolution*. Stanford: Stanford University Press, 1961.

Jayawardena, Kumari. *Feminism and Nationalism in the Third World*. London and Totowa, N.J.: Zed Books, 1986.

Jinian Xiang Jingyu tongzhi yinyong jiuyi wushi zhounian [Commemoration of the fiftieth anniversary of the death of the heroine Xiang Jingyu]. Beijing: Renmin Chubanshe, 1978.

Johnson, Kay Ann. *Women, the Family, and Peasant Revolution in China*. Chicago: University of Chicago Press, 1983.

Johnstone, William. *The Shanghai Problem*. Stanford: Stanford University Press, 1937.

Jordan, Donald. *The Northern Expedition: China's National Revolution of 1926–1928*. Honolulu: University of Hawaii Press, 1976.

Juewu [Awakening]. Supplement of *Minguo ribao* [Republican daily]. Shanghai, 1919–1926.

Kandiyoti, Deniz. "Identity and Its Discontents: Women and the Nation." *Millennium: Journal of International Studies* 20, no. 3 (1991).

Kenez, Peter. *The Birth of the Propaganda State: Soviet Methods of Mass Mobilization, 1917–1929*. New York: Cambridge University Press, 1985.

Kruks, Sonia, Rayna Rapp, and Marilyn Young, eds., *Promissory Notes: Women in the Transition to Socialism*. New York: Monthly Review Press, 1989.

Ladany, Laszlo. *The Communist Party of China and Marxism, 1921–1985*. Stanford: Hoover Institution, 1985.

Lai Guanglin. *Qishi nianlai Zhongguo baoye shi* [A history of Chinese newspapers in the last seventy years]. Taipei: Zhongyang Ribao She, 1981.

Lan Shuwen. "Huiyi Hubeisheng funü xiehui jiqi huodong pianduan" [Some recollections of the Hubei Women's Association and its activities]. *Hubei fuyunshi ziliao* no. 2 (ca. 1985).

Laodong yu funü [Labor and Women]. Guangzhou, February–April 1921.

Laodong zhoukan [Labor weekly]. Shanghai, extant nos. 13–18, November 12, 1921–December 17, 1921.

"Laodongjie xiaoxi" [News in the labor world]. *Laodong zhoukan*, no. 13 (November 11, 1921): 3.

Leary, Charles L. "Intellectual Orthodoxy, the Economy of Knowledge, and Debate over Zhang Jingsheng's Sex Histories." *Republican China* 18 (April 1993): 99–137.

Lee, Leo Ou-fan, and Andrew J. Nathan. "The Beginnings of Mass Culture: Journalism and Fiction in the Late Ch'ing and Beyond." In *Popular Culture in Late Imperial China*, edited by David Johnson, Andrew J. Nathan, and Evelyn S. Rawski. Berkeley: University of California Press, 1985.

Leith, Suzette. "Chinese Women in the Early Communist Movement." In Marilyn B. Young, ed., *Women in China: Studies in Social Change and Feminism*, pp. 47–71.

Leung, John Kong-Cheong. "The Chinese Work-Study Movement: The Social and Political Experience of Chinese Students and Student Workers in France, 1913–1925." Ph.D. diss., Brown University, 1982.

Levine, Marilyn A. *The Found Generation: Chinese Communists in Europe During the Twenties*. Seattle: University of Washington Press, 1993.

Lewis, Charleton. *Prologue to the Chinese Revolution: The Transformation of Ideas and Institutions in Hunan Province, 1891–1907*. Cambridge, Mass.: East Asian Research Center, Harvard University; distributed by Harvard University Press, 1976.

Li Da. "Pingmin nüxue shi dao xin shehui de diyibu" [The Shanghai Pingmin Girls' School is the first step to a new society]. *Funü sheng*, no. 6 (March 5, 1921): 2–3.

———. "Zhongguo Gongchandang chengli shiji de sixiang douzheng qingkuang" [Ideological struggle during the period of the founding of the Chinese Communist party]. *'Yida' qianhou*, 2:50–55.

Li Da [He Ming]. "Gaodi hui nannü shejiao de xinxiang yuan" [An admonition to modern-style men who denigrate social contact between the sexes]. *Funü pinglun*, no. 7 (September 14, 1921): 3–4.

———. "Shehui zhuyi de funü guan" [A socialist view of women]. *Funü pinglun*, nos. 10–11 (October 5 and October 12, 1921): 1–2, 2–3.

Li Dazhao. "Geguo de funü canzheng yundong" [The women's suffrage movement in various countries]. *Yishibao*, February 19, 1921.

———. "Li Dazhao jun jiangyan nüquan yundong" [Mr. Li Dazhao speaks to the women's rights movement]. *Jiangsheng rikan* [Voice of the Yangtze Daily], February 2, 1923. *Zhongguo funü yundong lishi ziliao*, pp. 143–45.

————. "Lixiang de jiating" [Ideal family]. *Yishibao*, December 19, 1921.

————. "Xiandai de nüquan yundong" [The present-day feminist movement]. *Funü pinglun*, no. 25 (January 18, 1922): 1–2.

[Li] Hanjun. "Nannü shejiao yinggai zenyang jiejue?" [How to solve the dilemma of social contact between men and women]. *Funü pinglun*, no. 7 (September 14, 1921): 2–3.

————. "Nüzi zenyang cai neng dedao jingji duli?" [How can women achieve economic independence?] *Funü pinglun*, no. 3 (August 17, 1921): 3–4.

Li Tsung-jen. *The Memoirs of Li Tsung-jen*. Boulder, Colo.: Westview Press, 1979.

Li Yuning and Zhang Yufa, eds. *Jindai Zhongguo nüquan yundong shiliao, 1842–1911* [Documents on the feminist movement in modern China, 1842–1911]. Vol. 1. Taibei: Biographical Literature Publishing Company, 1975.

Liang Zhanmei. *Zhongguo funü douzheng shihua* [Discussions on the history of the Chinese women's struggle]. Chongqing: Jianzhong Chubanshe, 1943.

Liao Wang Editing Bureau. *Hongjun nüyingxiong zhuan* [Biographies of Red Army women heroines]. Beijing: Xinhua Publishing House, 1986.

Lin Yü-sheng. *The Crisis of Chinese Consciousness: Radical Antitraditionalism in the May Fourth Era*. Madison: University of Wisconsin Press, 1979.

Lin Yutang. *Letters of a Chinese Amazon and War-time Essays*. Shanghai: Commercial Press, 1930.

Link, E. Perry, Jr. *Mandarin Ducks and Butterflies: Popular Fiction in Early Twentieth-Century Chinese Cities*. Berkeley: University of California Press, 1981.

Litou zhoubao [Plow weekly]. Nos. 17–18 (1926).

Liu Jucai. *Zhongguo jindai funü yundong shi* [A History of the modern Chinese women's movement]. Liaoning: Zhongguo Funü Chubanshe, 1989.

Liu Qingyang. "Qingyang de baogao" [Qingyang's report]. *Funü ribao*, May 23–25, 1924. Reprinted in *Zhongguo funü yundong lishi ziliao, 1921–1927*, pp. 192–97.

Liu Tiansu. "Liangshi cimu—Huiyi zai He Xiangning xiansheng shenbian de rizi" [Good teacher and loving mother—Remembering a day spent with He Xiangning]. *Huiyi yu huainian* [Recollections]. Beijing: Beijing Chubanshe, 1982.

Liu Wang Liming. *Zhongguo funü yundong* [Chinese women's movement]. Shanghai: Commercial Press, 1933.

Lo, Ren Yen. *China's Revolution from the Inside*. New York: Abingdon Press, 1930.

Lu Fangshang. *Geming zhi zaiqi—Zhongguo Guomindang gaizu qian de xin sichao, 1914–1924* [Resurgence of the revolution—New intellectual trends before the reorganization of the Chinese Nationalist party, 1914–1924]. Taibei: Zhongyang Yanjiuyuan Jindai Yanjiusuo, 1989.

Lu Jingqing. "Zai He Xiangning xiansheng shenbian" [At the side of He Xiangning]. *Huiyi yu huainian* [Recollections]. Beijing: Beijing Chubanshe, 1982.

Lu Xun. "Guafu zhuyi" [Widowism]. *Lu Xun quanji* [Collected works of Lu Xun] 1:262–69. Beijing: Renmin Wenxue Chubanshe, 1981.

———. *Lu Xun: Selected Works*. 4 vols. Translated by Yang Xianyi and Gladys Yang. Beijing: Foreign Languages Press, 1980.

———. "Nü xiaozhang de nannü de meng" [The female principal's dreams about male and female]. *Lu Xun quanji* [Collected works of Lu Xun] 7:291. Beijing: Renmin Wenxue Chubanshe, 1981.

Lung-kee Sun. "The Fin de Siecle Lu Xun." *Republican China* 18, no. 2 (April 1993): 64–98.

Luo Fanggu. "Dageming shiqi Suixian de funü yundong" [The women's movement in Sui county during the time of the great revolution]. *Hubei fuyunshi ziliao*, no. 2, pp. 148–54.

Luo Zhanglong. "Luo Zhanglong tan Zhonggong 'Sanda' de qianhou qing-kuang" [Luo Zhanglong discusses the situation around the time of the Chinese Communist party's third congress]. In *Zhongguo 'Sanda' ziliao* [Materials on the third party congress of the Chinese Communist party], compiled by Guangdong geming lishi bowuguan. Guangdong: Guang-dong Renmin Chubanshe, 1985.

Lutz, Jessie Gregory. *Chinese Politics and Christian Missions: The Anti-Christian Movements of 1920–1928*. Notre Dame, Ind.: Cross Cultural Publications, Cross Roads Books, 1988.

Ma Chunqu and Zhang Yun, eds., *Huiyi Yang Zhihua* (Recollections of Yang Zhihua). Anhui: Anhui Renmin Chubanshe, 1983.

Mai Jun. "Wo duiyu Zhao nüshi zisha de ganxiang" [My feelings on Miss Zhao's suicide]. *Dagongbao*, November 21, 1919.

Mann, Susan. "'Fuxue' [Women's Learning] by Zhang Xuecheng (1738–1801): China's First History of Women's Culture." *Late Imperial China* 13, no. 1 (June 1992): 40–62.

Mao Dun. *See also* Pei Wei and Shen Yanbing

———. *Wo zougoude daolu* [The road I have travelled]. Shanghai: Renmin Wenxue Chubanshe, 1981.

McDonald, Angus. *The Urban Origins of Rural Revolution: Elites and the Masses in Hunan*. Berkeley: University of California Press, 1978.

McElderry, Andrea. "Woman Revolutionary: Xiang Jingyu." *China Quarterly*, no. 105 (March 1986): 95–122.

McMahon, Keith. "A Case for Confucian Sexuality: The Eighteenth-Century Novel *Yesou Puyan*." *Late Imperial China* 9, no. 2 (December 1988): 32–55.

Meisner, Maurice. *Li Ta-chao and the Origins of Chinese Marxism*. Cambridge: Harvard University Press, 1967.

Meyer, Alfred G. "Marxism and the Women's Movement." In *Women in Russia*, edited by Dorothy Atkinson, Alexander Dallin, and Gail Lapidus, pp. 85–112. Stanford: Stanford University Press, 1977.

Minguo ribao [Republican daily]. Shanghai, 1915–1931. Reprinted Shanghai, 1981; *Minguo ribao*. Guangzhou, 1924–1927; *Minguo ribao*. Wuhan 1926–1927.

Moghadam, Valentine M. "Revolution, Culture, and Gender: Notes on 'The

Woman Question' in Revolutions." Unpublished paper, United Nations University, World Institute for Development Economics Research, Helsinki, Finland, 1990.

Mohanty, Chandra Talpade. "Cartographies of Struggle: Third World Women and the Politics of Feminism." In *Third World Women and the Politics of Feminism*, edited by Chandra Talpade Mohanty, Ann Russo, and Lourdes Torres, pp. 1–47. Bloomington: Indiana University Press, 1991.

Mohanty, Chandra Talpade, Ann Russo, and Lourdes Torres, eds. *Third World Women and the Politics of Feminism*. Bloomington: Indiana University Press, 1991.

Molyneux, Maxine. "Mobilization without Emancipation? Women's Interests, the State, and Revolution in Nicaragua." *Feminist Studies* 11, no. 2 (summer 1985): 227–54.

Nivard, Jacqueline. "Histoire d'une revue féminine chinoise: *Funü zazhi* 1915–1931." Ph.D. diss., l'EHESS, Paris, 1983.

"Nüquan yundong de gefangmian" [Various aspects of the women's rights movement]. *Funü pinglun*, no. 61 (October 4, 1922): 3.

Ono Kazuko. *Chinese Women in a Century of Revolution, 1850–1950*. Stanford: Stanford University Press, 1989.

Pan Yun. "Yige nüzi yin beipuo hun tuoli jiating" [A girl who leaves home because she was forced to marry]. *Funü pinglun* 67 (November 15, 1922): 4.

Pei Wei [Shen Yanbing]. "Lian'ai yu zhenjie de guanxi" [The relationship between love and virginity]. *Funü pinglun*, no. 5 (August 31, 1921): 1–2.

Peng Pai. *Seeds of Peasant Revolution: Report on the Haifeng Peasant Movement*. Trans. Donald Holoch. Ithaca: Cornell University, 1973.

Peng Pai wenji [Collected Works of Peng Pai]. Beijing: Renmin Chubanshe, 1981.

Peng Pai yanjiu shiliao [Peng Pai historical research materials]. Guangdong: Guangdong Renmin Chubanshe, 1981.

Peng Pai zhuan [Biography of Peng Pai]. Beijing: Beijing Chubanshe, 1984.

Perry, Elizabeth. *Shanghai on Strike: The Politics of Chinese Labor*. Stanford: Stanford University Press, 1993.

Pi Yishu. *Zhongguo funü yundong*. Taibei: Fulian Shukanshe, 1973.

Pu Qingquan. "Wo suo zhidao de Chen Duxiu" [The Chen Duxiu I knew]. In *Chen Duxiu pinglun xuanbian* [Selections and comments on Chen Duxiu], edited by Wang Shuli, et al. Vol. 2. Henan: Henan Renmin Chubanshe.

"Pudong nügong bagong de jieju" [The situation in the women's strike at Pudong]. *Funü pinglun*, no. 44 (June 7, 1922): 2.

Qi. "Quanguo funü daibiao dahui de zhongyao" [The importance of a national representative women's congress]. *Zhongguo funü*, no. 14 (May 10, 1926): 1.

Qiu Canzhi. *Qiu Jin zhuan* [Biography of Qiu Jin]. Taibei: Lianhe Tushu Gongci, 1969.

Quataert, Jean H. *Reluctant Feminists in German Social Democracy, 1885–1917*. Princeton: Princeton University Press, 1979.

Rankin, Mary Backus. *Early Chinese Revolutionaries: Radical Intellectuals in Shanghai and Chekiang, 1902–1911*. Cambridge: Harvard University Press, 1971.

———. "The Emergence of Women at the End of the Ch'ing: The Case of Ch'iu Chin." In *Women in Chinese Society*, edited by Margery Wolf and Roxane Witke, pp. 39–66. Stanford: Stanford University Press, 1975.

Rigby, Richard W. *The May Thirtieth Movement: Events and Themes*. Canberra: Australian National University Press, 1980.

Ropp, Paul. "The Seeds of Change: Reflections on the Condition of Women in the Early and Mid Ch'ing." *Signs* 2, no. 1 (1976): 5–23.

———. "Women in Late Imperial China: A Review of Recent English-Language Scholarship." *Women's History Review* 3, no. 3 (1994): 86–153.

Rosenblum, Charles Eric. "The Last Lie nü, the First Feminist: Miss Zhao's Use as an Icon during the May Fourth Period: An Analysis of the Nature of Female Suicide in China." Senior Thesis, Department of East Asian Studies, Harvard College, 1992.

Saich, Tony. *The Origins of the First United Front in China*. 2 vols. Leiden: E. J. Brill, 1991.

Scalapino, Robert A. "The Evolution of a Young Revolutionary: Mao Zedong in 1919–1921." *Journal of Asian Studies* 42, no. 1 (November 1982): 29–61.

Schwarcz, Vera. *The Chinese Enlightenment: Intellectuals and the Legacy of the May Fourth Movement of 1919*. Berkeley: University of California Press, 1986.

———. *Time for Telling Truth Is Running Out: Conversations with Zhang Shenfu*. New Haven: Yale University Press, 1992.

Scott, Joan W. "Gender: A Useful Category of Historical Analysis." *The American Historical Review* 91, no. 5 (December 1986): 1053–75.

Seagrave, Sterling. *The Soong Dynasty*. New York: Harper & Row, 1985.

"Shanghai nüquan yundong tongmenghui qingyuanshu" [Petition of the Shanghai Women's Rights League]. In *Zhongguo funü yundong lishi ziliao, 1921–1927*, pp. 63–64.

"Shanghai sichang nügong quanti bagong" [The general strike by Shanghai women silk workers]. *Chenbao*, August 9, 1922.

[Shao] Lizi. "Shanghai sichang nügong bagongji" [A record of the Shanghai silk strike]. *Funü pinglun*, no. 53 (August 9, 1922): 2–4.

———. "Songjiang Jingxian zhongxue de jingshen" [Spirit at Jingshan Middle School in Songjiang]. *Funü pinglun*, no. 55 (August 23, 1922): 4.

———. "Jiushi hunzhi wenti de beiju" [The tragedy of the old style of marriage]. *Minguo ribao*, September 13, 1921.

———. "Nannü shejiao yu jiu lijiao" [Social contact between men and women and old ethics]. *Funü pinglun*, no. 7 (September 14, 1921): 4.

[Shao] Lizi and [Shi] Cuntong. "'Feichu hunzhi' taolun zhong de liangfengxin" [Two letters pertaining to the discussion on 'the abolition of marriage']. *Juewu*, May 15, 1920.

———. "Feichu hunzhi wenti de taolun" [A discussion on the issue of abolishing the marriage system]. *Juewu*, May 23, 1920.

Sheean, Vincent. *Personal History*. Boston: Houghton Mifflin, 1969.

[Shen] Xuanlu. "Taolun nannü tongxiao wenti" [A discussion of the co-educational school issue]. *Laodong yu funü* [Labor and women], no. 4 (March 6, 1921).

Shen Yanbing. "Baofengyu—Wuyue sanshiyi ri" [Tempest—May Thirty-First]. *Wenxue zhoubao*, no. 180 (July 5, 1925). Reprinted in *Wusa yundong shiliao* [Historical materials on the May Thirtieth Movement], edited by Muo Yongming, 1:743–46. Shanghai: Renmin Chubanshe, 1981.

[Shen] Yanbing. "Du *Shaonian Zhongguo* funü hao" [Reading the issue on women in *Young China*]. *Funü zazhi* 6, no. 1 (1920): 1–4.

———. "Funü jingji duli taolun" [A discussion of women's economic independence]. *Funü pinglun*, no. 3 (August 17, 1921): 1.

———. "Nüzi de juewu" [Women's consciousness]. *Funü zazhi* 6, no. 5 (May 1920).

[Shen Yan] Bing. "Ailunkai xueshuo de taolun" [A discussion of the theories of Ellen Key]. *Funü pinglun*, no. 3 (August 17, 1921): 4.

———. "Gao Zhejiang yaoqiu shengxian jiaru san tiaojian de nüzi" [Advice to the women of Zhejiang who are demanding the inclusion of three articles in the provincial constitution]. *Funü pinglun*, no. 4 (August 24, 1921): 2–3.

———. "Nüxing de zijue" [Women's consciousness]. *Funü pinglun*, no. 1 (August 3, 1921): 4.

———. "'Shengyu jiezhi' de shengjia" [A correct evaluation of birth control]. *Funü pinglun*, no. 40 (May 10, 1922): 2–3.

———. "Suowei nüxing zhuyi de liang jiduanpai" [Two extremes in the so-called feminism]. *Funü pinglun*, no. 15 (November 9, 1921): 4.

Shen Zemin. "Nüzi de juewu" [Women's consciousness]. *Funü zazhi* 6, no. 5 (May 1920).

———. "Nüzi jinri de diwei" [The position of women today]. *Funü pinglun*, no. 27 (February 8, 1922): 1–2.

[Shen] Zemin. "Duiyu 'feichang yundong' shuo yijuhua" [Some words about the anti-prostitution movement]. *Funü pinglun*, Special supplement (January 1, 1922): 3.

Shen Zemin. "Sanjiao lian'ai de wenti" [The issue of a love triangle]. *Funü zhoubao*, no. 80 (March 29, 1925).

Shenbao, Shanghai, 1872–1949.

[Shi] Cuntong. "Jiejue hunyin wenti de yijian" [Opinions on how to solve the issue of marriage]. *Juewu*, May 17, 1920.

———. "'Wuru nüzi renge' de jieshi" [An explanation of 'humiliating women's personality']. *Juewu*, May 15, 1920.

Shou Chang. See Li Dazhao.

Sima Changfeng. *Xin Zhongguo wenxueshi* [A history of new Chinese literature]. Qiuming Chubanshe, 1975.

"Sixth CCP Congress Resolution on the Women's Movement." *Chinese Studies in History* 4, no. 4 (Summer 1971): 229–32.

Smedley, Agnes. *The Great Road: The Life and Times of Chu Teh*. New York: Monthly Review Press, 1956.

Snow, Helen Foster. *Women in Modern China*. Hague: Mouton & Co, 1967.

Spence, Jonathan D. *The Gate of Heavenly Peace: The Chinese and Their Revolution, 1895–1980*. New York: Penguin Books, 1982.

———. *The Search for Modern China*. New York: W.W. Norton & Co, 1990.

Stacey, Judith. *Patriarchy and Socialist Revolution in China*. Berkeley: University of California Press, 1983.

Stites, Richard. "The Russian Revolution and Women." In Marilyn J. Boxer and Jean H. Quataert. *Connecting Spheres: Women in the Western World, 1500 to the Present*. New York: Oxford University Press, 1987.

———. *The Women's Liberation Movement in Russia: Feminism, Nihilism, and Bolshevism, 1860–1930*. Princeton: Princeton University Press, 1978.

Stockard, Janice. *Daughters of the Canton Delta: Marriage Patterns and Economic Strategies in South China, 1860–1930*. Stanford: Stanford University Press, 1989.

Stranahan, Patricia. *Yan'an Women and the Communist Party*. Berkeley: Institute of East Asian Studies and Center for Chinese Studies, University of California, 1983.

Strand, David. *Rickshaw Beijing: City People and Politics in the 1920s*. Berkeley: University of California Press, 1989.

Strong, Anna Louise. *China's Millions*. New York: Coward-McCann, 1928.

Su Qing nüshi. "Henan Xin" [Letter from Henan]. *Zhongguo funü*, no. 9: 6.

Sun, Yen-chu. "Chinese National Higher Education for Women in the Context of Social Reform, 1919–1929: A Case Study." Ph.D. diss., New York University, 1986.

Tan Sheying. *Zhongguo funü yundong shi* [A history of the Chinese women's movement]. Shanghai: 1936.

Tan Zhushan. "Huishu funü de wenhua yu shenghuo diaocha" [Investigations into the education and lives of women in Huishu, Dongjiang]. *Funü zhisheng*, no. 20 (1920): 3–8.

Tang Dongqing. "Tang Dongqing de huiyi" [Memoirs of Tang Dongqing]. *'Yida' qianhou* 2 (1980): 458–59.

Teng, Ssu-yü. "Introduction, A Decade of Challenge." In *China in the 1920's: Nationalism and Revolution*, edited by F. Gilbert Chan and Thomas H. Etzold. New York: New Viewpoints, 1976.

Tilly, Charles. "Reflections on the History of European State-Making." In *The Formation of National States in Western Europe*, edited by Charles Tilly. Princeton: Princeton University Press, 1975.

Topley, Marjorie. "Marriage Resistance in Rural Kwangtung." *Women in Chinese Society*, edited by Margery Wolf and Roxane Witke. Stanford: Stanford University Press, 1975.

Udaka Yasushi. *Shina rōdō mondai* [Labor problems in China]. Shanghai: Kokusai bunka kenkyukai, 1925.

van de Ven, Hans J. *From Friend to Comrade: The Founding of the Chinese Communist Party, 1920–1927*. Berkeley: University of California Press, 1991.

Vishnyakova-Akimova, Vera Vladimirovna. *Two Years in Revolutionary*

China, 1925–1927. Translated by Steven I. Levine. Cambridge, Mass.: East Asian Research Center, Harvard University; distributed by Harvard University Press, 1971.

Vogel, Lise. "Questions on the Woman Question." *Monthly Review* 31, no. 2 (June 1979): 39–59.

Wang Guangyuan, ed. *Chen Duxiu nianpu* [A chronology of Chen Duxiu]. Sichuan: Chongqing Press, 1987.

Wang Huiwu. "Gexuexiao xiaoxi huizhi" [A collection of news items on each school]. Shanghai *Minguo ribao*, September 3, 1922, p. 11.

———. "Jiandang chuqi de yixie qingkuang" [Some circumstances surrounding the initial period of constructing the party]. *'Yida' qianhou* 2 (1980): 76–78.

———. "Ru pingmin nüxiao shangke yixingqi zhi ganxiang" [Reflections on the Pingmin girls' school after a week of classes]. *Funü sheng*, no. 6 (March 6, 1922): 3.

———. "Zhongguo funü wenti: Quantao jiefang" [The Chinese woman question: Liberation from a Trap]. *Shaonian Zhongguo* [Young China] 1, no. 4 (October 1919): 6–10.

———. "Zuzhi gongzuobu de wo jian" [My views on organizing a work study section]. *Funü sheng*, no. 2 (December 28, 1921): 1.

[Wang] Huiwu. "Dui bagong nügongren shuo de hua" [A speech to women workers on strike]. *Funü sheng*, no. 10 (June 20, 1922): 3.

———. "Wo duiyu chan'er xianzhi de yijian" [My views on birth control]. *Funü sheng*, no. 9 (May 5, 1922): 2.

Wang Jianhong. "Duyao" [Poison]. *Funü zazhi* 6, no. 5 (May 1920).

[Wang] Jianhong. "Jiezhi shengyu yu baochi lian'ai" [Birth control and the preservation of love]. *Funü sheng*, no. 9 (May 5, 1922): 1–2.

Wang Jianying, ed. *Zhongguo Gongchandang zuzhishi ziliao huibian* [Compilation of materials on the organizational history of the Chinese Communist party]. Beijing: Hongqi Chubanshe, 1983.

Wang Yizhi. "Wusi shidai de yige nüzhong" [A women's school in the May Fourth era]. In *Wusi yundong huiyilu* [Memoirs of the May Fourth Movement]. Beijing: Zhongguo Shehui Kexue Chubanshe, 1979.

———. "Xiang Jingyu tongzhi." In *Lieshi Xiang Jingyu* [Martyr Xiang Jingyu]. Beijing: Zhongguo Funü Zashi She, 1958.

———. "Zimeimei kuailai gan nüquan yundong ba" [Sisters, quickly undertake the women's rights movement]. *Funü pinglun*, no. 60 (September 27, 1922): 1.

Wasserstrom, Jeffrey N. *Student Protests in Twentieth-Century China: The View from Shanghai*. Stanford: Stanford University Press, 1991.

Watson, Rubie S. "Girls' Houses and Working Women: Expressive Culture in the Pearl River Delta, 1900–1941." In *Bondage, Rescue, and Escape Among Chinese Women*, edited by Suzanne Miers and Maria Jaschok, pp. 25–44. Hong Kong: Zed Books, 1994.

Weili Ye. "Crossing the Cultures: The Experience of Chinese Students in the U.S. from 1900–1925." Unpublished manuscript.

————. "'Nü Liuxuesheng': The Story of American-Educated Chinese Women, 1880s–1920s." *Modern China* 20, no. 3 (July 1994): 315–46.

Wenshi ziliao yanjiu weiyuanhui, ed. *Guangdong wenshi ziliao*, nos. 30, 34. Guangzhou: Guangdong Renmin Chubanshe, 1981.

Wilbur, C. Martin. "The Influence of the Past." In *Party Leadership and Revolutionary Power in China*, edited by John Wilson Lewis, pp. 35–68. Cambridge: Cambridge University Press, 1970.

————. *The Nationalist Revolution in China, 1923–1928*. Cambridge: Cambridge University Press, 1983.

————. *Sun Yatsen: Frustrated Patriot*. New York: Columbia University Press, 1976.

Witke, Roxane. "Mao Tse-tung, Women, and Suicide." In Marilyn B. Young, ed. *Women in China: Studies in Social Change and Feminism*, pp. 7–31.

————. "Transformation of Attitudes towards Women during the May Fourth Era of Modern China." Ph.D. diss., University of California, Berkeley, 1970.

————. "Women as Politician in China of the 1920s." In Marilyn B. Young, ed., *Women in China: Studies in Social Change and Feminism*, pp. 33–43.

"Women's Liberation in the Hunan Peasant Association." *China Reconstructs* (March 1975): 40.

Wusi shiqi qikan jieshao [Introduction to the periodicals of the May Fourth period]. 3 vols. Beijing: Sanlian Shudian, 1979.

Xia Songyun. "Funü yundong he guomin geming" [The women's movement and the national revolution]. *Guangming* (ca. 1926) pp. 14–16.

Xia Zhiyu. "Huiyi Li Hanjun laoshi" [Recollections of teacher Li Hanjun]. *Geming shi ziliao*, no. 14 (1984): 176–78.

Xian Pi. "Hubei quansheng funü yundong." *Hubei funü yundong shi ziliao*, no. 2, pp. 169–94.

Xiang Jingyu. "Gao sichang laoku nütongbao" [Appeal to the toiling women compatriots working in the silk factories]. *Funü zhoubao*, no. 6 (September 26, 1923).

————. "Nüzi jiefang yu gaizao de shangque" [Discussions about women's emancipation and transformation]. *Shaonian Zhongguo* 2, no. 2 (May 26, 1920). Reprinted in Zhonghua quanguo funü lianhehui funü yundong lishi yanjiushi, comp., *Wusi shiqi funü wenti wenxuan*, pp. 69–77.

————. "Zai Shanghai nüjie guomin huiyi cuchenghui chengli dahuishang de jianghua" [A speech at the founding meeting of the Shanghai committee to promote women's participation in the national convention]. *Funü zhoubao*, no. 65 (December 27, 1924).

————. "Zhili di'er nüshi xuechao zai nüzi jiaoyu gexin yundong shang de jiazhi" [The value of the student education reform movement in the student unrest at Zhili's Second Provincial Girls' Normal School]. *Funü zhoubao*, no. 33 (April 9, 1924): 2–3.

[Xiang] Jingyu. "Cong pingmin jiaoyu zhong huafen nüzi pingmin jiaoyu de wo jian" [My views on differentiating common girls' schools from common people's education]. *Funü zhoubao*, no. 24 (January 30, 1924). Reprinted in Xu Rihui, ed., *Xiang Jingyu wenji*, pp. 145–47.

———. "Duiyu Beijing nüshi daxue chao de ganyan" [Reflections of the tide at Beijing Women's Normal University]. *Funü zhoubao*, no. 80 (April 5, 1925).

———. "Duiyu genben gaige Beijing nüzi shifan daxue deyijian bing zhi Beijing nüzi shifan daxue quanti tongxue [Views on the basic reform of Beijing Normal Women's College delivered to the entire student body of Beijing Normal Women's College]. *Funü zhoubao*, no. 71 (February 9, 1925).

———. "Duiyu Nüqingnianhui quanguo dahui de ganxiang" [Thoughts on the National Y.W.C.A. Congress]. *Funü zhoubao*, October 31, 1923. Reprinted in Xu Rihui, ed., *Xiang Jingyu wenji*, 109–110.

———."Jiu guniang fanle hezui!" [What crime did ninth sister commit!]. *Funü zhoubao*, no. 6 (September 9, 1923).

———. "Minguo huiyi yu funü" [The national convention and women]. *Funü zhoubao*, no. 64 (December 14, 1924).

———. "Ping Wang bihua de nüuan yundong tan" [Comments on Wang Bihua's views on the Women's Rights Movement]. *Funü zhoubao*, no. 8 (October 10, 1923). Reprinted in Xu Rihui, ed., *Xiang Jingyu wenji*, pp. 103–6.

———. "Shanghai funü tuanti jiang lianhe yuanzhu sichang nügong" [Women's organizations in Shanghai will unite to support the women workers in the silk factories]. *Funü zhoubao*, no. 13 (January 14, 1924). Reprinted in Xu Rihui, *Xiang Jingyu wenji*, pp. 114–16.

———. "Shanghai nüquan yundong hui jinhou ying zhuyi de sanjianshi" [Three matters which the Shanghai Women's Rights League ought to pay attention to in the future]. *Funü zhoubao*, no. 12 (November 8, 1923): 1–2. Reprinted in Xu Rihui, ed., *Xiang Jingyu wenji*, pp. 111–13.

———."Sichang nügong tuanjieqilai" [Silk workers unite]. *Funü zhoubao*, no. 14 (November 21, 1923). Reprinted in *Zhongguo funü yundong lishi ziliao*, pp. 135–36.

———. "Zhongdeng yisheng nüxuesheng de dushu wenti" [The problem of women students above the middle school level]. *Funü zazhi* 10, no. 3 (March 1, 1924).

———. "Zhongguo zuijin funü yundong" [The recent women's movement in China]. *Qian feng* [Pioneer], no. 1 (July 1, 1923). Reprinted in Xu Rihui, ed., *Xiang Jingyu wenji*, pp. 84–92.

Xiangdao zhoubao [The Weekly Guide]. Shanghai, 1922–1926.

[Xiao] Chunü. "Qudi nüxuesheng lihun wenti" [The problem of preventing women students from getting a divorce]. *Juewu*, nos. 10, 18, 19 (1924).

Xiaofeng [Chen Wangdao]. "Hun zhidu zui'e de beigan" [The deplorable evils of the marriage system]. *Juewu* (June 24, 1921).

Xie Bingying. See Hsieh Ping-ying and Lin Yutang.

Xin qingnian [New youth]. Shanghai, Beijing, and Guangzhou, 1915–1926.

Xingqi pinglun [Weekly review]. Shanghai, 1919–1920.

Xu Chengmei. "Huiyi wusa yundong" [Recollections of the May Thirtieth movement]. *Fuyun shi ziliao* [Materials on the history of the women's movement], no. 3 (1982): 22–34.

Xu Meikun. "Canjia Zhonggong 'Sanda'" [Participating in the Third Congress of the Chinese Communist party]. *Geming shi ziliao* [Revolutionary historical materials], no. 8 (September 1982): 44.

Xu Rihui, ed. *Xiang Jingyu wenji* [A collection of Xiang Jingyu's writings]. Changsha: Hunan Renmin Chubanshe, 1980.

Xu Ruo. "Duiyu muqian funü yundong shuo jijuhua" [A few words on the future of the women's movement]. *Funü sheng*, no. 5 (February 10, 1922): 1.

Xu Zhizhen. "Guanyu Yuyangli liuhao de huodong qingkuang" [The situation regarding activities at No. 6 Yuyang Lane]. *'Yida' qianhou* 2:58–70.

Xue Xishen and Tang Cunbiao. "Hou Shaoqiu." In *Shanghai yinglie zhuan* [Biographies of Shanghai martyrs] 1 (July 1987): 103–15.

Y. D. [Li Xiaofeng]. "Zhiye yu funü" [Occupations and women]. *Funü zazhi* 7, no. 11 (November 1921): 8–11.

Yang Shiji. *Xinhai geming gianhou Hunan shishi* [Hunan historical events during the period of the 1911 revolution]. Changsha: Hunan Renmin Chubanshe, 1953.

Yang Zhihua. "Yijiu erliu nian Shanghai sichang nügong yundong zhong zhi ganxiang" [Thoughts on the strike movement of female silk workers in Shanghai in 1926]. *Zhongguo funü*, nos. 16, 17 (June 30, 1926): 3–7.

[Yang] Zhihua. "Zhongguo sanba yundongshi" [The history of March 8 in China]. *Chinü zazhi* [Red women's journal], no. 6 (March 8, 1927): 23.

Yang Zhihua nüshi. "Jiu lunli dixia de kelian ren" [Victims of the old morality]. *Funü pinglun*, no. 55 (August 23, 1922): 4.

———. "Lilun wenti de wojian" [My views on divorce]. *Funü pinglun*, no. 56 (August 30, 1922): 1.

———. "Shejiao he lian'ai" [Social contact and love]. *Funü pinglun*, no. 51 (July 26, 1922): 1.

Yang Zilie. *Zhang Guotao furen huiyilu* [Memoirs of Mrs. Zhang Guotao]. Hong Kong: Zhongguo Wenti Yanjiu Zhongxin, 1970.

Ye Shengtao. *Ni Huanzhi*. Beijing: Renmin Wenxue Chubanshe, 1953.

Yeh Wen-hsin. *The Alienated Academy: Culture and Politics in Republican China, 1919–1937*. Cambridge, Mass.: Council on East Asian Studies, Harvard University; distributed by Harvard University Press, 1990.

Yi Yi nüshi. "Wo duiyu lun nüzi diwei liangze tongxin de ganxiang" [My feelings on the two letters about women's position]. *Funü pinglun*, no. 25 (January 18, 1922): 1.

'Yida' qianhou. See Zhongguo shehui kexueyuan xiandaishi yanjuishi.

Ying. "Nüxuesheng weishenma buhan 'jiehun lihun juedui ziyou' de kouhao?" [Why don't women students call out the slogan "absolute freedom in marriage and divorce"?]. *Funü xianfeng*, no. 2 (April 8, 1926): 2–3.

Yip, Ka-che. *Religion, Nationalism, and Chinese Students: The Anti-Christian*

Movement of 1922–1927. Bellingham, Washington: Western Washington University, 1980.

Young, Marilyn B., ed. *Women in China: Studies in Social Change and Feminism.* Ann Arbor: Center for Chinese Studies, University of Michigan, 1973.

You Yi. "Henan funü zhuangkuang" [Women in Henan]. *Guangming*, no. 8 (June 30, 1926): 18–21.

Yu, Miin-Ling. "Sun Yatsen University in Moscow." PhD. diss., New York University, 1995.

Yuan Puzhi. "Hubei shengwei taolunguo Li Hanjun huifu dangji de wenti [The discussions of the Hubei Provincial Committee on the restoration of Li Hanjun's party membership]. *Geming shi ziliao*, no. 14 (1984): 183.

Yuben. "Liubie Shanghai nüjie lianhehui." *Funü sheng*, no. 1 (December 13, 1921): 3–4.

Yun Daiying. "Bo yang Xiaochun 'fei ertong gongyu' " [A refutation of Yang Xiaochun's "Against Public Childcare"]. *Xuedeng* [Academic lamp], April 8, 1920. Reprinted in Zhonghua quanquo funü lianhehui funü yundong lishi yanjiu shi, ed., *Wusi shiqi funü wenti wenxuan*, pp. 195–99, 321–26.

———. "Jiehun wenti zhi yanjiu" [Research on the marriage question]. *Dongfang zazhi* [Eastern miscellany] (July 15, 1917).

———. "Yingzhe ershi lun jiating de qiyuan" [Engels on the origin of the family]. *Dongfang zazhi* [Eastern miscellany], nos. 17, 19, 20 (1920).

Zarrow, Peter. "He Zhen and Anarcho-Feminism in China." *Journal of Asian Studies* 47, no. 4 (November 1988): 796–813.

Zhang Guotao. "Huiyi Zhongguo Gongchandang 'yida' qianhou" [Recollections of the Chinese Communist party around the time of the first congress]. *'Yida' qianhou* 2:122–83.

Zhang Songnian [Zhang Shenfu]. "Nüzi jiefang da budang" [The great inappropriateness of women's emancipation]. *Shaonian Zhongguo* 2, no. 4 (October 1919).

Zhang Yunhou, et al., eds. *Wusi shiqi de shetuan* [Societies of the May Fourth period]. 6 vols. Beijing: Sanlian, 1979.

Zhao Zhang'an, et al. *Lao gemingjia de lian'ai hunyin he jiating shenghuo* [Love, marrige, and family life of veteran revolutionary families]. Beijing: Gongren Chubanshe, 1985.

Zheng Chaolin. "Wei aiqing er douzheng" [Struggle for love]. *Kaifang zazhi*, no. 3 (1991): 81–87.

Zhenyu [Xiang Jingyi]. "Guohui duiyu zaizhi Zhongguo de jiuguo xie yue gu he taidu?" [What attitude should the parliament adopt toward the nine-power agreement that tries to dominate China?]. *Xiangdao zhoubao* (November 8, 1922).

Zhonggong dangshi cankao ziliao [Reference materials for Chinese Communist party history]. Beijing: Renmin chubanshe, 1979.

"Zhonggong zhongyang funü weiyuanhui gongzuo baogao" [Work report of the Chinese Communist Central Women's Committee]. In *Zhongguo funü yundong lishi ziliao, 1921–1927*, pp. 696–700.

Zhongguo funü [Chinese Women]. Shanghai, 1925–1926.
Zhongguo funü yundong lishi ziliao, 1921–1927. See Zhonghua quanguo funü lianhehui funü yundong lishi yanjuishi, comp.
Zhongguo geming bowuguan, ed. *Xinmin xuehui ziliao* [Materials on the New Citizen's Study Society]. Beijing: Renmin Chubanshe, 1980.
"Zhongguo Gongchandang d'erci quanguo daibiao dahui guanyu funü yundong de jueyi" [The resolution on the women's movement to the second congress of the Chinese Communist party]. Reprinted in *Zhongguo funü yundong lishi ziliao*, pp. 29–30.
"Zhongguo Gongchandang zhongyangju tonggao" [A Circular of the central bureau of the Chinese Communist party]. Reprinted in *Zhongguo funü yundong lishi ziliao, 1921–1927,* p. 1.
Zhongguo shehui kexueyuan xiandaishi yanjiushi, Zhongguo geming bowuguan dangshi yajiushi [Modern History Research Department of the Chinese Academy of Social Sciences and the Party History Research Department of the Chinese Revolutionary Museum], eds. *'Yida' qianhou: Zhongguo Gongchandang de yici daibiao dahui qianhou ziliao xuanbian* [The period of the first party congress: Collection of source materials on the period of the first party congress]. Beijing: Remin Chubanshe, 1980.
Zhonghua quanguo funü lianhehui [All-China Women's Federation], ed. *Zhongguo funü yundong shi* [A history of the Chinese women's movement]. Beijing: Chunqiu Chubanshe, 1989.
———. *Zhonghua nü yinglie* [Chinese women martyrs]. Beijing: Wenhua Chubanshe, 1988.
Zhonghua quanguo funü lianhehui funü yundong lishi yanjiushi [All-China Women's Federation, Research Department on the History of the Women's Movement], comp. *Wusi shiqi funü wenti wenxuan* [Selections on the woman question from the May Fourth period]. Beijing: Sanlian Shudian, 1981.
———. *Zhongguo funü yundong lishi ziliao, 1921–1927* [Historical materials on the Chinese women's movement]. Beijing: Renmin Chubanshe, 1986.
Zhongyang Dang'anguan, ed. *Zhongguo Gongchandang di yici daibiao dahui dang'an ziliao: Zengdingben* [Archival sources for the first congress of the Chinese Communist party: Revised and enlarged edition]. Beijing: People's Press, 1984.
"Zhongyang junzi zhengzhi xuexiao Wuhan fenxiao choubei jingguo gailue" [Outline of the establishment of the Wuhan branch of the Central Military and Political Institute]. *Huangpu junxiao shiliao, 1924–1927* [Materials on Whampoa Academy, 1924–1927]. Guangdong: Renmin chubanshe, 1982.
Zhou Jianfei. "Dageming shiqi de Wuhan junfenxiao" [The Wuhan Military Institute in the period of the great revolution]. *Hubei fuyun shi ziliao* [Materials on the history of the Hubei women's movement], no. 2: 45–57.
"Zuijin hunan zhi zhengzhi qingkuang he dangwu qingkuang" [The recent situation in Hunan political and party affairs]. *Zhengzhi zhoubao*, no. 13 (May 24, 1926): 11–14.

Interviews

Cai Bo. Interview by author. Beijing, July 23, 1983.
Ding Ling. Interview by author. Beijing, July 11, 1983.
Epstein, Israel. Interview by author. Boston, July 1992.
Jiang Jiaoshou. Interview by author. Shanghai, February 3, 1983.
Kong Wenzhen. Interview by author. Beijing, October 9, 1980.
Li Xiaoyun. Interview by author. Beijing, April 8, 1983.
Liu Yaxiong. Interview by author. Beijing, April 1983.
Lu Jingqing. Interview by author. Shanghai, February 6, 1983.
Mao Zhuqing. Interview by author. Changsha, Hunan, March 10, 1983.
Ou Mengjue. Interview by author. Guangzhou, February 18, 1983.
Qu Duyi. Interview by author. Beijing, April 8, 1983.
Ren Wuxiong. Interview by author. Shanghai, February 2, 1983.
Wang Huiwu. Interview by author. Beijing, June 25, 1983.
Wang Yaquan. Interview by author. Taibei, Taiwan, May 26, 1987.
Wang Yizhi. Interviews by author. Beijing, 1979–1983.
Xu Chengmei. Interview by author. Shanghai, February 1, 1983.
Zhong Fuguang. Interviews by author. Beijing, August 11 and August 23, 1983.
Zhou Min. Interview by author. Taibei, May 1987.
Zhou Yueying. Shanghai All-Women's Federation. Interview by author. Shanghai, February 1, 1983.

Index

Compositor: Asco Trade Typesetting Limited
Text: Galliard
Display: Galliard
Printer: Thomson-Shore, Inc.
Binder: Thomson-Shore, Inc.